THE POLITICS OF ANTI-WESTERNISM IN ASIA

COLUMBIA STUDIES IN INTERNATIONAL AND GLOBAL HISTORY

MATTHEW CONNELLY AND ADAM MCKEOWN, SERIES EDITORS

CEMIL AYDIN

THE POLITICS OF
ANTI-WESTERNISM IN ASIA

Visions of World Order in Pan-Islamic and Pan-Asian Thought

Columbia University Press

New York

Columbia University Press
Publishers Since 1893
New York   Chichester, West Sussex

Library of Congress Cataloging-in-Publication Data
Aydin, Cemil.
    The politics of anti-Westernism in Asia : visions of world order in pan-Islamic
and pan-Asian thought / Cemil Aydin.
            p. cm. — (Columbia studies in international and global history)
    Includes bibliographical references and index.
    . ISBN 978-0-231-13778-2 (cloth : alk. paper)
    1. Panislamism.   2. Asia—Politics and government.   3. International cooperation.
I. Title.   II. Series.
    DS35.7.A95 2007
    303.48'2176701821—dc22   2007001759

∞

Columbia University Press books are printed
on permanent and durable acid-free paper.

Printed in the United States of America

c 10 9 8 7 6 5 4 3 2

CONTENTS

ACKNOWLEDGMENTS

THIS BOOK GREW out of my Ph.D. dissertation on Japanese pan-Asianism at the history department of Harvard University and my master's thesis on nineteenth-century Ottoman intellectual history at Istanbul University. A generous postdoctoral fellowship from the Harvard Academy for International and Area Studies allowed me to complete the research for this book by conducting further studies on pan-Islamism.

I owe a deep debt of gratitude to three outstanding dissertation advisers, professors Cemal Kafadar, Andrew Gordon, and Akira Iriye, who not only guided my research but also became role models as public intellectuals. Their intellectual vision in the fields of comparative and global history made working with them as a student, teaching assistant, and later colleague a formative experience. I should especially note the unfailing support and friendship of Cemal Kafadar, who encouraged me as his graduate student to get a break from the libraries by watching a soccer game with him once a week.

I would like to thank the adviser of my master's thesis, Professor Ekmeleddin İhsanoğlu, especially for inspiring my comparative research on Ottoman and Japanese histories. Even with his very busy schedule as the secretary general of the Organization of the Islamic Conference, Professor İhsanoğlu took the time to read and comment on portions of my research while sharing his insights about the contemporary relevance of the historical theme of my book.

During my undergraduate education at Boğaziçi University, I was fortunate to learn from a group of dedicated and interesting teachers. I am especially indebted to Faruk Birtek's inspiring seminars on questions of modernity and social theory. Throughout my undergraduate education, I also benefited from the academic program and lectures at the Bilim ve Sanat Vakfı of Istanbul.

During my studies at Harvard, I was blessed by the ideas and encouragement of many scholars, as well as by their insightful conversation. Mikhael Adolphson, Herbert Bix, Harold Bolitho, Sugata Bose, Daniel Botsman, Albert Craig, John Dower, Roger Owen, and Genzo Yamamoto contributed to this work at various stages. Selçuk Esenbel of Boğaziçi University not only wrote the first scholarly articles on the interactions between pan-Islamic and pan-Asian movements but also advised me during my graduate research. Many friends made life in Cambridge, Massachusetts, intellectually stimulating and interesting and contributed to the content of the book. I would like to mention by name here Danielle Widmann Abraham, Rahim Acar, Mustafa Aksakal, Sahar Bazzaz, Kim Beng Phar, Evan Dawley, Mark Farha, Rusty Gates, Akbar Hyder, Davesh Kapur, Ilham Makdisi, Erez Manela, Eiko Maruko, Tosh Minohara, Ghada Osman, Mike Reynolds, Dominic Sachsenmaier, Chiho Sawada, Nilufer Shaikh, Cengiz Şişman, Himmet Taşkömür, Jun Uchida, Hikmet Yaman, and Hüseyin Yılmaz. I also want to thank James Clem and Beth Baiter at the Harvard Academy, Ruiko Connor at the Reischauer Institute, and Clare Putnam at the Weatherhead Center for their administrative support.

In Japan, while based at the University of Tokyo as a visiting student, I benefited from the support and advice of Merthan Dündar, Hiraishi Naoaki, Karita Toru, Mitani Hiroshi, Naoki Sakai, Ôtsuka Takehiro, Sakai Tetsuya, Suzuki Norio, Suzuki Tadashi, Christopher Szpilman, Tamamoto Masaru, and Yamauchi Masayuki. During my two years stay in Tokyo, Hosaka Shuji, Misawa Nobuo, Morimoto Kazuo, Nakajima Takeshi, and Yamada Chioi became friends who not only advised me on my research but also served as host families. In Istanbul, Tufan Buzpınar, Gökhan Çetinsaya, İsmail Kara, and Azmi Özcan shared their notes, comments, and insights about the history of pan-Islamism.

Over the years, I have exchanged papers and corresponded with scholars in various parts of the world regarding the topic of this book. Engin Akarlı, Houchang Chehabi, Sebastian Conrad, John De Boer, Kevin Doak, Prasenjit Duara, Vasant Kaiwar, İbrahim Kalın, Hasan Kösebalaban, Sucheta Mazumdar, Michael Penn, David Steigerwald, Stefan Tanaka, Gesa Westerman, Renee Worringer, and Hayreddin Yücesoy were very generous in sharing their research results and critically reading my own writings. At UNCC, history department chair John Smail arranged my teaching schedule to allow maximum time for writing, while John David Smith served as an experienced faculty mentor.

In the last couple of years, I have received great inspiration from two transnational communities of scholars, with whom I met regularly for joint research projects. I would like to thank the members of the Global History Network, supported by the Deutsche Forschungsgemeinschaft, and the study group "Japan's Challenge to the International Order during the 1930s," sponsored by the Shibusawa Foundation, for exciting discussions and conversations that generally influenced my thinking on the subject of this book as well.

I would like to add my thanks to the following institutions for their financial support. The Center for Islamic Studies (ISAM) in Istanbul gave the initial grant for my doctoral study. At Harvard, the Center for Middle Eastern Studies, the Reischauer Institute of Japanese Studies, and the Weatherhead Center for International Affairs not only served as academic hosts but also provided financial assistance in different research and writing stages. The Japanese Ministry of Education and the Toyota Foundation sponsored my research in Japan. My friend Vural Ak supported my research activities during several trips to Istanbul.

I also owe thanks to Columbia University Press editor Anne Routon for her coordination of the publication of this book and the reviewers of the manuscript for their critique and suggestions. Two editors of the International History series of Columbia University Press, Matthew Connelly and Adam McKeown, critically read the manuscript and proposed valuable suggestions for its final format. I am very grateful to Sarah St. Onge for her meticulous and patient copy editing, and Carolyn G. Weaver for indexing.

My deepest gratitude is for my parents for a lifetime of love, support, and pride in my achievements. My brother Ertan Aydın, as the other Ph.D. student and then professor in the family, always provided the necessary moral and intellectual support. Finally, I owe the greatest thanks to my wife, Juliane, for our conversations, woven into the beauty of everyday life, that inspired and encouraged me in this project. She not only helped me organize the book sections and manage the writing schedule but also edited all the chapters, even during the last days of her pregnancy. Our daughter, Leyla, brought a new sense of joy to our life in the last year of this project. It is to the love and companionship of Juliane and Leyla that I dedicate this book.

THE POLITICS OF ANTI-WESTERNISM IN ASIA

1

INTRODUCTION

I WAS IN the middle of a research project on Japanese pan-Asianism when the events of September 11 sparked an unprecedented scholarly and nonscholarly discussion about Muslim rage against the West. What surprised me, as a student of modern Japanese intellectual history, was that the issues covered in historical materials about Japanese-Western relations from 1905 to 1945 seemed very similar to what journalists and news program editors were discussing with regard to the contemporary relationship between the Muslim world and the West. Both before and after the Pearl Harbor attack of 1941, almost half a century before September 11, there were similar questions about anti-Westernism in Japan, with equally similar arguments among both Japanese and Western intellectuals. As a historian with specializations in both Middle Eastern and Japanese studies, I could not help thinking about anti-Westernism in the Muslim and non-Muslim parts of Asia in a comparative context and about the implications of such a comparison for understanding and responding to the questions of today. Thus the idea for this book was born as a quest to understand the significance of anti-Western ideologies in modern international history.

A historical comparison between Japanese and Muslim critiques of the West is significant beyond the peculiarities of my academic training because it reveals the paradoxes of contemporary controversies about anti-Westernism. While a politically influential paradigm argues that the Muslim revolt against the West derives either from Muslims' inability to harmonize their religion with Western modernity or from their primordial conservative reaction to a Christian-dominated globalization process, a counternarrative emphasizes that this rage was and still is a natural response to Western imperialism and hegemony.[1] Yet this polarized literature on the roots of the clash of civilizations between Islam and the West raises more questions than it answers. If anti-Western critiques in the Muslim world had something to do the with the eternal conflict between the religious traditions of Islam and Christianity, why do we see equally strong traditions of anti-Western critiques in the non-Muslim societies of Asia, such as China and Japan?[2] Similarly, if modern anti-Western critiques were a natural response to Western colonialism, why did they not fade away in the postcolonial period?[3] Why did noncolonized parts of Asia, such as Ottoman Turkey and Japan, also develop strong traditions of anti-Western critique? If anti-Western ideologies were correlated to religious revivalism, why did so many secular and humanist thinkers formulate some of the most articulate critiques of the West?[4] More important, how can we explain the fact that many of the themes of anti-Western critiques were simultaneously formulated and expressed by European and American intellectuals as well?[5]

Existing scholarly literature on anti-Western critiques in Middle Eastern, Indian, Chinese, and Japanese histories demonstrate that anti-Western ideologies can neither be seen simply as derivative of the anticolonial struggles nor explained solely as conservative and religious reactions to global modernity.[6] Yet both religious traditions and the legacy of Western colonialism were nonetheless highly relevant for the formation of anti-Western images, discourses, and ideologies. It is thus necessary to examine historically how various religious traditions and the experience of European colonialism interacted with peculiar Muslim or non-Muslim discontent with globalization, the international order, and modernization to produce shared anti-Western discourses in the twentieth century.

With a comparative focus on Ottoman and Japanese histories, this book offers a global history perspective on modern anti-Western critiques in order to understand their genesis, content, and political significance in international history. It challenges the exceptionalist writings on the critiques of the West in the Muslim world, which have underlined the historical memory of the conflicts between Muslim and Christian political entities. This focus has led to an overemphasis of the role of confrontations between essentialized geographies of the Muslim world and the Christian West in the interpretation of anti-Western emotions and ideas at the expense of the modern global context of Muslim discourses on the West.[7] It has also led to a neglect of the largely secular critiques of the West in Middle Eastern history, because of the depiction of a misleading dichotomy between pro-Western secularists versus anti-Western religious revivalists in the Middle East when in fact in the long history of decolonization many humanist and modernist thinkers in Asia, some of them followers of Enlightenment thought, such as Namik Kemal, Mahatma Gandhi, Rabindranath Tagore, Okukara Tenshin, Celal Nuri, Ahmed Rıza, and Sun Yat-sen, formulated sharp critiques of what they considered to be the West.

It is largely due to the lack of attention to the international politics behind positive or critical images of the West that we still lack any sophisticated comparison of anti-Western thought in the Muslim world and non-Muslim Asia. The existence of a rich and diverse tradition of anti-Western critiques in the non-Muslim societies of Asia, especially in highly modern and capitalist Japan, indicates that anti-Western ideas in the Muslim world cannot and should not be reduced to the dynamics of a relationship between the followers of two interrelated faith traditions, Islam and Christianity.[8] There is a growing awareness of the need for an interdisciplinary and comparative approach to both critiques of the West and anti-Western ideologies that will take the global circulation of Western-originated anti-Western ideas into account as well.[9]

The histories of pan-Islamic and pan-Asian visions of world order provide excellent case studies for understanding the appeal and impact of anti-Western ideas in global history. Both pan-Islamic and pan-Asian ideas emerged around the same time, during the last quarter of the nineteenth century, and contained a strong element of anti-Westernism in their assessment of modernity, cultural Westernization, and the international order. Pan-Islamic and pan-Asian thought not only became very influential in the formative periods of Asian nationalisms, they were also part of the wartime ideologies of the Ottoman Empire and imperial Japan during both WWI and WWII. The literature on Western, Islamic, and Asian civilizations, as well as various political projects involving their solidarity and encounter, has always been intimately related to the debates on the normative values and power relations of a globalizing international order. Case studies of pan-Islamic and pan-Asian thought can help us explore the interrelationship of cultural debates on civilizational and racial identities, on the one hand, with diplomatic and international developments, on the other. How can we explain the rise of anti-Western ideas, emotions, and trends in Asia parallel to the globalization and Westernization of world cultures from the 1880s to the 1940s? Are anti-Western critiques a reflection of discontent with the international order or a nativist rejection of Western-originated universal modernity? What has been the impact of anti-Western ideas in modern international history?

Study of pan-Asianism and pan-Islamism necessarily involves a methodology that gives serious consideration to the role of transnational imagination and identity in international history. Since Benedict Anderson's groundbreaking work, the powerful influence of nationalist imagination has been given due attention in the study of international history.[10] Imaginations of race, religion, and civilization, however, also represent a significant force in modern world history, even though they have often been overshadowed by the emphasis on nationalism. For example, from the early Meiji period on, changing conceptions of Asia became a powerful cultural-geographical representation in relation to which the character and mission of the Japanese nation were defined and re-defined.[11] Similarly, the Muslim world as a geographical civilizational entity, not simply denoting a shared religious identity, emerged during the 1860s in relation to the evolution of the notion of the West. It is necessary to understand why the civilizational identities of Asia and the Islamic world, together with the omnipresent concept of the West, came to exist as essential components of the invention of national identity.

As a matter of fact, the predisposition to identify with an entity larger than the nation, be it a civilization, religion, or race, seems paradoxical for a histori-cal period retrospectively characterized as the age of rising nationalism.[12] The ideals of pan-Asianism and pan-Islamism were only two of the numerous simi-lar political and intellectual trends, including pan-Slavism, pan-Europeanism, and pan-Africanism. The transnational identity of being Asian, Muslim, Afri-can, or European was also significant in defining the nature of nationalism and international politics even when these were not formulated into a systematic ideology of regional, religious, or racial solidarity.[13] Moreover, these transna-tional identity constructions influenced international relations, as can be ob-served in the complex relationship between pan-Islamic and pan-Asianist ide-ology, on the one hand, and the foreign policies of two non-Western empires of the twentieth century, the Ottoman and Japanese empires, on the other.

Although there exists a rich literature on pan-Islamism and pan-Asianism, especially in the historical writings on the late Ottoman and the Japanese em-pires, scholarship on these questions contains several conflicting and compet-ing interpretations with regard to two major questions. The first question relates to the ideological significance of the anti-Westernism associated with these two non-Western visions of world order. Given that Japan was the most Western-ized and industrialized nation in Asia, with close diplomatic and cultural ties to Europe and America, how can we account for the strong current of anti-Western thought that historically characterized Japanese intellectual life in the first half of the twentieth century? Some postwar scholars have offered a sym-pathetic view of the Asianist critiques of the West, perceiving in Japan's prewar Asianist thinkers a desire to overcome the problems of Western modernity that resembled the attempts of such esteemed humanist figures as Tagore, Gandhi, and Lu Xun.[14] Another group of scholars, however, has pointed out that anti-Westernism in Japan not only undermined democratic values and party politics domestically but also encouraged the rejection of liberal international norms associated with the West, especially Wilsonian internationalism.

A similar division in historiography exists in the literature on pan-Islamism. Initially, pan-Islamism was seen as a reactionary "Islamic" response to the chal-lenge of global modernity and Western civilization as it was usually identified with international visions of Islamist individuals, whether Sultan Abdulhamid II or the Young Turk–era Islamists. It was also associated with the propaganda discourse of the Ottoman government during WWI. The existence of a larger group of secular and nationalist figures who advocated a pan-Islamic policy for the Ottoman state illustrates, however, that pan-Islamism cannot be reduced to the utopian and expansionist world order vision of some Islamist thinkers. The relationship between Turkish nationalism and pan-Islamism is much more complex, given the fact that many Ottoman intellectuals who were categorized as secular nationalists expressed pan-Islamic sympathies, ideas, and world order visions around the years of WWI. In fact, the consensus on pan-Islamic notions of solidarity among various segments of the Ottoman intellectual elite before WWI is a reminder that at one point pan-Islamism was seen not as a reactionary idea but as a realist policy option available for Muslim societies. After all, it was the Ottoman government elite, which had avoided military confrontations with the leading Western powers since the 1840s through its famous realist balance-of-power diplomacy, that ended up declaring a pan-Islamic jihad against the British, French, and Russian empires during WWI. Interpreting the official Ottoman endorsement of the anti-Western discourse of pan-Islamism during WWI as a natural response to Western imperialism is also an insufficient explanation, as the expansion of Western powers in the Muslim world had been ongoing since the 1830s. Why was there no pan-Islamism at the time of the French invasion of Algeria in 1830 or during the mutiny of Muslim soldiers against British rule in India in 1857? Why did the rise of pan-Islamism occur after the 1880s?

The second significant historical aspect of pan-Islamism and pan-Asianism is the role they played in the history of decolonization while at the same time offering justifications for the Japanese and Ottoman leaderships and their domination over East Asia and the Middle Eastern Islamic world, respectively.[15] The anti-imperialist credentials of pan-Islamism have been emphasized in the literature. After all, even Hindu nationalists such as Gandhi joined the pan-Islamic Khilafat movement of India to show solidarity with the Muslim struggles against Western imperialism. The Ottoman government also used pan-Islamism, both to call for the unity of all Muslim subjects of the empire against the nationalist demands of its Christian subjects and to assert Ottoman leadership in the Muslim world as leverage in its relationship with the European powers. During WWI, pan-Islamism was not only part of the propaganda rhetoric of the Ottoman state but also a tool used by the German Empire in its great-power competition with the British, French, and Russian empires.

Similarly, an emphasis on the anti-imperialist aspects of pan-Asianism has been part of the scholarly literature since Marius Jansen's study on the collaboration between Chinese nationalist leader Sun Yat-sen and Japanese Asianists, which demonstrated that many Japanese supporters of Sun Yat-sen acted under an idealistic anticolonial vision of solidarity between Japan and China. There is an especially rich literature on the anticolonial motivations of the Japanese who worked with Subhas Chandra Bose in the Indian National Army campaign against the British Empire during WWII. As Prasenjit Duara has suggested, during the late 1930s, pan-Asianism continued to inspire idealist individuals, groups, and religious movements with liberationist, anticolonial, and redemptive agendas even at a time when these same ideas were being utilized in the grand scheme of Japanese imperialism.[16] Yet the fact that pan-Asianism also came to be an ideological tool used in the Japanese occupation to suppress Chinese nationalism has been accepted by virtually all scholars. How do these two conflicting aspects of pan-Asianism relate to each other?[17] This question continues to be the subject of scholarly and public controversy, particularly in the context of the discussions provoked by the textbook revision movement of some Japanese groups who insist on the decolonizing legacy of Japan's wartime expansion in East and Southeast Asia, a claim that naturally attracted harsh protests from East Asian nations.[18]

These questions point up the fact that it is necessary to examine the changes in the legitimacy and inclusiveness of the Eurocentric international order, as well as transformations in the relationship between the Western center and the non-Western peripheries, to grasp better the genesis and appeal of the alternative visions of world order embodied in the anti-Western discourses of pan-Islamic and pan-Asian thought. This book argues that it was the legitimacy crisis of a single, globalized, international system that produced pan-Islamic and pan-Asian visions of world order. The content of both these alternative visions of world order was shaped by the peculiar challenge to the intellectual justifications of late-nineteenth-century imperialism, especially through discourses of Orientalism and racism. In terms of their political projects, trajectories of pan-Asianism and pan-Islamism were intertwined with the major turning points in international history that altered both the power configuration and legitimacy claims of the world order, such as the Russo-Japanese War of 1905, WWI, and Japan's occupation of Manchuria. As pan-Asianism and pan-Islamism contributed to the decolonization process and influenced the foreign policies of both the Ottoman and the Japanese governments, they also left a long-lasting legacy that influenced nationalist thought and the international relations of the post-WWII period.

This book approaches the histories of pan-Islamism and pan-Asianism in their chronological stages within the global narrative of one single Eurocentric international order in order to resolve the historiographic debates outlined above, and thus the following chapters are organized around historical turning points.

The next chapter discusses why there was no systematic anti-Westernism in Asia until the 1870s, despite the reactions to European expansion, and explains this absence by the reformist non-Western elite's ambivalent acceptance of a civilizationist worldview as legitimizing the new Eurocentric international order. The chapter discusses the emergence of the notion of a universal West, beyond the Christian and white race identity of Europeans, in the minds of Asian intellectuals and reformers. Ottoman and Japanese intellectuals during the nineteenth century attributed a quality of universality to Western civilization and constructed an abstract image of the West that became a central pillar in their visions of world order and their assessments of intensifying global interactions. Their acceptance of the normativity of the Eurocentric civilization of the nineteenth century derived from the decoupling of the narratives of European and American progress from any association with religion, race, and geography. Non-Western elites gradually became familiar not only with Enlightenment thought but also with various exceptionalist European explanations of their superiority over the rest of the world, such as those found in the writings of Montesquieu, Guizot, and Buckle. In this process, the reformist intellectuals and leaders of Japan and the Ottoman state formulated a more inclusive notion of global civilization and international order, believing that they should encounter no religious, cultural, or racial obstacle to being as civilized as the Europeans. They insisted that upon achieving a certain set of "civilized" reforms, their societies could attain not only prosperity and might but also security and equality in the emerging world order.

The appeal of membership in a secure and prosperous international society, centered in Europe and transforming the world through globalization, had been a major component of the idea of the West among non-Western elites during the nineteenth century. The reformist elites in Asia faced unequal treaties, colonial tutelage, and even some forms of discrimination by Western political entities, yet they believed that these would be temporary, disappearing once non-Western societies successfully completed the necessary civilized reforms. In other words, they imagined a potentially more inclusive international society than the one existing in the mid-nineteenth century.

The third chapter discusses the emergence of pan-Islamic and pan-Asianist ideas during the last quarter of the nineteenth century. Pan-Islamic and pan-Asian visions of world order emerged during the late 1870s in response to the perceived rejection by the European center of its own claims to the universality of modern civilization and inclusiveness of the world order. The main critique of pan-Islamic and pan-Asianist thought was directed against the "uncivilized" acts of European imperialism, which created obstacles in the process of self-civilizing reforms of non-Western societies. Thus it was a corrective critique of the world order, asking for the fulfillment of the promises of the global civilization process and the universalization of modernity.

Following the turn to formal imperialism in Europe's relationship with Asia and Africa, well observed in the scramble for Africa in the aftermath of the invasion of Egypt in 1882, Asian intellectuals became more concerned with the transnational power of the new European discourses on the Orient, race, and empire. Just when the reform projects of the Ottoman and Japanese elites were being tied to the idea of a universal West, highly rigid interpretations of civilizational and racial hierarchies that identified progress with the white race or the culture of Christianity became the dominant explanations for Western hegemony and superiority in Europe and America. This led to a crucial contradiction in the legitimacy of the Eurocentric world order: the universalist tones of the Enlightenment image of the West, well established in Asian thought until the 1880s and in many ways continuing afterward, contradicted the exclusion of the Muslim world and Asia from the liberal promises of the Enlightenment in the ideologies of the permanent racial and civilizational superiority of the West over Muslims and "yellow race" Asians.

The seeming failures of the economic and political reforms in the Ottoman state, Egypt, and China formed only part of the reasons for inspiring the thesis "the East will never be the West" and for strengthening Western discourses that coupled progress and civilization with Christianity or the white race. Although there were anti-imperialist and inclusive intellectual projects in Europe, the popularization of the cultures of imperialism in Europe strengthened the exclusion of "yellow race" and Muslim claims to equality and dignity in the world community. More important, the imperialist competition among the European powers, which initiated a period of colonization for the sake of colonization beyond the arguments of "civilizing mission," increased the sense of insecurity in the rest of the world. Yet Orientalist and race discourses were not a simple derivation of uneven power relations, as they survived beyond the power hierarchy in global relations between various societies. It is in this global context that Asian intellectuals first developed an alternative discourse of civilization and race, which continued to uphold the idea of a universal modernity while aiming to delegitimize the imperial power structures in the world order. Both Ottoman and Japanese intellectuals engaged in intense debates about notions of empire, race, civilization, progress, and humanity. Parallel to these intellectual efforts, some of them developed visions of world order springing from notions of pan-Islamic and pan-Asian solidarities in opposition to imperialist international order. Yet neither of these two anti-Western internationalisms envisioned a return to the previous isolated regional systems or deglobalization. On the contrary, pan-Islamic and pan-Asian alternatives aimed at a reunified global order divided into complementary and equal regional blocks, in which the West would be forced to abide by its own proclaimed standards in cooperation with a free and modern Islamic world and Asia. The notion of a clash between the Islamic and Christian worlds, as well as the idea of a conflict between the white and yellow races, emerged in this period. Pan-Islamic and pan-Asian intellectuals emphasized clash-of-civilization or race theories as a diagnosis and critique of European policies, not as a prescription for their vision of world order. This era also gave birth to the main argument of anti-Western discourse, namely, that the West was applying a double standard in its international relations by violating the very principles of civilized behavior that Western public opinion proclaimed.

In the fourth chapter, the emphasis is on the impact of the Russo-Japanese War of 1905 on the content and politics of pan-Islamic and pan-Asianist thought. Contemporary commentators characterized the period from 1905 to 1914 as the era of the "awakening" of the East against the Western hegemony, a slogan that became the symbol of an intellectual decolonization that preceded the political one. Worldwide responses to the Japanese victory over Russia in 1905 show how a globally interconnected public sphere interpreted the historical significance of the Japanese victory through shared notions of East-West civilizational relations and the balance of power between the white and colored races. This chapter emphasizes that the Russo-Japanese War became the key historical reference in resolving the tensions between the universalization of Eurocentric modernity, through the agency of non-Western elites, and late-nineteenth-century Orientalist and racist discourses that justified the Eurocentric imperial world order.

The Russo-Japanese War of 1905 empowered the claims of non-Western intellectuals in the debates about race, the Orient, and progress. It became the strongest evidence against the discourse of the white race's permanent and eternal superiority over the colored races. After 1905 no scholarly or nonscholarly discussion of racism and innate civilizational hierarchies in world politics could ignore the example of Japan. Anticolonial intellectuals could and did use the Japanese success to invalidate the discourse of the white man's superiority and his burden to civilize Asia. The Japanese example was similarly used in the critiques of European Orientalism, as it proved that Orientals were not inferior and the Orientalist discourse of Western superiority over other civilizations was not necessarily true. If the Japanese could achieve progress and development without colonialism, other colonized Oriental nations could do the same. The slogans about the awakening of Buddhism, Hinduism, and Islam, against the charges of the decline of these faith traditions, became part of the self-consciousness of this era. Beyond proving the equality of the colored races and Oriental peoples, the Japanese success helped Asian intellectuals to assert that the existing backwardness of Asian societies was not a result of deterministic factors, conditioned by race, culture, geography, climate, and religion. They emphasized that this underdevelopment was just a temporary delay in progress that could be altered by a set of reforms, such as the ones Meiji Japan had implemented in just three decades. Parallel to the widespread critics of the discourse of race and Orientalism as a challenge to the intellectual and moral justifications of the then-existing world order, in the aftermath of the Russo-Japanese War both pan-Asian and pan-Islamic ideas entered journalistic and scholarly writings on international affairs, signifying the revolt of rising Asia against the imperialist West and further strengthening their appeal among Asian nationalists.

The fifth chapter discusses the experience and transformation of pan-Islamic and pan-Asianist visions during WWI. Both pan-Asianist and pan-Islamist critiques of the West included an effort to define Japan's or the Ottoman state's national interest and international mission in a way that would appeal to the realist policy makers in those non-Western empires. These efforts gained special policy relevance during the crucial deliberations leading to the Ottoman Empire's decision to enter WWI. The chapter describes the triumph of pan-Islamic ideas among the Ottoman elite both as a repository of anti-Western emotions and as a new realist thinking about the Ottoman response to the geopolitics of world affairs. It argues that the pan-Islamic diagnosis of international relations as an encirclement of the Muslim world by Christian imperial powers and the fear of further isolation of the Ottoman state as a Muslim political entity created the conditions for the Ottoman decision to ally with Germany in WWI, paradoxically to express the desire to belong to European international society while fighting against the three big Western empires.

From the early 1880s to 1912, pan-Islamism was an important topic in Muslim intellectual networks and European writings on the rising nationalism and modernization movements in the Muslim world. But during this period it did not become an officially endorsed Ottoman policy, despite the fact that the Ottoman state and the caliphate institution remained a central focus of pan-Islamic imagination. The Ottoman state elite's approach to pan-Islamism gradually changed during the crisis of Ottoman international isolation initiated by the Italian invasion of Tripoli in 1911 and the Balkan wars of 1912–1913, when the Western great powers all supported Christian states in violation of their legal and diplomatic obligations. Believing that it was primal Christian solidarity, not civilization and international law, that led France, England, and Russia to support Greece, Bulgaria, and Serbia, louder voices in Ottoman public opinion debates argued for the adoption of a pan-Islamic foreign policy as the only viable response. The appropriation of pan-Islamic solidarity as a grand vision of Ottoman foreign policy during WWI shows to what extent this anti-Western vision of world order began to appeal to the realist elites in the context of the legitimacy crisis of the international system during the 1905–1914 period.

The chapter also examines how Japanese pan-Asianists redefined Asianist thought by combining a new confident discourse on the superiority of Asia/Eastern civilization with a realist policy vision of Japanese leadership in Asian awakening against the declining West. Japanese Asianists successfully campaigned for the idea that it was better for Japan to be the leader of a future free Asia than a yellow race partner discriminated against in the club of white great powers. It was during WWI that pan-Asianists sharpened their anti-Western discourse and extended the boundaries of Japan's Sinocentric vision of Asia to include India, Southeast Asia, and the Middle East. The chapter emphasizes the political conflicts between pro-British Japanese diplomacy and anti-British Asianist policy visions. While their efforts did not affect Japan's alliance with the British Empire during WWI, pan-Asianists nevertheless managed to influence Japanese public opinion, contributing to the Japanese government's decision to propose a race equality clause at the Paris Peace Conference. WWI experiences shed light on the often-overlooked roles played by pan-Islamism and pan-Asianism in the collapse of the imperial world order.

The sixth chapter emphasizes that the influence of WWI on anti-Western thought and visions of world order was paradoxical: on the one hand, the image of the decline of Western civilization eroded the political and cultural prestige of Western hegemony in Asia, strengthening the alternative civilizational discourse of pan-Asianist and pan-Islamic thought. On the other, the international appeal of pan-Islamic and pan-Asianist ideas was undermined by two powerful alternatives to the imperial world order, symbolized by the Bolshevik Revolution and the Wilsonian principles. In a sense, socialism and Wilsonianism inspired anticolonial nationalist movements by offering two Western solutions to the globally acknowledged crisis of international order. As a new world order emerged, pan-Islamist and pan-Asianist ideas were rearticulated and asserted in relation to Wilsonianism, socialism, and rising nationalist movements, allowing their visions of world order and discourse of civilization to remain relevant even though their political appeal and support diminished during the 1920s. During this process, there was a temporary alliance between the Wilsonian challenge to the imperial world order and pan-Islamic visions of solidarity in the Khilafat movement established in support of the Turkish national movement. Similarly, there were also early alliances between the anti-Western challenge to the imperial world order and socialist internationalism. Yet by 1924 both pan-Islamic and pan-Asian visions of world order had established a distinct mode of critiques and tradition in relation to the League of Nations–based liberal internationalism and socialist internationalism supported by the Soviet Union.

During the interwar period, anti-Western ideas of pan-Islamic and pan-Asianist trends relied on the failures of the League of Nations system, while intellectually utilizing the Occidentalist dichotomy of the moral East and the materialist West. Thus, even though activism in the name of Asian or Islamic solidarity did not have much influence on international politics, many non-Western intellectuals, including pro-Western liberals, began to share both a discourse of East-West civilization and a diagnosis regarding the conflict between the two.

Chapter 7 examines the nature of the revival and reinvention of pan-Asianism in Japan during the late 1930s as an official vision of international order in East Asia. The policy path the Japanese government took after its withdrawal from the League of Nations appears to have been a triumph for pan-Asianist ideas. The chapter discusses why the Japanese ruling elites, which had a long tradition of cooperation with Western powers, decided that it was rational realpolitik to embrace a pan-Asian notion of Japan-led East Asian solidarity. It was pan-Asianism's ability to justify projects of unity and assimilation within the multiethnic Japanese Empire, especially against the Chinese nationalist movement, that seemed attractive to the Japanese elites, which benefited from the anti-Western and anticolonial aspects of Asianism to solve their own crisis of imperialism in East Asia. The Japanese Empire thus could utilize the universalist and anticolonial aspects of the pan-Asian tradition of critique of the Eurocentric world order when that empire itself faced a crisis both from nationalist challenges and with regard to getting recognition from Western/white empires. It was the power of the Asianist discourse of East-West civilizational difference and the racial injustice of whites against the colored peoples that facilitated a general conversion among Japan's liberal and socialist figures to a pan-Asianist vision of world order during the 1930s, making their ideas very similar to those advocated by the pan-Asianists of the 1905–1914 period. Despite its contamination with Japanese imperial ideologies and strategies, the legacy of Asian internationalism shaped Japan's foreign policy in the era of the Greater East Asia Coprosperity Sphere and contributed to the decolonization of Asia by forcing the Allied Powers to respond to pan-Asian propaganda with a promise of a more inclusive and nonracial new world order in the aftermath of WWII.

By treating the parallel histories of pan-Islamism and pan-Asianism as a topic of international history and by situating them in their proper global context, this study aims to contribute to existing historiographic debates in both Ottoman and Japanese studies. The comparative analysis of pan-Islamic and pan-Asian thought will illustrate that certain aspects of these two alternative visions of world order should be understood beyond monocultural analysis of the Muslim or Japanese context, as products of a global constellation of ideas, power relations, and international problems. More important, this historical reassessment of the politics of anti-Western thought in Asia can hold valuable lessons for current debates on the role of cultural identity in both justifying and criticizing the existing power relations in the international order. By identifying the past achievements and obstacles in the globalization of world order from the 1880s to 1945, this historical study may also help in the current struggles to establish normative universal values for a new international order that is both legitimate and inclusive.

2

THE UNIVERSAL WEST

Europe Beyond Its Christian and White Race Identity (1840–1882)

THE HISTORICAL ORIGINS of modern anti-Western visions of world are rooted in the gradual emergence of the idea of the "universal West" in non-Western intellectual histories during the first half of the nineteenth century. The development of the image of a universal West was not a simple product of "previously ignorant" Ottoman, Chinese, or Japanese intellectuals "discovering" the superiority of European civilization.[1] Ottoman Muslim elites, for example, knew a lot about the European societies and political structures long before the nineteenth century via travelers, ambassadors, migrants, converts, soldiers, books, and other intermediaries. Yet it was only during the 1830s that Ottoman Muslim elites began to conceptualize a holistic image of Europe as a model for reform and as the potential future of the Ottoman polity. Since this rupture, imagining a universal Europe as a model of reform was no longer an issue of naive imitation or a blind rejection. A global Europe became an omnipresent topic in Ottoman thinking about politics, economy, culture, and society. This change in the thinking of non-Westerners about Europe was also not a simple product of Ottoman, or later Chinese and Japanese, military weakness vis-à-vis the European powers. An understandable focus on gunboat diplomacy in explaining the birth of the image of a universal West overlooks the global consciousness of non-Western intellectuals and political leaders. Ottoman and Japanese educated elites' enthusiastic and original ruminations about the universality and desirability of modern civilization show that the notion of universal Europe cannot be reduced to an imposition from Western powers. Revisiting the questions of how and why Ottoman and Japanese leaders imagined a universal West and recognizing their agency in constructing a more inclusive vision of civilization could help recover the global consciousness of non-Western actors beyond the paradigms of "discovery" and "diffusion."

THE GREAT RUPTURE: OTTOMAN IMAGINATION OF A EUROPEAN MODEL

The civilizational geography of the West, as an imagined intellectual center of the international community, has been the primary focus of attention in modern Asian thought since the mid-nineteenth century, creating responses ranging from admiration and emulation to visions of selective synthesis and radical critiques. As the West has not only been the historical origin of modernity and values with universal claims but also the source of a system of international norms and power politics, images of the West in Asia have always been interconnected with political attitudes to domestic reforms and international affairs. Of all non-European societies, Ottoman Muslims had the longest and closest contacts with Europe before the nineteenth century, as the Ottoman state had approximately five hundred years of encounter, exchange, cooperation, and conflict with several European states. In the period from the Congress of Vienna to the 1830s, there occurred a gradual yet radical transformation in the perception of Europe, which became the only model invoked in reorganizing the Ottoman state and in imagining the future of both Ottoman society and the world. The Ottoman state was also not isolated from the post–French Revolution or post-Napoleonic transformation in European politics and diplomacy. (An Ottoman-Russian alliance, after all, became part of the reasons for the second Napoleonic wars.) Ottoman bureaucrats had frequent interactions with their European counterparts, and the fact that they viewed late-eighteenth-century Russia as part of Europe indicates an awareness of the newly emerging European international society.

The timing of the rupture in the Ottoman perceptions of Europe in the early nineteenth century has been a controversial historical question mainly because both modern Muslims and Western scholars agreed that Ottoman elites were too late in discovering or recognizing the great cultural, scientific, and political revolutions in Europe.[2] Donald Keene, for example, briefly notes that Japanese scholars who lived in the relatively isolated world of Tokugawa Japan were more interested in European ideas during the eighteenth century than were their Muslim counterparts. He attributes this to Muslim apathy and contempt for the infidel Christians. From a global comparative perspective, however, Ottoman knowledge of the Western world was much larger than that of the Chinese, Indians, and Japanese. While Japan's Dutch scholars were trying to read European scientific books in relative isolation and difficulty, the Ottomans had ambassadors in Europe, and many Europeans who settled in Ottoman lands were given high-level bureaucratic positions.[3]

In the history of Ottoman relations with Europe throughout the seventeenth and eighteenth centuries, there was an increasing flow of information and images across the fluid Ottoman borders with Europe. During this period, the Ottoman approach to the ideas, techniques, and methods seen in Europe was selective, as they adopted some of them and dismissed or ignored others. For example, the Ottomans followed developments in military technology in Europe very closely and were able to keep pace with the innovations in Europe until the second half of the eighteenth century.[4] Similarly, Ottoman scholars accepted some of the new mathematical and astronomical theories they learned from European books without feeling any need to advocate wholesale importation of the new science.[5] The same selective method characterized the Chinese attitude toward European knowledge during the eighteenth century, as well the European approach to the Muslim and the Chinese worlds. Europe in the age of the scientific revolution and reform movements did not seem an overwhelmingly better place to live and superior place to emulate in the eyes of its Ottoman observers. Descartes, Sir Isaac Newton, and Emmanuel Kant became important for Ottomans only after the Industrial Revolution, when the Ottoman elite was trying to explain what made the Europeans very powerful.

With the intellectual efforts to understand the power generated in Europe by the Industrial Revolution and the emergence of a stable European international society after the Vienna Congress, Europe began to inspire more admiration and emulation in its Ottoman observers. A qualitative shift in the Ottoman perception of Europe occurred in the two decades after the Vienna Congress, and Europe became a constant reference for new ideas and reform agendas.[6] One can see this change clearly in the influential *Treatise on Europe,* published in 1840, by Ottoman bureaucrat Mustafa Sami Efendi.[7] Differing from the earlier selective approach to Europe, for example, Mustafa Sami Efendi does not make any negative observations about Europe. He offers a holistic assessment of the excellence of Europe and its superiority, connecting all the positive characteristics of European institutions and practices in a civilizational unity that merited emulation. Sami Efendi emphasizes that Europe's excellence in civilization derived not from its religion and climate but purely from its universal and imitable achievements in science, technology, and learning.

It is clear that the image of Europe created by Mustafa Sami Efendi represents a departure from earlier images of Europe, such as those presented in the seventeenth-century writings of Evliya Çelebi (1611–1682) on Vienna or the early eighteenth-century writings of Yirmisekiz Mehmet Çelebi (late 1660s–1732) on Paris. For instance, Yirmisekiz Mehmet Çelebi's highly positive report on French courts, libraries, hospitals, factories, fortresses, and social customs from his diplomatic mission to Paris in 1720 provided a comparison with the Ottoman world and an appreciation of French merits. But his report also included hints of social and cultural critique and refrained from presenting

Europe as the ultimate model for all Ottoman reforms.[8] In contrast, Mustafa Sami Efendi had nothing negative to write about Europe. Moreover, Ottoman intellectuals began to formulate their vision of the superiority of Europe in a new grand narrative about the linear progressive development of world civilization, which necessarily implied a hierarchy between Europeans and Ottomans in their level of civilized progress. In *A Treatise on the Circumstances of Europe*, written around the same time as Mustafa Sami Efendi's work on Europe, leading Ottoman reformist bureaucrat Sadik Rıfat Paşa even used the French word "*civilization*," without translation, to explain the political, economic, and social secret behind European power and superiority.[9]

Ottoman military weakness compared to the superior armies of major European powers and the need to emulate the methods of their European rivals to gain equality with them had clearly been an important reason behind the Ottoman interest in European science and technology. External threats and anxiety about the integrity of the Ottoman state, however, cannot explain Ottoman Westernism. The desire for a military balance of power did not mean that the ideal of catching up with the higher levels of civilization in Europe was merely tactical and soulless. After all, even the modernizing reforms in France, England, Russia, and Prussia were in one way or another related to security threats, and there was nothing exceptional about similar attempts by the Ottomans. By the 1840s, however, Ottoman interest in European civilization went far beyond military motivations. The Ottoman-educated elite became fond of the European lifestyle and the material comforts they had seen or heard about. Writings about Europe, including its histories, geography, peoples, and lifestyles, became popular reading for the Ottoman elite. More important, it was the appeal of joining a stable and prosperous family of states, a new international society, that shaped the early formulation of Ottoman Westernism.

OTTOMAN WESTERNISM AND THE EUROPEAN INTERNATIONAL SOCIETY

The Ottoman image of a universal West partly resulted from observing the stable and peaceful international order established by the Congress of Vienna and legitimized by new notions of civilization. In the aftermath of the Ottoman suppression of the Greek rebellion, the Ottoman elite developed a keen interest in how the new European diplomacy of civilization had worked against their state's interest. Although European leaders were not supposed to support a nationalist secession. European public opinion about the uncivilized nature of the Ottoman state became politically very significant, leading to European military intervention and pressures that resulted in Ottoman recognition of Greek independence in 1829 .[10] With this diplomatic crisis, a group within the Ottoman bureaucracy convinced the state elite that their image as an uncivilized or semicivilized Muslim state ruling over the grandchildren of Greek civilization played a crucial role in the negative public opinion that was influencing the political leaders of European powers. A new Ottoman political initiative proving the "civilized" nature of the empire could avoid further European hostility and intervention while securing European support for the process of domestic reform. Initially based on collaboration and a delicate balance of power among the five European powers (Britain, France, Austria-Hungary, Russia, and Prussia), the Concert of Europe system technically allowed the incorporation of new members such as the Ottoman state upon the fulfillment of "civilized" reforms by prospective members.[11]

The Gülhane Imperial Edict (Gülhane Hattı Hümayunu) of 1839, later known as the Tanzimat Proclamation, became the clear acknowledgment of the existence of a Eurocentric international society and its legitimizing discourse of universal civilization. It declared a set of legal, administrative, and fiscal reforms in order to strengthen the Ottoman state and make it a member of the new European diplomatic order. The edict was proclaimed on the accession of the new sultan, Abdülmecit I (1839–1861), on November 3, 1839. It was read by Grand Vizir Mustafa Reşit Paşa to an audience that included the sultan, ministers, top civilian and military administrators, religious leaders of the Greek, Armenian, and Jewish communities, and the ambassadors of foreign countries. After its proclamation, the edict was published in the official state newspaper, and its French translation was sent to various European states and the embassies in Istanbul.

By issuing the Tanzimat Proclamation, the Ottoman state challenged the Eurocentric international order to clarify its principles of inclusion. Could a multiethnic and multireligious empire, which occupied most of Eastern Europe, be a part of the European state system despite the fact that it was ruled by a Muslim dynasty? As early as the second half of the eighteenth century, Ottoman diplomats visiting Europe were already envisioning peace between the Christian states of Europe and the Muslim Ottoman state as a value in itself, beyond the benefit of providing the Ottoman Empire with protection from the threat of the alliance among Christian European states.[12] Once the Ottoman elite recognized the emergence of a European international society evolving around the diplomacy of the Concert of Europe, they hoped this society would function according to normative principles and customs without creating any discrimination against the Ottomans. In other words, they were in favor of a diplomacy based on civilizational principles, not on Christian solidarity.[13] After all,

Ottoman Muslims shared both the Hellenistic legacy and a monotheistic faith with contemporary civilized Europe and believed that civilization was the common heritage of humanity, not an exclusively European ideal.[14]

Several of the leaders of the European powers were supportive of Ottoman elites' desire to be part of European international society. Two of the leading Ottoman bureaucrats who played important roles in drafting the Gülhane Imperial Edict, Sadik Rifat Paşa and Mustafa Reşit Paşa, had experience as ambassadors in European capitals. They had had the chance to consult and discuss issues of civilization, religious identity, and international relations with leading European diplomats such as the Austrian foreign minister, Prince Metternich, and the British foreign secretary, Lord Palmerston. The latter supported the Tanzimat reforms, confidently asserting that "there is no reason whatsoever why [Turkey] should not become a respectable power" with ten years of peaceful reorganization and reform.[15] Despite the fact that Metternich championed a conservative European system while Palmerston was a liberal, they both agreed on the question of dealing with the Ottoman state as part of the European state system.

The ideas in the Tanzimat Proclamation originated in the tradition of reforms implemented by Mahmud II, who, during the 1820s and 1830s, had centralized the government, restructured the military and administration, established new educational institutions, and introduced European-style dress and head coverings. Mahmud II's reforms were also partly intended to shape the image of the Ottoman state as a civilized society, worthy of respectful treatment in Europe. For example, the reform of Ottoman bureaucratic attire, and especially headgear, started before the Tanzimat period.[16] Since the implementation of this reform, Ottoman bureaucrats had dressed almost exactly like their European counterparts. The fez, which, a century later, became the symbol of Ottoman Muslim identity, was initially intended to symbolize the Ottoman adoption of civilized European dress. Although there had been a strong line of continuity of reform since the beginning of the nineteenth century, the Gülhane Imperial Edict domestically empowered the Europhile bureaucracy and reduced the power of the sultan-caliph to assure full rights and equality to non-Muslims under the reinterpreted rule of *Shari'a* (Islamic law).

The frequent and underlined references to Shari'a and Islamic universalism in the Tanzimat Proclamation, the foundational text of Ottoman Westernization, are not paradoxical. This was no double language intended to prevent negative reactions from conservative elements. Rather, references to Islamic ideals in Tanzimat texts are an indication that, in the mind of the Ottoman reformist group, certain aspects of the European civilized polity, such as the rule of law, equality of religious minorities, and protection of property, did not contradict the traditions of Islamic legal thinking. The convergence between reinterpreted Islamic universalism and Westernism was characteristic of the era. In Egypt during the same time period, Rifaah Rafi al-Tahtawi (1801–1873) formulated a universal vision of liberal civilizationism in Islamic terminology, based on his observations during a long period of stay in Europe.[17] Similarly, Khayr al-Din Tunisi (1810–1889) implemented liberal reform ideas with the strong conviction that parliamentary government and modern European ways were compatible with the Islamic tradition.[18] Precisely because of the Ottoman agency in the construction of the image of universal West and the global consciousness underlying this image, Ottoman reforms based on European models were never an unfiltered mimicry of European culture at the expense of betraying tradition, especially Islamic tradition. Most of the Muslim reformers ruling the Ottoman state saw values, institutions, and international norms in Europe as universal, not peculiarly Christian.

A NON-CHRISTIAN EUROPE?

The Ottoman political elite's diagnosis of the European model as a universal example might seem odd in light of many educated European elite's own sense of the superiority of Christianity over Islam and of the white race over the colored peoples. It is even more surprising given that the Ottomans continuously witnessed diplomatic maneuvers by European powers with the goal or excuse of protecting Christian subjects of the Ottoman Empire. Yet the Ottoman observers of Europe consistently decoupled European civilization from its Christian roots.

From Europeans with whom they conversed, the Ottomans heard that Christianity was one of the reasons for Europe's superiority. Yet in diagnosing and explaining the secrets of Europe's achievements they avoided making any reference to Christianity, appropriating instead the more neutral terms "civilization" and "universal civilizing process." The new paradigm emphasized the inclusive aspects of the progress of humanity through a historical, developmentalist vision of world "civilization." The Ottoman rejection of any attempt to couple universal civilization with Christianity coincided with a dominant Enlightenment worldview in Europe during that particular period.[19] Ottoman bureaucrats soon became aware of the universalist thinking both in eighteenth-century Enlightenment thought and in the conservative thought of post–French Revolution Europe.

In the early nineteenth century, European self-perception of superiority exhibited an openness and universalism that it did not have after the rise of Social Darwinism and racism at the end of the century. The best example of this change can be seen in the early Orientalist literature in Europe, the discipline that is now identified with the discourse of European superiority over the Orient. As Vasant Kaiwar and Sucheta Mazumdar remind us, early conservative but universalist Orientalism, as seen in the writings of William Jones, exhibited a belief in the unity of all humanity with regard to some great and fundamental principles. Especially after the French Revolution, conservative universalism was revived in search of stability, which was found in the Orient.[20] Similarly, racism, though not in the late-nineteenth-century scientific form, was already part of the European discourse explaining its superiority over the rest of the world, but this racism initially did not disturb the Ottoman elite for two reasons. First, the Ottomans viewed themselves as belonging to the Caucasian race and thus were not offended by racist perceptions of the natives of Australia, Africa, and the Caribbean. Second, they could rely on the universalism of the Islamic tradition to embrace and modify Enlightenment universalism. The tensions between the universal humanism of Enlightenment thought and racism could be resolved by Ottoman observers of Europe partly because they, like their European counterparts, did not see humanism and racism as contradictory during the first half of the nineteenth century. The Muslim leaders of the Ottoman state thus believed they should encounter no religious, cultural, or racial obstacles to being as civilized as the Europeans, as long as they completed a set of reforms that would allow them to reach a higher level on the universal ladder of progress.

The Islamic intellectual tradition, especially through the writings of medieval Muslim traveler, historian, and social observer Ibn Khaldun, had its own way of explaining differences in wealth and power. Ottoman intellectuals, though aware of the cyclical Khaldunian view of history in their approach to the decline and rise of states, did not agree with his determinism and thus adopted reforms to get the Ottoman state out of its decline.[21] The earlier Khaldunian perspective definitely influenced Ottomans' observations of Europe, but their thinking on the history of civilization was shaped by European writings and a self-perception of Europe as being at the top of a linearly developing world history. Starting from Montesquieu's *De l'esprit des lois* to Guizot's *Historie de la civilization en Europe* and Buckle's *History of Civilization in England*,[22] European intellectuals outlined a theory of Europe's superiority over other geographies. Utilizing the same vision and framework of civilizational progress, several European writers, such as Alexandre Blacque and David Urquhart, asserted that Ottomans were capable of development similar to Europeans.[23] And although Montesquieu's ideas implied that climate was a determinant in Europe's superior progress, François, baron de Tott (1733–1793), noted that the negative influence of a climate could be overcome by moral force.[24]

Ottoman observers used a similar language of civilization to describe Europe's material progress in constructing new roads, hospitals, libraries, and hotels and their achievements in bureaucracy, dress codes, socialization, and public hygiene.[25] The term Ottoman intellectuals picked to translate the concept of "civilization" was derived from the Arabic word for city and civility: "*medeniyet.*" Though the meaning of the term evolved from the 1830s to the 1860s, around the 1860s "*medeniyet*" was not only a simple equivalent of the word "civilization" but also referred to every good thing contemporary European civilization represented: the highest stage in the progress of humankind and a sure path that was to be followed by the Ottomans.[26] The term connoted refinement and good taste and saw no contradiction with the classical Islamic notions of civility, chivalry, and social ethics.

The legacy of Islamic thought already contained a notion of a world history and civilizational vision, which made it easier to adopt the vision of a singular universal civilization.[27] Ahmed Cevdet Paşa, one of the most talented and long-serving Tanzimat bureaucrats, reformulated an Islamic vision of universal history after appropriating some elements of Enlightenment world history. According to Cevdet Paşa, civilization was the shared product of all religions and cultures.[28] He thought that universal civilization chose the best culture and society in a certain period as its residence. Thus civilization moved from India, Babylon, Egypt, and Greece, to Muslim Mesopotamia, and finally to Europe. Each stage preserved the characteristics and contributions of those that went before. The final state of civilizations could be shared by all, although its best habitation was now in Europe. Only God could know what would the best residence for civilization after its European period.[29]

Just as the antonyms for "civilization" in European languages were "barbarity" and "savagery," the term that the Ottomans usually preferred was "*bedeviyet,*" which if translated could be taken as offensive as it signified the lifestyle of Bedouin Arabs and nomadic Turks. The idea of a permanent superiority of civilized people over "savage" nomadic people contradicted Khaldunian sociology and general medieval Muslim thought, which often attributed positive qualities such as dynamism, hospitality, and solidarity to Bedouin Arabs.[30] The Ottoman elite's vision of the progress of "universal civilization" and their identification of the nomads with barbarism allowed them to blame the opposition to modernizing reforms on concepts of savagery and nomadism. It also reflected an Istanbul-based perspective on the cultures and customs of Ottoman populations that saw Ottoman populations as needing civilizing reforms by the central government.[31]

There were several strategic uses of this idea of a universal European civilization. The state elite could demand sacrifices and radical transformations from its population by justifying them in the name of Ottoman self-strengthening through Western style reforms, presented as a universal path of progress. Civilizing reforms could also be implemented autocratically, without popular participation, because the state elites, by virtue of their familiarity with European languages and lifestyles, could claim that they knew what was best for the future of Ottoman state and society. Thus it was in the interest of the Ottoman bureaucracy to be Europhiles and to insist on the universality and applicability of the European model.

Parallel to their recognition of a superior universal civilization in Europe, members of the Ottomans elite agreed that they themselves were less modern and less civilized than the Europeans and hence needed rapid reforms in order to develop in the same direction in a short period of time. They were ready to accept the conditions proclaimed by the European center for equal membership in the emerging global order. This internationalization of the historicist vision of civilizational hierarchies, combined with Islamic universalism, convinced the Ottomans that they could adopt European institutions and methods without abandoning their Islamic tradition.

Ottoman reformist elites from 1839 to the 1860s found their civilized image and their close cooperation with the leading power of European international society, Great Britain, working to their advantage in international affairs. The alliance with the European powers against Russia during the Crimean War (1853–1856) became the biggest achievement of Ottoman diplomacy. Just two decades after the Greek rebellion, when the European powers had sided with the Greeks, the Ottoman government was in alliance with Britain and France against Russia. Ottoman generals were fighting beside British and French generals in amazingly similar military uniforms. Ottoman membership in the club of European states provided a sense that the Tanzimat policies actually worked, and the Ottoman state gained a legitimate right to international existence as a recognized member of the Concert of Europe at the Treaty of Paris, signed at the end of the Crimean War in 1856.[32]

THE WEST IN EARLY JAPANESE REFORMIST THOUGHT

Late Tokugawa Japanese thought contained a strong trend of anti-Christian and anti-Western thought. Yet, in about half a century, the Japanese elite also began to look at Western civilization as a model for reform. Despite three decades between the Tanzimat Proclamation and the Meiji Restoration, the transformation of the Japanese perception of the Eurocentric international order and Western civilization followed a trajectory similar to the Ottoman path. Japanese intellectuals, too, invented and imagined a universal West until the mid-1880s. Islamic and Confucian universalism as well as the specificities of their relations with Western powers shaped the differences between the Ottoman and Japanese experiences. The shared global context and European influences would soon, however, make Ottoman and Japanese reformists think in similar ways.

Although Confucianism was the main philosophical inspiration behind negative images of Europeans as lacking in morals and virtues, protonationalist currents in Japan motivated antiforeignism among late Tokugawa intellectuals. Interestingly, this antiforeign trend went hand in hand with the increase in Western learning. The main fear of a group of Tokugawa-period Japanese political leaders was the Christianization of the Japanese islands, which, in their view, could result in the colonization of Japan, similar to the experience of the Philippines. Antiforeignism of the early nineteenth century relied on increased information about Europe and thus was not a simple retrograde cultural xenophobia. It was based on an informed analysis of changing world conditions. For example, Aizawa Seishisai identified Western national power with the unifying role of a civil religion, Christianity, and argued that Japan should mobilize its cultural resources to combat Western influence through an emperor-centered national religion.[33]

Despite the spread of antiforeign sentiments in Japan in the early nineteenth century, many Confucian thinkers began to appreciate aspects of Western civilization, judging them to be positive implementations of Confucian ethics. Division of the world into a civilized Confucian zone and the uncivilized barbarians outside of it did not mean that Confucian scholars could not perceive any values and merits in foreign societies. As the knowledge of Europe and America increased in Japan through the medium of Dutch studies,[34] some Confucian scholars began to note that European respect for knowledge, scholars, and books, as well as the principles of fair and just government that held sway in that continent, were all more characteristic of ideal Confucianism than were the existing practices of Tokugawa Japan. For example, Shiba Kokan (1738–1818) wrote appreciatively of the European custom of providing facilities for widows and orphans, hospitals, and poorhouses, practices harmonious with the Confucian notions of civilization. When the United States demanded Japan's much wider opening to the world, Sakuma Shôzan (1811–1864) suggested that the response to the American consul should reflect awareness of the convergence between proclaimed Western values and Confucian values. Even when Shôzan criticized the actual trade and military policies of European countries, symbolized in the act of the Opium War, in order to criticize the U.S. imposition on Japan, he contrasted these policies to the European ideals of cherishing humanity, justice, and courtesy. In 1860 Yokoi Shonan even recognized that the West was far superior to Japan in Confucian morals.[35]

Hence, when the Japanese state declared its commitment to Western-inspired reforms and recognized the legitimacy of the Eurocentric world order in the famous Five Articles of the Charter Oath of the Meiji Revolution, it could speak about the radical changes necessary in the country as a revival of Confucianism: "Abolish coarse customs from olden times and stand by the 'Fair Way of Heaven and Earth.'"[36] Highly similar to the persistent references to the Islamic universalism of the Shari'a in the Ottoman Tanzimat Proclamation, the references to Confucianism in the Meiji Charter Oath should not be taken as a tactical deception of the population. They were rather an affirmation of the universalism seen in Western civilization expressed through a Confucian language, a convergence that was long recognized by many late Tokugawa intellectuals. When the Meiji emperor declared that his subjects would "seek knowledge in the world and promote the conditions of the emperor's reign," all knew that this meant a recognition of the superiority of the civilization in Europe and America and the necessity to learn from it. Yet this moment of radical turn to the West was initially endorsed by Confucian worldviews as well.

To translate the European concept of "civilization," Japanese intellectuals picked a word from the Confucian classics, "*bunmei.*" Though initially the Confucian approach to the concept of civilization referred more to the traditional sense of refinement of human character and social life through learning and morality, soon "*bunmei*" gained the meaning of linear and limitless progress embodied in Enlightenment thought. Hence the support Confucian universalism gave to the idea of emulating and learning from the superior example of Western civilization led to a self-destructive intellectual transformation as a new generation of Western-educated Japanese thinkers turned against the Confucian tradition.[37]

Once Japan was forced to open its ports to international trade by the new international system, it had to send missions to America and Europe, both for diplomatic exchanges and to learn the secrets of Western military power. After the opening of the first embassy to the United States in 1860, the frequency and importance of diplomatic missions and other travels to Western countries increased. What is crucial here is the transition in the language used to communicate visitors' observations. Though the initial discussions were selective and critical, soon a literature of praise and admiration for Western civilization emerged. The first example of this pro-Western literature is Fukuzawa Yukichi's famous best-seller *Seiyô jijyô* (Conditions in the West).[38] There, Japanese readers read the first depictions of Western civilization as a total system, worthy of reflection and emulation. Fukuzawa even offered his own universal theory of world civilizations in his 1875 book *An Outline of a Theory of Civilization*.[39]

The importance of the Western model in the reform and renovation of Japan can best be seen in the official study tour of a delegation of top-level ministers and bureaucrats to America and Europe that spanned nearly two years, between 1871 and 1873. Even the idea behind the so-called Iwakura Mission was an indication of the inevitable path of Westernization. The question was only which countries to choose as models and which pace and degree of Westernization to aim for. Similar to Tanzimat leaders and Muslim liberals, early Meiji reformers in Japan hoped to join the international community with equal rights through rapid Westernizing reforms. Interestingly, symbolic aspects of Western civilization also mattered in the Japanese drive to join the Euro-American civilized world. Reminiscent of Sultan Mahmud II's dress reforms, the Meiji emperor changed his dress from elaborate Shinto clothing to Western-style tight pants and uniforms in 1871.[40] It was only appropriate that the Japanese emperor look "civilized" and "masculine" to symbolize Japan's aspiration to gain acceptance by the Eurocentric international community.

The initial overriding desire for Westernizing reforms to strengthen the Japanese state against foreign threats soon gave way to a fascination with the Westernized lifestyles Japanese visitors observed during the boom of travel to Europe and America. A large collection of books representing the European Enlightenment and nineteenth-century liberal thought was introduced to Japan through translations and foreign instructors.[41] While this Westernization wave led to antitraditionalism, it also sustained an optimistic view of Japan's future as an equal member of the civilized community of nations once the self-civilizing cultural revolution was completed. In fact, anxieties about an over-Westernization of domestic cultural and social life could only be countered and defused by the logic of necessity in international politics and the promise of a future prosperity in an interconnected global community. This internalized liberal civilizationism also justified unequal treaties, which were explained as natural results of the temporary inferiority in Japan's level of civilization. Liberal Westernists believed that the interventions of the Western powers would disappear as Japan progressed and fulfilled all the required principles of civilization.

The frequency of travels to Europe and America, as well as the government's commitment to Western style reforms after the Meiji Restoration further entrenched the image of superior Western civilization. Voyages inspired by diplomatic necessity and curiosity were followed by an immense student movement from Japan to America and Europe, especially Germany. Japan had issued approximately ten thousand student passports by the end of the nineteenth century. A large number of well-paid European and American scholars and professors were also invited to Japan. Even though these professors were replaced by their Japanese students in a decade, the Eurocentric content of knowledge in Japanese higher education remained firmly in place throughout the first three decades after the Meiji Restoration.

At this pro-Western reformist moment, Japanese leaders had to think about the Christian character of the core members of the international society in

Europe. Participants in the Iwakura Mission were confronted with questions regarding the freedom to practice Christianity in Japan. These questions and conversations alerted Japanese leaders to the issue of Christianity in their attempt to create a civilized image of Japan in Western countries. In fact, on the return of the Iwakura Mission, the previous prohibition on Christian missionary activities was lifted, and both practicing and proselytizing for the Christian faith became unrestricted.[42] Conversion to Christianity became very common among Western-educated youth during the first three decades of the Meiji reforms. Some intellectuals and political leaders even debated whether it would be necessary for Japan to convert to Christianity as a nation in order to gain equality in the international system. Fukuzawa Yukichi went so far as to suggest that Japan should formally declare itself a Christian state in order to gain international advantages: "We do not propose that a majority of our people should become Christians, a small proportion would be enough. All that is necessary is to accept that name of a Christian country."[43]

Aside from the personal decisions involved in any process of conversion to Christianity, however, Japanese leaders had to consider the politics of the representation of the emperor's religious character. The officially sanctioned belief in the Japanese emperor as a Shinto deity made him appear to be an uncivilized or less civilized leader in the eyes of Westerners. In the end, Japan's political leaders refrained from presenting the Shinto tradition of the emperor ideology as a religion. Rather, they depicted it as a national folk tradition and custom. Instead, Buddhism was eventually presented as a "civilized" religion that could be an alternative to Western Christianity in a secular modern Japan.[44] Japanese political leaders carefully observed the ties and tensions between the Eurocentric international order and the Christian culture of the core states and successfully managed to create a positive image of Japan in the predominantly Christian European public opinion.

For Japanese modernizers, the racial identity of advanced Western civilization soon became a more important question than Christianity in determining their acceptance into Eurocentric international society. Moreover, as Japanese knowledge about Western thought increased, the Japanese realized that Christianity, though a Western religion, was very much under attack from scientific and modern thinking. In this battle, more and more Japanese became attracted to the appeal of nonreligious and scientific thought, both on the merits of its arguments and because these non-Christian theories seemed more inclusive.[45] For example, in the Philosophical Ceremony, first conducted at Tokyo University in 1885, Japanese students, graduates, and teachers venerated the images of "Four Sages" of universal philosophy: Socrates, Kant, Buddha, and Confucius. The very fact that Jesus was deliberately omitted, with Socrates and Kant chosen instead to embody the West, while Buddha and Confucius embodied the East, shows the reluctance of Japanese intellectuals to make any association between the West and Christianity.[46]

Beyond their adoption of European ideas and self-perceptions relating to progress, enlightenment, and civilization, Japanese intellectuals soon developed their own universal theories regarding the diversity of global cultures and their relationship with the imagined universal civilization of the West. The best example of post–Meiji Restoration liberal civilizationism was Fukuzawa Yukichi's book *An Encouragement of Learning* (*Gakumon no Susume*)[47], which sold approximately a million copies. Fukuzawa wrote about the hierarchy of civilizations, whereby Europe represented strong, wealthy, and mature civilization while Asia and Africa were characterized by lower levels of civilization producing poor and weak nations. It was clear for Fukuzawa's readers that Japan had to climb on the ladder of civilization in order to reach the highest level, identified with the universal West.[48]

Reading these early liberal universalist Japanese writings, one may get the impression that they were mostly receiving their ideas from the great minds of the European Enlightenment. Though this is largely true, during the process of translation, Japanese reformists usually modified European theories to make them more universal and inclusive. They especially revised the deterministic conditions such as geography, culture, and race that European thinkers noted in explaining the superiority of the West and the backwardness of the rest of humanity. For example, Fukuzawa Yukichi's *An Outline of the Theory of Civilization*, written in 1875, presented a more universal vision of progress for all nations and geographies. Declaring his intellectual maturity and independence with regard to the Western origin of his ideas, Fukuzawa noted that Japanese intellectuals familiar with Western civilization were in a superior position to theorize about the conditions and progress of civilization, because they knew both the Western and non-Western world very well. Moreover, he criticized and modified Buckle's *History of Civilization in England*,[49] the inspiration for Fukuzawa's own book, because Buckle's theories argued that civilizations in Asia were doomed to stagnation because of their geography and climate. In his own alternative theory of civilization, Fukuzawa distinguished external elements of civilization from the "spirit of civilization" and attributed the real progress of civilization to the latter. Such a distinction allowed Fukuzawa to suggest that with globalization and the spread of the "spirit of civilization," all non-Western societies could progress in the path of civilization.[50] Fukuzawa's critique of Buckle shows that Japanese intellectuals were aware that European thinking about the history and theory of civilization usually noted that climate, geography, race, and culture could be an impediment to progress in non-Western societies. But they revised these theories to argue that, with globalization and the spread of modern ideas, every society could attain the level of civilization in the West. As a result, Japanese reformists also preferred to depict a West more universal than most Western thinkers would have accepted.

The widespread belief among Japanese Westernizers that progressive change was possible, desirable, and manageable everywhere facilitated the popularity of Samuel Smiles's *Self-Help,*[51] which was first translated into Japanese in 1870. This book, similar to the equally popular translation of *Robinson Crusoe,* provided the inspiration to believe that Japan, like a "poor boy in the family of nations," could be a land of power and wealth.[52]

When a group of young Japanese intellectuals started advocating a radical vision of cultural Westernization, they were framing their antitraditionalism through the appeal to liberal civilizationism, while assuming that no cultural and racial barrier would prevent the Japanese nation from gaining equality with the Western powers after the completion of reforms. This Westernist ideology of reform was best formulated by Tokutomi Sohô (1863–1957). The son of a wealthy peasant, Tokutomi was among the first group of Japanese students who received Western style education in the newly established schools run by Americans or Europeans. He came into conflict with his parents by embracing Christianity, believing that the propagation of Christianity would serve the Japanese nation by superseding outmoded traditional Japanese ways of thinking. He was convinced that Western civilization was the only universal civilization and that Japan should even adopt Christian ethics to embark on the universal path of progress and development. He read the works of great Western thinkers such as Macaulay, Tocqueville, Guizot, Spencer, Mill, and Rousseau as sources of universal guidance as to what the Japanese people should do. In his best-seller *Nihon no Seinen* (The youth of the new Japan), Tokutomi Sohô asked Japanese youth to emulate the qualities found in the liberal democratic societies of the West and to discard the old ways of Japan in this process of Westernization.[53] In *The Future of Japan,*[54] he confirmed his belief in liberal civilizationism, predicting that with free trade and Westernization, Japan would adapt to the "trends of the times" (*jisei*) and be part of a global order of advanced nations. His ideas were based on a belief in universal standards of development along the Western patterns. He did not assume that Japan's cultural difference and unique qualities would prevent its inevitable adaptation to the Eurocentric trends and the international order.[55]

Similarly, another influential thinker of Meiji Japan, Taguchi Ukichi, argued that Japan must adopt Western practices because of their universal value and applicability. This was simply the only way to establish equality between Japan and the advanced Western countries. For him, the path of unilinear progress to universal civilization was unaffected by national, religious, cultural, and environmental differences.[56] Even Fukuzawa Yukichi's controversial 1885 article "Datsu-A-Ron," which argued that it would be better for Japan to "leave Asia" and join the ranks of civilized Europe, demonstrates the Japanese appreciation of the universality of European civilization beyond its Christian and racial character, as it assumes that Japan would face no obstacle in joining the universal Europe.[57] Although Fukuzawa Yukichi's "leave Asia, enter Europe" thesis reflected his disillusionment with the failure of reform efforts in Korea and suggested that Japan should treat its Asian neighbors as European powers would do, it also signaled a tension between the metacontinental imagination and Eurocentric projects of civilizing reforms. While Japan was firmly situated in the continent of Asia according to nineteenth-century mapping and thus carried all the cultural affiliations of this map location, the aspirations of Japanese intellectuals were to transform Japan into a European–style civilized nation. It should be remembered that similar dilemmas existed for the pro-reform Westernizing elites of other non-Western nations. Khedive Ismail, who ruled Egypt between 1863 and 1879, is reported to have pronounced "my country is no longer in Africa, it is in Europe" to note the success of his reform projects.[58]

THE MODERN GENESIS OF PAN-ISLAMIC AND PAN-ASIAN IDEAS

The fact that pro-Western liberal civilizationism was the dominant reformist and intellectual agenda in both Ottoman Turkey and Japan during the first decades of their state-centered reform programs did not mean there were no critiques of the West during that time. On the contrary, both the 1839–1882 period in Ottoman Turkey and the 1853–1882 period in Japan witnessed strong protestations against the international policies of the Western powers, and there were many critical observations on European culture and politics. Respect for the Enlightenment West and the ideology of liberal civilizationism, however, became the dominant paradigm despite these critical observations. Civilizationism diffused the optimistic vision that unequal and unjust conditions between the West and the Islamic world or the West and Asia would disappear once Westerners and non-Westerners alike fulfilled the principles of civilization.

Moreover, in their critiques of the West from the middle of the nineteenth century onward, non-Western intellectuals began to make reference to abstract universal ideals and normative principles with which they thought the intellectuals of Western world would agree. Both Japanese and Ottoman critiques of Western policies began to point out the contradictions between the civilization claims of the European powers and their actual policies.

In the Ottoman case, discontent with European interventions on behalf of the Christian subjects of the Ottoman Empire became one of the major sources of critique of the reform process among Muslim populations. As Christian citizens of the empire gained equal rights with Muslims through Ottoman reforms, they were also allowed to keep the privileges accorded by earlier Ottoman-Islamic customs, such as exemption from military conscription. Non-Muslims involved in foreign trade also gained the right to have their complaints adjudicated by the embassies of Western powers rather than by Ottoman authorities. This condition practically put Ottoman Christians outside the discipline and the control of the centralized state apparatus and thus violated the essence of Ottoman legal and political modernization, which aimed at creating a central state capable of educating, taxing, and conscripting all Ottoman citizens, irrespective of religion, creed, or race. This issue became very sensitive when Ottoman authorities tried to control nationalist and secessionist movements among Christian subjects and later constituted a major cause for the upcoming diplomatic and military conflicts with the Russian Empire. Ottoman Muslim reformists were very open to European pressures for human rights and the equal treatment of Christian subjects. Yet they perceived these pressures as a denial of their claim that the Muslim rulers of the Ottoman state could be civilized enough to gain the loyalty of their Christian subjects. As long as the Ottoman Muslim dynasty was abiding by the standards of civilized rule, Muslim intellectuals reasoned, there was no need for Europeans to intervene to help Christians Ottomans secede from the empire. Muslim critics rightly asked why Muslim subjects of the British, Russian, and French empires had no political, social, and economic equality, while those powers asked the Ottoman Empire to give more rights and privileges to non-Muslim minorities. Gradually, Muslim public opinion raised concerns that European interventions in the name of implementing civilizing reforms were in fact biased attempts to strengthen Christians. It was a visible contradiction that the same European powers asking for liberty, autonomy, and equality for the Christian subjects of the Ottoman state were denying moral, civilized treatment to Muslim subjects in the imperial domains of India, Algeria, and Central Asia.

The Ottoman government itself, however, never took steps that would challenge the legitimacy of European empires and their expansion over Muslim lands. Even though Ottoman public opinion was generally sympathetic toward Muslim resistance against the civilized Western powers of the British, Russian, and French empires, the government could not do much to support them. During the 1857 Great Indian Rebellion led by Muslims, Ottoman rulers sided with the civilized British administration rather than the Muslim populations of India. The British government even got a letter from the sultan (or claimed to have received such a letter) urging Indian Muslims to cooperate with the civilized rule of the British government and not to rebel against it.[59] Similarly, the Ottoman government did not support the Muslim resistance to the Russian Empire in the Caucasus, except during the Crimean War.[60] Yet, despite the lack of any support from the Ottoman rulers to various Muslim resistance movements against Western colonialism, the Ottoman caliphate was becoming more popular in the Islamic world precisely because the caliph was perceived as the head of a civilized Muslim state with full and equal diplomatic relations with the European powers. It was this perception that prompted Acehnese leaders to ask for the support of the Ottoman government against Dutch attacks.

The first notions of Islamic solidarity emerged not as a traditional reaction to the modernization of the Ottoman state but rather because of the increasing prestige of the Ottoman caliph as the leader of a civilized state recognized as a member of the civilized international society. When the Ottoman caliph received a request for aid from the sultan of Aceh in 1873 to ward off Dutch attacks, the Aceh rulers were mobilizing the diplomacy of civilization, not any medieval Islamic notion of caliphate. Citing a document issued a century earlier by the Ottoman caliph recognizing Aceh as an Ottoman dependency, the Aceh rulers hoped that Ottoman protection would make the Dutch attacks illegitimate as the Dutch would have to honor their civilized diplomatic relations with the Ottoman state.[61] All the ambassadors of the European powers in Istanbul came together to protest the potential Ottoman support for Aceh, fearing this would set a precedent for other Muslim territories already colonized or on the verge of being colonized by the European powers. At the end of this diplomatic crisis, the Ottoman state had to withdraw even its earlier recognition of Aceh as a dependency.

From the perspective of the advocates of support for Aceh in Ottoman Istanbul, the issue was not a matter of reactionary Muslim alliance but of moral obligation to protect backward Muslim areas from colonial control so that the Ottoman center in turn could lead them to a higher level of civilization and progress. In other words, Ottoman advocates of support for Aceh were utilizing the notion of the civilizing mission by noting that it should be the duty of a Muslim state, not the Dutch empire, to help raise the level of civilization in Aceh. Meanwhile, the Aceh debates increased Ottoman curiosity about Muslims in different parts of the world and helped create a trans-state Muslim identity. The Young Ottoman intellectual Namik Kemal noted with a hint of irony that, during the 1870s, the Ottoman public began to ask for solidarity with the Muslims of Western China, in whom they had little interest twenty years earlier.

When the number of references to the idea of Islamic unity increased in the Ottoman press, the Dutch and British governments protested against these writings to the Ottoman government, which led to a governmental warning to the press that it should avoid references to anti-Western unity in the Muslim world that could arouse suspicion among the Western powers. It is in this context that, in August 1873, the British Foreign Office asked all its representatives in the Muslim world to do research and send assessment reports about the religious and political revival, especially with respect to its connection to the Ottoman caliphate. The twenty-nine reports produced by British Foreign Office representatives in the Muslim world indicated that there was no organized pan-Islamic movement for the caliphate. They noted, however, that Muslims were becoming more aware of the conditions in other Muslim lands and that they had more contacts as a result of improving communication and transportation opportunities. Although the British Foreign Office reports concluded that pan-Islamic solidarity was not an immediate threat, as Dutch colonial authorities of the time had exaggeratedly asserted, they noted that the rising international awareness of Muslims had to be followed with special attention.[62]

Ideals of pan-Asian solidarity emerged around the same time as pan-Islamism. Early Meiji pan-Asianism also developed as a critique of the reforms based on the ideology of civilizationism and date back to the era of the Freedom and People's Rights Movement of the 1870s.[63] During the 1840s and 1850s, Japanese intellectuals were very critical of the British policies toward China during the Opium Wars. In fact, Japanese antiforeignism, symbolized by the slogan "expel the barbarians," became a motto of the Meiji Restoration partly because of the mistrust of Western intentions. Ironically, those leaders who came to power with the slogan "expel the barbarians" implemented a comprehensive reform program in order to achieve all the European standards of civilization. Yet, in the first two decades of Meiji era self-civilizing reforms, there was an authoritarian Westernization in the sense that all reforms were implemented from the top down without any recourse to participatory rule. In terms of Japan's foreign policy, the emphasis was on cooperation with the Western powers to gain their trust as a newly civilized nation and finally to eliminate unequal treaties. Early ideas of pan-Asianism arose out of a liberal opposition to Meiji Westernization and combined its criticism of Japan's foreign policy toward East Asia with opposition to the elitist nondemocratic process of modernization then under way at home. Ôi Kentarô (1843–1922), one of the leaders of the Freedom and People's Rights Movement of the 1870s and 1880s, called on Japan to support the reform and strengthening of Korea, pointing out that such an action would serve to promote the security and prosperity of the entire region, while instigating democratization in both Japan and Korea. Ôi Kentarô's vision of Asian solidarity contrasted with Fukuzawa's "Leaving Asia" argument, although both had the same belief in the universal process of civilization and progress.

The predominant Ottoman Muslim response to the rift between the power politics of Europe and perceived normative principles of civilization was to radicalize and universalize civilizationism as a protection from European interventions. Also significant was the awareness that the moral principles of the international society were under the protection of a balance-of-power dynamics that compelled Britain to support the Ottoman reforms.[64] Even when several British policies led to disillusionment among Ottoman rulers, the Ottoman state continued to rely on the good will and leadership of the British Empire. When the balance of European power politics and the British policies toward the Ottoman state changed after the unifications of Germany and Italy in 1871, Ottoman leaders lost the British protection of their state sovereignty and territorial integrity against the Russian threats. The crisis of the 1870s resulted in the disastrous and traumatic wars of 1877–1878 with Russia and Austria-Hungary, at the end of which the Ottomans had to agree that the majority of its European territories would be annexed or become independent. What should be remembered, however, is the Ottoman response to the perceived alliance of European powers against its territorial integrity: an appeal to the moral principles of European international society with the declaration of a constitution in 1876, at a time when European powers were convening in Istanbul to decide the fate of its Christian-majority territories in the Balkans. It was the Ottomans who preferred the principles of European international law that required respect for the borders and sovereignty of each civilized state. The ideal of a constitution as the ultimate symbol of the Ottoman self-civilization process had a long history of intellectual and political support within the empire. The international crisis only gave reformist groups in the bureaucracy added advantages over their opponents. Irrespective of European pressures, the liberal civilizationist camp in the Ottoman bureaucracy, as well as among the rising Ottoman intelligentsia, believed in the equality under law of all subjects of the empire and tried to create a modern notion of citizenship.[65] Similarly, an Ottoman constitution was a dream of the rising intellectual elite of the time, evidenced by the popularity of Young Ottoman thought during the 1870s.

In both the Ottoman state and Japan, the first generation of Westernized intellectuals asked for a more participatory constitutional reform process and larger solidarity with other Asian-Muslim nations. The Freedom and People's Rights Movement in Japan and the Young Ottoman movement in Turkey championed a rethinking of what the criteria of civilization should be both domestically and internationally. Domestically, they criticized the top-down reforms for lacking the spirit of civilization, which they depicted as popular participation and constitutional rule. Internationally, they noted that some sort of Asian or Islamic solidarity was vital to achieving the self-civilizing reforms, because European interventions were preventing the success of such reforms all over Asia. Intellectuals of the Young Ottoman movement in Turkey and the Freedom and People's Rights Movement in Japan were more knowledgeable about Western thought than the first-generation modernizing elite. They also perceived tensions between their cultural identity and some aspects of the adopted

Western thought and aimed to resolve these by radicalizing the universalist thinking on modernity, international order, and globalization. Their ideals of radicalization and nationalization in the process of self-civilizing reforms espoused an Islamization and Asianization of the ideal of universal modernity but never an abandonment of the commitment to vision of global civilization.

First ideas of Islamic and Asian solidarity during the late 1870s embraced both the notion of universal modernity perfected in Europe and the notion of an interdependent community of states sharing a world order. Advocates of Muslim or East Asian solidarity were staunch modernizers, despite their reference to "East Asian-ness" or "Muslim-ness," and it was this generation that helped to distinguish ideal universal civilization from European practices.[66] The ideas of Mehmet Namık Kemal (1840–1888) epitomize the modern global context of early pan-Islamic notions. He had great familiarity with Western culture through the medium of French writings, in addition to a strong grounding in Islamic education and Ottoman bureaucratic culture. After serving as a member of the translation bureau of the Ottoman government and as editor of a sociopolitical commentary, *Tasvir-i Efkâr*, Namık Kemal left Turkey in 1867 to live in Paris and London in order to escape imprisonment for his involvement in the Young Ottoman Society. After his return to Istanbul in 1870, he spent the rest of his bureaucratic career mostly in exile in remote cities.

As a member of the Ottoman bureaucracy, Namık Kemal's main critique of the new Westernizing political elite of the early Tanzimat was the loss of legitimacy of the pro-Western reformist government according to both Islamic and Western norms. He argued that most of the reforms implemented by the Ottoman state were for the sake of seeming civilized through superficial Westernization at the expense of "real" civilization and modernity, which had to include democracy, participation, a parliament, and political freedom He urged the Ottoman government and the public to grasp the real meaning of civilization and progress beyond the Ottoman elites' interest in European attire, dance parties, and other aspects of contemporary Western culture.[67] Namık Kemal was one of the first Ottomans to use the term "Muslim Unity" (*İttihad-ı Islam*), in an article in the journal *Ibret* on June 27, 1872.[68]

The other leading Young Ottoman figure, Ali Suavi, had also observed European socieites firsthand and was familiar with the writings of Enlightenment figures and contemporary European thinkers. He wrote about the benefits of North African Muslim unity as the necessary condition to prevent Europe's overwhelming power from reconquering Africa. Suavi expressed bitter resentment against European foreign policies carried out in the name of a civilizing mission by reference to the ideals of liberty, equality, and freedom that the West was supposed to cherish. "Strangely enough, while the republicans in England and France speak about democracy, equality and freedom, they have no wish to relinquish their hold over Canada, India and Algeria. Just look how those Frenchmen talk pretentiously about freedom and equality, all the while seeking world domination like Caesar."[69]

CONCLUSION

The first generation of Ottoman and Japanese reformists did not see their reformist Westernism as contradictory to their national, religious, and cultural identity. They saw global unevenness and disparity as a result of the natural and moral consequences of the civilizational hierarchies in science and civilization. They accepted that there were new norms of international relations in which a state's image as a civilized polity was crucially important. As a result of their civilizational worldview, for them, colonial tutelage, unequal treaties, and some limited form of racial discrimination were partly legitimate aspects of the globalizing world order. Japanese Westernists such as Tokutomi Soho could even see the unequal treaties imposed on Japan as positive outside pressure to apply rapid domestic reforms beneficial to Japan's progress. Initially, this discourse allowed Ottoman and Japanese reformers to be optimistic that they would one day gain equality by completing all the necessary reforms.

The period from the 1830s to the 1880s witnessed the emergence of an image of the West in Ottoman and Japanese thought. This image not only inspired reform movements in both countries; it was also identified with humanist liberalism, Enlightenment thought, and the new global structures of world order. Throughout the nineteenth century, there was never a monolithic idea of the characteristics, achievements, virtues, and vices of the West. Yet there were dominant paradigms and explanations in each period. In their first three decades of reform, the most influential description of the West in the Ottoman and Japanese societies revolved around the liberal and universal notions of civilization and Enlightenment. When non-Western reformists became familiar with the main ideas of Enlightenment thought, they also became aware of the various forms of European ideas about the uniqueness and essential superiority of European societies stemming from religion, race, climate, or other peculiar characteristics. Ottoman and Japanese intellectuals preferred, however, to modify and reformulate these ideas to insist on the "universal" secrets of Europe's progress and to make "civilization" more inclusive of non-Western cultures and traditions.

Ottoman and Japanese leaders were equally aware of the global structures of uneven economic relations and balance-of-power politics in international relations. Yet, they imagined and hoped that the universal moral principles of international law and civilized behavior would be the future direction of globalization. Even those who criticized the West did so only in the context of the international policies of particular Western powers. In those critiques, there was no rejection of the universal ideals identified with the West, nor could any important political leader or intellectual ignore the appeal of Western civilization. The image of the West has since become a contested and controversial topic, but it was always present in the discussion about the conditions, future direction, and even the assessment of the past of both Ottoman and Japanese societies.

3

THE TWO FACES OF THE WEST

Imperialism Versus Enlightenment (1882–1905)

PAN-ISLAMIC AND PAN-ASIAN ideas emerged after the liberal Westernist moment in Ottoman and Japanese reformist thought. Their genesis was closely related to the break in the Asian elite's perception of the west. The global image of the West changed dramatically during the 1880s following the European scramble to colonize Africa in the aftermath of the British occupation of Egypt. On a global scale, the period from the early 1880s to 1914 was both the peak of European imperial expansion and the formative period of modern social sciences in Europe. Michael Adas describes this period as an era of high imperialism, typified by an "unprecedented closure for the human community and consequently all of the life and lands of the earth."[1] Emphasizing the uniqueness of this period, Hannah Arendt considered the three decades from 1884 to 1914 separate from the nineteenth century, which, for her, "ended with the scramble for Africa and the birth of the Pan-movements".[2] With this categorization, Arendt underlined that the three decades before WWI exhibited a rupture, and even a deviation, from the larger trends of the rest of the nineteenth century.

During these three decades, there was also a tension between the universalist and particularist trends in the center of international society. The Christian and white race aspects of international law and international society, which already existed in the system created by the Vienna Congress, became more noticeable toward the end of the nineteenth century. There was also a contradictory trend to open the Eurocentric international society to non-Western areas to create a "spaceless universalism" of indiscriminate international law.[3] The Hague Peace Conference of 1899 was a sign of the universalization of the system. That same year, however, Rudyard Kipling wrote the most succinct and poetic expression of the imperialist ideology, "The White Man's Burden," in celebration of the American annexation of the Philippine islands.[4]

Another conflicting signal about the inclusive norms and the exclusive Christian and racial character of the international society came only three years after the American colonization of the Philippines, when Britain concluded the Anglo-Japanese Alliance with Japan. This alliance symbolized the end of the unequal treatment of Japan by the Western powers and the unprecedented acceptance of a nonwhite nation into the club of white-Christian great powers. Yet, despite Japan's inclusion into the international society as an equal member, European and American public perceptions of Japan as belonging to the yellow race and thus not equal to the superior Christian and white nations continued, leading to a tension between Japan's legal status in international law and popular Western perceptions of Japanese racial inferiority.[5]

The elective affinity between the "formal imperialism" turn in Europe's relationship with Asia and Africa and the changes in European thought with regard to hierarchies of race, religion, and culture was more than a matter of coincidence and causality. There is continuing debate in scholarship on whether the British Empire had to turn some of its informal colonies into formal ones or if its decisions were partly contingent on their response to the Urabi Revolt in Egypt in 1882. There is a similar debate on the economic and political rationality of the intense inter-European competition for land grabbing in Asia and Africa after the British occupation of Egypt.[6] A resolution to these debates is beyond the scope of this book. What is important for the history of anti-Western thought, however, was Asian intellectuals' perception of the new ethos of race and cultural superiority that celebrated European empires as agents of progress and civilization.

The increasing social and political mobilization of the imperial centers gave ideologies of self-civilizing mission not only a populist national character but also a Christian and racial identity. For Muslim observers, the symbol of the new era in Europe was the prime ministership of William Gladstone in England, who was a popularly elected leader and public opinion maker.[7] Gladstone's hostile remarks about Muslims and Turks reflected both a larger European sentiment about "infidel Muslims" and a more refined European Orientalist discourse on Muslim inferiority.[8] Observing the new anti-Muslim rhetoric coming from the top politician in the center of the European international society, Muslim reformists felt they were being pushed away by the very Europe they were trying to emulate. Gladstone's constant remarks about the uncivility of the Ottoman Muslim elite were sharp contrasts to the way Ottoman diplomats and statesmen were having cordial, encouraging conversations with the leaders of the Concert of Europe such as Metternich and Palmerston about their self-civilizing reforms.[9]

The new sense of Western self-reflection in relation to the non-Western world implied that no matter the success rate of non-Western reforms, non-

Christian and non-white nations would never perfectly fulfill all the required standards of civilization because of defects in their racial makeup, religious dogmatism, or cultural character.[10] In that sense, Orientalist and racist discourses in the last quarter of the nineteenth century began to contradict the idea of the universality of European modernity and its civilizing mission. If non-Western societies were permanently relegated to an inferior status in the international hierarchy because of their faith or race, what could be the meaning and ultimate goal of their reforms? Would they have to live, forever, under the tutelage of European masters?

Ottoman intellectuals, like those in other parts of the Islamic world, reassessed their understanding of the relationship between Western civilization and universal modernity in the face of the perceived conflict between the two. The person who brilliantly formulated the Muslim modernist attempt to separate the universality of modernity from the Western experience was Ahmed Midhat Efendi, whose prolific writings on Western and Islamic civilization made him unquestionably the most influential Ottoman intellectual during the high age of imperialism.[11] By producing a large corpus on topics such as science and technology, Islamic civilization, the West's superiority in progress, and Eastern and Western cultures, Midhat Efendi not only confirmed the liberal modernism of the earlier generation and harmonized Islamic identity with the promodernist attitudes but also responded to the dominant European discourse on the inferiority of Muslims. Like many others in his generation, he had to discuss the backwardness of the Muslim world in relation to the West, the conditions of other Eastern civilizations in the face of the Western challenge, and finally the image of Muslims and Easterners in Western public opinion. While offering a moderate position on most of these issues, one that embraced both Islamic identity and the universality of Western civilization, Ahmed Midhat continued to spread the ethos of modernity by praising Western civilization with reference to its material achievements in areas such as city planning, public hygiene, parks and forests, transportation, travel convenience and hotels, youth and sports activities, and other aspects of life. Even Ahmed Midhat's observations on the norms of socialization, such as hosting and dinner manners, attire, the public role of women, and grooming in Europe were generally positive, although he did not suggest that the Ottomans should necessarily emulate the Europeans in all these social aspects.

In the generation of Ahmed Midhat Efendi, the literature of comparison between Western and Islamic civilizations was important partly because it was the venue for intraintellectual debate on formulating a distinctly modern Muslim identity and redefining the limits and criteria of Ottoman Westernization. In this process, Ahmed Midhat Efendi and many others condemned what they considered to be the perils of over-Westernization among educated Ottomans and the consequent loss of identity and nationality that would create an un-bridgeable gap between modern youth and the general population. In one of the most popular Ottoman novels at the end of the nineteenth century, *Felatun Bey ile Rakım Efendi* (Mr. Felatun and Mr. Rakim), Ahmet Midhat describes the difference between an imitative, cosmetic Westernization, which is ridiculed as superficial, and a preferred model characterized by a relentless effort to hold on to both Ottoman cultural tradition and the principles of the new age. Imitative Westernist Felatun Bey spends his life on the European side of Istanbul gambling and socializing with women while true Muslim modernist Rakım Efendi works diligently and cherishes modern life in a more modest and balanced manner. Rakım Efendi also knows French and is familiar with European civilization, but, in contrast to Felatun Bey with his consumerist decadence, he is presented as a true heir to both the real European and the Ottoman norms of hard work, seriousness, and morality. In his critique, Ahmed Midhat Efendi truly reflected a global climate of opinion. He was inspired by the very similar concerns of Russian intellectuals about the ills of over-Westernization and, around the same time, Japanese intellectuals associated with the group called Seikyôsha (Society of Political Education) also expressed like-minded fears of the erosion of national culture by over-Westernization. Midhat Efendi's distinction between real universal modernity and superficial Westernization indicated that he wanted to preserve loyalty to the former by warning his readers about the negative impact of the latter.[12]

The other major concern of Ahmed Midhat Efendi and other reformists in his generation was the European rejection of the potential success of Islamic modernity. After a visit to Europe to attend a congress of European Orientalists, Midhat Efendi personally noted the discomfort of European delegates when he, as an Ottoman participant, spoke to them in good French and dressed in modern attire.[13] His critique of Orientalism and European perceptions of Ottoman Muslims showed that his generation was very sensitive about what Europeans thought about them but were not passive disciples of European discourse. As Carter Findley succinctly formulated, the West was "omnipresent" in Muslim modernist thought, but "it was never omnipotent".[14]

Overall, however, in the renewed Muslim modernist commitment to both the Western-inspired universal modernity project and Islamic identity, there is no rejection of Western civilization or any conservative anti-Westernism. The Ottomans were highly aware of the different varieties of national modernity in Europe, especially after the German victory over France, and could find no contradiction in emphasizing their cultural and national differences even when they were aspiring to adopt the shared elements of European progress. Theirs was a search for a global modernity that would be in harmony with the multiple traditions of different religions and cultures, at a time when European discourses of Orient and race were trying to limit the achievements and future of modernity only to the Western race and Christian culture. A look at modernist Muslim literature shows that Muslim intellectuals sincerely believed in the universality of modernity.[15] There were no fundamentalist Muslims among Ottoman intellectuals of the time. During the age of high imperialism, however, Muslim reformists had to be critical of Western thought and policies in order to ask for equality in international affairs and affirm this very belief in the universality of modernity.

The fact that Japanese intellectuals showed similar intellectual tendencies during the 1890s, despite the sharp contrast in the rate and success of the Ottoman and Japanese modernization processes, indicates that debates on modernity, cultural identity and Western civilization had a global character. Contrary to the failures of the Ottoman reform process, the Japanese reforms were highly successful in creating an efficient centralized government, developing a modern economy, and establishing a strong army. Parallel to these achievements produced by Japanese Westernization, however, the first Meiji generation raised questions about their cultural and racial identity, Japan's relationship with Western powers, and the limits of Japanese Westernization. These second thoughts about Western civilization and the Westernization process at home should not be seen as a conservative reaction to modernity and a rejection of Japan's integration into the global community. Rather, they represent a critique of the changing Western attitudes to Japan and the global unevenness of the international order. The so-called Meiji Conservatives of the 1890s were more familiar with Western ideas, and it was they who perceived a greater threat from Western imperialism and Westernization despite the relative rise in Japan's international standing and military power.[16]

The first Meiji political novel, *Kajin no Kigu* (Strange encounters of elegant females), presents the characteristics of the new thinking on the West and Japanese identity. Written by Shiba Shirô (1852–1922) under his pen name Sanshin Tôkai, this novel reflects the universalism and global consciousness of the 1880s seen with the eyes of a world traveler.[17] Shiba Shirô studied in the United States, where he graduated from the University of Pennsylvania's business school. Although the narrative of his novel relates the encounter of a Japanese student in the United States with two beautiful female characters, the daughters of a Spanish constitutionalist and an Irish patriot, there is no developed romance in the novel. Instead, as the main characters tell their families' stories of resistance against the oppression of mostly Western governments both at home and abroad, the Japanese student connects them to present a picture of a universal struggle for justice against oppressive Western governments, imperialism, and global inequity. The novel even includes a conversation with the Egyptian nationalist general Urabi about British imperialism and the double standards of European powers. The author's sympathy for the weak nations of the world is partly related to his anxiety over Japan's fate in the face of the alarming encroachment of the European powers, but it is also a reflection of his universalist humanism. This work became the most popular novel during the mid-Meiji period, selling so many copies that it earned the reputation of "raising the price of paper" in Japan?[18] This popularity is evidence not only of concerns about Japan's position in the changing world order but of the well-established global sympathies of the educated Japanese public of that time and the emergence of the notion of the shared destiny of non-Western peoples.

It was in the early 1880s that the idea of Asian solidarity found its most eloquent formulation in a book by Tarui Tôkichi, titled *Daitô Gappôron* (Theory of uniting the great East).[19] The first draft of this book, written in 1885, argued for Asian solidarity in the context of the reformist movement in Korea and the Freedom and People's Rights Movement in Japan. Tarui then completed a rewritten version of the book in 1893, using classical Chinese in an effort to gain wider readership among Koreans and Chinese. Chinese progressive intellectual Liang Qichao wrote a preface in praise of Tarui's proposal of a federation of the East.[20] Tarui later noted with pride that his book sold as many as one hundred thousand copies and was read extensively in Korea and China.[21]

Tarui's book advocated cooperation between Japan and Korea accompanied by the modernization of both nations; it cited as an ultimate goal the unification of the two countries, which would herald the era of the revival of East Asia. Invoking both Western thought and classical Confucian learning, Tarui's vision for the future did not stop at predicting the federation of the East; he went on to argue that with increasing globalization the whole world might be expected to unite in some distant time. Tarui noted that technologies such as electricity and steam power acted to facilitate more interaction among different societies. Estimating that the unification of all states would be achieved within five hundred years, he urged the leaders of East Asia to take a proactive stance toward this inevitable process of globalization for the benefit of their populations. Tarui had great respect for Western thought and quoted John Stuart Mill, Herbert Spencer, and Robert Owen in his book. His theory was quite different from later, race-based international conflict theories in its optimism about the ability of globalization to bring about world harmony in the future. Until such a state could be achieved, he reasoned further, the East could protect its independence against the strength of the West with its own efforts at unification and cooperation.

Why would a member of the Freedom and People's Rights Movement, who opposed the Meiji leadership and asked for more popular participation and a less arbitrary government in Japan, develop a theory of East Asian solidarity?

Influence of the appropriation of European geographical knowledge, which divided the world into Europe and Asia, cannot alone explain Tarui's vision of East Asian unity as a step toward worldwide global unity. There was clearly a consciousness of belonging to a shared Chinese cultural zone, defined by Confucianism and a common writing style, in Tarui's identification with China and Korea. More important, however, was the influence of the intra–East Asian reformist network, which facilitated encounters of Japanese reformists with Korean and Chinese reformists.

A pan-Asian solidarity association already existed before the publication of Tarui's book; as Kôakai (Raise Asia Society) was established by Sone Toshitaro (1847–1910) in 1880. Kôakai was highly successful in attracting members of the reformist groups in China and Korea and in turn influencing their ideas.[22] This intra–East Asian interaction among like-minded Chinese, Japanese, and Korean reformists was crucial in the diffusion of the idea of Asian solidarity against Western imperialism or the Russian threat. Similarly intra-Asian interactions and dialogues facilitated by the travel of Buddhist monks and lay intellectuals in Japan, India, Sri Lanka, and other parts of Asia, in addition to their encounters with Europe and America, would help to expand the notion of a shared Asian legacy and anti-Western solidarity to India as well.[23]

The group of Japanese intellectuals that formed Seikyôsha (Society for Political Education) in 1888 gave anti-Western critiques of Japanese intellectuals additional philosophical grounding by formulating a new global assessment of Westernization, imperialism, and national identity. For them, nationalism contradicted full-scale, holistic Westernism. Seikyôsha writers were not cut off from the Western trends of the time. On the contrary, they evinced a deeper awareness of the complexity of Western thought and politics, recognizing that each European nation, as well as America, had a different cultural legacy and national identity. They were also open to the influences of the growing number of voices in Europe and America admiring the traditional arts and culture of Japan and hoped for their protection despite the need for Western-style reforms. For example, one of the early leaders of Seikyôsha, Miyake Setsurei, studied with Ernest Fenollosa, an American intellectual who urged the Japanese to follow an authentic path rather than a cultural Westernist one. Otherwise, Seikyôsha intellectuals had the same Western intellectual nourishment as their more Westernist colleagues, including a close familiarity with the writings of Herbert Spencer, Georg Wilhelm Friedrich Hegel, Francois Guizot, Henry Buckle, and Thomas Carlyle. Seikyôsha writers, however, aspired to combine Japanese traditions, Buddhism, and Confucianism with the modern Western ideas of parliamentary democracy, industrial development, and social progress. They objected to the prevailing tendency to prefer Western values over Asian ones, espousing instead a formulation of cultural diversity that would produce, through globalization, a universal world civilization. In "Shin-zen-bi Nihonjin" (The Japanese: Truth, goodness, and beauty), a treatise written in 1891, Seikyôsha intellectual Miyake Setsurei noted that the competition among diverse cultural views of truth, beauty, and goodness was necessary to produce the best form of world civilization, not the Westernization of diverse global cultures. While he accepted that the cultures of the Western nations were at the highest stage of civilization, he argued that the cultures of other nations had to be preserved in order to bring the progress of world civilization to higher stages.[24]

The paradox of Seikyôsha intellectuals' immersion in European thought and their partly anti-Western formulation of cultural nationalism can best be seen in Miyake Setsurei's promotion of European philosophy while continuing a harsh critique of Meiji Westernization. His veneration of Kant and Socrates, but not Jesus, together with his elevation of Buddha and Confucius to the status of universal sages, was partly an attempt to decouple the universal West from Christianity and partly an attempt to put Asia, via Buddha and Confucius, into the construction of this universality via the agency of Japan or Japan's intellectuals.[25] Seikyôsha intellectuals embraced and redefined Japan's Asian identity in the context of their quest to synthesize national cultural identity with Western-style reform. They established an "Oriental Society" (Tôho kyôkai) to raise awareness of the greatness and legacy of Asian civilization in order to counter the adulation of Western civilization.

Around the same period, Japanese historians had to rethink and reformulate Japan's position in Asia and the position of Asia in world history to offer an alternative to the Eurocentric vision of world history, a vision that relegated Japanese national identity to a marginal and insignificant position. A revised view of world history was crucial for the Seikyôsha group to explain what had gone wrong in Japan and Asia at large that made these regions become or stay backward and what made Europe more advanced. In developing this Japanese view of world history, the emphasis was on the historical relativity of the rise and decline of several world civilizations. It was noted that the Arabic, Indo-Egyptian, and Mongolian civilizations were the most advanced in the world previous to the European civilization. This meant that European superiority was not intrinsic to European culture, race, or even geography, although a set of contingent factors made Europe the most advanced civilization in the world during the nineteenth century. According to these thinkers, Japan always knew how to select and assimilate the best among the diverse world civilizations, and it should still have been able to adopt the elements of the highest level of civilization without loosing its cultural and national sense of self.

Although both Ottoman and Japanese intellectuals offered similar critiques of Orientalism, a Eurocentric view of world history, and racism, there were peculiarities in the way they formulated their visions of a universal modernity inclusive of their own traditions and cultural identities. One major characteristic of the predominantly Islamic discourse of modernity was its insistence on the essential compatibility between the fundamental teachings of Islam and the qualities of universal progress and science. In order to understand the genesis of this predominant Muslim interpretation of modernity, one must look at the politics and legacy of the Muslim intellectual responses to Eurocentric thought and Orientalism. The best historical laboratory for this examination can be found in the now-classical statement of Orientalist arguments on Islam by Ernest Renan in 1883 and the various Muslim refutations of Renan's ideas in the following two decades.

THE MUSLIM WORLD AS AN INFERIOR SEMITIC RACE: ERNEST RENAN AND HIS MUSLIM CRITICS

The representative statement of the imperial discourses of Orientalism and race that excluded Muslims from the universality of progress and civilization was a speech entitled "Islam and Science" that Ernest Renan delivered at the Sorbonne in 1883. Renan did little more than express the European notions of Islam's religious dogmatism, which he defined as the biggest obstacle to the progress of science in Muslim societies. He also added Aryan race theory to an explanation of Islamic backwardness to emphasize further the eternal incompatibility between the Semitic and Turco-Mongolian races (most of whom were Muslim at that time) and the production of modern science. In that sense, Renan linked the discourses on inferior races, whether Semitic-Jewish or colored, with Orientalist notions of the inferiority of Islam with regard to Christianity. Renan also championed a reinterpretation of the secular Christian culture of Europe as an Aryan culture and a refashioning of Jesus as a non-Semitic figure. Renan's intellectual output was thus a representative synthesis of imperial era discourses of race and Orient that would render Muslim reformists' dream of becoming members of the Eurocentric world order impossible.[26]

From the moment of the publication of Renan's "Islam and Science" in the *Journal des Débats* on March 30, 1883, Muslim students in Paris were infuriated by the speech's arguments, criticizing Renan for advocating misjudgments and fallacies about Muslims.[27] During the following years and even decades, several Muslim intellectuals from Russia, Ottoman lands, Egypt, and India wrote direct refutations or responses to Renan's claims.[28] Despite the obvious contradictions, weaknesses, and errors in Renan's thesis, his arguments became a transnational topic of discussion in the Muslim world and beyond, and ultimately earning a permanent focus in modern Islamic thought.[29]

Renan's reputation as a prominent secular European intellectual of the late nineteenth century cannot alone explain this intense Muslim response to his ideas on the history of Islamic science. Muslims took these arguments seriously because Renan's thesis about the history of Islamic science was seen as a symbol of a larger European justification for Europe's racial superiority of white and "Aryan" Christians over Semitic Muslims as a way to justify its imperial "civilizing mission" in the Muslim world. Therefore, Muslim refutations of Renan were intimately related to their discontent with European hegemony and their alternative visions of world order.

Renan's credentials as a famous secular European intellectual who nevertheless was proud of his Christian cultural legacy meant that he was not seen as part of the missionary campaign against Islam, a fact that contributed to the appeal of his ideas. Ernest Renan was born in France on February 28, 1823, and studied theology, philosophy, and Oriental languages, publishing his dissertation on Averroes and Averroism in 1852. Renan became a controversial yet influential European intellectual for his secular critiques of Christianity and the church. He was no marginal Orientalist whose reputation relied solely on his knowledge of the languages and cultures of the exotic, distant East. On the contrary, Renan was at the center of mainstream European intellectual life, and even today he is known more for his ideas on nationalism than for his reflections on Islamic civilization.

Ernest Renan's anti-Islamic comments, at their core, were no different from the widespread antireligious ideas of scientism and positivism predominant in Europe. He argued that Muslims could never reach the level of the European civilization while remaining loyal to their culture, religion, or even ethnicity.[30] He suggested that only by denying their religious dogmatism and getting rid of the influence of Islam could Muslims come to terms with rationality and science-based European modernity.

What made Renan's ideas different from the frequent anti-Muslim writings in the European media was their precise attack on the historical consciousness of optimist Muslim modernists, who saw their own history as part of the history of European civilization and progress. If Muslims had once achieved a golden age in science and technology, Muslim reformism believed, there was no reason why they could not reach similar achievements in scientific progress in the right circumstances. Muslim achievements in science in the first five centuries of Islamic history, at the time when their religious zeal was strong, gave encouragement to Islamic modernists from Jamal ad-Din al-Afghani to Namik Kemal that Islam and modern civilization were already compatible and supported their view that the argument of a conflict between science and religion was relevant only for Christian societies, not for Muslims (the debates on the conflict between science and religion were just intensifying in Europe as a result of the impact of Darwin's book on evolution). Furthermore, Muslim reformists saw the Christian legacy of Europe not as a disadvantage but rather as an advantage for Muslim reforms, since both Muslims and Christians had shared cultural and religious characteristics. If Christians could be civilized, there was no reason Muslims could not.

Renan was familiar with this optimistic Muslim reformism as well as with understanding how it was related to the pan-Islamic variety of anti-imperialism before he made his speech. In fact, initially, it was the European intellectual Renan who was reacting to this optimistic Muslim modernism. He personally met several Muslim reformists in Paris, such as Şinasi and Jamal al-Din al-Afghani, who was in France during 1883–1885. al-Afghani was publishing his pan-Islamic magazine *al-Urwa al-Wuthqa* (The firmest bond) in Paris between March and October 1884. He was championing both a vision of Islamic modernism and a call for the decolonization of the Muslim world. al-Afghani believed that independence and autonomy from Western colonial rule was a precondition for Muslim revival and for Muslims' gaining their rightful position on the international scene as equal and respected members. Ernest Renan later commented that al-Afghani's optimism about the potential success of modernizing reforms in the Muslim world was one of the reasons he gave his speech on the conflict between Islam and science.

What was so disturbing for Renan, and for new Orientalism in general, about the optimistic Muslim reformism and Muslims' belief in the compatibility of their faith and modern scientific progress? Muslim reformists easily appropriated the Eurocentric view of the history of world civilization with a slight modification that emphasized the contribution of Muslims to this civilization through the inheritance, protection, and transmission of the Hellenistic legacy for modern Europe. The nature of early nineteenth-century European supremacy made it easier for Muslims to accommodate Islam within Eurocentric world history, because the European belief in their own essential superiority was mostly based on the ability of the different races to produce science, technology, and arts. In that sense, it was mostly directed against the natives of new colonies and did not include the peoples of the Middle East.[31] Muslim intellectuals could accept that the Caucasian race was unique in terms of its high intellectual capacity and contribution to civilization, as long as they could count the Turks and Arabs as belonging to this superior Caucasian race. Hence some Muslim intellectuals even contended that the black race, "by its very nature and creation, was not capable of grasping the issues of science and philosophy."[32]

Similarly, Muslim modernists did not see Islam as an impending force against the development of science. Even when they read about the conflict between religion and science in European thought, they tended to think that this conflict was peculiar to Christianity or other religions and that Islam would have not shared it. Interestingly, this idea was formulated in the French language by a positivist French thinker, Charles Mismer, who served as a consultant to the Ottoman and Egyptian governments from 1867 onward.[33] Mismer devoted the third chapter of this book *Soirées de Constantinople* to the question of Islam and science, emphasizing Muslim contributions to the development of modern science and predicting the success of Muslim modernization projects in the future.[34]

Renan did not share Mismer's conviction about the future success of Muslim modernization. He first declared his general belief that religion in general and Islam in particular were hostile to science and progress. Challenging Muslim modernist beliefs that the golden age of Islam had proved that Islam and science were compatible, Renan argued that the scientific achievements in Islamic history were not "due to Islam" but in fact had occurred" in spite of Islam." In saying this, Renan was declaring the impossibility of Islamic modernism, as he was specifically attacking the Muslim appropriation of Enlightenment history within a form of Euro-Islamic-centric world history. According to Renan, the historical achievements of Muslims in the sciences did not contradict the science-versus-religion principle, since this success had nothing to do with either Islam or the Arab race.

Renan offered an alternative historical explanation for the past achievements in science and progress in Muslim societies, arguing that the flourishing of science in Islamic history was due either to Iranians, who were Aryan by race, or to Christian Arabs, whose religion carried elements of Aryan culture. Thus Renan cast a pessimist theory that Muslims, as long as they remained Muslims, could never fulfill the "standards of civilization". More important, Arabs and Turks did not have the capacity to develop science because of the characteristics of their race. The political saliency of this Orientalist argument, which meant that Muslims needed colonial tutelage to overcome their backwardness, explains the response of Muslim reformers.

Renan's assertions about the Arab and Turkish-Mongolian races being incapable of scientific progress led him to emphasize that most Islamic science was produced not by Arabs but by the non-Arab Aryan/Iranian race. In this second argument, Renan offered a set of inconsistent claims. The Iranian race could produce science even when they became Muslims, because, as the Aryan race, they could somehow protect their genetic genius from religious fanaticism. Moreover, Christian Arabs, despite the defects in the Arab race, still had the chance to achieve scientific activity and progress, because Christianity was less antirational than Islam. Hence, for the secular rationalist Renan, Christianity would always be superior to Islam in its contribution to modern progress.

Jamal ad-Din al-Afghani wrote the first public response from a Muslim modernist perspective to Renan's arguments. al-Afghani's letter sent to *Journal des Débats* was published within two months of the publication of Renan's text.[35] As the Arabic original of this text does not exist, there has been a controversy as to whether al-Afghani could be the author of some of the remarks conceding the obstacles of all religions, including Islam, to the progress of sciences. Yet, despite its apologetic character, al-Afghani's response still successfully underlined some of the contradictions in Renan's arguments. His main focus was rightly on the rejection of the political implications of Renan's thesis, which al-Afghani summarized by saying "several hundreds of millions of [Muslim] men, . . . would thus be condemned to live in barbarism and ignorance."[36] al-Afghani criticized Renan for not doing full justice to the Arab contributions to the legacy of Hellenistic sciences, which Arabs "developed, extended, clarified, perfected, completed and coordinated with a perfect taste and a rare precision and exactitude."[37] He successfully demonstrated several contradictions in Renan's claims, especially his assertion that all the great philosophers and scientists in Islamic history, such as Avicenna, Averroes, and Ibn Tufayl, were either Iranian or born into non-Arab races. Finally, even though al-Afghani affirmed Renan's argument about the conflict between religion and philosophy, he suggested that if Christians could overcome the burden of their faith to advance in modern civilization and science, with time Muslims would be able to do so as well.

Renan wrote a letter to the same journal two months later to respond to al-Afghani. This time, Renan pushed his argument forward, suggesting that only the decline and eradication of Islam from the minds and cultures of Muslims could liberate them from the chains of backwardness. This letter became the last comment by Renan on this issue, and his direct response to al-Afghani remained a rare instance in which a late nineteenth-century European intellectual directly responded to a critique by a Muslim intellectual.

Upon the translation of Renan's speech into different languages, a large group of Muslim modernists wrote on this issue, all emphasizing the following common points. First, Muslim modernists agreed that the Muslim world was in a grave state of decline and backwardness, yet they argued that the real cause of this was not Islam, which, they all insisted, was not against reason, thinking, progress, science, and technology. Second, they wrote that Muslims had a great civilization in the past and the main inspiration of this golden age was Islam itself. Third, they asserted that it would be a revival of this earlier, progressive Islam, not an abandonment of it, that could again bring Muslims close to progress.[38] These Muslim modifications of Eurocentric world history and Orientalism left an indelible mark on the modernist ideals not only of mainstream reformists but also revivalist (*salafi*) Muslims who merged their advocacy of adaptation to the inevitable path of progress with a call for the revival of the imagined "pure" and "original" Islam. Revivalist modernist Muslims hence conceded some of the arguments of Orientalist literature about the backwardness and decline of contemporary Muslim civilization but interpreted the cause of decline as a deviation from their imagined normative Islam.[39] More important, the defense of Islam by modernist Muslims, some of whom were not devout in their daily lives, demonstrates the extent to which Islam and the Muslim world conjured the meanings of race in the age of high imperialism. Similar to the identity of being Jewish, being Muslim was a quasiracial category. It is due to this racial implication that Muslim modernists had to defend Islam against Orientalist critiques of inferiority and backwardness, while conceding a certain level of civilizational backwardness and working for the "revival" of their fellow coreligionists.

The well-established conviction of several generations of Muslim modernists that Islam fosters progress was partly a product of the way refutations to Renan reversed his essentialist argument about Islam's relationship with science. By reversing Renan's argument and insisting that Islam fostered the rise of scientific activity, Muslim intellectuals also challenged the Orientalist justifications for Western imperial rule in the Muslim world. The fact that this debate started during the 1880s reveals much about the changing climate of opinion on a global scale regarding the relationship between religious-cultural identity and Eurocentric world order. While Muslim intellectuals in the age of high imperialism were contending with European Orientalism, they also popularized the concept of Islamic civilization as different from Western civilization, a distinction that could not be found in the early Tanzimat era reformist writings. In both the Orientalist and Muslim modernist arguments, the development of science and civilization was assumed to be directly related to the religious beliefs and mentality of a society. Since Renan's debate, not only the polemics but later even the historical scholarship on this issue were shaped around the issues of whether Islam stifled or fostered progress, in contrast to the earlier generation of Muslim reformists, who approached the issue of scientific progress in the Muslim world on a largely sociological basis.[40]

This new Muslim reformist discourse did not mean the abandonment of the vision of universal progress in science and technology. In fact, together with the globalization of economic forces, scientific progress was seen as an inevitable factor. Yet what post-Renan Muslim modernists created was a narrative of Islamic civilization, based on the religion of Islam, that was judged to be superior to the Christian faith simply because Islam was claimed to be more conducive to modern rationality and science. The most poignant example of this attitude can be seen in Ahmet Midhat Efendi's notes to the translation of John William Draper's book *History of the Conflict Between Religion and Science.*

Midhat Efendi agrees with Draper's argument that Christianity conflicted with the modern sciences. In his commentary to the translation, however, he observed that religious opposition to scientific progress was not an issue for Islam, which, as a proscientific and rational faith, never conflicted with science.[41]

From the early 1880s on, Muslim modernists tried to attend the Orientalists' congresses and other intellectual gathering to deliver their messages of dialogue and self-explanation directly to the European intellectuals whose misperceptions they were trying to correct. Ahmed Midhat Efendi's attendance at the 1889 Orientalist congress in Stockholm facilitated dialogue between him and various European Orientalists.[42] Sometimes, the Ottoman state would dispatch a bureaucrat to attend an Orientalist congress in Europe to present a semi-official paper.[43] For instance, Numan Kamil Bey went to the tenth Orientalist congress in Geneva in 1894 to read a paper that was later published in the Ottoman language under the title *Islamiyet ve Devlet-i Aliyye-i Osmaniye Hakkında Doğru bir Söz* (Several true remarks concerning Islam and the Ottoman state).[44] Kamil's presentation focused on proving the compatibility between Islam and modern civilization, as well as the modern image of the Ottoman caliphate. He first presented a summary of Islamic history with the agenda of refuting the European image that Islam was spread by the force of sword and violent jihad. In his narration of Islamic history, Kamil underlined the civilized behavior of powerful Muslim states toward their Christian adversaries. He describes the conduct of Salahuddin al-Ayyubi (Saladin) toward the defeated European commanders during the Crusades as conforming to both the international law (*hukuk-i beyne'l-milel*) of the time and the requirements of Islamic principles.[45] Kamil devotes a special section to what he calls "the origins of European scholars' opinions against Islam and the Ottoman state" and identifies Constantin Volney, François-René Chateaubriand, Ernest Renan, and William Gladstone as especially "fallacious" in their ideas in this regard.[46] The concluding sentence of this text almost invites European Orientalists to accept the arguments of Muslim modernists by asking them to be "objective" in their responses to the question of whether Islam is the "destroyer of civilization" or a "servant of civilization."[47] Here, Kamil's thesis on Islam and civilization was partly about the politics of the Ottoman state's international relations with the European powers according to the diplomacy of the "standard of civilizations."

The very fact that the Ottoman government sometimes picked a state official, instead of funding a scholar, to give a paper at an Orientalist congress indicates their awareness of the politics of Orientalist literature in Europe.[48] More important, various attempts by the Ottoman government and individual Muslim intellectuals to engage with their imagined European public opinion, generally through conversations with European Orientalists, reveal the nature of Muslim-European cooperation and contestation in the formulation of Western images of Islam, as well as modern Muslim images—and critiques—of the imperial era West.

YELLOW VERSUS WHITE PERIL? PAN-ASIAN CRITIQUES AND CONCEPTIONS OF WORLD ORDER

Despite the growing military and economic might of the Japanese state, and sometimes precisely because of it, Japanese ideas of Asian solidarity gained a new anti-Western character. Especially after the international recognition of the rising military power of Japan during the Sino-Japanese War of 1895, some European statesmen viewed Japan as a potential threat to Western colonial interests in East Asia. The German emperor Kaiser Wilhelm encapsulated this negative perception when he purportedly described this rising Japanese power as the "yellow peril" in a conversation with the Russian czar.[49] From then on, the term was repeated many times, by both European and Japanese papers. Because of the rising discourse on the yellow peril in Europe and America and the intensity of European competition for colonial hegemony in the world, a growing number of Japanese intellectuals began to be more suspicious of the West and advocated solidarity with China both to avoid the breakdown of that nation and to create solidarity within the yellow race. The gradually rising awareness of a conflict between the yellow and white races that resulted fueled a sense of Japanese identity and a consciousness of belonging to the colored races of Asia in relation to the white race of Euro-America.

The ideal of Asian solidarity was never officially endorsed by the Japanese government. Toward the end of the 1890s, however, even some high-level Meiji bureaucrats began to consider pan-Asianism as a potential alternative to the aggressive policies of Western powers in East Asia. The strong thesis by Prince Konoe Atsumaro (1863–1904) favoring solidarity with China exemplifies the appeal of pan-Asianist ideas among the Japanese political and diplomatic elite. Konoe Atsumaro was a member of the court nobility, carrying the title of prince by birth, and, according to the Japanese constitution of 1889, was a member of the House of Peers, one of the two legislative chambers. Konoe in fact became president of the House of Peers in 1896, after five years of study in Germany. In an article published in *Taiyô* in 1898, Konoe predicted an inevitable racial struggle in East Asia between the white and yellow races, with both the Chinese and the Japanese siding together as sworn enemies of the whites.[50] Konoe expressed concern over the partition of China by the Western powers. Observing the imperialistic activities of the white powers all over the globe, he asked the Japanese to prepare for a future alliance with China against the white race's attempts to dominate East Asia.[51] It is important to note that this concern over a

racist and aggressive West was coming from a figure at the top of the Meiji elite
who was personally acquainted with the leading political personalities of the
Western world. In 1898 Konoe founded *Dôbunkai* (Common Culture Association), renamed *Tôa Dôbunkai* after a merger with *Tôakai* in the same year, an
organization with the purpose of studying China and developing cultural policies with an eye toward a long-term alliance between the two nations.

The events in the years following the Sino-Japanese War provided the context for Konoe's call for racial solidarity in East Asia against the white powers.
The intervention by Russia, France, and Germany forced Japan to return the
captured Liaotung Peninsula to China in 1895. Only three years later, however,
the same territory was leased to Russia, an event that caused uproar in Japanese
public opinion at the idea that their nation was receiving second-class treatment
in the context of the international standards set by Western powers. Meanwhile,
the notion of the "yellow peril" showed its first negative effect on Japan's relations with America, where anti-Asian racism increased and a movement to
stop Japanese immigration arose. One major strand of Japanese response to this
"yellow peril" labeling was indignant, triggering the retaliatory coinage of the
term "white peril" as a description of Western hegemony in Asia.[52]

Konoe Atsumaro's anxiety over dangers from the West was indicative of a
paradoxical development. At the same time that Japan was growing stronger
through the Meiji reforms, its concern over the Western threat was also increasing. This situation can be attributed to both the emergence of a rivalry between
Japan and the expanding Western imperial powers and the political relevance
of racial identities. It also typified a long-lasting pattern in which Japan's relations with East Asia, even under slogans of solidarity with people of the same
culture and the same race, were always shaped by the tensions in its relations
with the Western powers.

As a practical political response to the perceived threat of Western aggression, Konoe Atsumaro formulated an Asian Monroe Doctrine that reflected
elements of both an idealistic mission to protect China on moral grounds and
a realistic foreign policy to pursue Japan's long-term national interest in East
Asia. In this Japanese application of the American Monroe Doctrine to the conditions of East Asia, it was maintained that Japan had an interest in any decision regarding the future of China, since geographic proximity and a shared
cultural and racial background dictated that the two nations be very closely
linked in their political destinies.[53] These ideas about an Asian Monroe Doctrine were to have an enduring legacy in the history of Japanese pan-Asianism.
The proposal, however, did not alter the general direction of Japan's foreign
policy of cooperation with Western powers over the affairs of East Asia. On the
contrary, Japanese diplomacy entered a new phase in 1902, when the Anglo-
Japanese Alliance was created, signaling that Japan's security and foreign policy

was officially linked with that of Great Britain and not with its fellow members of the "yellow race" of Asia.

In the context of increasing Japanese power in East Asia after its victory over China in 1895, the expansion of the Japanese Empire first to Taiwan and then to Korea led to several Japan-centered pan-Asianist visions of world order. Once Japan's world status changed from that of a non-Western nation under the imposition of unequal treaties to that of an ally of the British Empire and an imperialist power in its own right, the meaning of early liberal Asianist ideas in Japan was almost reversed along with the changing context of power relations.[54] Thus the legacy of liberal Asianism symbolized by Tarui Tôkichi, Ôi Kentarô, and Miyazaki Tôten could later be utilized to justify the Japanese annexation of Korea.[55] It was thus possible that the democratic Asianism advocated by Tarui could be appropriated as a moral justification for Japan's annexation of Korea in 1910 by a later generation of Asianists with a different political ideology.[56] Similarly, one can observe a shift in focus between the first and last parts of the first Meiji political novel, *Kajin no Kigu* (Strange encounters of elegant females). As this novel was written in short installments over a period of thirteen years, from 1885 to 1897, its author, Shiba Shirô, had the opportunity to reflect on Japan's transformation into a colonial power after defeating China in 1895 and seizing Taiwan. Hence Shiba Shirô's sympathy for oppressed peoples and their anticolonial struggles takes an interesting patriotic turn in the last installments of the novel, where he merges anticolonial resistance to European powers with the Japanese sense of mission as the leader of Asian awakening, meanwhile obscuring Japanese imperial interests. It is one of the main female characters of the novel who encourages the Japanese student not to be pessimistic about the conditions of Western hegemony in Asia, because Japan is reviving its nation and will one day lead the Asian peoples in their struggle against the colonial powers.[57]

The fact that anti-imperialist visions of world order embodied in early pan-Asianism were sometimes used to advocate Japanese rule over Korea should not, however, be taken as an indication that the Japanese political elite needed Asianism to justify the political process that led to the annexation of Korea in 1910. On the contrary, the progressive image of the civilizing mission of imperialism, combined with a discourse on Japan's security needs, constituted the official legitimization of the annexation of Korea, while Asianism served as a convenient but not crucial source of corroboration for this process.[58]

The process of transforming the anti-imperialist and democratic visions of world order in the Asianist ideas of the 1870s into an ideology of Japanese hegemony in East Asia was also symbolized by the relationship between liberal Tarui Tôkichi and ultranationalist Uchida Ryôhei, the founder of Kokuryûkai (Amur River Society). Together with Genyôsha (Black Ocean Society), Kokuryûkai turned the early Meiji ideals of Asian solidarity into a conservative doctrine of Japan-centered pan-Asianism and expansionism. Genyôsha was founded in 1881 by Hiraoka Kôtarô and Tôyama Mitsuru. Hiraoka (1851–1906) was a mine owner and a former samurai who had taken part in the rebellion of Saigô Takamori. Similarly, Tôyama Mitsuru (1855–1944) had links with both Saigô's samurai rebellion and the Freedom and People's Rights Movement, a political background he shared with Ôi Kentarô and Tarui Tôkichi. The aims that Genyôsha declared for itself were "to revere the imperial family," "to respect and honor the fatherland," and "to guard the rights of the people," yet they mostly focused on protecting and expanding Japanese interests in East Asia.[59] In spite of its initial links with the Freedom and People's Rights Movement, Genyôsha soon moved away from liberal ideas, promoting a right-wing political agenda in domestic politics and simultaneously advocating the continental expansion of Japanese power with the supposed moral mission of protecting the security and rights of the Koreans and Chinese. During both the Sino-Japanese and the Russo-Japanese wars, the society was involved in intelligence-gathering activities and covert operations. Kokuryûkai was formed by Uchida Ryôhei in 1901 as an offshoot of Genyôsha, with its purpose declared as the expulsion of Russia from the East Asian region up to the boundaries of the Amur River.[60]

Both Genyôsha and Kokuryûkai, whose members never numbered more than several hundreds, served as support centers for *tairiku rônin*, the idealistic Japanese adventurers who went to the Asian continent to take part in the Chinese revolution. Many of the *tairiku rônin* saw their Asianism as being in harmony with Japanese political interest and imperial expansion, but some of them, such as Miyazaki Tôten (1871–1922), did take the side of Asian nationalism against the interest of Japan when the two conflicted.[61] Despite their devotion to the cause of Japanese interests in Asia, Kokuryûkai and Genyôsha never came to represent the modern political elite of Japan.[62] The network of members of Genyôsha and Kokuryûkai, gathered around the charismatic personality of Tôyama Mitsuru, would often exercise its influence to assist Asian revolutionaries who visited Japan, giving them financial, political, and moral support.[63] These two organizations thus successfully fostered ties with nationalists and intellectuals from Asia, such as Sun Yat-sen of China, Emilio Aguinaldo of the Philippines, Resh Behari Bose and Rabindranath Tagore of India, and Abdurreşid İbrahim of Russia. By the end of the Russo-Japanese War, Genyôsha and Kokuryûkai had become symbols not only of conservatism and antiliberal nationalism but also of Japanese expansionism in East Asia in the name of pan-Asian solidarity. They thus represented the alliance between chauvinist nationalism and pan-Asian internationalism.

There were still expressions of a more progressive and nonchauvinistic Asianism. The Asian Solidarity Society, organized in 1907 by Chinese and Indian residents in Tokyo in cooperation with Japanese socialists and liberals, was one example. Its efforts to promote an Asian internationalism independent of the idea of Japanese hegemony in the region proved short-lived, however.[64]

The pan-Asianist vision of world order was not merely a Japanese invention. It had two major intellectual and political sources, both originating outside of Japan. One was the intellectual trend in Europe and America critical of the materialism and imperialism of Western civilization. The other was the nationalist movements in India, China, and elsewhere in Asia. Both of these sources influenced the Japanese vision of pan-Asianism through the writings of Okakura Tenshin. In the aftermath of the Anglo-Japanese treaty, Okakura Tenshin formulated the most sophisticated and internationalist version of pan-Asianism, critical of both the Anglo-Japanese alliance and Japan's Westernization.[65]

The greatest novelty in Okakura Tenshin's pan-Asianism was his rejection of Meiji era Westernization and the Eurocentric ideal of civilizational progress. He tried to establish the idea that the multiplicity of global civilizations, in which the West and Asia had equal claim to universal truth, had to be protected to save humanity from the excesses of global Westernization. Okakura also symbolized the beginning of the links between Japanese Asianism with both the admirers of Asian civilization in the West and Indian nationalists. He became a well-reputed figure among Asian art collectors in the USA as he worked for the Asian art section of the Boston Museum of Fine Arts.[66] Meanwhile, he maintained his contacts with the Bengali intellectuals around Rabindranath Tagore. Okakura's book *The Ideals of the East,* viewed as a pioneering formulation of Japanese pan-Asianism from its first sentence, "Asia is One," was completed within a circle of Indian intellectuals in India in 1902.[67] It was Sister Nivedita (Margaret Elizabeth Noble, 1867–1911), an Irish Theosophist follower of Swami Vivekananda and later an ardent Indian nationalist, who wrote the introduction to Okakura's *Ideals of the East* and placed his work within the framework of both anticolonial nationalism and Asiaphile criticism of Western civilization.[68]

Okakura could be confident in his call for a return to Asia, as his ideas were strongly inspired by the rising critiques against Western rationalism and materialism in Europe around the turn of the century. The following passage from Okakura Tenshin's *Ideals of the East* reveals how closely the notion of a return to Asian cultural traditions was tied to a perception of a larger crisis in European civilization: "Not only to return to our own past ideals, but also to feel and revivify the dormant life of the old Asiatic unity, becomes our mission. The sad problems of Western society turn us to seek a higher solution in Indian religion and Chinese ethics. The very trend of Europe itself, in German philosophy and Russian spirituality, in its latest developments, towards the East, assists us in the recovery of these nations themselves nearer to the stars in the night of their material oblivion."[69]

Okakura Tenshin saw the international affairs of the late nineteenth century as a conflict between East and West, taking the opinion that "the glory of Europe is the humiliation of Asia." He attributed European aggression to the "restless maritime instincts of the Mediterranean and Baltic, born of chase and war, of piracy and pillage" and contrasted it with the "continental contentment of agricultural Asia."[70] To belittle the modern vision of linear progress from barbarism to civilization, Okakura sarcastically noted that Japan used to be considered barbaric when it was an isolated peaceful state; only after the Japanese army began to commit mass killings of enemy soldiers on the battlefields of Manchuria did it begin to be described as a civilized nation.[71] For Okakura, it was not the decadent materialism of the West but rather the virility and energy of its own civilizational legacy that should become the basis of Asia's political revival and liberation. Okakura urged Asians to prepare themselves for an intellectual confrontation with Western colonialism by reviving their native civilizations.[72]

Before Okakura Tenshin, others, such as Tarui Tôkichi, Ôi Kentarô, and Uchimura Kanzô (1861–1930), had advocated a Japanese mission to support the liberation and development of Asian societies. In their thinking, however, Asia needed freedom not only from European hegemony but also from Asian tradition and despotism, a goal to be achieved through a process of civilization and enlightenment.[73] Okakura's most original contribution to pan-Asianist thought came through his rejection of a Eurocentric notion of Enlightenment and universal civilization. His Asianism was not based on the identity of the yellow race, of Chinese culture, or of the East Asian region but instead on a notion of Asian civilization. Although the content of this Asian civilization was defined by the universalism of Buddhism and Asian art, Okakura's anticolonial sensibilities and embrace of Asia as an alternative to the West rendered a metageographical image that sometimes included even the non-Buddhist parts of Asia. Okakura was confident in his view of Asia as a civilization distinct from, but also aesthetically and morally superior to, the civilization of the West. Finally, Okakura clarified the political implications of his view of Asian civilization and his critique of the West by writing anticolonial political essays in support of nationalism in India and other parts of Asia.[74]

CRESCENT VERSUS CROSS? PAN-ISLAMIC REFLECTIONS ON THE "CLASH OF CIVILIZATIONS" THESIS

Starting in the late 1880s, Ottoman intellectuals gradually began to perceive international relations as a global conflict between Christian Europe and the Muslim world. In order to overcome the unequal and uneven relationship with the Western powers, Abdulhamid II's regime had to establish the legitimacy and international recognition of a large Muslim empire ruling over millions of non-Muslim, especially Christian, populations. In that process, the Ottoman sultan continued to appeal to the notions of rights and legality for "civilized" states in the imagined, though Eurocentric, global public sphere.

It was not just the Ottoman sultan Abdulhamid II who expressed a sense of international isolation and insecurity in the face of the European competition to colonize the whole world.[75] Abdulhamid II's constitutionalist opponents, who were mostly in exile in European cities, also diagnosed international affairs as a dangerous encirclement of Muslim populations by an aggressive Christian West. Despite their admiration for the civilizations of France, England, and Germany, the Young Turk intellectuals condemned the Western powers' violation of the standards of civilization in international affairs, even while they were trying to achieve a revolution to implement some of the standards of civilization, especially a constitutional regime, in the Ottoman Empire.

The tensions that many Muslims perceived between the universal notions of global modernity and the immoral and imperialist politics of the Eurocentric world order led them to imagine an alternative vision of world order that would be more in harmony with their search for equality in the international sphere. The idea of a transnational solidarity of the Muslim peoples as a way to overcome their subjugation by the Western powers developed in this context as a pragmatic realpolitik option. Muslim modernists initially favored implementing the standards of civilization in a secure international environment based on the normative notions of the rights of states. Yet, against the dynamics of the power politics of imperialism and under the influence of the Darwinian idea that the weak will be eliminated by the powerful unless the weak parties cooperate and protect themselves, pan-Islamism seemed like a necessary defensive idea. Such a response to European aggressiveness was in fact predicted by the European imperial powers, which were aware of the reactions against the contradiction between imperial rule and their own slogans of liberty, civilization, and nationality.

Although the origin of the term "Muslim Unity" goes back to the mid-1870s, the transnational vision of pan-Islamic solidarity as a geopolitical concept belongs to the 1880s. The thesis of Islamic solidarity surged after the Ottoman loss of large territories in the Balkans and Eastern Anatolia in 1878, suggesting that the Ottomans could compensate for the loss of the Christian-majority areas in the Balkans by attracting Muslim-majority lands in South Asia into its orbit of international influence. In 1880 an Indian Muslim, Nusrat Ali Khan, succeeded in convincing Ottoman authorities to provide financial support for a journal, named *Peyk-i Islam* (Courier of Islam), addressing Indian Muslims from Istanbul. Although the British authorities in India did not find *Peyk-i Islam* dangerous, the British Foreign Office branch and embassy in Istanbul strongly protested its publication and pressured the Ottoman government to close the journal down.[76] The occupation of Tunisia by France in 1881 and of Egypt by Britain in 1882 further galvanized the emotional and intellectual attitudes of educated Muslims toward the Eurocentric world order and its legitimizing ideology of the "civilizing mission." It was during this period of rising Muslim protests over the increasing threat from the West that the great powers began to worry about a pan-Islamic solidarity, and the early articles and discussions on this issue began to emerge.

European newspapers began to refer to the idea of pan-Islamic reaction to Western expansion during the 1880s. In fact, one of the first uses of the term "pan-Islam" can be attributed to Gabriel Charmes, a prolific French journalist, in his description of the Muslim response to the French takeover of Tunisia.[77] From then on, numerous visions of pan-Islamism cropped up all over the Muslim world, either in the form of diplomatic cooperation among the Ottoman state, Iran, Afghanistan and other potentially independent Muslim states or in the sense of cultural awakening, economic development, and political solidarity.[78] The variety of visions, geographical locations, and diversity of its advocates indicates that no single person or institution can be credited with initiating and developing multiple versions of pan-Islamism. Several dominant characteristics and personalities did come to symbolize the movement, however.

The impact of the invasions of Tunisia and Egypt on the emergence of a global pan-Islamic vision can be seen in the biography of Jamal al-Din al-Afghani (1839–1897). al-Afghani traveled in the larger Muslim world extensively and already had ideas about the necessity for Muslim solidarity against the larger expansion of Western hegemony. It was immediately after the formal British occupation of Egypt that al-Afghani began to publish his pan-Islamic ideas in Paris in the journal he edited together with Muhammad Abduh (1849–1905), *al-Urwa al-Wuthqa* (The firmest bond), a highly influential publication that was distributed throughout the Muslim world. The journal invited all Muslims to overcome their political and theological divisions and establish Muslim unity, "*al-Wahda al-Islamiyya,*" in order to expel foreign intruders and establish their independence and dignity.[79]

From the mid-1880s on, several Muslim intellectuals tried to define the nature and content of Islamic solidarity. While European authors perceived it as xenophobic anti-Westernism that the Ottomans could use against British interests, Ottoman and other Muslim writers either denied the existence of any reactionary alliance against the West or defended the idea of Islamic solidarity as a peaceful and defensive method against the common threat of Western domination. For example, in 1881 Ahmet Midhat Efendi (1844–1912) argued in his article in the journal *Osmanlı* that the union of Muslims was not aggressive and was the only way to defend the Muslim world.[80] Midhat Efendi's arguments, inspired by his observations on pan-Slavism, pan-Germanism, and pan-Hellenism, were used in the context of international alliances based on geoculture. From this historical point until the 1908 Ottoman constitutional revolution, many in the Islamic world advocated ideas of pan-Islamic solidarity. Yet the practical projects derived from this vision had to consider the spiritual and political authority of the Ottoman caliph-sultan in Istanbul.

The ambivalence in the relationship between the modern notions of pan-Islamic solidarity and the seat of the caliphate in Istanbul led to a debate on the legitimacy and international influence of the Ottoman caliphate.[81] Once the notion of pan-Islamic solidarity emerged as a realistic geopolitical response to the tensions and potentialities in the imperial world order, it was natural that the issue of Ottoman leadership in any pan-Islamic project would raise several crucial political questions. Could the caliphate authority in Istanbul, which was hereditary through the Ottoman dynastic line, be reinterpreted and redesigned to become a power center in the changing global politics? Would the Ottomans be inclined to use the developing sentiments against colonialism and global consciousness regarding Muslim solidarity and cooperation to their advantage in the balance-of-power politics? Would a combination of pan-Islamic sentiments centered on the leadership of the Ottoman caliphate be advantageous or disadvantageous to the interests of the European great powers?

As early as 1873, British intelligence officer George Percy Badger questioned the prestige and legitimacy of the Ottoman caliphate among the Arabs in a report indicating a policy path for the British government in the case of a conflict of interest with the Ottoman caliphate.[82] Just three years after the initial British interest in this question, the Ottoman constitution of 1876 declared the sultan to be the caliph of all Muslims. From the European imperial point of view, two policy options were available to counter the increasing symbolic importance of the Ottoman caliphate in the Muslim world. They could either use the Ottoman caliphate for their own interests, or they could try to weaken it by encouraging intellectual and political challenges to the caliphate. These two competing points of view led to an international controversy over the legitimacy and political nature of the Ottoman caliphate. For example, the first book on this issue, written by J. W. Redhouse (1811–1892), a famous British scholar, linguist, lexicographer, and political adviser, was titled *A Vindication of the Ottoman Sultan's Title 'Caliph': Showing Its Antiquity, Validity, and Universal Acceptance*. It was published in 1877 in London to refute the arguments, popular in the British press and parliament, that the Ottomans had usurped the right to the caliphate.[83] In 1882 Wilfrid Scawen Blunt (1840–1922) wrote a provocative article on the illegitimacy of the Ottoman caliphate, leading to a series of responses to his ideas in the Muslim world.[84] There emerged a group of Muslim Arab intellectuals who doubted the future of the Ottoman caliphate and envisioned a potential Arab caliphate in the aftermath of the Ottoman defeat of Russia.[85] Later on, many figures from both the Islamic world and Europe joined this caliphate debate, taking sides for or against the legitimacy of the Ottoman caliph's fulfilling the requirements of the Islamic caliphate.[86]

Whatever the position of each participant with regard to the legitimacy of the Ottoman caliphate, they all had two shared assumptions: One was the politicization of the idea of a united caliphate for the Muslim world parallel to the globalization of information and transportation technologies and rising anti-imperialist sentiments in the Muslim world. The second was the recognition of the increasing prestige of the Ottoman caliph. It is in this context that one should evaluate Abdulhamid's pan-Islamic policy, which reflected more of the international context of the changing nature of the relations between the Muslim world and the Western powers than the sultan's own personal inclinations. Abdulhamid II refrained from identifying himself with any actively anti-Western ideology or rhetoric, as he believed in the necessity of continuing Westernizing-modernizing reforms without the destabilization threat of a parliament in the multiethnic and multireligious structure of the empire. For example, Abdulhamid II did not want to or could not support the nationalist Urabi revolt in Egypt, a revolt that facilitated the British military intervention in that country. In fact, reluctant to appreciate the nationalist mood of the uprising, Abdulhamid II blamed Urabi for facilitating it and thus serving the British intervention in Egypt.[87] Yet, despite his loyalty to the politics of Western-inspired reform in the high age of imperialism, Abdulhamid II also fostered the development of an Istanbul-based unofficial personal network of religious dignitaries and leaders in the Islamic world. Since this personal network was not official, it would not lead to an official diplomatic and military reaction from the Western powers, though it definitely aroused their suspicions.

The peculiarities of the anti-Western critiques and the political appeal of pan-Islamic visions of world order in the age of high imperialism can best be examined through the writings of Young Turk exiles in Europe. As they lived in Europe for a very long period of time and were highly familiar with both European intellectual trends and the network of Muslim and non-Muslim elites visiting European cities, the Young Turks had the opportunity to diagnose the global structures of power and ideas. They also had to resolve the tension between their emulation of the universal aspects of Western civilization and their vision of creating a well-recognized, civilized and equal Muslim political entity in the international society. One Ottoman intellectual whose biography best represents the shift to pan-Islamic ideas among disillusioned liberal Ottoman intellectuals in the high age of imperialism was Halil Halid, who wrote a classic book on the question of the conflict between the Christian and Muslim worlds in 1907. In addition to publishing three books in English, Halil Halid wrote numerous letters and opinion pieces in European papers on the question of the relationship between Europe and the Muslim world, clearly indicating his efforts to address the imagined international public opinion and the European intellectuals.[88]

Halil Halid was born in Ankara in 1869 and went through a madrassa education. In 1894 he left Turkey for Europe partly for fear of arrest in relation to his political opposition to the regime of Abdulhamid II, though he maintained good relations with the Ottoman embassy during his years in England.[89] He met the famous Orientalist Elias John Wilkinson Gibb and helped him in the preparation of his book *A History of Ottoman Poetry*.[90] In 1902 Halid was appointed to teach Turkish at the Special Indian Civil Service section of Cambridge University. Later he continued to teach Turkish for the Foreign Service Students Committee and the Board of Oriental Studies and became a member of the Royal Asiatic Society of Great Britain and Ireland. In the meantime, he completed a master's degree at Pembroke College at Cambridge University in the field of politics and law. In 1904–1905 he tried to organize a fund-raiser for the construction of a mosque in London. In that context, he traveled to Egypt and Sudan. In 1905 he participated in the fourteenth Orientalists congress in Algeria. In 1908 he initiated a campaign of popular economic boycott of Austria-Hungary to protest its annexation of Bosnia in that year. He left his teaching job in England in 1911 and returned to Turkey to assume parliamentary and diplomatic posts.[91]

Halil Halid's main disillusionment was Europeans' violation, by their imperialistic and Christian policies in the rest of the world, of the moral ideals that they proclaimed. He viewed European policies directed against the Muslim world as part of a general European imperialism that lacked moral values in its search for economic and material gain. As a solution, he advocated a moderate form of pan-Islamic alliance against European imperialist politics and their modern Christian crusade. His writings on issues relating to an Islamic response to Western hegemony found a large audience in English, Ottoman, Urdu, and Arabic. In them, Halid formulated the general Young Turk critique that European imperialism hid a Christian agenda behind its claim to establishing standards of universal civilization in international affairs.

Halil Halid's *The Crescent Versus the Cross*, published in 1907, received approximately sixty reviews and commentaries in the European press.[92] The critique of the "civilizing mission" ideology of Europe is the central theme of Halid's writings. He argued that the constant reference to the civilizing mission of the

European powers had lost its appeal and credibility through overuse, abuse, and malpractice. He was sure that this European discourse was just a ruse to intervene in the internal affairs of the Muslims and to violate their national honor and self-rule. He went on to explain two areas where this political discourse of a civilizing mission was utilized in the practice of colonialism. One was the conquest of natives of lower civilizations. Over time, colonized native populations were destroyed completely, while only a small group, unable to resist the lure of European civilization, was allowed to convert to Christianity to be used as servants. Halid cynically notes that if European colonization were limited to only uncivilized areas, no one would have objected. There was, however, a second area where the discourse of civilization was bound to fail because it faced the resistance of people who had their own sophisticated, superior civilization. Halid believed that those who already belonged to a well-established civilization such as Islam, India, or China could never be assimilated like primitive natives. Therefore, France could never achieve in Algeria what Britain had done in Australia.

To counter the politics of the European discourse of civilization, Halil Halid boldly declared that his book contained arguments and essays against the idea of the superiority of the European civilization. He noted that he himself had been a great worshipper-admirer of European civilization at one time, like so many people in Ottoman Turkey. Yet his fourteen years of residence in England, his travels to various European countries, and his position at Cambridge University had taught him that it was wrong to see European civilization as superior to his own in every respect. He hoped that his book would offer some advice and lessons for those who were pessimistic about everything Eastern and who always favored things Western.[93] Halid's purpose in shattering the myth of Western superiority in civilization was clearly more than just comparative cultural analysis. He made his challenge to the ideology of the civilizing mission very explicit. He was especially disturbed by the political language describing the Muslim world as a semicivilized or barbaric civilization that needed European guidance (6). In response to this discourse, he introduced the concepts of "material" and "spiritual-moral" civilizations, a distinction that would serve his challenge to the discourse of civilization of European imperial diplomacy.

Halil Halid devoted special attention to the European Christian biases toward Islam. For him, although Muslims and Christians could have cordial relations and Muslims had no historical enmity toward Christianity, zealot Christians created the issue of the "crescent versus the cross." He quoted William Muir's comment that Islam was the only religion resisting and competing with Christian missionaries (27). Similarly, he referred to Gladstone's characterization of Ottoman Muslims as "anti-human specimen[s] of humanity" as a reflection of this xenophobic anti-Muslim version of Christianity (14). In addition to the general Christian cultural bias of Europe, Halid also emphasized that the failure of missionaries to convert Muslims further fueled their anti-Muslim feelings. In his view, Christianity had many irrational practices and beliefs, something that made it hard to accept for those familiar with Islam (43). Muslims were not only resisting the attempts at Christianizing, they were also becoming more successful than Christian missionaries in attracting new believers (56). Halid believed that the relative success of Islam in converting nonmonotheistic peoples derived from its more humane and rational beliefs, an argument revealing of his anti-Christian emotions (70–81). Continuing his secular defense of Islam against Christianity, he provided a very extensive apology for several aspects of the Muslim tradition that Orientalists had shown to be reasons for the semi-civilized nature of Islam, such as the oppression of Muslim women in Islamic law and the historic practice of slavery. [94] He usually sided with the more liberal segments in the European intellectual spectrum in his polemical writings against Evangelical Christian missionaries and exponents of European imperialism. In his analysis of "English Turcophobia," he explained the anti-Turkish and anti-Islamic discourse in the British press as a consequence of the British perception of the Ottoman state as the most serious obstacle to its total hegemony over the Muslim world.[95]

Halil Halid then focused on three main arguments European powers used to legitimize their hegemony in the Muslim world, namely, bringing democracy to an authoritarian society, the elimination of Islam as an obstacle to progress, and facilitating free trade. First, with regard to the European claim to bringing democracy to despotic Muslim regimes, he argued that even if the Ottomans had very civilized and enlightened rulers, this would not be enough to change British Turcophopia, because the Ottoman Turks would still oppose the unfair hegemony of the European powers in the Muslim world. Halid still advocated fighting against oppression in Muslim societies but urged Muslims not let Europeans get rid of local institutions and traditions in the name of higher civilization. He compared a colonized state to a "toothless dog" and indicated his preference for the Abdulhamid II regime over any so-called enlightened colonial rule.

Second, with regard to the Orientalist discourse that Europeans would bring progress to Islamic societies, which had declined because Islam as a religion prevented secular progress, Halil Halid elaborated on evidence from European scholarship about the progressive nature of the Islamic faith in history. He underlined that Islam was never against progress, making reference to the writings of William Draper, a scholar famous for his ideas on the conflict between religion and science and on the positive role Islam played in the progress of Muslim Spain.[96] Halid explained the decline of the Islamic civilization by the military might of European alliances, which Ottoman power could not stop. In short, it was the economic rise and military victories of the West that had led to the stagnation of the East.[97] The East did not decline because of faith or fatalism. Muslims were not fatalists, but they also would not go around plundering nature and colonizing others.[98] Halid also wrote about the compatibility of Islam and modernity with reference to the question of women's rights and slavery to oppose the "necessity" of a European civilizing mission in these areas.

Third, with regard to the justification of European colonialism as a necessity to create free liberal trade, Halil Halid noted that no Muslim nation had refused to engage in fair free trade with Europe. Hence this could not alone explain colonialism. Historically, Muslims always welcomed European merchants, as could be seen in the history of Ottoman capitulations. In fact, Halid reminds his readers, it was only under the rule of colonialism that trade was no longer free in Muslim lands. European colonialists created a closed and illiberal system in which the British monopolized trade in Egypt and France controlled trade in Algeria and Tunisia to prevent the free activities of merchants from rival nations.[99]

Halil Halid discusses the question of Pan-Islamism in relation to the political tensions between rising nationalist demands for decolonization and Western attempts to continue their unjust hegemony over the non-Western world. He first attributes Western perceptions of Pan-Islamic unity and the yellow peril in Asia to the West's attempt to suppress an awakening of Eastern and Muslim nationalism. For Halid, there was only white/Western peril in the world, as Europeans collaborated to colonize Muslim areas and to mobilize world public opinion through the discourse of civilization.[100] It is ironic that the response of Ottoman nationalists to the Christian biases of the European powers, in the perceived conflict between the crescent and the cross, was a defense of Islam and the Muslim world through a secular language of Islamic "civilization" and the "natural rights" of Muslims to be free of colonialism. They developed a defensive Muslim internationalism. Especially the Young Turks believed that their ideas of Islamic unity were not a defense of Islam as a religion from a theological point of view but a refutation of the arguments of European fanaticism. For example, Halid rejected the depiction of Pan-Islam as a reactionary conservative xenophobia. He argued that it was Western hegemony itself that was leading to conservative reactions among some Muslims, because there were almost no free Muslims left. He quotes anti-Muslim statements by Baron d'Estournelles de Constant, a French diplomat and politician, as evidence of European aggressiveness: "The role of an officer who should undertake to disintegrate any forces of Islam would be the noblest and most useful that a man can play for his country".[101] The discourse of blaming Muslims for resisting oppressive foreign rule was only good for colonialists, he averred, lamenting the fact that ordinary people in Europe were easily deceived by the discourse of humanity and civilization and thus even good people in Europe were beginning to believe in the threat of Muslim unity.

Halil Halid calls on his European readers to try to understand why some Muslims under colonial rule resorted to armed resistance and had to rebel against their so-called civilized just rule. He notes that the European public did not have the chance to read about the problems of social decay, oppression, and material and spiritual poverty resulting from European colonial rule exercised in the name of civilization. He also offers a comparison of the French, British, Russian, and Dutch colonial regimes in the Muslim world. Though he finds British colonial rule to be a lesser evil in comparison to the other three, because of the absence of settler colonialism, he condemns all of them.[102] He finds the British and French support for the Russian and Dutch authorities' suppression of Muslims a sign of the absolute hypocrisy of Western civilization even within their own discourse of civilization. Similarly, he observes a kind of Pan-European solidarity in the European press's neglect of news of the sufferings of Muslim immigrants escaping from Russian rule.

The Young Turk exiles in Europe could be very receptive to critiques of the Ottoman regime with regard to the rights and freedoms of its subjects. But they could see no consistency and legitimacy in European attempts to liberate Bulgarians and Armenians when they were depriving Egyptians and Algerians of the same liberties. They concluded that, behind the European discourse of civilization, there was a strong Christian sentiment, a prejudice inherited from medieval times, against the Muslim world. They pessimistically noted that the crusading spirit in the modern form of the civilizing mission ideology and Orientalism were two of the main obstacles to a peaceful and just relationship between the Christian West and the Muslim world. They found it especially intriguing that the majority of British and French politicians, who were themselves not religious, supported missionary attempts to spread Christianity in Islamic lands. They despaired that the contemporary cultural misunderstanding was worse than the medieval one, because it was not due to ignorance but instead derived from deliberate distortion by a group of journalists, politicians, and scholars who were depicting the Muslim world in a certain way to serve their individual and collective Western interests.

Halil Halid's writings reflect the basic outlines of a critique of the West among Western-educated and modernist Muslims in the Ottoman Empire and beyond. He represented the larger trends, partly because he was a key member of the transnational Muslim intellectual networks, extending from Ottoman lands to India, but mostly intersecting in European capitals such as London or Paris. His writings were very much followed, translated into other Muslim languages such as Arabic and Urdu, and, more important, Halil Halid occupied important positions in Ottoman government on his return to Istanbul from exile. His intellectual biography shows that, by the beginning of the twentieth century, Western-educated Muslim elites were already debating the merits and possibilities of a larger solidarity and unity not only within the Muslim world but also with non-Muslim Asians in order to force European powers to revise and improve the normative and moral principles of the international order.[103]

CONCLUSION

Around the turn of the twentieth century, the perception of international relations as a conflict between crescent and cross or as a conflict between the white race and the yellow race became so acute that Muslim and East Asian nationalists searched to create alternative power combinations to protect themselves from the overwhelming might of the Western imperial nations. Ottoman and Japanese elites perceived the anti-Muslim statements of British prime minister William Gladstone or the anti–yellow race statements by German emperor, Kaiser Wilhelm, as emblematic of the rejection of their liberal reform attempts and evidence of the impossibility of their gaining equality with the Western nations. There was also growing pessimism and frustration stemming from the perception that the Eurocentric world order did not have any moral standards that could regulate conflicts of interest according to fair rules. Many non-Western nationalist intellectuals thus became convinced that each civilization had to gather its own power to balance the perceived unified power of the West, while benefiting from the existing inter-European rivalry as much as possible.

This dominant perception of the world order and its European center led to the formation of alternative universalist visions in the non-Western world both to define a more global form of modernity and to imagine a more inclusive international system. Pan-Islamic and pan-Asianist notions of solidarity were supposed to create the means to attain a new world order in which regional blocks, whether the Islamic world or East Asia, would regain their autonomy and dignity from Western hegemony as equal members of the global commonwealth of modernity. Their critique of the West was mostly limited to the imperialist West identified with the world order, and in fact anti-Westernism in this period continued to make reference to the proclaimed enlightenment values of the West.

4

THE GLOBAL MOMENT OF
THE RUSSO-JAPANESE WAR

The Awakening of the East/Equality with the West (1905–1912)

THE RUSSO-JAPANESE WAR in 1905 became a global moment of reflection on the legitimacy and structures of the imperialist world order. It was interpreted throughout the world as the first victory of an Asian nation belonging to the yellow race over a major white and Christian Western empire.[1] In fact, the world historical significance of the Japanese victory over Russia was noted by a wide array of contemporary observers writing in the immediate aftermath of the war.[2] This interpretation of the Japanese military victory transformed the character of reformist thought, perceptions of Western civilization, and critiques of the international order in the major centers of the non-Western world, from Egypt, Iran, and Turkey to India, Vietnam, and China.[3] The celebration by Asian and African intellectuals of the Russo-Japanese War as a turning point in their critique of the Eurocentric world order was highly paradoxical, however. Japan fought the war with Russia over control of Korea and Manchuria. It achieved its military victory partly as a result of the support it received from the Western superpower of the time, Great Britain. The Japanese elite were proud of the Anglo-Japanese alliance, which symbolized the civilized status of their nation.[4] Why, then, would Asian nationalists and intellectuals, who were aware that the Japanese victory over Russia was strengthening the pax Britannica in the Far East, still perceive it as a turning point in the history of decolonization from British and French imperial rule?[5]

We can only answer this question by analyzing how the war affected the terms of the global debates on race, civilization and progress, the three legitimizing pillars of the imperialist world order, and how it strengthened both modernist reformism and anti-Western critiques of pan-Islamism and pan-Asianism.

The immediate political and cultural responses to the Japanese victory all over the world were a reflection of the scope and synchronicity of the global intellectual sphere at that time. There was a surprising worldwide consensus on the larger historical and cultural meaning of the first modern war of the century throughout the world. While many Asian and colored intellectuals, including African-Americans in the United States, were welcoming Japan's military achievements as a moral contribution to their struggles, European observers predicted a potential threat to their interests from the rising Japanese power.[6] Asian newspapers were filled with articles on Japan, discussing either the positive implications of Japanese military victories for the "awakening" of Asia or the possible lessons other Asian societies could learn from the Japanese reforms.[7] It is important to note that there had been references to the Japanese model of reform since the mid-1890s in the writings of Turkish, Egyptian, and Chinese reformists and nationalists. Furthermore, especially after Japan's military victory against China in 1895, European newspapers and journals began to depict Japan as the singular successful case of Westernization and reform on the larger Asian continent, which overall was failing to reform itself. Even some European authors felt they had to examine Japan to rethink whether its achievements could teach European states anything.[8] Mostly relying on the European press coverage of Japan, nationalist thinkers of the Middle East also developed a keen interest in Japanese successes. Middle Eastern writings often included discussions of modernity, Western civilization, and international order via references to the Japanese model.

The Russo-Japanese War represented a truly global moment as a world historical event that had a transformative impact on the intellectual and political histories of the following decade. It propelled all anticolonial nationalists to be more assertive and confident, strengthened the constitutional movements, and invalidated several key legitimacy discourses of the Eurocentric world order. First of all, the scope of the responses to the war was great proof that the circulation of news and ideas had already created a global public sphere. The reading public consumed news about the Russo-Japanese War in a multitude of languages, thanks to the availability of accurate and fast reporting from the fronts through the telegraph network and international news agencies.[9] While the newspapers covered different battles of the war almost on a daily basis, the interpretations and discussions of the war were immediate among the reading public. Indian nationalist leader Jawaharlal Nehru noted in his autobiography how every morning he would impatiently check the English papers for recent news from the battles of the Russo-Japanese War and commented that he felt sympathetic and proud of the Japanese victories.[10] Chinese nationalist leader Sun Yat-sen was amazed and pleased to receive congratulatory gestures and messages from Egyptians during his passage through the Suez Canal during the war. He reported how, as a Chinese nationalist, he established bonds of solidarity with ordinary Egyptians, who also thought it appropriate to congratulate a Chinese passenger on the news of a Japanese victory.[11] The numerous articles and commentaries of Turkish, Arab, Persian, Indian, Vietnamese, and Chinese nationalists on the meaning of the Japanese victory popularized the shared interpretation of the war as proof of an Asian awakening and disproof of the Western claim to permanent racial and cultural superiority.

The similar interpretations of the world historical significance of the war making reference to racial and cultural identities such as "yellow race," "white race," "East and West" were yet more proof of the existence of a shared global intellectual sphere. Nehru was not an exception when he eagerly discussed the positive implications of the Japanese victory for Indian nationalism. Alfred Zimmern, who later became one of the founders of UNESCO, interrupted his Oxford University lectures on Greek history to speak to his students about the "most important event which has happened, or is likely to happen, in our lifetime; the victory of a non-white people over a white people."[12] One aspect of the various interpretations of the Russo-Japanese War was that, from Turkish and Indian nationalists to European intellectuals and African American leaders, there was a surprising convergence in the references to the notions of race and civilization in interpreting the political meaning of the war. Globally shared but European-originated terms such as "East and West" and "yellow race and white race" became a transnational force, utilized in legitimizing and delegitimizing structures of international politics and competing visions of world order at the turn of the twentieth century.

In chapter 2, I discussed the appropriation of the European concepts of "civilization" and "savagery" into the Ottoman and Japanese languages and how this process involved the transformation of the Islamic and Confucian concepts of civility, virtue, and perfection. Until the 1880s, most Ottoman intellectuals did not see Japan and the Ottoman world as part of the same general identity "Eastern."[13] In fact, Ottoman Muslims perceived themselves as closer to Europe than Asia. It was only after the 1880s that the Ottomans began to think of global cultures through the concept of "Şark ve Garp" (East and West). Throughout the 1890s, Ottoman references to Japan indicated that Muslim intellectuals had begun to perceive both the Ottomans and the Japanese as belonging to the category of East, defined in relation to their contrast with the civilization of the West. Ottoman intellectuals, who never perceived themselves as belonging to the yellow race, nevertheless began to identify themselves with the destiny and situation of the colored peoples in Southeast and East Asia around the turn of the century.

On the Japanese side, the concept of "tôyô" (East), originally adopted from the Chinese concept of the eastern seas, began, around the 1890s, to correspond to the concept of East and Orient in the European languages.[14] Previously, the Japanese imagination of the East was limited to the Chinese cultural sphere of East Asia and thus did not include the Muslim populations of Asia or the Ottoman state. For example, even as late as 1890, when the Ottoman battleship *Ertuğrul* visited Japan, staying there for three months, it did not lead to any discourse of Asian solidarity or any discussion of shared Eastern identity in the Japanese press.[15] When a typhoon off the coast of Japan sank the Ottoman battleship on its return journey in September 1890, the Japanese government and people showed great interest in the story of the death of five hundred Ottoman sailors. Through humanitarian aid and government initiative, sixty-nine Ottoman survivors of the *Ertuğrul* were returned to Istanbul by two Japanese battleships. Yet, even during the great media coverage of the disaster and Japanese aid campaign to the families of the lost Ottoman soldiers, there was no theme of shared Asian identity. On the contrary, as Michael Penn argues, the civilized image of Japan in the eyes of assumed Western observers was a major motive in the large-scale governmental and nongovernmental assistance to the victims of the sunk ship.[16] It is only after the turn of the twentieth century that the scope of "East" (*tôyô*) was first extended from the Chinese cultural zone of East Asia to include India and then finally all of Asia. By the time of the Russo-Japanese War, the meaning of "*tôyô*" was shaped by the dichotomy of the Orient versus the Occident and compelled even the most pro-Western Japanese intellectuals never to doubt that Japan was an Asian nation belonging to the yellow race and Eastern civilization. The synchronization of the meanings of East and West in different Asian languages was possible because each language community was intimately connected to the Western-centered global intellectual sphere. They all knew what European authors, media, and politicians wrote and thought about them. Hence the shared engagement with the European center led to the emergence of a common Eastern identity between Ottoman Muslims and Japanese despite a minimum level of direct contact and shared cultural legacy between these two societies.[17]

Another reason for the global impact of the Russo-Japanese War derived from the fact that major nineteenth-century wars were taken as test cases and proofs of the validity of the ideals and moral values of the conflicting parties. The Opium War was not simply a military defeat but remembered as the collapse of a great Confucian civilization at the hands of Western modernity. Similarly, the Ottoman defeats by Russia were interpreted not only as proof of the Ottoman Empire's status as the "sick man of Europe" but also as an indication of the decline of Islam. Within Europe, the German victory over France was seen as the defeat of the "soulless and technical" French civilization by the vitality of German national culture. More important, the successive series of European military victories in the process of worldwide colonization seemed to affirm the confident European perception of the global sphere as a hierarchy of races and civilizations. From the British show of superior military technology in suppressing the Egyptian nationalist movement at Tel al-Kabir in 1882 to the looting of the Chinese capital by a coalition of civilized nations in 1900, the high age of imperialism witnessed a series of military affirmations of Western hegemony.[18] Even when non-Western intellectuals challenged the legitimacy of global Western hegemony, all knew that Western military power could not as easily be defied. Japan's military power therefore gained great significance from this historical perspective, as it demonstrated that a non-Western nation could achieve parity in military power with (and even a superiority over) a European empire after only three decades of successful reform.

The global moment of the Russo-Japanese War influenced international history by shattering the established European discourse on racial hierarchies once and for all, thus delegitimizing the existing world order and encouraging alternative visions. For instance, when Abdullah Cevdet, the leading Ottoman Westernist and a believer in European ideas of race hierarchies, met Gustave Le Bon in 1905, he questioned Le Bon about where European thinkers had erred in their placement of the Japanese at the bottom of the racial hierarchy.[19] After 1905 no discussion of racism and innate civilizational hierarchies in world politics could avoid the example of Japan, because it clearly challenged all that had been written by European social scientists and European newspapers on this issue in the last quarter of the nineteenth century. The powerful interconnection among the trinity of Eurocentric world order at the end of the nineteenth century—namely, imperialism, modernity, and Orientalism/racism—forced anticolonial nationalists to redefine the prevailing notions of the relationship among civilization, race, and modern progress to claim their rightful position as equal members of the international system. The Russo-Japanese War clearly contradicted the racial arguments and the moral universe that had justified the world order from 1882 to 1905, and thus it could be utilized to invalidate the idea of Western invincibility.[20]

Frequent references to the rapid rise of Japan as the first Eastern nation to attain great-power status inspired the imagination of a new world order in which Asia would be decolonized and become an equal partner to the West. Ottoman intellectual Ahmed Rıza summarized this aspect of the war in the following paragraph:

How to explain the pretension of Europe, then, of wanting to civilize Asia, since, when a people of these regions endeavors to raise itself, [Europe] condemns it immediately as a "peril" of such and such color? . . . There are multiple well-merited lessons that the war permitted the Japanese to give to the "superior races". . . . One cannot doubt the preeminence of the social and political institutions of Japan, a so-called inferior race by most of those peoples upon whom the patent of superiority is conferred. The splendid victory of the Japanese has proved the Christian world arrogant; that it is not indispensable for a people to embrace Christianity in order to acquire morality, civilization, and an aptitude for progress. . . . Likewise events of the Far East have put forth evidence of the uselessness of interventions, frequent if pernicious, of Europe reforming a people. On the contrary, the more isolated and preserved from contact with European invaders and plunderers a people is, the better is the measure of [its] evolution toward a rational renovation.[21]

The Russo-Japanese War became especially pertinent in discussions of the equal treatment of Asian nations in the international sphere. In the conception of international law in the early twentieth century, each country could have full legal rights in the international society if it was deemed "civilized" by the core European countries. The discourse of civilization was not only used by European newspapers and politicians to justify colonial adventures but also became a scholarly tenet in mainstream texts on international law. For example, Iran, Siam, China, and Ethiopia were identified as states not "fully civilized" and thus not qualified to earn full legal equality in international law.[22] Even though the Ottoman state had technically been part of European international society since 1856, it was still treated as a non-Western and unequal member of the world nations in the European media and by European diplomats.

Because of the legal and political implications of the civilization discourse, Asian intellectuals were very sensitive about the politics surrounding the European colonial literature that had created an image of the Orient that, for them, bore no resemblance to the "real" Orient they knew or wanted to create.[23] Thus they saw the European representation of the Orient as one of the greatest barriers to normal, healthy international relations based on mutual understanding and respect, because it proffered the image of a society unfit for equality with the Occidental cultures. After the Japanese victory, Asian intellectuals became more confident in their campaign against the image of a decadent inert East. Their concerns and critiques of Western viewpoints of Asia and the Orient, as well as the invalidation of Western images with reference to Japan, were embedded in the belief that correction of misperceptions about Asians could in turn correct their problems in international affairs.

Asian nationalists were also aware that the correction of Western misperceptions of the Orient alone would not be sufficient to create a just international order, as they recognized power relations as equally important. Thus some Asian nationalists maintained a parallel conviction that only military power and industrial modernization could save the weak Asian nations from the so-called mercy of the powerful Western nations. For example, several leading Ottoman nationalists maintained that the Ottoman government should give up relying on diplomatic initiatives and appeals to international morality and instead follow Japan's path of industrial and military self-strengthening. The Japanese achievement was proof that only military victory, not just knowledge of legal rights and civilized ideas, could secure the path of equality and recognition in the chaotic and insecure international environment of the early twentieth century.[24] This ideal compelled many Asian nationalists to search for power alliances through pan-Islamic and pan-Asianist visions to counterbalance the perceived cooperation and unity of European powers in their policies toward Asian and African societies.

The inspiration of the Japanese model of modernization, especially its achievements in constitutional government, inspired a wave of constitutional revolutions in Asia from 1906 to 1911, exemplified by the Iranian (1906), Ottoman (1908), and Chinese (1911) revolutions. Constitutionalists in all these societies utilized models and metaphors of Japanese modernity, that country's constitution, and its military victories in mobilizing supporters and weakening authoritarian regimes.[25] The very fact, however, that the Japanese model inspired not only anti-Western critiques of world order but also constitutional movements that were equally modernist and Western demonstrates the ambivalence of Asian admiration for Japan. On the one hand, recognition of Japan's great-power status inspired nationalist movements in India, Indonesia, Vietnam, and Egypt tremendously.[26] Nationalists in those nations adopted a vision of Asian or Eastern solidarity, potentially under Japanese leadership, as a possible path to overcoming Western hegemony. On the other hand, Japan inspired a radicalization of modernizing reforms, including a desire to establish a constitutional government.

The influential French journal *Revue du Monde Musulman,* published after 1906 under the auspices of the French Scientific Mission in Morocco, carried articles on the revival of Islam and pan-Islamic emotions in the post–Russo-Japanese War period.[27] Pan-Islamism, nationalist thought, and the revival of the East were major themes of this journal, which saw the dynamism and transnational networks in Asia as a confirmation of the triumph of modernity in those Westernizing world regions.[28] The energy, leadership, and dynamism of Western-educated modern Muslims, who were both nationalistic and anti-Western, became very apparent throughout the Muslim world. The presence of these groups challenged Orientalist assumptions and the civilizing mission ideology and thus prompted a twofold reaction from European observers. Progressive Europeans revised their old assumptions.[29] A more racist camp, however, saw pan-Islamism as a new peril for the West against which the West should unite. One example of this reiterated racist ideology, expressed in a rather blunt and pseudoscientific fashion, was a book on the inferior racial psychology and irrational faith of the Muslims by Andre Servier.[30]

Interestingly, together with nationalism, three major non-Western world religions, namely, Islam, Buddhism, and Hinduism, seemed to experience a re-awakening and revival in the aftermath of the Russo-Japanese War. The revival of a transnational Islamic identity thus was not an exceptional phenomenon in Asia, as Buddhism and Hinduism also underwent revival. There were signs of pan-Buddhism and a revival of Hindu universalism. Anagarika Dharma-pala's reputation represented the appeal of international Buddhism, and Swami Vivekananda became the symbol of a new Western interest in Asian spirituality and Hinduism. Both Vivekananda and Dharmapala became figures of interna-tional reputation after attending the Chicago World Religions Conference in 1893. They encouraged nationalist movements and decolonization and symbol-ized an assertive and dynamic notion of Asian civilization with regard to the West.

Given the way the Japanese victory over Russia energized and strengthened both nationalist movements and alternative visions of world order, it is evident that the Russo-Japanese War was an important turning point in the history of Asia's decolonization before WWI. In its effect on international public opin-ion, discourses on Japan's modern achievements, and the subsequent consti-tutional revolutions in Iran, Turkey, and China, it came to be defined as the moment of the "awakening of Asia." As a matter of fact, slogans about the "rise" or "awakening" of the East associated with the Russo-Japanese War predate the image of the "decline" or "retreat" of the West, which only gained prominence after World War I.[31] The "awakening of the East" during the 1905 to 1914 period coincided, however, with the ultimate victory of Westernization and the idea of universal modernity. The triumph of Western modernity as a model in Asia, paradoxically, is most evident in Asian observations on the Japanese model of modernization.

AN ALTERNATIVE TO THE WEST? ASIAN OBSERVATIONS ON THE JAPANESE MODEL

The rise of Japan as the only nonwhite power spurred an increase in Asian interest in the Japanese experience of modernization. Gradually, Japan began to serve as a metaphor for Asian modernity for the Ottomans, Egyptians, and Indians. Many reformers wanted to know what would be necessary for their own societies to copy in order to match Japan's achievements in the three de-cades of reform after the Meiji Restoration. This question led to a search to understand the reasons, or "secrets," behind the rise of Japan and to reflections not only about the Meiji reform experience but also the character of the Japanese people. The Japanese model became a pedagogic tool for almost all the conflicting ideological currents in the Ottoman state, Egypt, and India, ranging from Social Darwinist secularists to Muslim and Hindu modernists and from supporters of a strong monarchy to constitutionalists. Given that the educated Japanese elite had been emulating Western civilization since the 1870s, the new Asian interest in the Japanese model of modernization had to reflect on Japan's Westernization as well.

The "secrets" of Japanese progress were commonly attributed to Meiji state policies regarding compulsory public education, participatory politics, and the constitution, as well as policies of industrial development. After describing these secrets, one Egyptian paper expressed the hope that Japan would become Asia's teacher in terms not only of the tangible skills of successful military technology, commerce, and agriculture but also of the importance of education and patriotism.[32] Ottoman, Egyptian, and Indian writings on the reasons for Japanese progress reflected a dilemma of interpretation on the issue of attributing Japanese success either to exceptional Japanese traits or to universally applicable policies that the Meiji leadership had executed. If the Japanese success was solely due to Japan's peculiar traditions and national culture, as several well-known European and Japanese interpretations emphasized, Japan could only be the exception that proved the rule of Asia's permanent backwardness. For example, Nitobe Inazo argued that the ethical training of Japanese individuals, inherited from the martial tradition of the samurai, Bushido, explained Japan's extraordinary success in modernity. For Nitobe, understanding the principle and single driving force behind the success of Japan's transformation after the Meiji Restoration required more than a focus only on education or technological and industrial advances. "It is the spirit that quickeneth, without which the best of implements profiteth but little."[33] This meant that other Asian nations were still incapable of reaching the same high levels of progress and civilization. Avoiding such a pessimistic conclusion, and in hopes of affirming an awakening of Asia through the symbol of the Russo-Japanese War, Asian commentators usually concluded, however, that Japan's path to progress could be repeated by other Eastern nations, even if there remained certain peculiar aspects of the culture that explained Japan's achievements.

An example of the tension between the particularistic and the universalistic interpretations of Japan's achievement arose in the discussion stemming from a conference on the renaissance of Japan organized by the Committee of Union and Progress, the party of the 1908 Constitutional Revolution, in Istanbul in 1911. The audience included high-ranking and influential figures such as the Ottoman prince Abdülmecid Efendi and the minister of foreign affairs, both of whom would naturally have been interested in hearing secrets of the Japanese success that could serve as policy-oriented lessons for the Ottomans. The main speaker was the Austria-Hungarian adviser to the Ottoman Ministry of Justice, Comte Leon Ostrorog (1867–1932). Ostrorog explained the Japanese success not as a miracle but as a consequence of the fundamental inclinations of the Japanese people, the most important of which was the recognition of the value of adopting the ways of a superior foreign civilization. In addition to underscoring Japan's historically unique ability to assimilate foreign cultures, Ostrorog's explanations touched on major ideas accounting for the exceptionality of Japan's modern successes, among them, Bushido ethics. Ostrorog concluded that the Japanese had achieved constitutional reform, instituted military conscription and compulsory education, founded universities, and reorganized the economy as a result of their exceptional national character.[34]

For Ottoman policy makers, the emphasis on Japan's uniqueness could be translated into an argument of fatalism and predetermination. If Japanese culture explained the country's progress, Ottoman-Muslim culture must have prevented progress and reform efforts. This kind of culture praise and culture blame implied that it would not be possible for the Ottomans to repeat the great achievements of their Oriental brothers in Japan.[35] Aware of these implications, and contrary to Count Ostrorog's emphasis on the role of peculiar Japanese characteristics, the conference organizer Salih Gourdji thus avoided mentioning cultural factors in his introductory speech. Instead, he made comparisons between Japan and the Ottoman state, concluding that had the absolutist regime of Abdulhamid II not stopped constitutional progress, the Ottomans could have reached similar achievements. The Ottomans could succeed like the Japanese if they took lessons from the political participation and constitutional leadership of Japan.[36]

Despite the immense proliferation of writings on the Japanese model, however, Asian discourses on the Japanese achievements in modernization did not offer any alternative to the view of modernity symbolized by Western societies. Modernity was still seen as essentially one and universal, and Meiji Japan's achievement was to prove that this process was not unique to the West but possible in an Asian society. What Asian admirers learned from Japan was in fact no more than a Japanese interpretation of Western modernity and a confirmation of the earlier Asian interest in universalizing modernity. The experience of Asian students in Japan is a good example of this trend. For instance, for the more than ten thousand Chinese students who studied in Japan until WWI, the experience was regarded primarily as a cheaper and more effective way to learn the Western-originated but universal modernity from a nearby country that had already adopted it successfully. While Chinese intellectuals were much influenced by Japanese interpretations of Western modernity through this student network, the fact remains that their ultimate goal was to learn what Japan had previously learned from the West rather than any Japanese alternative to the West. Among Indian, Vietnamese, Turkish, and Arab students, those who chose to come to Japan must have done so more out of ideological inclinations than financial and geographical convenience. Most became admirers of Japan's synthesis of Western modernity with its own cultural traditions. But they would also see Japanese modernity not as an alternative to the West but rather as its most successful application.[37] Students who returned to their home countries from Japan therefore did not find themselves in contradiction to those who came back from European countries, because Europe remained the ultimate model of modernity and reform.[38]

Nevertheless, the Japanese model of modernization was valuable for Asian observers for three main reasons. First, it presented a shortcut to the Western level of civilization. According to the predominant views of modern world history, advanced Western nations had achieved their civilizational level over the course of several centuries. Non-Western intellectuals seeking to raise their own societies to an equal standard had to find some way to replicate the long years of Western development in a shorter period of time, especially given the widening power gap between the Western imperial powers and Asia. The success of the Japanese reforms since the Meiji Restoration was thus important as a demonstration that progress could be achieved over just a few decades by cultivating patriotism, dedication to the nation, and social morality. If thirty years of rapid and selective state-led reforms had brought Japan to a level equal with the West, many nationalists in Asia could also be optimistic about the future power and wealth of their own nations. The will to change, the energy to reform, and the availability of earlier models eliminated all the geographical, cultural, and historical constraints and conditions that European thinkers had identified as the causes of the rise of civilization in the West.[39]

Second, the Japanese example showed that non-Western cultural and religious traditions did not necessarily have to be regarded as obstacles to modern progress. By the turn of the century, the nature of the relationship between traditional culture and universal modernity had already become an important question for the nationalist agenda. In the literature on Japan's modernization, the prevailing consensus held that Japan had successfully and intelligently selected the useful and essential aspects of Western civilization for adoption, without the need to appropriate "superficial and harmful" Western habits and deny its cultural heritage. In truth, the heritage that was preserved was more an invented image of traditional Japan than a reflection of the actual continuity of pre-Meiji Japanese culture.[40] This concept of a "Japanese selectivity," however, which could effectively synthesize Western and Eastern knowledge, was very significant from the perspective of Asian nationalism, which had been preoccupied with the question of the East-West encounter and civilizational harmony since the 1880s.[41] For example, the "good wife, wise mother" ideology that Japan had adopted from European culture was regarded as a successful preservation of the Japanese tradition in a modernizing context, since women could actively serve the self-strengthening of the nation through Westernizing reforms without losing their traditional cultural role.[42] Throughout the Middle East, imagery focusing on the creation of this progressive role for Japanese women in social life in harmony with the preservation of their traditional duties became a constant reference point among nationalists.[43] For intellectuals thinking within the paradigms of a synthesis between East and West, then, Japan presented a far better model than Germany or France, since it offered proof that native cultural traditions could indeed be compatible with modern civilization. For instance, the most prominent theorist of Turkish national identity, Ziya Gökalp, often referred to the Japanese historical experience in relation to his arguments that modern Turkey need not be afraid of losing its Muslim religion and national culture in the process of appropriating universal modernity.[44]

Third, the rise of Japan engendered optimism that it was not too late for Ottoman, Egyptian, and Indian reformers to bring their own societies to modernity and international equality. At the time of Japan's rise, Egypt and India were under colonial rule, while the Ottoman state, though politically independent, was still subject to unequal treaties and Western intervention in domestic affairs and had been dubbed the "sick man of Europe." A widespread mood of pessimism over the failure of the Ottoman reforms was combined with the newly popularized Darwinist ideologies of racial and civilizational hierarchies, leading to the conviction that not only the Ottoman failures but the overall backwardness of Asian societies could be attributed to the inherent incapability of Easterners, as opposed to Westerners, to civilize themselves.[45] In that context, Japan's example of catching up with Western civilization in just three decades served as an inspiration to Ottoman reformers to rejuvenate radical reformism with renewed optimism.[46] Similarly, in colonized societies such as Egypt, Indonesia, and India, an emphasis on the racial and cultural similarity they shared with the Japanese under the banner of Eastern identity made it possible for the nationalist movements in those societies to find new legitimacy in their struggle against colonialism. After all, if "the Japanese could succeed, the Javanese could do it, too," and thus they would not need the civilizing mission of the Dutch colonial rule.[47]

DEFINING AN ANTI-WESTERN INTERNATIONALISM: PAN-ISLAMIC AND PAN-ASIAN VISIONS OF SOLIDARITY

In terms of the history of pan-Islamic and pan-Asian visions of world order in the aftermath of the Russo-Japanese War, two aspects were very visible. First was the further internationalization of the imagination of non-Western solidarity and world order, as evidenced in the attempt to establish links between Muslim West Asia and non-Muslim Japan. Second, there were new realist formulations of pan-Islamic and pan-Asianist solidarity, though both the Japanese and Ottoman governments avoided identifying with alternative visions of world order that could jeopardize their cooperation with the Western powers.

Pan-Asianism and pan-Islamism became the main internationalist visions of world order for many nationalists in Asia in the aftermath of the Russo-Japanese War. As these ideas circulated in the new global journalism, disseminated by the many travelers, adventurers, and activists, Tokyo became a center in the network of pan-Asianist and pan-Islamic thought. When the *Revue du Monde Musulman* carried an article about the impact of the Russo-Japanese War on the Muslim world in 1906, it predicted that the number of Muslim students going to Japan would increase.[48] Before any students arrived in Tokyo, however, the leading pan-Islamist activist and intellectual of this period, Abdurreşid İbrahim, visited Tokyo, hosted by Japan's pan-Asianist groups for several months. İbrahim was not the only Muslim who visited Japan to learn the secrets of its progress and establish solidarity. Yet his contacts with Japanese pan-Asianists became the most influential and long-lasting relationship of a Muslim figure with this intellectual and political movement.[49]

The stories of the meetings of the representatives of the pan-Islamic and pan-Asianist movements in Tokyo and their attempts to create global cooperation demonstrate the internationalist aspects and limitations of both these movements. Abdurreşid İbrahim and several prominent Japanese Asianists, including Toyama Mitsuru, Inukai Tsuyoshi, and Uchida Ryohei, formed Ajia Gi Kai (Association for the Defense of Asia) in 1909 to institutionalize their contacts and hopes for future cooperation. The new Asianist organization had ties with Konoe Atsumaro's Tôa Dobunkai (East Asian Common Culture Society) as well as Kokuryukai and Genyosha, two major ultranationalist organizations advocating a more assertive Asia policy in Japan. There were several other pan-Asianist organizations in Tokyo in the first decade of the twentieth century because of the large number of students, political activists, exiles, and merchants from China, India, the Philippines, Vietnam, and other Asian countries. Differing from the earlier organizations, Ajia Gi Kai specifically focused on improving the ties between the Muslim world and the Japanese Empire. Its objectives included the establishment of branches in China (meant for Chinese

Muslims), India, Persia, Afghanistan, and Turkey to achieve the goal of "Asia for Asians." Ajia Gi Kai succeeded in registering nearly forty members from different parts of the Muslim world in addition to more than one hundred Japanese members.[50]

The intellectual and political charisma of Abdurreşid İbrahim, as well as his pan-Islamic networks in Russia, Ottoman Turkey, and Egypt, led to significant coverage in the Muslim press of Ajia Gi Kai's establishment in Japan.[51] Born in Russia and educated in Kazan, Mecca, Medina, and Istanbul, İbrahim was involved in Islamic reformism and had a reputation for activism as a journalist and pan-Islamic modernist thinker. During the troubled years of the first Russian Revolution and its aftermath, İbrahim was the leading figure in the national movement among Muslims of the Russian Empire. When the political activities of all non-Russian minorities in the Russian Empire were curtailed during the Third Duma (1907–1912), Abdurreşid İbrahim had to leave Russia. He set out on a long journey that covered much of Asia, from Central Asia, to Mongolia, China, Korea, and Japan, and then back to Istanbul by way of China, Singapore/the Malay Islands, India, and Mecca. He was one of the most traveled Muslim activists in modern times, visiting more Muslim lands than many other prominent pan-Islamic figures, such as Jamal ad-Din al-Afghani. Wherever Abdurreşid İbrahim visited, he was always focused on the questions of the progress and development of Muslims and other Asians, as well as their despair under colonial rule and the necessity for their unity.[52] He stayed in Japan for seven months, and his writings and speeches advocating Japanese-Muslim collaboration shaped both the initial Japanese Asianist perception of the Muslim world and Muslim perceptions of Japan.

It is important to note the most notable Muslim publication on Japan, the book *Shams al-Mushriqa* (The rising sun),[53] written just before the Russo-Japanese War by Mustafa Kamil (1874–1908), a nationalist leader who was also known for his pan-Islamic visions of world order. Kamil believed in the necessity of international solidarity between Egyptians and the rest of the Muslim world as well as non-Muslim Asia in the struggle against the hegemony of the British Empire. As the British Empire was truly a global force, the opposition to it had to have a global vision as well. Mustafa Kamil asked for Ottoman support for the cause of Egyptian independence from British rule through a vision of pan-Islamic solidarity. In his article "Europe and Islam," published in the French daily *Le Figaro* in 1901, Kamil predicted that, as European aggression against the Muslim world continued, Muslims would rise to protect their faith and the Ottoman state.[54] For him, modern Europe's hidden Crusade against Islam would impel Muslims to unite around the leadership of the Ottoman caliph. In his search for international allies that would aid the Egyptian and Muslim cause against British colonialism, Mustafa Kamil also advocated

Muslim cooperation in a larger Asian solidarity under the potential leadership of Japan.

Just a year before İbrahim's visit to Japan in 1908, his fellow Muslim modernist from Russia, İsmail Bey Gaspıralı (1851–1914), tried to establish the first major pan-Islamic congress in Cairo. Gaspıralı's project was partly inspired by his observations of the methods of the pan-Slavic movement and his experience with the Muslim Congresses of Russia in 1905 and 1906.[55] Gaspıralı's appeal was for a cultural and social renewal and the search for a solution of the common issues of Muslims in the field of education, economy, and social solidarity. He was careful to add that such a congress likely would not arouse the suspicion of the great powers, because its primary concern would not be international politics. For example, in his petition to the Ottoman caliph, Gaspıralı assured him that the congress would not cause any negative image of a reactionary Islamic alliance in European public opinion.[56] In his speech in front of hundreds of leading Egyptian intellectuals, Gaspıralı called for a reform and the awakening of the Muslim world, blaming Muslims themselves for their crisis of military weakness, colonial despair, and economic backwardness. Rashid Rida, the influential salafi modernist thinker, made comments agreeing with Gaspıralı on the importance of Muslim commercial revival. Despite the enthusiasm behind the first meeting of the Cairo pan-Islamic congress, however, the planning for future conferences became the victim of intergroup rivalries among Egyptian intellectuals. The most salient aspect of the first pan-Islamic congress was the unsupportive and cautious approach of the Ottoman government of Abdulhamid II, who was otherwise known in the Western media for his informal pan-Islamic policies.

Abdurreşid İbrahim's visit to Tokyo and the establishment of Ajia Gi Kai represented a search for new power centers by a leading pan-Islamic activist, and it was followed by a boom of Asianist publications in both Tokyo and Istanbul. Ajia Gi Kai published a journal in Japanese called *DaiTô* (The great East) that included many articles on Islam and the Muslim world.[57] Muhammad Barakatullah, an Indian revolutionary and a pan-Islamist himself, started the publication of *Islamic Fraternity* in the English language, solidifying Tokyo's position as a center for pan-Islamist and Asianist journals.[58] Muslims were not alone in their contacts with Japanese pan-Asianists, who established contacts and networks among various nationalist groups from the Philippines, Vietnam, and China to India.[59] For a while, Tokyo became an attractive destination for students, revolutionaries, intellectuals, and adventurers, especially from East Asia.

Barakatullah's collaborator, Hasan Hatano Uho, a pan-Asianist convert to Islam, published other Islamic journals contributing to the positive image of Japan in the Muslim world.[60] Hatano's book on Asian solidarity was later translated into Ottoman Turkish by Abdurreşid İbrahim under the title *Asya Teh-likede* (Asia in danger) and published in Istanbul by a pan-Islamist publication house, Sebilürreşad.[61] Meanwhile, in Istanbul, İbrahim's own memoirs about his travels in Asia were published, and his highly didactic and political Asian-ist perspective proved a great influence on the Muslim perception of Japan.[62] A Japanese pan-Asianist and Kokuryukai member named Yamaoka Kôtaro ac-companied Abdurreşid İbrahim on his return to the Muslim Middle East. He converted to Islam, visited Mecca, and gave lectures in Ottoman cities.[63] The activities of this small group gradually shaped the visions of pan-Asianists and pan-Islamists to encompass a notion of international solidarity that went be-yond the zones of the Islamic world or the Chinese cultural sphere.

This Muslim-Japanese cooperation needed intellectual justification on both sides as to their shared ideas and visions. In Japan, Muslims of West Asia were not usually considered part of the yellow race. In fact, the memoirs of Yamada Torajirô (1866–1957), a young Japanese who stayed in Istanbul for around two decades after 1892, show that, as a member of the first-generation Western-educated Meiji elite, he did not initially have strong ideas about a shared Asian identity, despite his romantic interest in Ottoman culture. He developed the notion of an Asian identity encompassing both the Ottoman world and Japan only during the first decade of the twentieth century.[64] It was the modernist and constitutionalist revolution in the Ottoman state in 1908 that convinced Yamada Torajirô to emphasize the shared characteristics of Japan and Ottoman society, in relation to the larger Asian awakening of the post–Russo-Japanese War period.[65] The Japanese members of Ajia Gi Kai embraced an Asian identity including the Islamic world, beyond the usual references to Chinese cultural heritage or Buddhist religious heritage.

Similarly, pan-Islamism was initially a movement concerned with Ottoman connections with Muslim populations all over the world and Muslim solidar-ity against European colonial rule. Cooperation with Shinto/Buddhist Japanese and other non-Muslim East Asians by an influential pan-Islamist figure ne-cessitated an explanation for the basis of this transreligious and transnational vision of solidarity.

A primordial conception of civilizational legacy cannot explain the emer-gence of a shared identity exhibited by the members of Ajia Gi Kai. At the turn of the century, pan-Asianism as defined by Okakura Tenshin and Rabindranath Tagore presented a vision of international solidarity grounded in the shared Buddhist legacy of India, China, and Japan.[66] Interestingly, one of the earlier pan-Asianist organizations established by Chinese, Indian. and Japanese figures around 1907 had classified Muslims as one of the outsider occupiers of Asia, whose boundaries were defined by Buddhist legacy and the yellow race.[67] Yet the trend was toward a more global consciousness of belonging to an Eastern and Asian unity that superseded religious and cultural legacies. Rebecca Karl has described the interest of Chinese intellectuals in the experiences of other non-Western societies, viewing them as global sharers of the traumatic experience of Western hegemony.[68] Similarly, Muslim intellectuals extended their vision of solidarity beyond the scope of the Islamic world, showing interest in the fates of Japan and China. For instance, Abdurreşid İbrahim wrote about his dialogue with the eighth Jebtsundamba in Mongolia, his sympathies with the Tibetan and Mongolian peoples, and his hopes for the revival of China. Thus the ideal of solidarity against Western expansion gradually transcended religious identities, as pan-Islamists began to see the Chinese and Japanese as potential allies, while Japanese Asianists imagined the Muslim world as an essential component of Asian awakening and solidarity.

This broad identification with the non-Western world did not mean the elimination of religious, national, or communal identities, for Asian identity was not incompatible with any of these other identities. The accidental fact that Christian Ethiopia, the Muslim Ottoman state, and Buddhist-Shinto Japan were seen as three nominally independent nations resisting the West helped internationalists go beyond their religious affiliations. The basis of Eastern-Asian identity was defined not by religion but by the historical experience with Western expansionism that each Asian society had shared since the mid-nineteenth century. As Abd al-Rahman Shahbandar, an Ottoman intellectual and later a Syrian nationalist, said: "We do not want to unite with Easterners just for aggression against the Europeans but rather to save humanity."[69]

The perception of a Western danger was fundamental to the anti-Western internationalism of Ajia Gi Kai. Pan-Islamist Abdurreşid İbrahim, like many others in his generation, sometimes expressed despair or fear that Asian societies and cultures would not survive because of global Westernization. Like his Muslim modernist contemporaries, İbrahim was very harsh in his condemnation of the existing Muslim cultures for their late embrace of the process of modernity. For him, the tide of modernization and Western expansion was unstoppable. If only Western civilization had used its power according to moral principles, it could have benefited all humanity. The West, however, had abandoned morality in the pursuit of power politics, and non-Westerners had to act immediately and in solidarity to avoid extinction while working in the long term for self-strengthening via modernization. This perception became the basis of a mission to defend the autonomy and dignity of Asian societies and to establish equality between Asia and Western civilization both politically and intellectually. The founding documents of Ajia Gi Kai demonstrate this missionary aspect of the pan-Asian internationalism:

Earlier, Asia was incomparably the richest continent in terms of nature, population, and agricultural products, and thus in history they gave birth to various civilizations and sages. But recently, because of internal discord, jealousy, and hate,
Asia has been exposed to Western expansion and become weak. If this situation
is not solved, the future of Asia will be grim and darker. Because we Asians have
common customs and manners, common spirit and character, we must make
a hard struggle ourselves for the betterment and development of Asia. For this
purpose, we established Ajia Gi Kai, and we ask for the cooperation of our fel-
lows in all Asia.[70]

In terms of their vision of modernity and international affairs, pan-Asianists
and pan-Islamists of the post–Russo Japanese War period continued the already
existing critiques of the imperialist West with reference to the ideals of a universal civilization. For Abdurreşid İbrahim, the concept of "civilization" functioned
as the key term in his critique of Western hegemony and in his vision of a new
order in Asia. By presenting numerous examples illustrating how colonialism
had violated all the Enlightenment ideals espoused by the West, he underlined
the hypocrisy and barbarity behind the idea of the white man's mission to bring
civilization to Asia. İbrahim's critiques referred to the ideals of human dignity,
racial equality, and national autonomy as the values of a real, humane civilization. To illustrate his critique of the "civilizing mission," he narrates a conversation with a French traveler who commented to İbrahim on how Russian behavior toward non-Russians was uncivilized and unjust. İbrahim responded to this
comment by saying, "When there is might, there is no question of rights and
truth. You French people treat Algerians like animals, insult their religion, and
violate their human rights. If 'civilized' nations like France are guilty of such a
degree of injustice, oppression, and lack of clear consciousness, what can we expect from the Russians?"[71] In this discursive strategy, there was still a commitment to the idea of the universal progress of world civilization. There was also
a hope of addressing the European public opinion in order to generate pressure to end colonialism. For example, Muhammad Barakatullah, who published
Islamic Fraternity in Tokyo, hoped to convince an imagined European reader
when he wrote the following about the Dutch colonial rule in Java: "We do not
desire to make political capital out of the unfortunate situation and hold the
Dutch nation to the contempt of the civilized world. Our object in giving pub-
licity to this account [of the barbarity of Dutch rulers in Indonesia] is simply to
appeal to the conscience of the Dutch people that they may realize the enormity
of the evil perpetrated by their representatives in the East Indies under the in-
human and barbarous system, or want of system, called government which they
have sanctioned to exist in their possessions in the Indian Archipelago."[72]

Abdurreşid İbrahim's admiration for Japan was sometimes accompanied by almost Darwinist comments about the laziness and political weakness of other Asian societies, including Muslim nations. Occasionally he uses the example of Japan's achievements to condemn the leaders and even the mass culture of the Muslim world for not resisting European colonialism. Yet İbrahim also hoped that once Asian societies reached a level of civilization comparable to Japan's, they could demonstrate the real standards of civilization by a moral approach to international affairs. The new Asian or Eastern standards for a better human civilization implied the possibility of merging the best aspects of both East and West as a privilege of Asians. On the issue of Asian contributions to world civilization, affinity and agreement among Muslims and Japanese were more in formulation than in detail, because what each considered genuine Asian values and Eastern spirituality relied on different cultural traditions. In the most general framework, they could agree on several ambiguously defined and sometimes self-Orientalizing values such as the importance of family, a religious outlook on life, cleanliness, mercy for the weak, respect for elders, ethical behavior in international affairs, tolerance for people from all races and religions, cultural and religious diversity, and spiritualism.

JAPANESE PAN-ASIANISM AFTER THE RUSSO-JAPANESE WAR

The early Asian Monroe Doctrine of Konoe Atsumaro was of a defensive nature, reflecting Japanese concerns about increased imperialist activity on a global scale and interventions in China, without making any grand claim to Japanese leadership in liberating Asia from colonialism. The Japanese victory over Russia in 1905, however, allowed the defensive concerns that motivated Konoe Atsumaro's Asian Monroe Doctrine to evolve into a confident assertion of Japan's regional hegemony and its overarching mission in the world. As Japan came to be seen as the pioneer of Asian awakening and the model illustrating the compatibility of Asian culture with universal modernity, a new vision of Japan's national mission emerged accordingly.[73]

Although the Asian Monroe Doctrine claimed to serve Japanese national interests and appeared at a time when the idea of Japan's mission of leadership in Asia was beginning to penetrate public consciousness, it was still far from being a part of Japan's official foreign policy. Japanese policies toward Asia remained in harmony with the Anglo-Japanese Alliance, in spite of the Japanese elite's support for Asianist ideals or their sense of Asian identity. In some cases, differing visions of the role of Asianism in foreign policy led to disagreements among high-level bureaucrats. One well-known conversation between Itô Hirobumi and Gotô Shinpei illustrates this division within the elite.

In September 1907, the president of the South Manchuria Railway Company, Gotô Shinpei (1857–1929), described his vision of Japan's world policy to Itô Hirobumi, then serving as resident general in Korea. At the beginning of this policy report, Gotô expressed his belief that helping Chinese leaders to create *Tôyôjin no Tôyô* (Asia for Asians) represented the true aim of "Great Asianism" (*Dai Ajia Shugi*) and the best means of establishing a real peace in East Asia (*Tôyô*). On hearing this, Itô interrupted Gotô and asked him to stop and explain what he meant by the term "Great Asianism." He cautioned Gotô against carelessness in expressing such ideas, pointing out that no benefit could come to Japan from the idea of Great Asianism. Itô also warned that such references to Asianism would cause a misunderstanding in the eyes of Westerners, leading them to associate Japanese power and policies with their prejudiced concept of the "yellow peril."[74]

From this conversation, which took place in the context of defining a long-term policy toward Russia, it is clear that some top-level Japanese officials in the period following the Russo-Japanese War supported an Asianist orientation in foreign policy for the national interest of Japan. They shared a belief in the nation's cultural affinity with China and a feeling of pride that Japan alone had achieved a successful civilizational synthesis of East and West. They also perceived world events as constituting a racial conflict. Influential political figures such as Konoe Atsumaro, Inukai Tsuyoshi, Gotô Shinpei, Ôkuma Shigenobu, and Yamagata Aritomo all expressed Asianist ideals during their political careers.[75] In fact, Asian nationalists visiting Japan met with some of these leading Japanese statesmen.[76] On the whole, however, Japanese leaders cautioned that any kind of overt Asianist emphasis would threaten Japan's relationship with the Western powers and might provoke anti-Japanese views.[77] They made a deliberate effort to avoid appearing friendly to Japan's Asian nationalist admirers. Rather, they demonstrated Japan's pro-Western diplomacy by complying in 1909 with a request from the French embassy to expel a group of Vietnamese students who had come to Japan to study the secrets of Japanese progress.[78] Similarly, it is highly instructive that in 1910 Prime Minister Ôkuma Shigenobu wrote a preface to a translation of Lord Cromer's *Modern Egypt* emphasizing that the British colonial experience in Egypt could serve as a model for Japan's management of Korea, at the same time that Egyptian nationalists were looking to Japan for inspiration in their national awakening.[79]

In Japanese intellectual life, however, Japan's Asian identity was firmly established. There were two major political approaches to Asian identity. One group thought that Japan had become a world power despite its Asian legacy and because of its unique Japanese spirit. For them, then, Japan was a successful exception to the general rule of Asia's inherent backwardness.[80] In contrast, another group attributed the roots of Japan's modern achievements to its Asian cultural heritage, interpreting the rise of Japan as the harbinger of a larger Asian awakening.[81] Between these two perspectives, the idea of a dual Japanese mission was gradually born. One was a mission toward the West as the representative of the East for the purpose of harmonizing the best of both civilizations, and the other was aimed at Asia, with the goal of raising that continent's level of civilization. Incorporating these two missions, a popular formulation making reference to the "harmony between East and West" (*Tôzai Bunmei no Chôwa*) became both an explanation for the rise of Japan and its new national mission.[82] Two competing missions embedded in the ideal of the synthesis of East and West gave it two distinct political faces, however. On the one hand, it could be interpreted to mean that only Japan out of all Asian nations could achieve this synthesis, thus endorsing a civilizing mission toward Japan's colonies in Asia. On the other hand, using a similar idea of East-West synthesis in a different fashion, Asianist thinkers began proposing a global alternative to Western civilization, advocating an end to the Western colonial order. As no concrete theorizing had been carried out to explain this duality, the idea of a civilizational synthesis of East and West remained one of the most popular but least clarified slogans of cultural nationalism in Japan.

CONCLUSION

The Russo-Japanese War was a turning point in the history of both modernist ideologies and anti-Western critiques. From the Russo-Japanese War until WWI, the contradictions in the legitimacy structures of the international order, namely, the civilizing mission ideology, became more obvious. Globally, the debates on the concept of racial hierarchies and the ideas of Eastern and Western civilizations became more intensified and politicized. Three aspects of these debates are especially important for the historical trajectory of anti-Western critiques and alternative visions of world order. First, the Russo-Japanese War sealed the existing Eurocentric world order's loss of legitimacy. Anticolonial nationalists and intellectuals successfully utilized the Japanese victory to counter the earlier discourse of white race supremacy and the backwardness of Oriental cultures. Second, pan-Islamic and pan-Asianist visions became part of the realpolitik discourse of world politics. Many nationalist movements all over Asia embraced the anti-Western internationalism of pan-Asian and pan-Islamic thought as a potential form of empowerment in their demands for autonomy and equality in the international system. Third, the Russo-Japanese War and the subsequent series of constitutional revolutions in Asia (Iran in 1906,

Turkey in 1908, and China in 1911) established a consciousness of the era as the "awakening of the East," preceding the era of WWI described as the "decline of the West." Gradually, the meanings of "Asia" and "East" in relation to the West were redefined, in a reverse Orientalist strategy, to match the political realities of the period. The global moment of the Russo-Japanese War became not only a turning point in the history decolonization of Asia, but also the precondition for the interpretation of WWI as the "decline of the West." In the long trajectory from the 1880s to the 1930s, recognizing the moment of 1905 can help us to rethink the subjectivity of the non-Western world in the transformation of imperial world order in the first two decades of the twentieth century.

5

THE IMPACT OF WWI ON PAN-ISLAMIC AND PAN-ASIANIST VISIONS OF WORLD ORDER

WWI PRESENTED CHALLENGES and opportunities for the alternative visions of world order embodied in pan-Islamic and pan-Asian thought. As the arguments and proposals of both pan-Islamic and pan-Asianist thought relied on the illegitimacy of Western hegemony and its civilizing mission ideology, WWI clearly confirmed the moral crisis of the Eurocentric world order. The protracted and destructive Great War thus strengthened the political and intellectual appeal of pan-Asian and pan-Islamic ideas. The civilizational discourses of both trends were confirmed by the perceived decline of the Western civilization and the breakdown of the diplomacy of imperialism.

The wartime political destinies of pan-Islamic and pan-Asianist projects were shaped, however, by the decisions of the Ottoman and the Japanese governments. While the Ottoman government decided to utilize pan-Islamic ideas during WWI, the Japanese government entered into a complex conflictual relationship with pan-Asianist trends. A wartime pan-Asianist campaign in Japan had a significant impact on the race consciousness of Japanese public opinion, even if it failed to reorient Japanese foreign policy. In both the Ottoman and Japanese cases, pan-Islamic and pan-Asian challenges to the legitimacy of the imperial world order contributed to global self-reflection on the new world order in the aftermath of WWI.

PAN-ISLAMISM AND THE OTTOMAN STATE

Since the 1880s, Ottoman political leaders had cautioned that any official indication of pan-Islamic solidarity would lead to further suspicion of the Ottomans in the minds of the European powers and took care not to identify the

Ottoman State with pan-Islamic movements and projects. They insisted that the Ottoman state had to focus on solving its own problems and give priority to its relations with the European powers before it could think of other Muslims. After all, "while dreaming to save India from the British rule, the Ottoman State could lose Western Thrace just fifty miles away from its capital city."[1] This cautious policy of avoiding direct challenges to the Eurocentric imperial world order in the Muslim world and focusing on the security and territorial integrity of the Ottoman state reflects the legacy of Tanzimat diplomacy until the 1910s.

On the eve of WWI, however, and especially after the Ottomans joined the Great War, the liberation of colonized Muslim lands was cited as one of the aims of the war, and the Ottoman government utilized pan-Islamic networks and ideals extensively in its war effort. It was obvious that the Ottoman political elite, known for their realist assessments of world trends and the European balance of power, had abandoned the legacy of Tanzimat diplomacy and adopted a pan-Islamic discourse. This was not because the Ottoman elite came under the influence of utopian ideals of Islamic solidarity but rather because pan-Islamism itself become a realist policy option for them.

The Ottoman entry into WWI and the subsequent mobilization of pan-Islamic ideas and networks have retrospectively been interpreted as the result of the political will of a group of utopians and expansionists led by Enver Paşa.[2] According to this theory, the ideological extremism of a small group of pro-German and pan-Turkist leaders of the Committee of Union and Progress (CUP) Party, who controlled the decision-making mechanism of the Ottoman state, conspired to push Turkey to enter the Great War. They hoped to regain lost Ottoman territories in an alliance beneficial to both Germany and the Ottoman state. Similarly, pan-Turkism and pan-Islamism are seen as additional ideological motivations behind Enver Paşa and his clique's "irrational" decision to enter WWI on the side of Germany. Enver Paşa's death in 1922 in Central Asia during his participation in the Muslim resistance to the Soviet regime contributed to the association of his name with both pan-Turkish and pan-Islamic activism.[3] Since the postwar leaders of both Ottoman Turkey and the Turkish Republic felt the need to detach themselves from the decision to engage in a long and costly war that ended with a disastrous defeat, they tended to put the blame not only on the pro-German conspiracy of a group of top CUP leaders but also on the influence that pan-Islamic and pan-Turkist ideals might have had on the decision-making process.

This official historical view in Turkey long discouraged careful study of the intellectual, emotional, and political bases of the decision to go to war. Several scholarly revisions of this perspective do exist, however.[4] In a thorough examination of the decision-making process, Mustafa Aksakal has demonstrated the larger elite consensus and agency in the making of the Ottoman alliance with Germany. Aksakal not only analyzed what he described as general nationalist feelings of revenge against the West in Ottoman public opinion after the Balkan wars but also the consensus of the Ottoman elite beyond the CUP leadership or Enver Paşa.[5] Yet there is a discrepancy in the new historiography between the accounts of rational calculation leading to the Ottoman decision to forge an alliance with Germany and the outburst of nationalist awakening and "irrational" feelings of revenge against the imperialist powers in the post–Balkan War period. Why did the intellectuals and political leaders who were later identified with secular nationalism endorse a pan-Islamic interpretation of Ottoman international relations?[6] Similarly, what was the relationship between the intellectuals with Islamist inclinations, such as Mehmet Akif Ersoy and Şehbenderzade Ahmed Hilmi, and the anti-Western nationalist mood of the Ottoman public opinion in the post–Balkan War period?[7] It is clear that there was no contradiction between the nationalist awakening and the triumph of a pan-Islamic interpretation of world politics on the eve of WWI. The role of a realist reinterpretation of pan-Islamic geopolitics as a moral critique of the existing system could explain the connections between the Ottoman perceptions of a hostile imperialist alliance against the Muslim world and the reassessment of pan-Islamism as a viable tool of Ottoman international policy.

A series of policy books on the topic of pan-Islamism written by journalists and CUP-connected intellectuals before WWI indicates the increasing appeal of a pan-Islamic alternative to Ottoman foreign policy. During the reign of Abdulhamid II, both the caliph and his Young Turk opposition knew about and partly adopted ideas of pan-Islamic solidarity in their critique of the Eurocentric world order. Both sides, however, rejected any idea of an anti-Western union for two main reasons: First, their critique of European policies did not support an abandonment of the diplomacy of civilization. While Abdulhamid II promoted the image of the Ottoman state as a progressive and civilized Muslim empire that had the right to rule over non-Muslims because of the nature of its enlightened stature, the Young Turks criticized the sultan for avoiding the essence of modern civilization: constitutional rule and participatory government.[8] Neither imagined a radical break with the legacy of the Tanzimat diplomacy, namely, the fulfillment of the standards of civilization, the avoidance of military conflicts, and cooperation with the European powers.

When the Young Turks came to power in 1908, they hoped that European hostility to Islam and the Ottomans would gradually subside as they proved that Islam and constitutional and parliamentary government—or, in essence, Islam and modern civilization—were compatible under their rule. They also hoped that the new constitution would eliminate the secessionist demands of the Christian minorities and European interventions in order to protect the Christian citizens of the empire. In fact, the popularity of the Young Turk movement in the Islamic world showed the Muslim embrace of modernism in addition to the predominant belief that the modernization of Muslim societies would help establish their equality in the world order. The anti-imperialist aura of the Young Turk leaders was not incompatible with the belief that the new constitution and rapid reforms similar to those implemented in Japan would bring about the equal and respectful treatment of the Muslim Ottoman state by the European powers.[9] The Young Turk slogan about making the Ottoman state the "Japan of the Near East" partly reflected a wish for closer relations with England and other Western powers after a series of rapid reforms and economic developments.[10]

There were intellectuals, mostly Islamists during the first years of the Second Constitutional Period from 1908 to 1911, who advocated the strengthening of Islamic solidarity and increased attention to both Muslim and non-Muslim societies in the non-Western world. Prominent among them were Mehmet Akif Ersoy (1873–1936), Abdürreşid İbrahim (1857–1944), Şehbenderzade Ahmed Hilmi (1865–1914), who all opposed Abdulhamid II's regime and supported the 1908 constitutional revolution. They advocated rapid and radical modernization, though at times the social content of their reform projects was rather socially conservative compared to other modernist groups in the Ottoman state.[11] Abdürreşid İbrahim voiced the concerns and nationalistic feelings of Muslims living under Russian rule, urging the Ottoman state to develop policies in this regard, and Şehbenderzade Ahmed Hilmi similarly expressed the pan-Islamic visions of Egyptian and North African Muslims. None of these intellectuals, however, advocated a radical anti-Western foreign policy, and neither did they ask for a pan-Islamic mobilization. They drew attention to the problems of the Muslim world and urged the Ottoman state to take leadership in solving them and help Muslims gain political liberation within a realistic framework that would be in harmony with the Ottoman state's interests and relationship with the West. Mostly gathered around the journals *Sirat-i Müstakim* and other Islamist publications, they became influential in public opinion but did not represent the policies of the Ottoman government between 1908 and 1911.[12] Even though they had influential friends and sympathizers in the CUP leadership, their pan-Islamic ideals (or the pan-Turkic version of pan-Islamism) did not alter Ottoman foreign policy until the crisis of the 1912 Balkan wars.

The general Ottoman perception of their relationship with the European powers changed after the Italian invasion of Libya in 1911. During this crisis, the Ottomans expected international censure of Italy for its illegitimate actions under international law. The alliance system among the European powers and feelings of Christian solidarity in European public opinion prevented any European power's intervention, however, even for the sake of realpolitik, and Italy was allowed to seize a Muslim majority territory from the Ottoman state. Because of Italian naval superiority, the Ottomans could not act directly to aid the resistance in Libya. Instead, the Ottoman government dispatched a group of military officers, which included Enver Paşa and Mustafa Kemal (Atatürk), to organize the nationalist resistance against the Italians. The very fact that the Ottoman officers had to rely on the resistance of the Libyan Arabs demonstrated that—contrary to what occurred during the French invasion of Tunisia in 1882—collective action based on principles of nationalism and Islamic solidarity had already become an effective international force by the early 1910s.[13]

During the period when the Ottoman government was busy organizing resistance against Italy and working on the diplomatic front, the Balkan states that had previously gained independence from Ottoman Turkey—namely, Greece, Serbia, Bulgaria, and Montenegro—made an offensive alliance and attacked the Ottoman state in October 1912. At the end of the bitter fighting, which included the ethnic cleansing of a large Muslim population from the Balkans to the interior of the Ottoman lands and a series of massacres, the Ottoman State had to agree to cede almost all of its European territories to the coalition of the Balkan states.[14] Despite the European powers' proclamations that they would not accept any changes in the status quo as a result of this war, at the end, the expansion of the Christian Balkan states at the expense of Ottoman lands was internationally recognized at the London Peace Conference of 1913.[15] European support for the massacres the Christians committed against the Muslim population in the Balkans and the inability of the European state system and international law to prevent them buttressed the general perception among the Ottomans that there was a new Christian crusade against Muslims and that Ottoman Turkey had to consider new policies.

The figure who best represents the changes in the character and arguments of pan-Islamic thinking and its influence on Ottoman public opinion from 1908 to 1914 was Şehbenderzade Ahmed Hilmi (1865–1914).[16] A Sufi thinker with a keen interest in other mystical traditions and an opponent of Abdulhamid II's regime,[17] Ahmed Hilmi lived in Egypt and Fizan (Southern Libya) as an exile. On returning to Istanbul after the 1908 constitutional revolution, he published a journal titled İttihad-i İslam (Islamic unity). After eighteen issues, the journal was closed down because of Hilmi's opposition to the CUP government, though he was allowed to continue publishing in other journals.

In his writings on Ottoman foreign policy and international relations, Ahmed Hilmi combined the perspectives of the Muslim populations in the periphery, who were mostly under the threat of Western colonial rule, and the interests of the Ottoman state. He argued that a vision of cultural, economic, social, and finally political solidarity among Muslims, at least the ideal of it, was not simply a moral duty but also an opportunity for the Ottomans to gain leverage in the international balance of power. Hilmi knew very well that the idea of a single, united Islamic state was a utopian fantasy. He did not advocate such a one-state global Islamic polity. What he aimed for was cooperation and solidarity to create a viable economic and military power for the Muslim world. A work he wrote just before the Italian invasion of Libya, titled *Yirminci Asırda Alem-i İslam ve Avrupa* (The Muslim World in the Twentieth Century and Europe),[18] was revealing in its realism, as he suggested, parallel to Islamic unity, Ottoman participation in the European alliance system to avoid international isolation.

Even more surprising were Ahmed Hilmi's cautious assessment of the European alliance system and his policy recommendation that an alliance with the camp of the British, French and Russian empires could be possible. Although he found an alliance with the Germany-led Axis coalition more natural and acceptable, he recommended rational and realist analysis to decide what was best for the Ottoman state.[19] Regarding an alliance with the European imperial powers that had colonized Muslims, Ahmed Hilmi noted that, for Muslims under colonial rule, the best strategy would be to work quietly for these societies' modernization and progress until the time was ripe for their liberation. This Muslim cooperation with their colonizers, under the condition of their freedom to pursue economic, social, and cultural development, was also something favorable and preferable to colonizers. The Ottoman caliph could thus offer it in his negotiations to enter the alliance system. In any case, the Ottomans would have to choose one of the two alliance systems in Europe, which would been more beneficial than isolation in view of the aggressive interests of the European powers.

Ahmed Hilmi's work on pan-Islamism in 1911 is particularly interesting in its affirmation of the universality and desirability of European civilization in material, economic, and social progress. Yet he found contemporary European politics to be the worst in human history in terms of immorality and inhumanity. The contrast between Europe's civilizational progress and savage political morality made Europe adopt a scientific theory to explain its immorality in terms of Darwinism and the survival of the fittest.[20] Hilmi predicted that the relativism and moral apathy of materialism would spur a crisis in European civilization and connected the fear of the awakening of Asia and Africa in the speeches of European leaders, who increasingly talked about yellow and black perils, to their recognition of Europe's moral decline.

Italy's invasion of Libya and the subsequent Balkan wars helped in making the ideas of Ahmed Hilmi more a part of mainstream thought. On the one hand, Hilmi could appeal to the nationalist sentiments of Turkish Muslims. He wrote one of his most influential works, *Türk Ruhu Nasıl Yapılıyor?* (How is the Turkish spirit formed?), in 1913.[21] In it, he urged the Muslim "Turks" left in Anatolia after the European territories of the Ottoman state were lost not to give up and to revive their national consciousness to recover the dignity and power of the Ottoman state. These statements did not mean that Ahmed Hilmi had become an ethnic nationalist. For his generation, the nationalism of the Turkish-speaking Muslims of the Ottoman state and a pan-Islamic foreign policy were not contradictory. While advocating a mobilization of the Anatolian Muslims, with further nationalist socialization, he envisioned that solidarity with Muslims living outside Ottoman Turkey would be a way for the Ottomans to escape their isolation and encirclement by the Christian great powers. Ottoman intellectuals who did not belong to the Islamist camp also began to consider pan-Islamism a rational and realistic option for Ottoman international policy. Ironically, it was Celal Nuri (İleri) (1882–1936), one of the Ottoman intellectuals whom Şehbenderzade Ahmed Hilmi once severely criticized as being materialist,[22] who offered the most sophisticated and influential formulation of pan-Islamism as a realist assessment of world politics in the post–Balkan War period.

THE REALIST PAN-ISLAMISM OF CELAL NURI AND İSMAIL NACI PELISTER

In his book titled *İttihad-i İslam* (Islamic unity), Celal Nuri formulated the most elaborate combination of a moral critique of the Eurocentric world order and realpolitik suggestions for pan-Islamism as a useful policy to overcome the international isolation of the Ottoman state.[23] Celal Nuri was not an Islamist in terms of his vision of domestic policy; rather, he was sided with secular Westernists on many domestic reform policy issues. He had a vision of pan-Islamic solidarity under Ottoman leadership, however, and in fact saw non-Western solidarity extending from Japan and China to the Ottoman lands as the only possible means to overcome the colonial hegemony of the West and the isolation of the Ottoman state in international affairs. Nuri's book illustrates how the anti-Western mood convinced many Ottoman intellectuals that the Ottoman state could increase its leverage in international affairs by assuming leadership in the Muslim world.

Celal Nuri, the son of a high-level Ottoman bureaucrat, was educated at the Mekteb-i Hukuk (School of Law). He worked first as a lawyer and then became a journalist, writing articles for journals such as *Courrier d'Orient, Le Jeune Turc, Tanin,* and *Hak* on topics ranging from international law and Muslim modernism to Ottoman diplomacy and Islamic solidarity.[24] In an early book on international law, published in 1911, Nuri discussed the works of James Lorimer, Friedrich von de Martens, Henri Bonfils, and Paul Fauchille on the concept of international legality in relation to the actual "double standard" policies of Western powers toward the Ottoman state.[25] After underlining that the European powers did not follow moral norms and the principles of international law consistently in their dealing with Muslim nations and the Ottoman state, Celal Nuri advocated the natural rights of state entities in international system. At the end of the book, Celal Nuri appended his article "Islam and the Necessity of Renewal," thus demonstrating the intimate connections between the Ottoman demands for equality in international law and the long legacy of Muslim modernism, both trying to make the Islamic tradition conform to the standard of civilization and to defend (apologetically) Muslim cultures against the Orientalist judgment of inferiority. Celal Nuri's prolific writings on questions of Islam and modernity and on the reasons for the decline of Islamic civilizations reflected the continuing relevance of the discourse of civilization in issues related to international law.[26]

In 1913 Celal Nuri published his major work on Islamic unity, *İttihad-i İslam*, presented as a discussion of the history, present, and future of the Muslim world. *İttihad-i İslam* starts with an extraordinary sense of anxiety about the increasingly insecure international order. Nuri mentions the division of Iran into spheres of influence by England and Russia, Morocco's becoming a French protectorate, the Italian invasion of Libya, the expulsion of the Ottomans from Europe by the Balkan Christian alliance, and the support given to them by the great European powers. To these indications of the Western powers' assault on Muslim societies, he adds the polarized division in Europe completed by the alliance among Britain, Russia, and France, which he feared could lead to a great confrontation between the forces of pan-Germanism and pan-Slavism.[27] Finally, Celal Nuri noted the awakening of the Far East, as evidenced not only by the rise of Japan but also by the establishment of a republican regime in China. All these contemporary events were put in an interpretative framework of the confrontation between an "Awakening East" and the "Imperialist West." For him, the years of 1913–1914 heralded in a new era, a turning point in history, after which the international scene would definitely change and the world would never be the same. The whole world was preparing for a war, and the nature of imperialism was changing as the colonized nations were awakening to ask for their legal rights. Some nations were getting old, like France and England. Western public opinion was in fear of the awakening of some peoples, such as Muslims and Ethiopians (blacks). And, overall, financial and economic considerations were becoming crucially important in shaping the destiny of world history (3–4).

Celal Nuri reinterpreted the new scene in international affairs through the prism of a conflict between the East and the West, believing that the Western powers were provoking the Eastern nations. This interpretation led him to raise the major questions of his book (5): Was the gap between East and West eternal and unbridgeable? Could there be a rapprochement and détente between the two? Moreover, what would be the role of Muslims in this new relationship between the East and the West? What kinds of efforts should Muslims, who constituted one-sixth of humanity, as a nation defined by their religion, exert in order to liberate themselves from the chains of oppression and gain their rightful place in the civilized world? In all of Celal Nuri's major questions, "Muslims" and the "Muslim world" were racial and civilizational categories comparable to the "black race" and the "yellow race," not terms designating a community of believers. His questions show how the debates on the new world order in the global public sphere on the eve of WWI were framed and clarified through a language of Eastern and Western civilizations and how anticolonial and anti-Western critiques gained an advantage by using a discourse of pitting the moral East against the materialist Western civilization for their political causes.

His questions brought Celal Nuri to the issue of pan-Islamism in the sphere of international relations. He felt qualified to write a book on the Muslim world and pan-Islam because he had been involved in ideas of Islamic solidarity since the constitutional revolution in 1908—for about five years—and had communicated with Muslims from Egypt, Tunisia, Algeria, Morocco, the Ottoman lands, India, Russia, and China about this topic (9). Nuri criticized those who immediately associated pan-Islamism with ideas of religious obscurantism and unrealistic utopian political visions (10–11). He wrote that those who thought in such overcautious ways would never understand what *İttihad-i İslam* meant. First of all, the Ottomans already shared the same destiny with the rest of the Muslim world, and thus they had to understand the reality of other Muslim societies, even if they could not help them. Whatever the final decision about policies would be, the Ottomans should know everything about the conditions in the Muslim world in order to decide whether pan-Islamic policies would lead to great dangers or to great benefits for them. Second, Nuri rejected the identification of pan-Islamism with either Abdulhamid II's regime or with the conservative reaction against constitutionalism and modernity. After noting that he himself had joined the struggle for freedom and a constitution, he emphasized that the international problems of the three hundred million Muslims in the world were questions of their progress and liberty and thus should be approached as a political issue, not a religious one.

Third, Celal Nuri insisted that the question of the destiny of the Islamic world could not be separated from the Ottoman efforts to gain full equality in international relations. He observed a change in the trends of the time and developments in Europe that could render the vision of Islamic unity highly relevant for "how the Ottoman government could achieve full equality, both in theory and practice, with the other governments" (479). In this Ottoman search for equality, the Ottoman state should continue and even radicalize the domestic policies of Westernization and modernization, which were essential not only for the well-being of the Ottomans but also for the elimination of the problems that had led to outside interference. For example, the court system should be improved to such high levels that even the enemies of the Ottoman state would not be able to find any defects in it. The idea of Islamic unity becomes necessary to achieve this European modeled progress (480–482). Moreover, Muslim solidarity could help the Ottomans gain the necessary strength to avoid any pretensions of outside protection, as the Ottomans could not trust the promises and actions of the Western great powers.

The secular side of Celal Nuri's pan-Islamic ideas can best be seen in his vision of solidarity with non-Muslim Asian nationalists in China, India, and Japan. He saw a potential alliance between the Japanese and the Chinese deriving from their shared problems with the penetration and hegemony of the West.[28] He noted that, were it not for the rise of Japanese power in East Asia, China would also be divided and colonized to be the second India in Asia.[29] Japanese success in modernizing and self-strengthening had not only stopped the further decline of Asia but had also heralded the age of Asia's, and especially China's, awakening. Nuri thought it unfortunate that Japan and China had conflicts with each other. If only Japan would improve its policy toward China to gain the hearts of the Chinese nationalists, the future of Asian awakening would be much brighter. Instead of fighting with each other, China and Japan should cooperate, in accordance with the "second principle of Darwin," so that they could both survive against the outside threats.[30] Beyond Chinese-Japanese cooperation, Celal Nuri also envisioned a larger solidarity of all Asians (143).[31]

Celal Nuri's ideas on Islamic civilization were similar to salafi modernism in the sense that he condemned the Muslim decline after the medieval ages with reference to an idealized image of a normative original Islam. Thus he did not accept that Islamic civilization was essentially inferior to European civilization. For him, Islamic civilization was capable of attaining a stature equal to Europe's if Muslims would only recover its original merits. Thus Celal Nuri wrote extensively about the decline of Islamic civilization, the deviation of Muslims from the true standards of civilization, their decay, and the urgent need for them to change. For him, Muslims had to renew the process of independent thinking, *ijtihad,* in their own traditions. An Islamic renaissance and revival were still the essential components in Celal Nuri's vision of Muslims taking their rightful role in the international community, and in that sense he was ironically internalizing some of the Orientalist arguments that sustained the European discourse of civilization (see, especially, 166–175). Nevertheless, Nuri also made a distinction between the industrial-technical civilization and the spiritual civilization of Europe to emphasize that, while Muslims were behind in the first arena, they were superior to Europe when it came to spiritual and moral issues.

Celal Nuri presented a highly detailed account of the state of various Muslim nationalities such as the Arabs, Turks, Iranians, and the Indian and South East Asian Muslims. He emphasized the already existing ties that bound and united all Muslims. These were the institution of caliphate, the pilgrimage, transnational Muslim educational institutions and curricula, and also transnational Islamic literature (292–320). These shared ideas and institutions constituted the minimal requirement for Muslim unity. For him, however, the essential unity of the Muslims still derived from their common need to respond to European Orientalism and imperialism at the same time. Thus he wrote extensive chapters on European colonial policies and negative Christian and European images of Muslims in order to outline the potential strategies to oppose them. His discussion of European colonial policies underlined differences in assimilation and discrimination policies. In arguments similar to those of Halil Halid, he suggested that if the British Empire had given the same rights and autonomy it had accorded Australia, Canada, and South Africa to all its colonies, the empire would have been respected by all people under its rule as the champion of real civilization, and it would have itself benefited economically and politically (150). In his critique of the predominant practices of international relations, Nuri made frequent references to "*hukuk-u düvvel*," the rights of nations, and to normative international laws.

Celal Nuri's book discussed issues that were most salient for Ottoman public opinion in the years between the Balkan wars and WWI. This was a work addressed to the Ottoman public to define the intellectual and interpretive basis of grand policy in the situation of a world war. In fact, Nuri stated his expectation of a clash among imperial powers, which, he thought, could allow colonized people to change their destinies if they could seize the opportunity (242). In that sense, his anti-imperialist call for Islamic and Asian unity could only mean an alliance with Germany against the three major imperial powers in the Muslim world when the Ottoman government had to decide to choose a side after the outbreak of such a war.

Celal Nuri's book is telling evidence that Ottoman intellectuals did not accord identical meanings to "pan-Islamism" and "Islamism," as he took the side of Westernists against conservative Islamists on several issues, such as the question of women's rights.[32] Even when Celal Nuri wrote a book on the Prophet Muhammad to show his greatness, in response to the unfair and biased depiction of him in European writings (such as those by Reinhart Dozy, Aloys Sprenger, and Ernest Renan),[33] he tried to underline that he also disagreed with some Muslim writers who perceived the Prophet as superhuman.[34] His defense of Islam against Orientalism did not qualify him as an Islamist in the domain of domestic reform politics.

Finally, it is important to underline his disagreements with Westernists like Abdullah Cevdet, who did not agree with Nuri's anti-Western stance during the Balkan wars, which reached the level of hatred and revenge. In a polemic between Abdullah Cevdet and Celal Nuri, it became clear that Cevdet did not support a radical condemnation and hatred of the imperialist West, as this might lead to a rejection of the Enlightenment West as well. In response, Celal Nuri noted that he made a distinction between the good Enlightenment West and the bad imperialist West, and that his anti-Westernism did not extend to everything about Western culture, much less to modernity.[35]

In short, Celal Nuri's ideas represent the shift in the modernist segment of Ottoman intellectuals toward pan-Islamism as a realpolitik option that would be beneficial to Ottoman international relations. His anti-Westernism was limited to the perceived lack of morality in European policies in world affairs and was accompanied by a radical belief in the modernization of Muslim societies according to the Western model. Similar to the Islamist critiques of the world order as seen in the writings of Ahmed Hilmi, there was still a strong affirmation of the universality of modernity and European-modeled modernization projects.

Another good example of the Ottoman elite's interest in pan-Islamic policies as a way to overcome international isolation in the face of the perceived Christian and Western threat can be seen in the policy papers of İsmail Naci Pelister, a very prolific Young Turk leader who used the pen name Habil Adem. A philosophy doctor, journalist, and well connected CUP member working for the intelligence apparatus of the Ottoman state, İsmail Naci Pelister became the most articulate advocate of a new realist pan-Islamist policy for the Ottoman state after the Balkan wars. He published most of his policy papers under a dual cover, always citing a fake European scholar as the real author and attributing the translation to "Habil Adem." İsmail Naci wrote three important books between the era of the Balkan wars and WWI, all related to the foreign policy of the Ottoman state. The first, *Mağlub Milletler Nasil İntikam Alirlar* (How defeated nations take revenge), called the Ottomans to remember the achievements of the German nation after its conquest by the armies of Napoleon. The Germans recovered fast and took their revenge by defeating the French armies and taking their lost territories back.[36] İsmail Naci (Habil Adem) suggested that the Ottomans should take instruction from the German experience of defeat and empower themselves to regain their lost territories and dignity. His second book, *Londra Konferansindaki Mes'elelerden Anadoluda Türkiya Yaşayacak mi? Yaşamayacak mi?* (One of the matters of the London Conference: Will Turkey survive in Anatolia?), discussed the European policy debates, after the Ottoman defeat in the Balkan wars, about the final status of a small Turkish state in Anatolia.[37] His third, and for my purposes the most important book, was *Muharebeden Sonra: Hilafet Siyaseti ve Türklük Siyaseti* (After the [Balkan] wars: The policy on the caliphate and Turkism).[38] It merits closer scrutiny, to grasp the triumph of pan-Islamic policy notions among the Ottoman government elite. The Arabic translation of the book was published in Istanbul in 1913, probably with the sponsorship of the government, to be used for propaganda purposes among Arabic-speaking Muslims.[39]

Like Celal Nuri, İsmail Naci tried to offer a realistic policy option for the Ottoman Empire by combining the discourse of pan-Islamism with the Ottoman grand policy against the European colonial powers. What he proposed was a complete restructuring of Ottoman foreign policy to adapt to the new reality that the Ottoman state did not have any territory left in Europe, arguing that the previously neglected Muslim populations in Asia would be the basis of Ottoman survival and revival. In many ways, İsmail Naci criticized the Ottoman elite for being too Eurocentric in their focus on the Christian majority provinces of their state and asked them to forget about the European losses and concentrate instead on the heartland of Ottoman Turkey. With this perspective, he condemned the traditional Tanzimat policies of cooperation with the Western powers, blaming them as the roots of the contemporary weakness of the Ottoman Empire.[40] İsmail Naci's condemnation of the legacy of the Tanzimat exemplifies the post–Balkan wars pessimism about the prospects of the Ottoman state's surviving through appeals to international law and the diplomacy of cooperation with Western powers.

İsmail Naci emphasized the sadness that the Ottoman defeats in the Balkan wars had caused in the hearts of Muslims in India, Egypt, Afghanistan, Tunisia, Algeria, Morocco, and Tripoli (Libya). As a solution to the Ottoman crisis of international isolation, he suggested an Islamization and nationalization of Ottoman foreign relations with a focus on Asia. Very observant of the inter-power rivalries in Europe, he predicted that Germany would support a new pan-Islamic policy in the Ottoman state because of its competition with Russia. İsmail Naci expected Britain to respond negatively to the new policy because of its dislike of the connections between the Ottoman caliphate institutions and Indian nationalism. He refused, however, to separate the institution of the caliphate from Turkey's foreign policy, despite the risk of attracting the British Empire's ire. He perceived pan-Islamic internationalism under the leadership of the Ottoman caliphate as not being contradictory to the nationalist awakening of specific Muslim countries such as Egypt and Iran, as such transnational solidarity would strengthen their nationalist struggles against the colonial regimes. İsmail Naci noted that the British had responded to Ottoman-centered Islamic solidarity by positing the idea of an Egyptian-based caliphate and provoking anti-Ottoman sentiments in Syria under the pretext of uniting all Arabs within the British Empire. But he was confident that Arab Muslims would come to see the fallacy of a plan of unity within the British Empire. Even if the Arab peoples gained independence without the protection of the caliphate in Istanbul, as long as this happened outside the protection of the British Empire, it would still be beneficial to Ottoman Turkey. He thus proposed stronger international cooperation between Iran and the Ottoman state, as both could benefit from such solidarity. With regards to India, he noted that the revival of the caliphate would give Muslims in India dignity, glory, and fame and would strengthen their determination and resistance to British colonialism. Finally, İsmail Naci wrote about Afghanistan's importance in the new Ottoman policy, evoking the dream of making that country something like the industrial and neutral Belgium of Asia. He praised Russian Muslims for their achievements in combining faith and modernity and counted their economic and political power as one of the potential benefits to the Ottomans of a pan-Islamic policy.[41]

The appeal of İsmail Naci's modernist and secular interpretation of the caliphate as a means to increase Ottoman international power derived from the problems in the relationship between the Ottoman state and the European powers. The Ottoman relationship with the rest of the Islamic world became secondary and derivative of the primacy of its relationship with the Western powers, not a religious obligation or an internationalist value in itself. After all, it was not Ottoman pan-Islamism that initially caused problems in the Ottoman relationship with Europe but the crisis of Ottoman relations with the European powers that led to an interest in pan-Islamism as a realpolitik alternative. İsmail Naci's depiction of the caliphate as an instrument of the grand policy of the Ottoman state led to its secularization and was perhaps indicative of the path that ended with its abolition during the 1920s.

PAN-ISLAMIC MOBILIZATION DURING WWI

One major issue for the Ottomans in imagining a military confrontation with Britain and France, which were usually seen as the cradle and most developed examples of Western civilization, was the sour feeling of fighting with a society from whom they had learned modernity. In fact, a patriotic and pan-Islamic play depicting discussions among Ottoman military academy students around the time of the Ottoman decision to join the Great War in Europe, titled *Halife Ordusu Mısır ve Kafkas'da* (The caliph's army in Egypt and Caucasia), contains a scene expressing this Ottoman dilemma. In response to the excitement over the hope that the Great War would bring doom to Europe and could mean the salvation of the Ottoman state, a student named Subhi, who had previously studied in Europe, asserts that he is not happy to see the "bankruptcy of a great civilization of Europe" from which the Ottomans learned so much.[42] The dilemma facing Westernized Ottoman intellectuals advocating a war against the cradle of the modernity they emulated could only be overcome by the fact that by 1914 the Ottomans had already made a sharp distinction between the ideal of universal modernity and its European homeland. One intellectual who wrote extensively about overcoming European-centered modernization projects and creating an authentic Islamic modernity was Said Halim Paşa.

Between 1913 and 1917, at the time when a realist vision of pan-Islamic solidarity was becoming dominant in Ottoman public opinion, Said Halim Paşa (1864–1921) was the prime minister of the Ottoman cabinet. A respected Islamist intellectual, Said Halim Paşa expressed criticism about the legacy of the Ottoman emulation of Europe and the notion of Muslim modernity and cultural Westernization among the Ottoman elites.[43] By 1914, however, his ideas about Western civilization and Islamic solidarity were no longer exceptional in Ottoman public opinion.

Said Halim Paşa was born in Cairo in 1863. He was the grandson of Mehmed Ali Paşa (the founder of the modern Egyptian state) and the son of Vezir Halim Paşa, who had been exiled to Istanbul by the Khedive İsmail. He completed his higher education in Switzerland in the field of political science during the mid-1880s and, on his return to Istanbul, held government positions at various offices. Because of his ties with the Young Turks, he had to leave Istanbul under the pressure of Sultan Abdulhamid II and lived in Cairo and Europe. He supported Young Turk activities financially and intellectually during his exile and returned to Istanbul in 1908 after the constitutional revolution. As a member of the inner circle of the Committee of Union and Progress, Said Halim Paşa was appointed to the senate and worked for the Young Turk cabinets in high-level positions, culminating in his appointment as prime minister in 1913. Having also named himself foreign minister in the cabinet he formed after 1913, he was in positions of power when the Ottoman cabinet decided to enter the Great War on the side of Germany. During the war, his influence declined, and he resigned from his post in 1917. He was interrogated after WWI to investigate his responsibility for the war and the Armenian genocide. Exiled to Malta in 1919, Said Halim Paşa was assassinated by an Armenian in Rome on December 6, 1921.

Said Halim Paşa's main ideas on an Islamic alternative to Western modernity were formulated in seven essays originally written in French and later translated into the Ottoman language.[44] He presented his vision of creating authentic Islamic political institutions, which would merge the spirit of modernity with the cultural values of Islam and avoid any superficial imitation of the West. For him, creating an authentic Islamic modernity was a precondition for the decolonization and awakening of the Muslim world. In other words, political independence from Western hegemony in the international sphere had to be accompanied by independence from copying Western civilization in domestic reforms. Yet his rejection of cultural Westernization was not antimodern, as he believed in the necessity of reviving Muslim civilization by modernizing it. He proposed a deeper and better understanding of universal modernity beyond its implementations in Christian European societies. This would liberate the Ottomans from the necessity of imitation and allow them to create their own synthesis between Islam and modernity.

It is important to note that making a distinction between universal modernity and the Christianity of Europe had always been a main characteristic of the Ottoman observation of Europe. Said Halim Paşa, however, felt that the previous generation of the Ottoman elite had failed in this effort, mostly because of their ignorance about the essence of modernity and their own personal interest. He recommended a new effort at cultural de-Westernization, accompanied by a revival of the universal norms of Islam in harmony with the spirit of modernity. Halim's critique of the West and Westernizing reforms was based on a universalist and humanist mission. He believed that a rediscovery of Islamic norms and values and their implementation would help the Muslim world gain a noble and equal role in the community of world civilizations and begin to make a positive contributions to the world.[45]

In terms of the more immediate historical context, Said Halim Paşa wrote against the background of the Great War. He saw the ethnic-racial conflicts as evidence of an inappropriate and in fact dangerous Western notion of nation and considered nationalism to be a dangerous idea not only for Muslims but for the whole world. A perception of the decline of Western civilization was implicit in his arguments. He was for internationalism in general, and he saw Islam as one of the positive internationalizing forces, both in history and in the future.

Despite his ideas about authentic Muslim modernity, there is no indication that Said Halim Paşa implemented any specific policy decisions as prime minister that differentiate him from the other modernists he severely criticized in his books. On the eve of WWI and during the war, his pan-Islamism did not stand out as radically anti-Western compared to the dominant trends among Ottoman intellectuals. There is no indication that Said Halim Paşa took any personal initiative in policies regarding the Islamic world against the opinions of the other members of his government. His ideas about the international order and Muslim internationalism, however, were more in harmony with the post–Balkan War trends in the Ottoman public opinion. Thus, at the top of the Ottoman decision-making process, Said Halim Paşa gave consent to the anti-imperialist and pan-Islamic decisions of Young Turk leaders such as Enver Paşa.

After the Ottoman government entered WWI in early November 1914 and started the mobilization, it initiated propaganda efforts directed at the Muslim populations under colonial rule and utilized the pan-Islamic ideas and networks for its war efforts. With the establishment of Cemiyet-i Hayriye-yi İslamiye (Benevolent Society of Islam) in January 1913, some organizational preparations were already under way to make Istanbul the center of a pan-Islamic network in the aftermath of the Balkan War. The organization was meant to be an organ of cultural interaction and humanitarian cooperation in the Muslim world. The Cemiyet's cadre included Said Halim Paşa, its first secretary general; Abd al-Aziz Shawish (d. 1929); Salih al-Sharif Tunisi (1866–1921); Shakib Arslan (1869–1946); and Sharif Ali Haydar Pasha (the senator representing Mecca; d. 1935).[46] During WWI, all the major personalities of pan-Islamic thought of the preceding two decades ended up cooperating with the efforts of the Ottoman government. Those who were from the Islamist camp and leading figures from the Arab world were especially active in giving Ottoman Turkey's pan-Islamic campaign a high intellectual profile and prestige: Abd al-Aziz Shawish, Muhammad Farid, Halil Halid, Mehmet Akif Ersoy, Shakib Arslan, Salih al-Sharif al-Tunisi, Al-Hadj Abdullah, and Abdurreşid İbrahim[47] were some of the key participants in this campaign.

The wartime Ottoman government mobilized pan-Islamic activists and ideas to foment Muslim disobedience against its Christian-colonizer enemies, while ironically calling for cooperation with its Christian-colonizing allies such as Austria-Hungary. Previous research has already documented various examples of Ottoman and German propaganda.[48] What is important for the purposes of this study are the implications of the propaganda battle between Ottoman Turkey and Germany, on one side, and the British, French, and Russian empires, on the other, for the legitimacy of Western colonial rule and the normative principles of the new world order that would emerge at the end of the conflict.

First of all, Ottoman efforts to gain the support of nominally independent Muslim nations such as Iran, Afghanistan, and Morocco failed as none of these countries was in a position to challenge the hegemony of Britain, France, and Russia. Thus Ottoman propaganda had to appeal to public opinion, to the anonymous Muslim individual and his religious beliefs. In a play titled *Halife Ordusu Mısır ve Kafkas'da* (The caliph's army in Egypt and Caucasia), for example, it was the ordinary sincere Muslims of Egypt or Caucasia who resisted the British and Russian armies and welcomed the armies of the Ottoman caliphate.[49] The play also depicts Muslim soldiers in the British army deserting and joining the Ottoman side. This type of patriotic play was instrumental in convincing the Ottoman public that pan-Islamic notions of solidarity could be beneficial to the Ottomans to compensate their disadvantages in terms of military power and capability.

Second, Ottoman propaganda primarily appealed to the doctrines of the Islamic faith with regard to fraternity with believers, the rejection of non-Muslim oppressive rulers, and obligations to the caliphate. All these propaganda items implied a deviation from the Ottoman tradition of international relations since the Tanzimat period and contradicted the fact that Turkey was the ally of two Christian powers that were also infamous for their treatment of their Muslim subjects. For example, the Ottoman government first commissioned a proclamation of jihad from the chief religious authority of the empire, declaring it on November 11, 1914.[50] This proclamation was not a logical result of earlier pan-Islamic thought. Up to WWI, pan-Islamism was not an ideology of hatred toward the West or a philosophy of wholesale Muslim revolt. It was rather a moral and later practical-political critique of the injustices and double standards of the Eurocentric world order. Its goal was to create a world system in which the Muslim world could gain a respected position of equality with other regions and civilizations and join humanity's progress in economy, social life, and political maturity. In that sense, the Ottoman propaganda pamphlets diverged from the main internationalist outlook of pan-Islamism in emphasizing the religious duties of all Muslims to wage jihad and obey the caliph. In fact, some of the anticolonial Hindu nationalists of India who aimed to collaborate with the Ottoman campaigns against the British Empire during WWI were very disturbed by the faith-based language of Islamic solidarity that characterized the Ottoman propaganda in India.[51] Although the jihad proclamation was distributed in the Muslim world in the Arabic, Persian, Urdu, and Tatar languages, it was soon understood that such a call alone could not lead to any organized rebellion of Muslims under colonial rule unless it was backed up by a victorious Ottoman army.

Nevertheless, Ottoman propaganda was instrumental in further eroding the legitimacy of the colonial powers in the Muslim world by emphasizing religious and national self-determination against foreign rule. In general, Ottoman pan-Islamic ideas succeeded in popularizing a notion of self-determination for the whole Islamic world. The main idea ran parallel with the anti-imperialist demands of nationalists. "Egypt for Egyptians," "Africa for Africans,"[52] and "Asia for Asians" could all be contained within the pan-Islamic emphasis on solidarity and liberation, which meant that the Muslim world should belong to Muslims. This propaganda also helped to radicalize the already existing anti-Western critiques.

The British, French, and Russian empires had to respond to Ottoman pan-Islamic propaganda, not simply by preventing communication and contact between their subjects and Ottoman leaders but also by reacting to the accusations of the oppression of Muslims and maintaining military reserves against a potential Muslim revolt. Thus the empires ruling Muslim populations had to claim that their rule was good for Muslim rights and demands. Moreover, t¹ British government played with the idea of Arab national independence from Ottoman rule and the possibility of an Arab caliphate as an alternative to the Ottoman caliphate. The idea of an Arab caliphate had intellectual origins that are traceable to the early 1880s, and this project could be revived by encouraging its Arab supporters.[53] British agents succeeded in facilitating an Arab rebellion against the Ottoman state under the leadership of Sherif Hussein.

Although the Ottoman center turned to pan-Islamism when its relationship with the Western powers deteriorated and it needed an alternative alliance to strengthen its international position, it did not invent pan-Islamism but rather utilized already existing ideas and emotions. The Ottoman turn to pan-Islamism was partly a result of the failure of Eurocentric international society, which had pushed an important member of the system since the 1840s to formulate a radical alternative. The exclusion of the Ottoman state was also an indication of deep crisis within the existing international system. The Ottoman state's turn to pan-Islamic mobilization proved that the appeal of Eurocentric international society had expired and could never return to its old shape after WWI. In that sense, despite their defeat of Germany and the Ottoman state in WWI both the British and French empires had to accept a renegotiation and redefinition of the world order. The pan-Islamic challenge thus played an important role in the emergence of new normative values and power structures after WWI.

THE TRANSFORMATION OF PAN-ASIANISM DURING WWI: ÔKAWA SHÛMEI, INDIAN NATIONALISTS, AND ASIAPHILE EUROPEAN ROMANTICS

Although the Japanese government entered WWI as an ally of the British Empire, toward the end of the war, British intelligence reports noted a surge in anti-British and pan-Asianist ideas and activities in Japan and elsewhere in East Asia.[54] There emerged a stronger and more articulate formulation of pan-Asianism, insisting on moral critiques of the colonial world order and combining them with realist arguments for Japan's leadership in a desirable state of Asian solidarity.

Japanese pan-Asianism, together with the larger trends in Asia, went through a period of transformation during WWI. Two aspects of this transformation are crucial: the first was the formulation of Japan's international mission to support nationalist movements in Asia and the definition of this support as the most beneficial path for Japanese national interests. Based on this argument, Japanese pan-Asianists, in collaboration with nationalist leaders in Asia, hoped that Japan would end its alliance with Britain to form a race-based alliance in an awakening Asia. The second was the influence of anti-Western ideas coming from romantic critics of Western civilization in Europe and America. This influence strengthened the idealist conception of Asian civilization as an alternative to the "decadent West."

Both these developments are evident in the formative period of the thought of Ôkawa Shûmei, (1886–1957), who was the most prominent and influential Asianist ideologue of imperial Japan in the three decades from WWI to the end of WWII. As the leading theoretician of Japan's mission in the leadership of Asian unity, Ôkawa Shûmei dedicated his life to the cause of Asian revival and Japan's national reconstruction.[55] Among the Asianist intellectuals, Ôkawa formulated the fiercest anti-Western arguments, and he became famous for his "clash of civilizations" thesis, forecasting a military confrontation between the United States and Japan as early as the mid-1920s. It was Ôkawa Shûmei whom occupation authorities singled out at the Tokyo War Crimes Tribunal as the chief civilian ideologue of Japanese expansionism.[56] Furthermore, Ôkawa's prolific writings on Asian nationalism incorporated India and the Muslim world into the Japanese conception of Asia, and he was one of the pioneers of the field of Islamic studies in imperial Japan.[57] In addition to his influential position as the most prolific intellectual of Japanese pan-Asianism, Ôkawa also played an important role as a radical nationalist thinker. As a scholar of Asian studies, he held high-ranking research positions at the Manchurian Railway Company. Given his ability to combine scholarship with activism, Ôkawa's career during WWI provides us with a unique chance to investigate the ideas of pan-Asianism in their political context.[58]

Ôkawa Shûmei was born in 1886 in northern Japan and received a good education typical of the children of the local elite in the late Meiji period. After mastering the Chinese classics and improving his knowledge of European languages, Ôkawa immersed himself in reading Western classics ranging from Plato and Aristotle to Kant and Hegel during his high school education.[59] As was common for well-educated youth in his time, Ôkawa became familiar with the religion of Christianity as early as his middle-school student years and was influenced by Christian universalism, though he did not become a full Christian by accepting baptism. During his youth, Ôkawa also became interested in socialism and anarchism.[60] Soon, however, he began to feel a tension between his nationalism and socialist ideas, criticizing and rejecting the pacifist stance toward the Russo-Japanese War adopted by many leading socialists.

Ôkawa chose to enroll in the Oriental philosophy section of the Faculty of Letters when he entered Tokyo Imperial University in 1907. During his university years, he focused particularly on Indian philosophy and religion, guided by the famous scholar of Buddhism and religious studies Anesaki Masaharu. Ôkawa's involvement in Dôkai, an indigenized Christian church, from 1910 to 1913 is exemplary of the cosmopolitan intellectual inclinations that marked his university years. Dôkai was established by Matsumura Kaiseki (1859–1939) in 1907 in order to offer a Japanese and Confucian interpretation of Christianity.[61] To this end, Ôkawa edited the journal *Michi* (The way), which espoused the integration of Eastern and Western cultures as one of the main missions of Confucianized Christianity. Dôkai's flexible and tolerant approach to different religions and its criticism of the imposition of Western values through Christianity influenced Ôkawa's search for alternative universal values.

The most important turning point in Ôkawa's life came in the year 1913, when he exhibited a dramatic change of purpose in life after reading Sir Henry Cotton's *New India or Indian in Transition,* which he had bought by chance at a secondhand bookstore in Kanda.[62] According to Ôkawa's autobiographical account, reading about the injustices of British colonial rule in India in Sir Henry Cotton's *New India* changed his apolitical interest in Indian religions into a political commitment to the liberation of Asia. The book made him realize "the tragedy of India under British rule," transforming him "from a complete cosmopolitan into an Asianist."[63] Ôkawa often recalled how he was angered and grieved by the contrast between the greatness of the ancient Indian civilization that he had studied and the tragic condition of contemporary India; this anger made him "a warrior who dedicated his life to the revival of Asia."[64] Thus, at the age of twenty-seven, Ôkawa started his long career as an activist and prolific Asianist scholar.

Okakura Tenshin is usually referred to as the pioneer of Japanese pan-Asianism and Japan's intellectual "revolt against the West."[65] In reality, Okakura's books were not widely known in Japan until the 1930s. Published in English, they were addressed to educated Westerners interested in Asian art and to the Indian nationalists with whom Okakura had become familiar during his trip to India in 1902.[66] Until the 1930s, Okakura Tenshin's ideas penetrated Japanese Asianist discourse mainly through Ôkawa Shûmei's appropriation and interpretation of them. Okakura Tenshin greatly influenced Ôkawa, who became familiar with his view of Asia while attending Okakura's lectures at Tokyo University during the 1910 academic year.[67]

Just a few months after he became interested in Asianism, Ôkawa published articles by two Indian nationalists who were in Tokyo, Anagarika Dharmapala and Muhammad Barakatullah, in the journal that he was editing.[68] Both of these articles were about Indian nationalism and patriotism and contained a critique of colonialism and racism. Anagarika Dharmapala was a leading intellectual of the Buddhist revival and the independence movement in Sri Lanka.[69] He went to Japan several times en route to the United States. Dharmapala's article was devoted to a critique of the "white supremacist" ideology, affirming the equality of colored races with the white race. Muhammad Barakatullah was a Muslim

Indian nationalist who arrived to Japan in 1909 in order to assume the professorship of Hindi-Urdu languages at the Tokyo School of Foreign Languages. Remaining in Tokyo until 1913, Barakatullah published an anti-British journal called *Islamic Fraternity*. His article in *Michi* was a short history of the Indian national awakening and included strong condemnations of British colonial policies. It was translated from English into Japanese by Hatano Uhô, a graduate *of* Tôa Dôbun Shoin,[70] who cooperated with Barakatullah in the publication of *Islamic Fraternity*.[71] That fact that Ôkawa could solicit and publish articles by Indian nationalists indicates that he had already become connected with both the Japanese network of Asianists and the circle of Indian nationalists in exile.

In July 1914, about a year after Ôkawa became interested in Asian nationalism, the Great War broke out in Europe, and Japan entered on the side of Great Britain in fulfillment of its commitments to the Anglo-Japanese Alliance. During WWI, Ôkawa Shûmei synthesized the critique of Western civilization he inherited from Okakura Tenshin with the policy vision of an Asian Monroe Doctrine to formulate an anti-Western conception of the Japanese national mission to aid the anticolonial nationalist movements. Two experiences shaped Ôkawa's ideas dramatically during this period. The first was his cooperation with the Indian revolutionaries, and the second was the influence of romantic criticism of Western civilization, especially through his association with the French poet Paul Richard.

ASIA AS A SITE OF NATIONAL LIBERATION

The particular features of Ôkawa's Asianism can best be seen in his political campaign seeking Japanese support for the Indian nationalist movement. In actuality, the idea of supporting Indian nationalism against Great Britain was unrealistic and unthinkable for the Japanese government, given Japan's commitment to the Anglo-Japanese Alliance. To influence government policy and public opinion, Ôkawa Shûmei and the Indian revolutionaries visiting Japan redefined the Asian Monroe Doctrine to insist that a decline in the strength of the Western powers in Asia should make Japan more confident in demanding regional leadership. They also proposed that, given its yellow race identity, Japan would gain more by becoming the "elder brother" and leader of a free Asia than by remaining an isolated member in the club of great powers. Meanwhile, Ôkawa promoted a historical interpretation of WWI as the harbinger of Asian awakening and the decline of Western civilization, suggesting that the revival of Asia would shape the future of humanity and the new international order.

When the Great War started in Europe, the revolutionary Ghadar Party of Indian nationalists, with German financial backing, hoped to create a base in

Japan for the shipment of arms to India and dissemination of anti-British propaganda.[72] They assumed that, because of their shared Asian and colored race identity, the Japanese public would support Indian nationalists. Two Indian nationalists who came to Japan during the war, Rash Behari Bose and Herambalal Gupta, contacted Ôkawa Shûmei through their connection with Muhammad Barakatullah. When Ôkawa, Bose, and Gupta met in Tokyo in 1915, they planned activities aimed at influencing Japanese public opinion. Before Bose and Gupta could do much in Tokyo, however, the British intelligence service became aware of their activities, and soon the British embassy asked the Japanese authorities to arrest or deport the Indian revolutionaries from Japan. This demand forced the Japanese government to act against Japan's Asianist groups supporting Indian nationalists.

When a very prominent leader of the Indian nationalist movement, Lala Lajpat Rai, visited Japan in November 1915, his presence gave Ôkawa and the Indian nationalists a chance to organize larger meetings to attract the participation of prominent Japanese intellectuals and politicians.[73] On November 27, 1915, the Indian Association in Japan held a large function under the pretext of celebrating the coronation of the Taishô Emperor. This event was attended by many Indian and Japanese participants, the latter mostly chosen by Ôkawa Shûmei.[74] In his speech during the reception, Lala Lajpat Rai mentioned his respect for Japan's imperial family and then proceeded to call on Japan to take the leadership role in Asia and work for Asian liberation. Anesaki Masaharu, a scholar of Buddhism and Ôkawa's supervisor at Tokyo University, and Oshikawa Masayoshi, a member of the Japanese parliament, spoke in a tone sympathetic to the cause of Indian nationalists, emphasizing the close historical ties between Japan and India, their common culture, and the need to improve their relationship.[75]

The day after this event, which Indian revolutionaries considered a big success for their cause, Japan's Home Ministry issued orders to deport both Rash Behari Bose and Herambalal Gupta, giving them such short notice that they could only leave on ships going to a British-controlled territory. Knowing that their deportation could mean a possible death sentence for them, the Indian nationalists and their Japanese supporters tried to convince the authorities to extend the deadline so that Gupta and Bose could depart on an America-bound ship. They also attempted to influence public opinion by visiting Japanese newspapers. Finally, after their efforts to change the deportation order had failed, Gupta and Bose asked for the protection of Tôyama Mitsuru, the charismatic leader of Japan's ultranationalist Asianist groups. Tôyama arranged a hiding place where they could evade police arrest. This case illustrates the ambivalent relationship and tensions between Asianist groups and the Japanese government, as the Japanese police could not challenge Tôyama Mitsuru and the whole network of the Kokuryûkai to capture Bose and Gupta. Public interest in this escape story led members of the Japanese parliament from all political parties to criticize the government for treating the Indian nationalists as common criminals and for complying submissively with the requests of the British embassy.[76]

Wartime Japanese interest in India did not end with this escape story. When Rabindranath Tagore, a celebrated Indian poet and the first Asian to be honored with a Nobel Prize in literature, visited Japan in 1915, he sparked a lively debate about Japan's Asian identity with his provocative speeches.[77] Tagore's highly publicized speeches introduced to the Japanese audience the vision of Asian unity that he and Okakura Tenshin shared during their conversations and correspondence until 1912. Ôkawa and Indian nationalists were very pleased with the political implications of Tagore's message. Benefiting from the Japanese public's rising interest in India after Tagore's visit, Ôkawa published his first book on Indian nationalism, *Indo ni Okeru Kokuminteki Undô no Genjyô oyobi sono Yurai* (The current state of the nationalist movement in India and its origins).[78] To prepare the book, Ôkawa primarily relied on Lala Lajpat Rai's writings and on the accounts he heard from Indian revolutionaries in Tokyo.[79] Ôkawa's main argument was the same as that of the Indian nationalists, namely, that the cause of unrest in India was general dissatisfaction with British rule, as opposed to the terror and propaganda efforts of a small group of revolutionaries to which the British side attributed responsibility. Ôkawa also emphasized the double standard and deception in Britain's propaganda claims that it was fighting for democracy and freedom in WWI, given the oppressiveness of British rule in India.[80] Ôkawa concluded his book by reiterating the necessity of Asian unity and of Japanese assistance in the struggle for Indian independence, quoting Tagore's famous pro-Japanese comments in an interview with the *Manchester Guardian* as evidence of the Asian expectation for Japanese leadership:

It does not surprise one to learn that the Japanese think it their country's mission to unite and lead Asia. The European nations, for all their differences, are one in their fundamental ideas and outlook. They are like a single country rather than a continent in their attitude towards the non-European. If, for instance, the Mongolians threatened to take a piece of European territory, all European countries would make common cause to resist them. Japan cannot stand alone. She would be bankrupt in competition with a United Europe, and she cannot expect support in Europe. It is natural that she should seek it in Asia, in association with a free China, Siam and perhaps in the ultimate course of things with a free India. An associated Asia, even though it did not include the Semitic West, would be a powerful combination. Of course that is too long a way ahead, and there are many obstacles, languages and difficulty of communication. But from Siam to

Japan, there are, I believe, kindred stocks and from India to Japan there is much of religion and art and philosophy which is a common possession.[81]

Tagore's Asianist ideas would not get strong endorsement from official circles in Japan, however, in spite of the great interest he commanded as the first Asian poet to receive a Nobel Prize. Many believed that Japan's national interest lay in its alliance with the British Empire, and both the ideal of Asian unity and the hope of raising support for Indian nationalism seemed utopian. Against this predominant perception, Ôkawa Shûmei cooperated with Taraknath Das, another Indian revolutionary who came to Japan during WWI, to disseminate the idea that Japan's national interest actually contradicted British interests in the Far East. As a result, they argued, it was in Japan's best interest to initiate a policy of leadership in Asia rather than continuing the Anglo-Japanese Alliance.[82]

The Indian Revolutionary Committee of America organized by the Ghadar Party sent Taraknath Das to East Asia in September 1916 to engage in propaganda work against Britain and to solicit possible armament shipments from China to India. Das was a talented scholar who later in life taught Indian history at Columbia University and enjoyed a prolific writing career. During his stay in Japan, Das consulted with Rash Behari Bose and Chinese nationalist leader Sun Yat-sen and conducted interviews with Inukai Tsuyoshi and Ôkuma Shigenobu, two influential figures in Japanese politics. He also established a pan-Asiatic association with Ôkawa Shûmei.[83] Das first published a book in Shanghai called *Is Japan a Menace to Asia?* in which he argued that the interests of Britain and France conflicted with Japanese interests in the region. He claimed that both of these white great powers were provoking anti-Japanese sentiments in the Far East in an effort to limit Japanese influence. Das urged Japan to act against British interests in the region by allying itself with Asian nationalist movements. According to his argument, the Western powers had imposed an international isolation on Japan, and Asian solidarity was the only way to overcome this. Das also proposed that the Chinese should cooperate with Japan for the benefit of both nations. The book was discussed extensively at the time and received much attention in Japanese Asianist circles. A Japanese-language summary was published by the leading nationalist journal, *Nippon Oyobi Nipponjin*.[84] A pro-British daily, the *Far Eastern Review*, denounced Taraknath Das, together with Sun Yat-sen, as promoters of Japanese colonial rule in Asia in the name of pan-Asianism and the Asian Monroe Doctrine. British authorities banned the book and tried to prohibit its distribution in friendly countries.[85]

During 1917 Das gave several lectures in Japan and, with the help of Ôkawa Shûmei, published another book to affirm the main arguments of pan-Asianists against the Anglo-Japanese Alliance. The book, entitled *The Isolation of Japan in World Politics*, focused on an inevitable conflict of interest between the yellow race and the white race in Asia, thus arguing that a long-term alliance between Japan and England was impossible.[86] It added that since Japan would never be treated equally by the Western powers, it should try to initiate a different regional order in Asia to break its international isolation. The opposition leader in the Japanese parliament, Oshikawa Masayoshi, wrote an introduction to Das's book, criticizing the pro-British policies of the Terauchi Masatake cabinet. Influential political figures in Japan such as Gotô Shinpei and Ôkuma Shigenobu praised the book. Restrictions on the distribution of the Japanese version, enforced by the police at the request of the British embassy, had the reverse effect of serving as an advertisement.[87]

Meanwhile, among Indian nationalists, there was anxiety that if there were a revolt in India against British rule, Japan would aid England to suppress Indian demands for national liberation. As a matter of fact, in the mutiny of Indian soldiers in Singapore in 1915, Japanese residents helped the British authorities, evoking the Anglo-Japanese friendship to justify their actions.[88] To prevent Japanese support for Britain in the event of a future Indian nationalist revolt, Ôkawa Shûmei focused on the dissemination of information on Indian nationalism. He published a book written by William Pearson, *For India,* as part of the publication series of the Asiatic Association of Japan.[89] Pearson was an enthusiastic British supporter of Tagore's education projects and traveled to Japan as Tagore's secretary in 1916. Advocating that the "home rule of Asia" and the Asian Monroe Doctrine should be the supreme aims of Japan, Pearson offered several arguments explaining why Japan should support Indian nationalism rather than British colonialism:

> India is bound to Japan by ties closer than those of political alliance, and for Japan to help in crushing a revolution in India would be for her to fight against a part of that great Unity of which she is a member, and not only so but also against the possibility of ever becoming the recognized head of Asia. . . . The whole of Asia would regard her as a renegade instead of as their natural leader. . . . For Japan will be fully respected by the Great Powers of the world only when Asia becomes free and is also respected by those same powers. Materially also the safety of Japan will be assured only when all the forces of Asia are organized behind her and thus constitute a unity capable of resisting all the aggressive covetousness of the world.[90]

As he cooperated with Indian nationalists during WWI and campaigned against the Anglo-Japanese Alliance, Ôkawa began to formulate his peculiar form of pan-Asianism. The first article Ôkawa wrote after the start of the Great War was about an alliance of the yellow race, with Japan as its leader, against the white race, which included both Germany and Britain on the same side.[91] In his second article, Ôkawa clarified how his Asianism was based on a new vision of civilization and history.[92] He first affirmed that the contemporary European hegemony in Asia was not a statement about innate European racial superiority, for its historical reality was limited to the past three hundred years. Ôkawa contended that, throughout history, the colored peoples of Asia had made greater contributions to world civilization than the white peoples of Europe and that they had been politically more powerful as well. He then went on to describe how the Russo-Japanese War of 1905 and WWI had acted to change the balance of power between the West and the non-West, shattering the myth of the racial superiority of whites. Proudly emphasized was the fact that in the wake of Japan's victory in 1905, the colored races all over the world—whether black or yellow—were showing signs of awakening and rebelling against white domination, signaling the end of European hegemony in Asia. Moreover, the ongoing "barbaric" war in Europe was cited as exposing the fallacy of the European claim to represent a superior civilization. Rejecting the self-representation of the allied powers as defenders of civilization and freedom against German savagery, Ôkawa castigated Britain, France, and Germany alike as "scientific barbarians," as evidenced by their policies in Asia. He called for a positive Japanese mission in the revival and liberation of Asia. But he also felt the need to give assurances that Japan was not going to be another great power with imperial interests:

> According to our conviction, heaven has assigned to the empire the mandate of becoming the leader of the new world. We are not arguing for Japanese conquest of the world as some imagine it. Nor are we arguing for Asian unification. To act in these ways would be just a repetition of the mistakes of the Western nations. Our duty is to rescue those peoples that are being oppressed by Western nations. It is definitely not to replace the Western nations in oppressing them. Rather, our desire is to help all people gain freedom, which is one of the most valuable rights given to mankind, thus to free them from external, unjust oppression, and to cultivate their original cultures.

(111–112)

Ôkawa was not alone in expressing such anti-Western ideas combined with the notion of the Japanese mission. Tokutomi Soho, who converted to a form of nationalist Asianism from Westernism around the 1900s,[93] also advocated an Asian Monroe Doctrine as a long-term policy of leadership in Asia that would make Japan the tutor of its Asian "brother" states, with hopes of restoring the equilibrium between the white and yellow races. While defining an idealistic mission for Japan as the only non-Western great power, Tokutomi refrained from denying the realistic policy of the government elite. His Asian Monroe Doctrine promised the aggrandizement of Japanese influence and interest without alluding to any risk of discord with the Western powers. He wrote:

> The mighty object of the Restoration was to place Japan on a par with the great powers. In other words, it consisted of safeguarding the independence of this country. The question of today is not the independence of the Japanese Empire but her expansion. This leads to the birth of the Eastern autonomy theory. Now that the national rights of this country are recovered, it is incumbent on the Yamato race to try to recover for the weaker nations of the East their rights, which have been trampled underfoot by other powers. If once Japan attains these objectives, we must refrain from abusing our influence to bring pressure to bear on the whites, but we must exert ourselves to break down the racial and religious prejudices to which the whites are wedded and show the world that the civilizations of the East and the West are reconcilable, that the white and the yellow races are by no means natural enemies to each other, and that if they join hands on an equal plane, the ideal of universal brotherhood is not necessarily impossible to realize.[94]

The Asian Monroe Doctrine of Tokutomi Sohô, though supported by some Chinese and Indian nationalists, thus effectively became a political vision to make Japan a great power on an international scale, defining its own exclusive sphere of influence in East Asia. Different from Ôkawa Shûmei, however, Tokutomi Sohô had a realistic view of Japanese diplomacy and refrained from advocating full independence for Asian nations. Sohô also never opposed the Westernization of Asia.

Kodera Kenkichi (1878–1949) was another Japanese intellectual advocating a realist pan-Asianism. He presented the most scholarly formulation of the arguments for racial solidarity in his *Dai Ajia Shugi Ron* (On great Asianism), a book he wrote after his study in America, utilizing all the major works on international politics in European languages. Kodera wrote:

> Is it not strange that in the Europe that has come to control or overwhelm Asia, the talk of the yellow peril is loudly heard, whereas from among the colored peoples who have been conquered or intimidated by the white nations, little has been spoken out loud about the white peril? This, when the yellow peril is no more than an illusion while the white peril is real. . . . Some people denounce Greater Asianism as being based on a narrow, racist frame of mind. But racial prejudices are what the white nations have taught us. This trait is more especially

pronounced among them. The fact of discrimination in the New World is substantial evidence. To speak out against the white peril and to advocate Greater Asianism cannot touch the malicious propagation by Europeans and Americans of the white peril and their calls for a white alliance. While the former is defensive, passive, and pacifist, the latter is offensive, aggressive, and imperialistic.[95]

In summary, Ôkawa Shûmei's campaign for Japanese support for Indian nationalism emphasized the long-term benefits of breaking the Anglo-Japanese Alliance to prepare the basis of Japanese leadership in Asia. This argument relied on the perception of Japan's international isolation stemming from its status as the only nonwhite great power. Ôkawa's redefinition of the Asian Monroe Doctrine, extending its scope from East Asia to India, cannot, however, explain the origins of his call for the de-Westernization of Asia and the revival of national cultures as an alternative to the Western civilization. Ôkawa's anti-Western ideas were shaped by the influence of romantic and pessimist criticism of Western civilization coming from Europeans themselves.

ASIA AS THE HOPE OF HUMANITY

During his first visit to Japan in 1916, Rabindranath Tagore was disappointed to find that most Japanese intellectuals did not share the Asian identity he observed and admired in Okakura Tenshin's writings. Rather, Tagore found Japanese intellectuals too nationalistic to share the humanist vision of Asian unity he and Okakura envisaged. It was Ôkawa Shûmei who appropriated Tagore and Okakura's cosmopolitan civilizational critiques of the West and incorporated their ideas into his pan-Asianist purview and his nationalist vision of Japan's international mission. Ôkawa's intellectual ties with Paul Richard, a European poet, offer an exemplary glimpse of the contribution that antimodernist thinking in Europe made to both Asianism and cultural nationalism in Japan.

Born in 1874 into the family of a pastor in southern France, Paul Richard studied philosophy and theology.[96] As a young thinker, he criticized the stagnation and decline of Western civilization from a spiritual point of view, condemning the extreme materialism he saw and advocating a new spiritual culture that relied on the intellectual legacies of Asia. He and his wife, Mirra, went to India and became the most important followers of Aurobindo Ghose, founding the philosophical journal *Arya* with the goal of harmonizing a variety of religious traditions to reach a more universal wisdom. Paul and Mirra Richard went to Japan in May 1916, staying for about four years. Paul Richard urged his Japanese friends to revive their Asian heritage for the benefit of all humanity, including

Europe. He gained great respect as a thinker among Japanese Asianists such as Tôyama Mitsuru, Uchida Ryôhei, and Miyazaki Tôten. Ôkawa, who translated all Richard's major books into Japanese, was his closest Japanese associate.[97]

Paul Richard became the European figure most beloved by Japanese nationalists because of his book *Nipponkoku ni Tsugu* (To the Japanese nation), translated into Japanese by Ôkawa Shûmei and published in January 1917.[98] In this work, Richard praised Japan as the best candidate to become the "just nation and the nation of the future," which would fight not for conquest, like European nations, but for the liberation of oppressed peoples. He stressed that, as the sole developed Asian nation, Japan could combine modern science with ancient wisdom and European thought with Asian philosophy, thus uniting a divided humanity. Paul Richard's vision of a new Japan as the leader of Asia was well received by Japanese Asianists. For example, Ôkawa Shûmei's belief in Japan's national mission was strengthened by his conversations with Europeans like Paul Richard, who were also expecting Japanese leadership to foster the establishment of a better Asia and a better world.

Richard's praise was for a hypothetical Japan of the future, however, and it did not relate to the Japan that actually existed. For example, on the issues of the return of the Tsingtao to China and Japan's rule in Korea, he was highly critical of Japan, even asking for Japan's withdrawal from Korea. Richard was aware of his differences with Japanese Asianists on the issues of Korea and China, but instead of condemning their nationalism, he hoped to convince them to see his point of view. When Richard accepted the position of general adviser to the English magazine *Asian Review,* published by Kokuryûkai, he justified his collaboration with Japanese Asianists by voicing his search for a new humanism to rescue Western civilization from its crisis:

> The Hero, the Leader of the East, Japan wishes to be. I agree with her in this grand aim. But, in return, she must also agree with me that the only way to fulfilling this aim is to be the first to find and follow the heroic path leading the nations of the East to a new civilization, a new wisdom. . . . We will work for this magazine because it will work for Japan. We are working for Japan in order to make her work for Humanity. We are working for Asia—for a free and united Asia—to prepare in her and through her the world for the great Dawn, the Dawn of Man.[99]

Paul Richard's main ideas were based on his condemnation of contemporary European nationalism and colonialism. He emphasized Europe's betrayal of the universal ideals of equality and justice during the race for colonialism. In order to "save Europe," and in fact all of humanity, from the "corruption of contemporary European civilization," Richard advocated a restoration of Asian wisdom and philosophy:

The days will come when all the peoples shall be free. . . . For this war [WWI], while judging the peoples, settling old accounts, and preparing new destinies, offers the captives, if they are worthy of it, an occasion for breaking their chains. . . . Russia has started, India will follow. . . . Colonization is indeed the mortal sin of Europe, who say "Equity" and commit iniquity; who say "Liberation," and keep in subjection entire races; —"Democracy" and submit multitudes to the autocracy of force, —"Rights of nationalities" and deny to the three hundred million people who inhabit India the right to be a nation. . . . Peace will come from Asia, when Asia will be free. It is not then solely for the uplift of Asia and in the interests of the world to come, but in the interests of Europe herself. . . . The hour has come for her [Europe] to die to the old life that she may be born again anew. But for [sic] this rebirth of Europe has for its condition the restoration, the restitution of Asia.[100]

In spite of Paul Richard's critique of Japanese policies in Korea and China, his search for an alternative humanity in Asia had the general effect of feeding the fires of nationalism and traditionalism in Japan. His insistent criticism of contemporary Western civilization invariably ended up reaffirming the very traditional and nationalist convictions of Ôkawa Shûmei and other Asianists. Richard referred to the Japanese emperor metaphorically as descending from an immortal lineage and invited the Japanese people to work for the unity of the world under the rule of heaven. Similarly, he criticized modern democracy by making references to the problems associated with democracy in Europe; he then concluded that the emperor system, if it worked ideally, could in fact be better than democracy, given its capacity to complement individual rights and freedoms with group solidarity and goals.[101] In this way, not only Ôkawa Shûmei but even leaders of the ultranationalist Kokuryûkai found encouragement in Richard's writings. For example, Kuzuu Yoshihisa wrote the following comment on Paul Richard's message to Japan after Richard left for India in March 1920:

It is Dr. Richard's conviction that too much hypocrisy and too little justice are the figuring factors in the present civilization. He unhesitatingly asserts that because of certain unique and special make-for-civilization qualities in our nationals that we Japanese are the chosen people, whose work for the world is to effect the spiritual union of Asia, and he exhorts us to glorify our time honored nationality. We Japanese are going to do our best to live up to his expectations and join with him in his mission of purging civilization of its hypocrisies and injustices.[102]

His interactions with both Indian nationalists and Asiaphile European romantics contributed to Ôkawa's formulation of a highly confident strand of anti-Westernism in pan-Asianist thought. In addition, his collaboration with the Indian nationalists strengthened his radical vision of a new order in Asia based on complete decolonization, at least from Western colonial rule.

More important, the widespread interpretation of WWI as the beginning of the decline of European hegemony in the world helped Ôkawa Shûmei successfully to combine an Asian Monroe Doctrine with a discourse calling for an alternative Asian civilization. The anti-Westernism Ôkawa espoused went beyond a rejection of colonialism, extending to a cultural program of de-Westernizing Japan and the rest of Asia in the name of civilizational revival. Ôkawa's call for a civilizational synthesis between East and West was not unique to Japan, for a similar civilizational identity was also becoming dominant in China and other parts of Asia at the end of the Great War.[103] It was his ability to merge a perceived global consensus on the "Rise of Asia" and the "Decline of the West," with the idea of the Japanese national mission and Japan's national interest that would have lasting influence on Japanese pan-Asianism.

Ôkawa Shûmei's employment of a new civilizational discourse about the "awakening East" versus the "decadent West" demonstrates how, during WWI, the idea of an East-West encounter had already become a tool of anticolonial nationalism and pan-Asianism, although the idea of East and West was originally a product of the "civilizing mission" discourse of Western colonialism.

CONCLUSION

Both pan-Islamic and pan-Asian visions of international order were tremendously affected by the upheavals of the Great War, to the point of gaining greater policy influence. Pan-Islamic arguments were partly responsible for convincing the Ottoman elite to enter the Great War on the side of Germany. Italy's invasion of Libya and the loss of the European territories of the Ottoman Empire to a coalition of Christian Balkan states convinced many in the Ottoman state that the old policy of "diplomacy of civilization" and cooperation with the European powers was disadvantageous and that the Ottoman state had to reconsider its international relations. In that context, ideas of pan-Islamism merged with a rising sense of assertive nationalism and turned into a grand vision of an Ottoman state and Turkish nationalism. Pan-Islamic movements and figures cooperated with the Ottoman government in an intense campaign to mobilize the Muslim world against the British, French, and Russian Empires, an experience that accelerated the intellectual appeal of this ideology all over the Muslim world but tied its political destiny to the Ottoman defeat. Meanwhile, the Japanese government's decision to enter the war on the side of the British, French, and Russian empires did not alter the predominantly anti-British and anti-Western activism of pan-Asianist groups. In fact, Japanese pan-Asianists, in cooperation with various Asian nationalists, campaigned for the breakup of the Anglo-Japanese Alliance during WWI.

The Great War ended with the victory of the British Empire and thus frustrated all the political expectations of the pan-Islamic and pan-Asian trends. In terms of the legitimizing ideology of the British Empire, however, the results were contradictory, and in fact the reverse of what they first appeared. The imperial world order of the 1882–1914 period had lost its legitimacy even at the centers of the Western powers, and a new world order had to be negotiated. In the process of delegitimizing the old order, both pan-Islamism and pan-Asianism played roles as important as those of anticolonial nationalism, Wilsonianism, and the Bolshevik Revolution. In the post-WWI moment of global reflection about the ideals and reality of a new world order, pan-Islamic and pan-Asian ideas continued to be relevant.

6

THE TRIUMPH OF NATIONALISM?

The Ebbing of Pan-Islamic and Pan-Asian Visions of World Order During the 1920s

COMPETING VISIONS TO reconstruct the ambivalent post-WWI international system shaped the political and intellectual trajectory of pan-Islamic and pan-Asian thought. The British and French empires had won the war and were thus able to try to implement their imperials designs, some of which were specified in secret treaties such as the Sykes-Picot Agreement.[1] Imperial Russia, a member of the Entente alliance, was transformed by a revolution, however. The new revolutionary government in Russia not only repudiated imperial diplomacy but also proclaimed its support for anticolonial national liberation movements. Moreover, some of the war aims proclaimed by American president Woodrow Wilson, especially the principle of "national self-determination," raised the expectations of nationalist movements all over the world that a new League of Nations could be supportive of their anticolonial demands.[2] In terms of the cultural basis of the world order, the unexpectedly long war shattered the image of Western civilization, an image that was crucial for the "civilizing mission" ideology of the imperial world order.[3]

Both pan-Islamism and pan-Asianism participated in the worldwide reflections on the new world order and its justifications through ideologies of race, civilization, and nation. Despite their effective responses to Wilsonianism and socialism and the empowerment arising from new doubts about Western civilization, however, pan-Islamic and pan-Asian visions of world order seemed to lose their realpolitik appeal by the late 1920s.

THE WILSONIAN MOMENT AND PAN-ISLAMISM

Wilson's reference to the principle of national self-determination as a way to resolve the conflicts in the post-WWI period was welcomed by non-Western nationalists as an abandonment of the "standard of civilization" ideology of imperial diplomacy. Muslim and non-Muslim Asians living under the imperial control of the British and French empires could now claim national self-determination and appeal to the legitimacy of their natural rights. As such, this ideal invalidated the arguments that the inferiority of their faith, civilization, or race would prevent Asian societies from having full political autonomy and equality in the international sphere.[4] In reality, imperial powers would keep the notion of standards of civilization in the newly established mandate system, but national self-determination would soon become the most prominent anticolonial argument.

Despite the defeat of the Ottoman Empire, the Ottoman elite found the new world trends favorable to their interests. They hoped that the twelfth point in Wilson's "Fourteen Points" would allow the Ottoman Muslims to establish secure and recognized state boundaries in areas where they were a majority, even if they had to lose the Arab-majority provinces of the Ottoman state.[5] When the Ottoman government signed the armistice at Mondros on October 30, 1918, Ottoman public opinion carried an air of relief and optimism. The heavy conditions of the armistice were counterbalanced by the belief that the idea of national self-determination as the organizing principle of the new world order could finally allow the acceptance of a new Ottoman state into the international community as an equal member. Leading Ottoman intellectuals urged the Ottoman government to create a favorable peace based on the Wilsonian principles. Many of them believed that, with a fair implementation of the Wilsonian principles by the League of Nations and with the support of a liberal British Empire, the Ottoman leaders could try to negotiate a caliphate ruling over a politically independent Ottoman state in Anatolia that had a Muslim majority, be it Turkish, Arab, or Kurdish Muslims.[6]

This new Ottoman expectation could be seen as an abandonment of the previous realpolitik pan-Islamism, which was identified with the CUP government and the defeat. Before WWI, the Western powers seemed to be a monolithic bloc, and there were no international institutions from which to demand justice based on normative principles true for all races and cultures, especially non-Western ones. By 1914 the imperial policies of the Western powers led the Ottoman elite to see the collective cooperation of Muslims or Asian nations against the Western powers as the most logical strategy for survival and self-strengthening. Given this pre-WWI background, postwar Ottoman Wilsonianism was largely an optimist vision that embraced the promises of a new world order as a way out of the restrictions, limitations, and problems the Ottoman state had faced during the high age of imperialism (1882–1914). Similarly, Muslim nationalist leaders in the Arab world could also make use of the new normative principles in their struggle against the British and French empires.[7]

It is not surprising to see that most articulate advocate of realist pan-Islamism before WWI, Celal Nuri, become a strong advocate of Wilsonianism. Celal Nuri was one of the founders of the Wilsonian Principles Society, established in Istanbul on December 4, 1918. The other founders of the society included the editors of the major newspapers and leading public intellectuals of the time, such as the famous female novelist Halide Edip Adivar (1884–1964), as well as prominent journalists like Ahmet Emin (Yalman) (1888–1972) and Yunus Nadi (Abalioğlu) (1880–1945). The society sent a telegram to Woodrow Wilson, asking him to mediate between the Ottoman government and the Entente powers for a just peace. The content of the telegram also included a request for the United States to protect Ottoman Turkey from new assaults and to offer economic assistance to facilitate domestic development and the establishment of a new regime.[8] Some even suggested that the United States should assume a mandate over Ottoman Turkey during the transition to its full independence, with the belief that such a mandate would be preferable to direct administration by the British or French empires.

In his pre-WWI writings on international law, Celal Nuri had emphasized a natural rights theory for equal treatment of each recognized state entity in the international community. Thus the twelfth Wilsonian principle, interpreted as the natural right of each nationality to self-determination, seemed very familiar and acceptable to him. The Wilsonian notion of national self-determination, however, rendered ethnicity, not the state, a legitimate entity in claiming rights and equality from the imagined international community. In that sense, there was already a potential problem with presenting Ottoman Muslims, composed of Turkish, Kurdish, and Arab ethnicities, as a single ethnic nation, rather than a religious community.

The Ottoman Muslim leaders were aware of the alternative claims to the right to national self-determination over the territories of Ottoman Turkey. Armenian nationalists claimed that Eastern Anatolia and many other cities in the Cilicia region belonged to their national homeland even if Armenians had lost their population in the area as a result of wartime massacres and Ottoman policies of forced emigration. Their claim of self-determination to a historic homeland had the support of U.S. public opinion and even Woodrow Wilson. Meanwhile, some Kurdish nationalists claimed national rule in the same territories that the Armenians wanted as a homeland. Ex-Ottoman ambassador to Stockholm, Şerif Paşa, went to the Paris Peace Conference to represent the Kurdish national claims. On March 22, 1919, the Kurdish Progress Society (Kürt Teali

Cemiyeti) was established in Istanbul to advance the claims for Kurdish autonomy. More important, the Greek president Eleftherios Venizelos presented a demand to the Paris Peace Conference on December 30, 1918, claiming that the majority of Western Anatolia was Greek and thus should be given to Greece according to the principle of national self-determination.

The power to interpret what national self-determination meant for Ottoman Turkey belonged to the four European powers at the Paris Peace Conference: Britain, France, Italy, and the United States. Italy had already been promised areas in Anatolia during the secret treaties of WWI, and it took unilateral action by invading portions of Anatolia. Following this Italian invasion, Britain, France, and the United States agreed to give Western Anatolia to Greece as a mandate. The beginning of the Greek invasion of Anatolia on May 15, 1919, mobilized Turkish public opinion.

The Greeks were not the majority in Western Anatolia. The great powers at the Paris Peace Conference, however, authorized the Greek request partly based on the predominant discourse that the Turks were not capable of ruling a multiethnic and multireligious society in a civilized manner and thus the Greeks were better suited to the task. In response to the occupation of Anatolia by Greece and Italy, the Muslim populations of Anatolia and Thrace mobilized in various organizations, all of which appropriated the Wilsonian principles as the main basis of moral legitimacy in their appeal to international public opinion and in political attempts to negotiate a favorable peace treaty. In fact, most of the organizations established by Muslims against the occupation of Anatolia carried the name of Müdafaai Hukuk Cemiyeti, the "Society for the Defense of the Rights" (of the Muslim-Turkish population to national-self-determination), emphasizing legal rights and self-determination. The very idea of the "defense of the rights" assumed an international community and international legality as the constitutive principles of the new world order. Some of the mass demonstrations were followed by a ceremonial telegraph message to Woodrow Wilson, reminding him of the principle he had declared as defining the United States' war aims and the conditions under which his country entered WWI. Muslim leaders asked for the implementation of a plebiscite to determine whose self-determination would decide the future of an area. Meanwhile, Ottoman intellectuals urged the government to send an Ottoman delegation to the Paris Peace Conference.[9] In short, the Muslim-Ottoman vision of a world order and Turkey's place in it remained within the discourse and framework of the Wilsonian principles, and the primary emphasis was not on pan-Islamic solidarity.

When the Ottoman government finally received a belated invitation to the Paris Peace Conference on May 30, 1919, its official memorandum, unsurprisingly, asked for a peace based on the Wilsonian principles.[10] The memorandum still carried traces of the discourse of civilization in the sense that it affirmed the civilized character of the Muslim Ottomans, which necessitated their equal membership in the international community. The main argument, however, revolved around a natural rights theory supported by the norm of national self-determination, which was interpreted as a guarantee for a homeland for the Muslims of the Ottoman Empire. Interestingly, the memorandum refuted the perception that there was any anti-Westernism among the Ottoman Muslims. Indicating the emerging post-WWI revisionism, the memorandum attributed the Ottoman decision to enter into WWI to the conspiracy of a small group of Young Turk leaders. According to this theory, the Ottoman Muslims, who were closely linked to Western civilization, had become victims of the clique in the Union and Progress Party and should hence not be punished. The memorandum accused the same Union and Progress Party leadership of being responsible for the atrocities against the Armenians, while emphasizing that this policy was an imitation of the ethnic cleansing policy perpetuated by the Christian Balkan states against their Muslim populations during the Balkan wars. It also noted that there had been no massacres against the Greek citizens of the Ottoman state during the war (202).

The fourth item of the Ottoman memorandum to the Paris Peace Conference noted that the Ottoman state was now deprived of its means for self-defense but that it trusted the justice of the civilized world and expected the fair implementation of Wilson's moral principles. While requesting that Muslim-majority areas should fall under Ottoman rule, it suggested that, in some mixed-population areas, a population exchange policy be implemented to eliminate future problems and to solve the age-old Eastern question forever. The reference to "Peace in the East" implicitly linked the Paris Peace Conference and the Wilsonian principles as the only way to overcome the diplomacy of frequent European interventions in Ottoman domestic politics with the proclaimed aims of protecting the rights and privileges of its Christian populations. With regard to the Arab provinces of the Ottoman state (Syria, Iraq, Hijaz, and Yemen), the memorandum again called for the implementation of the twelfth point of the Wilsonian principles, national self-determination, but mentioned that, because of Muslim bonds with the institution of the caliphate, these areas could still have political ties with Ottoman Turkey. The memorandum also insisted that Ottoman rule over a sovereign territory would represent the rule of the contemporary civilization of the West. Finally, it asked for the elimination of unequal treaties and capitulations with the demand that all the civilized (international) laws of the West be fully applied to Turkey in international relations. In return, the Ottoman government would promise to shoulder its share of the Ottoman debts of the pre-WWI period and keep the Bosporus open to all. At the end, the Ottoman government reiterated its protest against the occupation of Western Anatolia and its territories on the Mediterranean shore. With these conditions, the Ottoman government expressed the wish that an independent Turkey be part of the League of Nations and stated that, for this, it would always be grateful to the great-civilized powers of the West (205).

In response to this Ottoman memorandum, Entente powers produced a harsh statement on June 28, 1919, reminding the Ottoman government that it had entered the war on the German side without any provocation, and, as a defeated party, it had to accept the conditions imposed by the victors. The response also included a statement regarding the civilizational inferiority of the Turks, indicating that the Muslim Turks had not been very good at ruling other nations and religions. The response also hinted at the Ottoman claim to leadership in the Muslim world against the Western imperial powers during WWI, suggesting that the Turkish-Muslim government in Istanbul should become a good model for other Muslims, which "they were not for many decades." The Turkish delegation was then asked to leave the Paris Peace Conference on June 28 to await decisions about the Ottoman state.[11]

It is in the context of the Ottoman demands at the Paris Peace Conference that post-WWI pan-Islamic visions were revived. The main focus of this campaign was the continuation of a seemingly Christian hostility toward the Muslim world at the Paris Peace Conference. The arguments of this pan-Islamism differed from the pre-WWI form, however, in the sense that it merged with the legitimacy of the Wilsonian principle of national self-determination and focused on the independence of the Muslim-majority areas of the Ottoman state rather than the broader challenge to Western imperialism in the Muslim world during WWI.

A prominent pan-Islamist of the earlier era and a leading Indian nationalist of the time, Shaikh Mushir Hosain Kidwai (1878–1937),[12] wrote two books in English to formulate the new pan-Islamism critical of the Paris Peace Conference.[13] Kidwai's arguments included a synthesis of the pre-WWI idea of a caliphate-centered geopolitical pan-Islamism and the new notions of national self-determination. In *The Future of the Muslim Empire: Turkey,* he argued for the recognition of Ottoman territorial sovereignty over multireligious and multiethnic populations on two grounds. First was the national self-determination principle, as Muslims were the majority. The second was an argument that the Ottoman government, with a caliph at the top, would be more civilized in its treatment of subjects that were not of the same religion and ethnicity than the imperial powers of Britain and France had been. Clearly refuting the British and French depiction of Ottoman rule as Muslim despotism, Kidwai argued that the British Empire refused to give civilized rights to Catholic Ireland and Hindu-Muslim India, hence it had no legitimacy to criticize the Ottoman treatment of Christians, who had representatives in the Ottoman parliament in Istanbul.

Kidwai's second book on the same issue was written within a couple of months of the first but carried a more pessimist and anti-British tone because of the harsh response given to the Ottoman demands at the Paris Peace Conference. Lamenting that the "materialistic Europe respects the sword alone" and "force alone can cure her of her pride," Kidwai resorted to the pre-WWI perception of European policies as deriving from their Christian biases and the mentality of the Crusades. He thus condemned the European statesmen who had gathered in Paris as continuing the old imperial policies, violating the promises of the Wilsonian principles, and laying the foundations for new wars.[14] Kidwai's book became an articulate expression of both the early pan-Islamic embrace of Wilsonianism and pan-Islamic disillusionment with the Paris Peace Conference.[15] Kidwai's and other Indian leaders' campaign for the national self-determination of the Muslims in Ottoman Turkey through letters to British officials reveals, however, a Wilsonian dilemma in the sense that it was the Indian Muslim subjects of the British Empire who were demanding the national self-determination of Ottoman Muslims on behalf of a transnational Muslim solidarity with the caliph at its head. It was also mixed with the politics of Indian resistance against the legitimacy of the British Empire.

Muslim mobilization around the demands of Turkish Muslim leaders led to a more popular India-based pan-Islamic organization. Various Indian Muslim organizations first met in a Khilafat conference in November 1919, during the full-scale expansion of the British-supported Greek armies in Anatolia.[16] The Khilafat movement aimed at pressuring the British government to change its attitude toward Turkey; other goals were the protection of Islam's holy places and financial assistance to the national struggle in Anatolia. It was joined not only by the Sunni Muslims but also by Shi'a Muslims and even Hindu nationalists such as Mahatma Gandhi, who saw in the Khilafat Congress a just cause for India's Muslims.

In the early 1920s, the prominent leaders of the Khilafat movement, chief among them Muhammad Ali and Shaukat Ali, visited London to pressure the British government and garner public opinion support for Ottoman Turkey. Both during their interviews with prominent British politicians and in their speeches and writings aimed at influencing European public opinion, the leaders of the Khilafat movement emphasized a realpolitik argument, in addition to the then commonplace Wilsonianism, to the effect that Britain needed a friendly Turkey and the support of the Muslim world against a potential alliance between Russia and Germany. This realist suggestion for a rapprochement between the British Empire and Ottoman Turkey to create a balance of power with Germany and Bolshevik Russia was especially striking given some of Indian Muslim leaders' sympathies for both Russia and Germany. Similarly,

Muhammad Ali warned that if Muslim majorities were not given self-deter-mination but ruled by Christian minorities, India's Muslims might refuse to fight for the British Empire in future wars.[17]

Even when the pan-Islamic network was mobilized in support of the de-mands of Ottoman Turkey in 1920, both the last Ottoman parliament and the rising nationalist movement in Anatolia clarified Ottoman Muslim demands for national self-determination in a more detailed and realistic document called the National Pact. The Ottoman National Pact of February 17, 1920, envisioned a Muslim nation composed of Turks, Arabs, and Kurds living in Anatolia, thus avoiding the question of national self-determination for the Kurdish people. It also aimed to minimize the number of Christian populations in future Otto-man Turkey through border adjustment and population transfers to eliminate the legacy of the "Eastern question" and thus the potential for further European interventions. After asserting the right to independence for Ottoman Turkey within the parameters of the armistice, the Ottoman National Pact abandoned any claims of sovereignty over the Arab-majority provinces of the Ottoman Empire lost during WWI. While the definition of a more limited boundary for Ottoman Turkey partially meant the abandonment of Turkey's claim to leader-ship in the Muslim world, the pact described Istanbul as the seat of the caliphate and thus implied the continuation of this institution.

Worried about the rise of the nationalist movement in Anatolia embodied in the unanimous support for the National Pact in the Ottoman parliament, the Entente powers, under the leadership of Britain, occupied Istanbul on March 16, 1920. In the context of the occupation of Istanbul by the Entente powers, the notion of pan-Islamic solidarity as a basis of alternative international support for Turkey grew even stronger. The editor of the journal *İzmir'e Doğru* succinctly formulated this new conception: "Now the whole world is convinced that only naked force is regulating international affairs. Turks and Muslims agreed to sur-render because they trusted the principles proclaimed by the honorable repre-sentatives of the great American nation. If that same American nation is now keeping quiet in the face of this horrendous event [the occupation of Istanbul], then the only solution for the Turks is to ask for help from the Muslim world with all its power and capacity."[18]

The Entente powers finalized their conditions for peace at the San Remo Conference (April 18–26, 1920). It was agreed that Ottoman Turkey would not only recognize the political entities of Kurds and Armenians but also accept a Greek-ruled political entity in Western Anatolia. The Entente conditions for peace required the continuation of the Ottoman capitulations to the Western powers, hence protecting the unequal treaty system of the era of imperialism.[19] All these conditions were expressed in the Sèvres Peace Treaty (August 10, 1920) that the Istanbul government finally signed, but the national government in

Ankara never recognized the treaty. The Ankara government initiated not only a military campaign against the Greek forces and other occupying powers in Anatolia but also promoted a public opinion campaign in European capitals to explain the cause of Ottoman Turkey through the language of the Wilsonian principles and the understanding between Eastern and Western civilizations. Parallel to that, the national liberation movement in Turkey utilized both the sympathies of the Bolshevik government in Russia and pan-Islamic sensibilities in the Muslim world to its advantage.

Pan-Islamic ideas and networks had several benefits for the Ankara government: First of all, they could bolster the idea of a Muslim nation composed of Turks, Kurds, Arabs, and other ethnicities. Second, the general support of the Muslim world, especially the Indian Muslims, would strengthen Turkey's position against the British and French empires. It is in this context that one can understand the interest of Mustafa Kemal Paşa in the pan-Islamic movement and its important figures. It was Mustafa Kemal Paşa who asked an Islamist, Mehmet Akif Ersoy, to organize a pan-Islamic conference in Ankara, while inviting a reputed Muslim leader of North Africa, Ahmad al-Sharif al-Sanusi (1873–1933), to join the Independence War in Anatolia. Ahmad al-Sharif al-Sanusi was the third grand master of the Sanusiyya Order in Libya. As a reputed fighter for Muslims against Italian, French, and British colonialism in Africa, he was well received in Istanbul when he arrived in the city in a German submarine in August 1918. He was given the honor of officiating at the ceremonial girding of Caliph Omar's sword for the new Ottoman sultan-caliph Vahdettin. When al-Sanusi was in Bursa, a representative of the Ankara government asked him to support the national movement in Ankara against the religious condemnation of the caliph-sultan. Al-Sanusi decided to support the movement led by Mustafa Kemal and worked for its propaganda in Anatolia until he left Turkey in 1924. When he went to Ankara, Mustafa Kemal received him with a banquet in his honor, praising his importance in the pan-Islamic movement. In early 1921, al-Sanusi presided over a Muslim congress in Sivas (not the same as the Sivas Congress).[20] The text of Ahmad al-Sharif's *khutba* (Friday sermon) in Sivas was published in the influential Islamist journal *Sebilürreşad* on March 31, 1921.[21] Not much more international activity came out of this Islamic congress in Sivas, but it shows that the Ankara government kept its options open with regard to using a transnational Muslim network in its struggle against foreign invasions and a British-French–led new world order.

The Ankara government remained in full contact with the Khilafat movement in India. It is important to emphasize that the national government in Ankara received the bulk of the Khilafat movement's financial and political support, overshadowing the Istanbul government of the caliph the movement tried to save. During this period, the Ankara government itself separated the institution of the caliphate from its critique of the policies of the Istanbul government under the tutelage of foreign military occupation.

While the core of the public opinion campaign of the pan-Islamic Movement in support of the Turkish national movement focused on Britain, there were attempts to influence French and Italian public opinion. The Khilafat committee visited these countries and supported a French-language journal, *Echos de l'Islam,* to express the opinions of Muslims regarding the new world order.[22] Mustafa Kemal asked Ahmed Rıza,[23] a prominent Young Turk leader who had spent long years in Paris as an exile during the Abdulhamid II period, to go to Paris to solicit backing from his international network of contacts and to write in support of the cause of the Turkish national movement. In the immediate aftermath of WWI, Rıza was one of the advocates of Wilsonianism as a normative principle of the new world order, expressing the hope that a well-defined limited American mandate could help to save Ottoman Turkey from the unfriendly intentions of British and French empires.[24] Until the signing of the Lausanne Treaty in 1923, Ahmed Rıza carried out a campaign of lectures, articles, and letters in the French press.[25]

Rıza's arguments in support of the Turkish national movement primarily focused on the idea of national self-determination, the Turkish ambition to have a nation similar to that of the French. Yet he also focused on the anti-Muslim prejudices evident in European public opinion and tried to emphasize that Western biases against Muslims and other Eastern peoples constituted one of the major obstacles to a just world order. His most famous work, *La faillite morale de la politique occidentale en Orient* (The moral bankruptcy of Western policy toward the East), was written in Paris during this period and published in 1922.[26] This book also emphasized that the anti-Western emotions in the Muslim world were largely a product of the moral hypocrisy of Western policies toward the East. In fact, even Mustafa Kemal, in an interview with a French newspaper at the beginning stages of the Turkish war for independence, emphasized that it was the policies of France and Great Britain that had pushed the Ottoman Muslims away and led them to take the enemy side in the Great War.[27]

The Ottoman Muslims' national movement, under the leadership of Mustafa Kemal, benefited from the material and moral support of the pan-Islamic movement in its final success. Once the Turkish national movement in Ankara achieved a series of military and diplomatic victories, expelling the Greek army from Anatolia and signing separate diplomatic treaties with Bolshevik Russia and France, the British Empire had to abandon the Sèvres Treaty and make a new peace with Turkey at Lausanne. The Lausanne Treaty, signed in July 1923, gave the Turkish boundaries international recognition. Though the borders agreed to in Lausanne did not include all the territories declared part of

Turkey in the Turkish National Pact, the compromises that the Entente powers made were significant: National self-determination for Anatolia was to be for the Muslims, not the Greeks. Moreover, the Turkish and Greek governments agreed in Lausanne to a comprehensive population exchange involving most of the Christians in Turkey and the majority of the Muslims living in Greece. Supervised by the League of Nations, this population exchange was welcomed by the Ottoman Muslim elite as a way to solve not only communal tensions but one of the major causes of European political interests in Turkey for about a century, namely, the perceived need to protect "civilized" Christians from the oppressive rule of Muslims.

For the Muslim leaders of Turkey, the Lausanne Treaty represented the triumph of the natural rights theory of the Wilsonian principles, as it finally gave full equality in the international system to a Muslim-majority area without any reference to the discourse of civilization. Yet the confirmation of this national self-determination was partly achieved by the military preparation and victories of the Ankara government rather than implementation of the Wilsonian principles by the League of Nations. The leader of the Turkish national movement, Mustafa Kemal, described this in the following way: "I was certain that we would achieve a positive result. . . . What we demanded from the [Lausanne] Conference was nothing more than the confirmation in a proper manner of what we had already gained. We only claimed our well-known and natural rights. In addition, we had the power to preserve and protect these rights."[28]

The achievements of Turkish Muslims in gaining full international recognition without the stigma of unequal treaties and colonial interventions made the leaders of the Ankara government heroes in the eyes of the Muslim world, which was already energized by the campaign of the pan-Islamic movements. In fact, the Khilafat congress in India bestowed the title "the Sword of Islam" on Mustafa Kemal, the leader of the Ankara government and the famous Muslim poet and pan-Islamic thinker of India, Muhammad Iqbal, was inspired to write poems in praise of Mustafa Kemal and Turkish national movement.[29]

In the aftermath of the Lausanne Treaty, however, Muslim leaders of new Turkish Republic decided to abandon pan-Islamic networks and visions in favor of a negotiated Wilsonian truce with the Eurocentric world order. The abolition of the Ottoman caliphate by the Turkish National Assembly on March 3, 1924, came as a shock to many pan-Islamic supporters of Turkey and shaped the destiny of pan-Islamic thought during the interwar era.[30] A complete analysis of the domestic reasons and legal arguments for the abolition of the institution of the caliphate is beyond the scope of this study. It was partly related to the vision of a secular modern state in the mind of President Mustafa Kemal. It is important to note three aspects of this event from the perspective of the history of pan-Islamic thought and activism.

First of all, the caliphate was abolished at the peak of its popularity and in two stages. In the first, the Turkish national assembly abolished only the sultanate and declared a republic. When the new republic asked the last sultan-caliph, Vahdettin, to leave the country, it named the eldest member of the Ottoman royal family, Abdülmecid Efendi, as caliph only, to serve as the spiritual leader of the Muslim world without any political power in domestic and international politics. Predictably, various Muslim public-opinion leaders opposed the separation of the sultanate from the caliphate. Even so, Muslim organizations from nations as diverse as Albania, China, Russia, and Romania sent letters and telegraphs of support to the new spiritual caliph in Istanbul. For example, in a meeting held during the week of December 21–27, 1922, the Indian Caliphate Congress recognized the new spiritual caliph, Abdülmecid Efendi, in Istanbul. In many ways, the Indian Caliphate Congress was between a rock and a hard place. On the one hand, if it accepted the abolishment of the sultanate and spiritualization of the caliphate institution, it was retreating from one of its main claims against the British authorities: namely, that the caliphate was a universal Muslim institution with both religious and political powers. On the other hand, if it did not accept but rather openly opposed the decision of the Turkish national assembly, it would weaken Turkish national movement. It was at this critical conjuncture that many Muslim leaders, from Palestine and Arabia to India, wrote letters to Mustafa Kemal or the Ankara government, urging them not to separate the political and spiritual powers of the caliphate, with implicit or explicit threats to pick another caliph outside of Turkey if their requests were not taken seriously. The national government in Ankara was, however, aware of the acceptance of the caliph in Istanbul from reports that his name had already been mentioned in Friday prayers all over the Islamic world, with even the ulama at al-Azhar University of Cairo proclaiming their allegiance to the new caliph.[31]

A second important aspect of the process that led to the abolishment of the caliphate was the realpolitik calculation as to whether keeping it would be a burden or an opportunity in terms of both challenging British colonialism and asserting Turkey's transnational power and influence. It should not be forgotten that there were strong voices among the Muslim Turkish elite to keep this institution, from both religious and secular perspectives, in order to gain prestige and influence in the Islamic world and leverage in relations with European powers.[32] Yet negotiations with the British Empire during the framing of the Lausanne Treaty already indicated problems with any transnational claim of the caliphate in an age of rising nationalism. In various clauses of the Lausanne Treaty, the new Turkish national government legally declared that it withdrew all its rights and privileges in Egypt, Sudan, Libya, and other lost territories of the Ottoman Empire. The new international arrangements accepted by Turkey thus gave little legal space for the caliph in Istanbul to intervene in Muslim societies outside Turkey. With the conclusion of the Lausanne agreement and with the confidence of gaining recognition from European powers as a national entity, Turkish leaders began to raise concerns about the international responsibility of the caliphate institution for the new Turkish nation. As Mustafa Kemal later noted, the paradoxical fact was that Egypt and India had much crowded Muslim populations than Turkey had. He commented on how unreasonable it was for the eight million Muslims of Turkey to host an internationally significant caliphate, capable of interfering in the affairs of British colonial domains in India and Egypt to protect the more than eighty million Muslims living there.

A third important aspect of the abolition of the caliphate was the inability of the colonial Muslim world to institute a new elected caliphate. The immediate international response to news of the abolition of the Ottoman caliphate demonstrates the legacy of the 1910s, in the sense that many sides commented on the decision from realpolitik perspectives, measuring who gained and who lost and even conjecturing whether the French Empire would try to institute a new caliphate under its control in North Africa. Muslim leaders from India to Egypt and from Mecca to Berlin protested the decision and immediately searched for an international gathering to establish a new caliphate. The destiny of the alternatives to the abolished Ottoman caliphate demonstrated the problems of pan-Islamic solidarity in the ambivalent era of the interwar years. Just two days after Turkish national assembly's decision, on March 5, Sherif Hussein of Mecca proclaimed his status as the new caliph but did not receive much support in the Islamic world. The Egyptian ulama, on March 10, declared that there needed to be a congress to discuss the issue of the caliphate. The deposed caliph, Abdül-mecid Efendi, also supported this idea of a congress. Meanwhile, Sherif Hussein organized a caliphate congress in Mecca in July 1924, without much success of getting his claim to be approved. Although Sherif Hussein was planning another caliphate congress in Mecca, coinciding with the pilgrimage season of 1925, Mecca came under the control of the Saudis. Meanwhile, Egypt's King Fuad sponsored a different caliphate congress in Cairo in May 1926, ending with a similar failure to forge an agreement. In the same year, the Saudi family organized a Muslim congress in Mecca, but, as Wahhabis, they had even less chance than Sherif Hussein of getting larger Muslim support for the idea of a new caliphate.

In many ways, the leaders of republican Turkey contributed to the broader transition from the era of imperial world order to a new international order based on the legitimacy of nation-states by abolishing the caliphate and ending a high moment of pan-Islamic solidarity. Yet this did not eliminate identity of belonging to an Islamic civilization or future efforts to create transnational Islamic solidarity. As an attempt to secure Muslim liberation for one national state, the Turkish experience did offer a model for other nationalist movements in the Muslim world. Moreover, despite their contributions to the legitimacy of the League of Nations, the Muslim leaders of Ottoman Turkey kept a detached attitude toward the new league, which they saw as an instrument of British and French imperial interests. An editorial in the Turkish newspaper *Vakit* in on December 22, 1922, stated that European intrigues had done much harm to the League of Nations, which had first appeared on the world scene as an organ with considerable powers.[33] After all, Lord Balfour, from his chair at the league, had described the Turkish Muslim nation as a collection of "brigands." Turkish public opinion perceived the league's interest in Turkey as one-sided and very pro-Christian.

The League of Nation's decision on the status of the Mosul provinces became another reason why Turkey did not become a member of the league even after the peace treaty at Lausanne.[34] A three-member League of Nations commission report (September 1925) decided that the Mosul province belonged to Iraq and extended the British mandate over Iraq for twenty-five years. Despite strong protests, Turkey finally signed an agreement with England on June 5, 1925, accepting the cession of Mosul to Iraq. Since Turkey did not join the league, during the 1920s, the League of Nations had only two Muslim members, Iran and Albania. The absence of representatives from the Muslim world made the league relatively irrelevant for the expression of discontents in the Muslim world.

Most of the Ottoman intellectuals who were famous for their anti-Western critiques perceived the new league as a confirmation of the British and French colonial schemes under a different guise. For example, Ahmed Rıza found the league insufficient as a new institutional setting because of its Eurocentric leadership and bias. His solution was a radical internationalism that would try to eliminate religious and cultural prejudices in the global community as a precondition for a just implementation of international law. He wrote: "Real disarmament should be based on moral principles and be preceded by the disarmament of public opinion. The public must be properly informed and convinced by observed and demonstrated facts. Politicians do not usually help the people of goodwill in this regard. They make no attempt to dispel the memories of religious hatred and to weaken racial prejudice, the real sources of antagonism and war."[35]

For Rıza, the main problem of the international order was still the issue of mutual understanding between the East and the West. According to him, "the experience of ten centuries has made it inevitable that the East should mistrust and distrust the West" (210–211). His concrete suggestion was to create an institution of intellectual and cultural exchange, a sort of world cultural-exchange-and-dialogue association, that would complement other institutions' work in creating a fair and just world order. The emphasis on Western "misperceptions" of the East and the Muslims as an impediment to justice in the new international order was also mentioned by Halil Halid, who warned that, given the rising power of the United States, Americans' Christian prejudices toward the Muslim world could constitute a new problem. Thus he urged Turkish Muslims to act preemptively to change American misperceptions about Turks and Muslims.[36]

THE WILSONIAN MOMENT AND PAN-ASIANISM

As post-WWI pan-Islamism relied on the perceived Christian and imperial bias of the Paris Peace Conference as exemplified in its failure to give justice to the Muslims, post-WWI pan-Asianism in Japan perceived "white supremacy" solidarity among Western powers in their rejection of Japan's "racial equality proposal" (*jinshu sabetsu teppai*) at the same conference. Although Japanese pan-Asianists saw the Wilsonian principles as a moral intervention aimed at creating a just and equitable international order,[37] the rejection of Japan's proposal for "racial equality" at the Paris Peace Conference became a test case used by them to formulate an Asianist critique of the League of Nations.[38]

Complex diplomatic and political motivations lay behind the Japanese proposal for racial equality at the Paris Peace Conference.[39] For the purposes of this book, it is important to mention that the Japanese proposal reflected partly the idealism of the Wilsonian moment and partly a sense of Japanese national mission.[40] Japan benefited immensely from its wartime alliance with the British Empire by capturing German colonies in the Pacific, invading the German-leased territories in the Shandong Province of China, and improving its economy.[41] Yet the Japanese public and parts of the elite had perceived that racial discrimination, an integral part of the then-existing international order, could stand as an impediment to the achievement of Japan's full membership in the club of great powers. Meanwhile, Japanese diplomats began to worry about changes in the balance of power in Asia as the United States, which had an anti-Japanese immigration movement, emerged from the Great War as the most powerful nation in the world. In this context, the Japanese delegates in Paris proposed the racial equality clause, hoping to quell the fear of global racial conflict by demonstrating the possibility of cooperation with white Western powers within the new framework of the League of Nations. The incorporation of racial equality as a founding principle of the League of Nation would also provide an international legal framework for resolving the problem of discrimination against Japanese immigrants in the United States.

When the racial equality proposal was rejected, all of Japan's Asianists took this as an opportunity to call for an end to the pro-Western diplomatic framework and to condemn the League of Nations as devoid of moral legitimacy.

While the cause of the failure of the proposal was much more complex, Japanese public opinion attributed it to the intransigence of white Western powers bent on continuing their discrimination against the colored races. Thus the rejection of the proposal became a great symbolic event especially from the pan-Asianist point of view, used throughout the 1920s to argue that the League of Nations had not solved the problem of racial discrimination against nonwhite races in international relations.[42]

For example, pan-Asianist thinker Ôkawa Shûmei wrote articles to agitate the Japanese public against Japan's participation in the League of Nations, arguing that the league was simply a neocolonial institution benefiting Anglo-American strategic and economic interests and affirming white supremacy in the world.[43] Subsequent pan-Asianist critiques of the League of Nations focused on the continuing relevance of racial discrimination and civilizational hierarchy. This was best summarized in an editorial in the *Asian Review,* published by Japan's Asianists. The editorial starts with an optimistic view of the league, suggesting that it would be "a real blessing to humanity, in that it will do much to prevent future wars." It goes on, however, to enumerate the reasons to be skeptical of the league's chances at success. The main reason is the defeat of President Wilson by "the forces of reaction," namely, the European diplomats, which managed to smother the hopes and aspirations of Asians in order to perpetuate "white domination" in Asia. Highly interesting in this article is the use of quotations from Norman Angell, the author of *The Great Illusion* (1909) and the recipient of the Nobel Peace Price in 1933, to demonstrate that even "a respected scholar and known pacifist" could still harbor a surprising adherence to white supremacist beliefs. As quoted in the *Asian Review,* Angell said the following in an interview on the eve of the Paris Peace Conference:

> We have been led to give great emphasis to the fact that this is a war for democracy, for equality of right; that is, for all men. That emphasis has not been lost upon the non-European races. The Japanese, the Chinese, some of the populations of India, to say nothing of certain African peoples have been welcomed as Allies. . . . Imagine the possibilities of the development of such a situation if Japanese, Chinese, Indians and other Asiatics were to interpret our ideals of democracy as entitling them to a real equality of treatment. . . . So, we may be within measurable distance of a unified Eastern and a disunited Western world.[44]

Based on this interview, the editorial concluded that, despite his credentials as a humanist, even "Mr. Angell seems to be a staunch advocate of the old policy of whitemenism" (348) because he seemed to be advocating for the League of Nations to unite the Western world against the awakening of the Eastern world, not to create a world based on racial equality and international justice.

Paralleling the Asianist critique of the League of Nations, several young bureaucrats such as Konoe Fumimaro began to voice apprehension that the Western powers, using the league and the process of disarmament as a pretense, were acting to maintain the status quo of the international order and to perpetuate their own global dominance. Konoe's reservations about the league system derived more from the limitations imposed on further imperial expansion and armament by the new international framework than from the rejection of the racial equality proposal.[45] But, in the end, no matter what reservations Japanese diplomats had about the league system, Japan joined the League of Nations as one of the founding members, demonstrating its enthusiasm by staffing the league secretariat with leading liberal internationalists such as Nitobe Inazô and even providing financial backing for the activities of the ostensibly private Japan League of Nations Association. At the same time, Japan pursued its national interest through mutual and multilateral cooperation with Western powers, symbolized by the Washington Conference system.[46] This policy of cooperation with the Western powers in an era of capitalist internationalism was seen to pay off as Japan expanded economically in the Asian continent and the United States became Japan's largest trading partner. It was this system of cooperative diplomacy and capitalist internationalism that Japanese pan-Asianists considered the greatest obstacle to their vision of liberating Asian under Japanese leadership. Throughout the 1920s, Japanese Asianists would remain in opposition, utilizing any indication of racial discrimination in international affairs to intensify their attack on the League of Nations and Japanese liberals.

While Japan's pan-Asianists emphasized the neowhite imperialism of the League of Nations, Wilsonianism revealed the latent imperial logic of Japanese pan-Asianists. Ironically, when the Japanese delegates were advancing a moral agenda for racial equality, the Japanese Empire was challenged by the rising momentum of Korean and Chinese nationalism, both of which complained about the failure of the Paris Peace Conference to pressure the Japanese Empire. Thus Japanese Asianists had to reflect on the contradiction between their arguments for Asian liberation and their nationalist loyalty to the Japanese Empire, especially when Korean nationalists demanded national self-determination and rebelled against Japanese rule. In this context, the majority of Japanese Asianists tried to legitimize Japanese imperial rule over Korea by insisting on its difference from Western colonialism in Asia.

The tensions between Japanese pan-Asianism and Wilsonian nationalism can best be seen in the writings of Ôkawa Shûmei. In 1919 Ôkawa joined the General Meeting to Abolish Racial Discrimination (Jinshuteki Sabetsu Teppai Kisei Taikai), a group organized by the Genyôsha and supported by the major political parties of Japan.[47] It was the largest Asianist pressure group aimed at influencing Japanese diplomatic attitudes during the Paris Peace Conference, and at several meetings participants favored a decision not to enter the league if the Japanese proposal were rejected.[48] The Asianist mobilization over the racial equality proposal revealed, however, a major contradiction in their demand for international morality: while they were advocating Asian liberation and racial equality, they did not endorse the Korean demand for national self-determination. They were also not vocal about Chinese protests over the Japanese imperial policies in their country. Paul Richard, a guest at the second and third conferences of the Society to Abolish Racial Discrimination, in March and April 1919, asked his Japanese audience to be consistent in their moral claims by embracing the idea of the brotherhood of Asians, instead of maneuvering for Japanese superiority in Asia. Richard called for Japan's moral leadership in the construction of a League of Asian Nations rather than a League of Nations; such an organization could then become the first step toward a true League of Nations that would encompass all peoples regardless of the color of their skin. For Paul Richard, however, Japan needed to liberate all its colonies before it could be regarded as a just nation deserving of a position of moral leadership in Asia.[49]

Ôkawa Shûmei, like the majority of pan-Asianists, would not agree on the issue of Korean self-determination, despite his intellectual admiration for Paul Richard. He offered an explanation for his contradictory position on Korean nationalism in the introduction to his later work on Indian nationalism.[50] Ôkawa insisted that Japanese rule in Korea was different from British rule in India, claiming that the motives behind Japan's colonial control were peaceful and noneconomic, that Japan's geographical proximity to Korea gave rise to security concerns it could not ignore, and, most important, that the two nations were connected by close historical, racial, and cultural links.[51] Ôkawa never commented on British rule in Ireland, a situation more comparable to Japanese colonialism in Korea, although he was a prolific writer on issues of European colonialism. Given the closeness of Ôkawa's relationship with Indian nationalists, who followed the history of the Irish nationalist resistance, his silence on the issue of Irish nationalism could well be attributed to his anxieties over Korean nationalism.

Ôkawa Shûmei's refusal to recognize Korean nationalism contradicted not only his enthusiastic advocacy of Indian nationalism but also contrasted with his assessment of the rise of nationalism in post–Great War Asia. Ôkawa saw the tide of Egyptian and Indian demands for independence as unstoppable, irrespective of British policies to improve the economy and political structure. For example, it was his opinion that Lord Cromer's policies in Egypt were helping the Egyptian economy. Yet, no matter how positive a change was brought about by these policies, Ôkawa argued, Egyptian nationalism was still bound to reject British rule. For him, nationalism in Asia after the Great War was more about political and cultural pride than economic and social problems in the colonies.[52] In spite of his acute observations on the nature of rising nationalism and his status as an expert of colonialism, however, Ôkawa was never able to face the reality of the Korean search for national self-determination because of his nationalist belief in the righteousness of the Japanese Empire. There were several pan-Asianists, such as Miyazaki Toten, who sympathized with Korean demands, but overall Japanese pan-Asianists developed a notion of racial harmony within Asia to deny the Wilsonianism-inspired national self-determination claims in Japan's colonies.

PAN-ISLAMIC AND PAN-ASIANIST PERCEPTIONS OF SOCIALIST INTERNATIONALISM

The relationship between pan-Islamic and pan-Asianist visions, and the socialist internationalism of the Bolshevik government went through several stages from 1919 to 1923. Although there were hopes of collaboration between the pan-Islamic and pan-Asian movements of the Asia, on the one hand, and the Bolsheviks, on the other, soon both sides assumed a more cautious approach, trying to use the other but not be used by it.

The activities of the Ottoman leader Enver Paşa after the surrender of the Ottoman state on October 30, 1918, demonstrated the complex relationship between pan-Islamic ideas and the anti-imperialism of the Bolshevik government. Enver Paşa tried to lead a pan-Islamic resistance against the British Empire through a new cooperation with the Bolshevik government in Russia. Having developed contacts during his stay in Berlin around late 1918 and 1919, he arrived in Moscow in 1920, receiving positive responses to his anti-British pan-Islamic cause from the Bolshevik leaders, including Lenin.

The new Bolshevik government in Russia hoped to benefit from the pre-existing anticolonial sentiments of Asian nationalists and undertook to organize the First Congress of the Peoples of the East in Baku in 1920, attempting to appeal to a sense of colonized Eastern identity.[53] While trying to lobby for military and financial aid from the Bolshevik government for the nationalist movement in Anatolia, Enver Paşa formed the Union of Islamic Revolutionary Societies to facilitate the coordination of the pan-Islamic network. In September 1920, Enver Paşa attended the Baku Congress of the Peoples of the East to represent the international Muslim movement he claimed to have established.[54] It is important to observe that during the year of 1920, both socialist internationalism and pan-Islamic internationalism were in harmony with each other in their goal to defeat the British and French imperial interests in the region. Similarly, the two were in agreement on the question of national self-determination, as their vision of world order assumed the coordinated struggles of each national movement against imperialism to establish the sovereignty of each national zone. During Enver Paşa's attempt to form a pan-Islamic network and his cooperation with the Soviets, the main concrete goal was strengthening the national movement in Ankara. Until September 1921, Enver Paşa tried to gather international support for this movement, while looking for the right moment to return to Anatolia. The military victories of the new Ankara government against the Greek forces in early September empowered the leadership of Mustafa Kemal, who did not want Enver Paşa back for personal and realpolitik reasons. Once the Ankara government had concluded peace treaties and direct links with the Bolsheviks in Moscow, Enver Paşa's pan-Islamic vision lost its value for the Bolsheviks.

Meanwhile, the tensions between the Bolshevik plans for Central Asia and the Muslim nationalist demands became sharper when there emerged a strong Muslim resistance against the expansion of Bolshevik rule to Central Asia. Soon, the early confluence between the anti-Western visions of pan-Islamic and socialist internationalism was broken. It is in that context that Enver Paşa decided to lead the Muslim national resistance against the expansion of Bolshevik control in Central Asia.[55] Theoretically, the Second Congress of the Comintern urged the Communists "to fight against Pan-Islamism, Pan-Asiatic and similar movements which try to combine the fight for liberation from European and American imperialism with the strengthening of Turkish and Japanese imperialism and the strengthening of their large landowners, nobility, clergy, etc."[56] Although this recommendation was practically asking communists in Asia not to transform their struggles into movements that could serve pan-Islamism or pan-Asianism, Indonesian Marxists—Tan Malaka (1897–1949), for example—protested that such a policy would practically destroy the social recruitment efforts of communists in a predominantly Muslim country.[57]

Despite its suppression of the demands of the Central Asian Muslim resistance, the Soviet Union continued to support nationalist movements and independent nations in Asia, thus strengthening the decolonization efforts to break free from British and French imperial rule through the legitimacy of national self-determination. For example, it concluded its peace treatise with the Ankara government on March 16, 1921, thus becoming the first country to recognize the new Turkish national government in Ankara. After the Soviet Union reasserted Russian imperial control over Muslim areas in Central Asia, different from the czarist era, this entire region was given a semblance of national autonomy and self-determination first and then tied to the Soviet Union.

The early assessments of the Bolshevik Revolution by Japanese pan-Asianists were also generally positive. The sympathy of leading pan-Asianists such as Ôkawa Shûmei toward the Bolshevik Revolution and the policies of the new socialist government was indicative of the shared challenge of both Asianism and socialism to the Eurocentric world order. Like other anti-Western critics of the period, Ôkawa Shûmei welcomed the news of revolutionary turmoil in Russia in 1917, regarding it as another instance of Asian awakening and a further testament to the liberating impact of the Great War. The Russian Revolution confirmed Ôkawa's expectation that the new world order after the Great War would indeed be different from the previous white domination in Asia. Ôkawa Shûmei's sympathy for the Russian Revolution as a sign of Asian awakening demonstrates his ambivalence about the position of Russia in the East-West confrontation. In the context of the Russo-Japanese War, not only Japanese Asianists but also the world at large had regarded Russia as a Western power expanding in the Far East. In 1917, however, Ôkawa Shûmei considered the Russian Revolution a part of the larger Asian awakening. In addition to viewing the Bolshevik challenge to the European colonial order very positively, he also hoped that the foreign policy of the Bolshevik government would contribute to the decolonization of Asia.[58]

Ôkawa Shûmei praised the policies of the new government in Russia toward Asian nationalist movements, sympathizing with the Bolshevik challenge to the international system. He argued that if a strong state like Russia could support the rising pan-Islamic movement in the Middle East and India, European hegemony in Asia would be brought to an end. Ôkawa saw just such a possibility for an Asian alliance in the friendly policies adopted by the Bolshevik government toward Turkey, Persia and, Afghanistan in 1921.[59]

The Bolshevik Revolution had its most visible impact on Japanese Asianism by triggering the polarization of right-wing and left-wing ideologies around two different versions of internationalism, dividing them to the extent that, by the early 1920s, Asianism had begun to be associated with Japanism and ultranationalism.[60] As explained in chapter 2, Asianism before the Great War was not always the monopoly of right-wing nationalist figures; it was embraced by liberals and socialists as well. The identification of pan-Asianism with the radical nationalist groups in Japan was a phenomenon of post-WWI period.[61] Liberals and socialists were generally inclined toward Wilsonianism and Comintern internationalism after the Great War. Meanwhile, the Japanism and the cultural nationalism of the ultranationalists made them more sympathetic to a vision of international solidarity based on civilizational and racial identity. Japanism and Asianism were allied, moreover, in their critical stance toward the Westernization of Asian cultures.[62]

When Ôkawa Shûmei established Yûzonsha in 1919 as the first radical nationalist organization of Japan,[63] one of the main pillars of the ideology of this organization was the claim to offer a Japanese and Asian alternative to Western universalism, and the organization did have the practical function of countering newly emerging socialist activism in Japan.[64] The founding charter of Yûzonsha specified several pan-Asianist goals for itself, such as "working for the national liberation movements in Asia," although the primary commitment of the organization focused on the radical structuring of Japan domestically. As Ôkawa envisioned a special role for Japan in the Asian revival, he did not find contemporary Japan ready to assume the real leadership of Asia.[65] In fact, he made Asian revival not only a mission for Japan but also the purpose of radical reconstruction within Japan by combining his ideal image of the Meiji Restoration with a vision of Asian solidarity:

> We should make efforts for the revival of Asia. This is my prayer all day and night. But what causes deep sorrow is that today's Japan still has not reached the level of Mahayana Japan. There are too many devils around. If Japan continues to be like this, it cannot take on the great responsibility of saving Asia at all. Similarly, Asian countries can never trust and rely on Japan. . . . The sword in our hand is a double-edged sword: while this sword has to be very sharp against the injustices in Asia, at the same time, it has to be very strong against the wickedness that is building its nest in Japan. Thus a fighter for Asian Revival, without any hesitation, must be a fighter for the reform of Japan, too.[66]

Despite the general pairing of Japanese socialist with socialist internationalism and radical nationalists with pan-Asian internationalism, one should not assume that early Asianist views of the Bolshevik Revolution was negative. On the contrary, sharper pan-Asianist critiques of socialist internationalism formed gradually, in reaction to Soviet foreign policies.[67] Only when the Soviet military presence increased in northern Manchuria and Siberia in the late 1920s did pan-Asianists like Ôkawa Shûmei began to perceive the Soviet Union as a potential threat to Japanese interests (the idea of this Soviet threat became important in Asianist suggestions for Japan's policy in Manchuria). More than from a strategic viewpoint, however, Asianist critique of socialist internationalism came mainly from the perspective of the clash of Eastern and Western civilizations. For example, Ôkawa Shûmei criticized the socialist assumption that a class-based revolution would eliminate conflicts among nations and create a just international order. Referring to Bertrand Russell's *The Roads to Freedom*, he argued that struggles among nations and civilizations would continue to occur even if socialist revolutions did take place in Europe.[68] According to Ôkawa, not only struggles among nations but also the greater struggle between the colonized East and colonizing West were destined to continue so long as Europe failed to return "stolen Asia" to its rightful owner.[69] Moreover, Ôkawa saw cultural Westernization as the most significant event in modern world history, establishing the basis of white hegemony in Asia. He regarded it as just as important to reject Western cultural domination in Asia as to resist economic exploitation and political hegemony. As he saw the revival of native cultural traditions and the reversal of Westernization as essential preconditions for the success of nationalist movements, for him, socialism, as a Western ideology, by its very nature could never transform the state of Western cultural supremacy in Asia.

In short, the relationship of pan-Asianist and pan-Islamic visions of world order with socialist internationalism moved from a stage of friendly cooperation to hostile competition. Despite their support for anticolonial national movements, Bolsheviks could not accept the idea of an alternative Eastern civilization entrenched within pan-Islamic and pan-Asian discourses, and gradually socialists distanced themselves from these movements, for fear that, instead of using them, they could become instruments of these two rival internationalisms. Similarly, after their initial sympathy toward the Bolshevik challenge to the Eurocentric imperial world order, both pan-Islamism and pan-Asianism underlined the importance of national and civilizational identities in international politics against the idea of class struggle and criticized the Soviet Union for its foreign policy during the interwar era. In the long term, pan-Islamic and pan-Asian ideologies lost a great deal of appeal for rising nationalist movements because of the attraction of Socialist internationalism. For example, pan-Asianist trends within the Indian, Chinese, and Vietnamese national movements from 1905 to 1914 were replaced by the attraction of socialist alternatives for later generation nationalists.[70]

"CLASH OF CIVILIZATIONS" IN THE AGE OF NATIONALISM

Evaluating the trajectory of pan-Islamic and pan-Asian thought during the 1920s requires close attention to their relationship with the rising nationalist movements. Anticolonial nationalist movements were popularly interpreted as a revival of Asia and thus associated with a vague notion of Islamic and Asian triumph over the West. Yet there were no practical projects to create an alliance or solidarity among Asian nations, and overall the political destiny of pan-Islamic and pan-Asian movements did not match the intellectual vibrancy of their critiques of world order.

Turkey's success in renegotiating its boundaries and gaining membership in the new international system rendered it a great inspiration and model for anticolonial nationalists in Asia. In India, China, and the rest of Asia, the success of the Turkish war for liberation became a model for nationalist movements.[71] It was in this context that many Western observers interpreted the success of Turkey as the revival of Islam and the East. Where the term "pan-Islamism" continued to be used in the postwar period in the vocabulary of international affairs, it referred more to the general activism of the nationalist movements in specific Muslim nations and their moral and material solidarity, rather than ex-pressing concern about the emergence of a united Islamic state. Thus contem-porary observers perceived the 1920s as the era of the rising tide of anticolonial nationalism. For example, in 1921 Lothrop Stoddard, an American white su-premacist and keen observer of anti-Western ideologies, presented an analysis of Muslim nationalism in a book titled *The New World of Islam*. He argued that the revival of Muslim nationalism and internationalism could not be reduced to the interest in Ottoman caliphate but instead was much broader and deep-rooted.[72] A similar interpretation of Turkish nationalism and pan-Islamic revi-val came from Ôkawa Shûmei, in his *Fukkô Ajia no Shomondai* (Problems of a resurgent Asia), first published in 1922. Ôkawa hailed the movements initiated by Gandhi in India and Mustafa Kemal Paşa in Turkey as new types of Asian revival, though different in character, rooted in national cultures and traditions. For Ôkawa, the trend to emphasize cultural pride and civilizational revival sym-bolized a double effort toward independence in Asia, simultaneously spiritual and political and rejecting the legacy of Westernization.[73]

In the same work, Ôkawa demonstrated his idealist Asian internationalism by describing the rising nationalist movements in Asia and the conservative reaction of the Western imperial powers. Focusing on regions of non-Chinese Asia such as India, Thailand, Afghanistan, Persia, Turkey, Egypt, Mesopotamia (Iraq), Saudi Arabia, Tibet, and Siam, Ôkawa outlined two key aspects of pan-Asianism usually overlooked in the historiography, namely, its internationalism and its universalist claims based on a reverse Orientalist discourse of civiliza-tion. Ôkawa's Asianism celebrated the history of anticolonial national awaken-ing in Asia, characterizing the period from 1905 to 1920 as the era of "the rising tide of color against the white world supremacy."[74] For him, Asia was the site of a universal struggle for freedom from colonial "slavery." After describing the internationalism represented by the League of Nations as no more than a reaction to Asia's nationalist awakening that sought to guarantee the colonial possessions of Britain and France, he reiterated that pan-Asian solidarity was a necessary first step in the creation of an internationalism based on the equality of the Asian and Western nations.[75]

Ôkawa Shûmei contributed to the expansion of the international vision of Japan's pan-Asianism by redefining Asia to include all the areas of the Asian continent that were usually covered by the European concept of the Orient.

This was much larger area than that represented in the more traditional Japanese view of Asia, which limited it to the Chinese cultural sphere. It also went beyond Okakura Tenshin's Buddhist-centered view of Asian civilization, which included only India, China, and Japan. Ôkawa's Asianist projects were based on his definition of Asia as a civilizational alternative to the West, a claim that implied a program of de-Westernization and indigenization as an essential precursor to liberation from Western rule. He noted that the trend of relying on Asia's own native traditions in the nationalist struggle for freedom and liberation had intensified after the Great War. Ironically, Ôkawa's sympathy for the language of civilizational revival led him to praise Indian nationalists such as Aurobindo Ghose and Tagore for expressing the "true" Indian spirit, even though they were British-educated intellectuals. Similarly, he saw the Young Turk movement, which was actually more pro-Western in its ideology than the Ottoman sultan had been, as the embodiment of the Turkish national spirit that allowed Turkey to gain true liberation and escape from Western hegemony (206–210).

Ôkawa Shûmei's Asianist celebration of the rising tide of anticolonial nationalism did not mean that there was any hope of a pan-Asianist political program in Asia in the 1920s. On the contrary, in the early part of that decade, liberal internationalists and Japan's policy of cooperation with Western powers overshadowed any Asianist thesis that Japan should be the leader of an independent Asia rather than a racially marginalized partner in the club of great powers. It wasn't until 1924, in the aftermath of the immigration law that excluded Japanese immigration to the USA, that pan-Asianists in Japan found the political context suitable to reassert their main thesis that race mattered in world affairs and it would be better for Japan to be the leader of the East against the West.

When the Immigration Act passed the U.S. Senate in April 1924, Japanese immigration to America—already limited to a quota of five hundred immigrants annually—was banned altogether.[76] The reaction from Japan was strong and widespread. What was humiliating for the pro-Western Japanese elite was the necessary implication that, despite Japan's civilized status and proven record of Westernization, Japanese people would continue to face discrimination on the basis of their identification with the yellow race and Eastern culture.[77] This event had a great impact on the psychology of young diplomats in the Japanese Foreign Ministry, who considered the passing of the act a national humiliation.[78] It also strengthened race consciousness among some Western educated intellectuals, who began to develop notions that challenging the "white peril" in Asia was Japan's global mission.[79] Pan-Asianist groups in Japan capitalized on the issue of discrimination against Japanese immigrants in the United States to assert their agenda of foreign policy change.[80] Pro-Western liberals, on the other hand, attempted to make use of a cultural diplomacy based on the concept of East-West harmony to solve the problem of discrimination against Japanese immigrants in the USA. For example, the U.S.-Japan Relations Committee, which represented the mainstream of the business and political elite with links to both the Japanese and American governments, couched its efforts to overcome the immigration controversy within the paradigms of harmony between Eastern and Western civilizations.[81] The idea of dialogue between East and West as a solution to race distinction in the world order, as liberal internationals promised it would be, was countered by a new, Hegelian vision of conflict between East and West in the writings of Asianist Ôkawa Shûmei.

For Ôkawa Shûmei, dialogue between East and West did not offer a solution to the problem of racial discrimination against Japanese and other Asians in America. He immediately wrote a provocative article ridiculing pro-American liberals for "shaming" themselves by seeking cooperative diplomacy with a nation that clearly saw the Japanese as members of a second-class race. Despite their opposing policy suggestions, however, Ôkawa and liberal internationalists shared the same civilizational paradigm in their approach to the problem. The difference lay in the fact that Ôkawa argued for the necessity of solidarity among the colored races against white supremacy, suggesting world unity after a final conflict, while liberal internationalists insisted on pursuing harmony and dialogue between civilizations, hoping that a long-term cultural policy would solve the problem of discrimination against the Japanese in the United States.[82]

In the same year that Japan saw its Westernized and modern identity rejected in the Immigration Act, a well-publicized speech by the Chinese nationalist leader Sun Yat-sen reminded the Japanese of the Asian dimension of their identity. This famous lecture, titled "Greater Asianism" and delivered in Kobe in November of 1924—just a few months after the passage of the Immigration Act—formulated a strategic critique of Japan's China policy and referred to the ideal of Asian values, with no reference to Wilsonian or socialist internationalism.[83] Sun urged Japan to follow the moral Confucian politics of the East and abandon the unethical Machiavellian power politics of the West.[84] His speech and its reception in Japan indicated the continuing salience of the Asianist discourse of civilization in both China and Japan during the 1920s[85]

It was in this context that Ôkawa Shûmei combined the political implications of the ideas of Western decline and Asian awakening to formulate his well-known "clash of civilizations" thesis, which served as both a diagnosis for the conflicts in international affairs and a prescription for solving them. In 1925, in his article titled ""Ajia, Yoroppa, Nihon" (Asia, Europe, and Japan), Ôkawa turned his vision of an inevitable clash of civilizations into a prophecy of a final war between Japan and the United States:

Now, East and West have respectively attained their ultimate goals. Indeed, they could no longer go any further if each pursues its own way. World history clearly shows that they have to unite in the end. This, however, can never be attained by peaceful means. . . . As history fully proves, in creating a new world, a life-and-death struggle between the champion of the East and that of the West is inevitable. This logic proved true when America challenged Japan.[86] She is in Europe what Japan is in Asia. . . . These two countries are destined to fight each other as Greece had to fight against Persia, and Rome against Carthage.[87]

The prophecy of an Armageddon between East and West was partly shaped by the influence of Vladimir Sergeyevich Soloviev (1853–1900), a prominent Russian mystic philosopher whose work *The Justification of the Good* Ôkawa regarded as spiritual nourishment.[88] In his pessimist diagnosis of the evolution of modern history, Soloviev predicted that a confrontation between East and West would become its main dynamic force. Ôkawa, however, turned Soloviev's idea into a normative and prescriptive characterization of the future of the relationship between Asia and the West, confident in his expectation of victory for the East over the decadent West. His prediction also relied on his assessment of war as a positive factor in human history, which was again an idea borrowed from the philosophy of Soloviev.[89]

More than two decades after Ôkawa published this vision of the clash of civilization during the mid-1920s, the prosecution at the Tokyo War Crimes Tribunal naturally emphasized Ôkawa's prophecy of a war between the United States and Japan in their argument for a Japanese conspiracy to attack America. When Ôkawa wrote his famous "clash of civilizations" thesis, however, the prediction that conflict would inevitably arise between Japan and the United States was not peculiar to pan-Asianists. As Mark R. Peattie points out, the anti-Japanese Immigration Act endorsed by the U.S. Congress in 1924 provided the impetus for a wave of literature "forecasting a Pacific war" between the United States and Japan.[90] More important in Ôkawa Shûmei's "clash of civilizations" thesis was the fact that he crafted from the circumstances surrounding the anti-Japanese Immigration Act an attack on liberal internationalism, using it to reaffirm his Asianist views.[91]

Asianists of the 1920s were not alone in spinning apocalyptic visions of a clash with the USA. In any case, they soon abandoned this focus on the United States until 1940s. In fact, many Pan-Asianists, including Ôkawa Shûmei, focused their attention on challenging the British Empire in Asia, and, for that reason alone, it would be wrong to interpret their post–Immigration Act "clash of civilization" theories as a systematic plan to foment Japanese-American conflict.

THE WEAKNESS OF PAN-ISLAMIC AND PAN-ASIANIST POLITICAL PROJECTS DURING THE 1920S

Responses to the Immigration Act of 1924 strengthened the colored race identity of many young Japanese intellectuals and diplomats. Moreover, the idea of synthesis or dialogue between Eastern and Western civilization, a discourse essential to pan-Asianist thought, held appeal for liberal internationalists during the 1920s. Yet, despite the intellectual relevance of the construction of national and international identity discourses, pan-Asianism was weak as a political movement throughout the decade. Pan-Islamism also showed a similar destiny in that its discourse of civilization became more popular, appropriated by new generation of intellectuals, while its political projects lacked any state support. In the case of pan-Islamism, the abolishment of the caliphate in Turkey led to a period of soul-searching during which the idea of a Muslim League of Nations and Muslim cooperation through international conventions became significant, while the attempts by several Muslim leaders to assume the caliphate utterly failed.[92] Many Muslim activists and intellectuals attended conventions in Mecca (1926), Jerusalem (1931), and Geneva (1935), and the discussions revolved around the international problems affecting the Muslim world. It was natural that, without the support of a state structure and without any legitimate and accepted leadership, these conventions would not produce effective results. The attempts of pan-Islamic gatherings and the writings they spurred reflect the general dissatisfaction of Muslim intellectuals about the interwar-era world order, which was still characterized by imperial domination. Yet, as long as no Muslim state entity was willing to utilize and mobilize these discontents, attempts at pan-Islamic solidarity did not go beyond intellectual critiques and proclamations of intent.

Pan-Asianist activities during the 1920s were not much different from the pan-Islamic networking during the same period. Though continuing to criticize the ineffectiveness of the existing world order and providing a vision of race solidarity and a discourse of civilization, pan-Asianist conventions, too, did not produce any significant political results. It is important to underline the weakness of pan-Asianist groups and projects during the later half of the 1920s because pan-Asianism was revived in Japan during the 1930s. A careful analysis of the character, participants, and results of the 1926 pan-Asiatic conference in Nagasaki demonstrates that the history of Japan's pan-Asianist thought in the 1930s should consider the rupture that separated 1926 from 1933 in Japan.

The flourishing of pan-Asianist ideas after Sun Yat-sen's "Greater Asianism" lecture in Kobe, combined with the concern over U.S. discrimination against Asian immigrants, led to the convening of an international pan-Asiatic conference in Nagasaki in August 1926, officially organized by the Pan-Asiatic Association in Japan (Zen Ajia Kyôkai) with the cooperation of the Asiatic Peoples League (Ajia Minzoku Dai Dômei) in Beijing.[93] The organization committee was led by Imazato Juntarô, a member of parliament representing Nagasaki from the Seiyûkai Party.[94] The conference expected to attract about one hundred delegates from China, Korea, India, Afghanistan, the Philippines, Turkey, and Persia, but only about a third of that number attended. It was followed by a gathering in Shanghai in November 1927, but third and fourth conferences, proposed to take place in Afghanistan and Dairen (China), respectively, were never held.[95]

The overall message of the conference was solidarity among Asian nations to achieve decolonization and economic prosperity. Given the participation of delegates from China, mention of an Asian Monroe Doctrine that advocated Japan's regional hegemony was absent from the speeches and declarations. The speeches by Indian, Filipino, Japanese, and Chinese delegates condemned Western colonialism and racial discrimination in international relations, making reference to the moral universalism of justice and equality among nations. Several speakers emphasized that their goal was not to encourage hatred for the white peoples or to instigate retaliation against them but rather to affirm the fundamental moral values of humanity.[96]

The conference emphasized that the League of Nations and the post–Great War international system continued Western colonial rule in Asia and neglected the question of race in international affairs. Rash Behari Bose repeated the argument that a pan-Asiatic league would be a step toward the development of a real world league where each nation would be an equal member. Japanese delegates noted that if there had been strong international support for Japan at the Paris Peace Conference, the racial equality proposal would have been adopted by the League of Nations. In spite of the criticism of the League of Nations expressed by the conference delegates, however, the *Osaka Asahi* newspaper rightly observed that the principles and ideals of the Nagasaki pan-Asiatic congress were almost the same as those underlying the League of Nations. In contrast to earlier pan-Asianist predictions of a final confrontation between Eastern and Western civilizations, the delegates at the Nagasaki conference avoided any reference to the idea of a clash of civilizations. They specified as their long-term goals the "renaissance of Asia's culture and civilization; the ultimate liberation of all foreign dominated peoples of Asia; the abolition of all unequal treaties existing among Asiatic nations; and the establishment of the League of the Asiatic Peoples."[97]

The participants in the Nagasaki pan-Asiatic conference discussed several long-term economic goals and projects, their shared assumption being that economic cooperation and exchange would strengthen bonds among Asian societies, an idea that was typical of the mood of capitalist internationalism of the 1920s. Proposals and suggestions ranged from recommending the "use of goods made in Asia as far as possible" to highly utopian projects that would have required huge investments and large-scale governmental cooperation, such as "the construction of a trans-Asiatic railway from Mukden to Turkey in 20–30 years" and the "establishment of an Asian Development Company and an Asiatic Monetary Organ."[98]

The Nagasaki conference revealed two major obstacles facing the pan-Asiatic internationalism in Japan, namely, lack of any political support and an increasing gap separating the Japanese perspective on Asian solidarity from the nationalist perspectives in China and Korea. The Japanese government took an unfriendly and detached attitude to the conference, because of its unwillingness to offend Western colonial powers, especially Great Britain. In fact, the Home Ministry did not allow the congress to convene in Tokyo, forcing its relocation to a smaller city and limiting the number of participants from Japan.[99] Japanese authorities also created problems for Mehandra Pratap, an Indian nationalist representing Afghanistan, by refusing his entry into Japan from Kobe on the grounds that he lacked travel papers.[100] Moreover, no other government in Asia was supportive of this pan-Asiatic conference. China's nationalist leaders showed their own unfriendly attitude, especially during the Shanghai pan-Asiatic conference in 1927. Many of the Nagasaki conference participants were individual political exiles with previous connections to Japan's pan-Asianist networks. They did not, however, have ties with the leadership of the nationalist movements in their home countries. People like Rash Behari Bose and Mehandra Pratap of India and General Ricardo of the Philippines were nationalists who had been important in the era of pro-Japanese Asian internationalism from 1905 to 1917, but they had begun to be overshadowed during the 1920s as a result of the changing nature of the nationalist movements in their home countries.[101]

The most serious problem of the Nagasaki conference, however, was the conflict between the Japanese vision of Asian solidarity and that of China and Korea. From the very beginning, there was concern on the Japanese side over the issue of Korean nationalist participation in the conference, and in the end the Japanese organizers invited only a pro-Japanese delegation from the League of Korean Journalists.[102] Several Korean nationalists telegraphed Japanese newspapers to denounce the conference on behalf of the Korean people. Of the four representatives from the Japanese parliament who attended the conference, two withdrew in reaction to a Chinese proposal calling for the unconditional abrogation of the Sino-Japanese treaty based on the Twenty-One Demands.[103] Despite the initial protests of the Japanese delegates, however, the Chinese proposal for the condemnation of the Twenty-One Demands came to represent a prominent achievement of the conference once the mediation of Rash Behari

Bose succeeded in producing a compromise between the Japanese and Chinese sides. According to the final statement, which received the full support of the Japanese delegation, it was declared that "all unequal treaties, discriminatory treatment and other unequal conditions existing between Japan and China or between all other countries should be abolished."[104] This joint declaration shows that pan-Asianists in Japan could be receptive to the demands and criticism raised by Chinese nationalists.

The main contradiction among the Japanese, Chinese, and Korean visions of pan-Asianism was made apparent in the nature of the media coverage of the conference. From the very beginning, the mainstream Japanese media commented on the conference in a negative manner, paralleling the cynical but relatively extensive coverage of the conference in the English-language media in the United States and Japan. Korean commentaries were not only furious over the hand-picked Korean delegates who would not condemn Japanese colonialism in Korea but also raised suspicion about the Japanese discourse of Asian unity against the West. Chinese newspaper coverage of the conference indicated the fallacy of Asian solidarity when parts of China were under Japanese domination. Japanese papers were condescending and critical toward the conference, yet even their negative commentaries showed an agreement with the discourse of civilization that attributed to Japan the leadership of the Asian peoples against the supposed civilizational unity of the West. Critical Korean and Chinese media reports on the conference thus did not even agree with the Japanese perception of world reality within the framework of "Euro-America versus Asia" (*Oubei tai Ajia*), or "white race versus colored races." Rather, they gave primacy to the dichotomy of "imperialism versus oppressed peoples" to implicate Japan within the category of imperialism and rejected the notion of their sameness and common identity with Japan under the name of "Asia." This did not mean denying the framework of civilizational discourse in Korea and China but giving primacy to the problem of Japanese hegemony in East Asia and rejecting the Japanese interpretation of the shared Asian interest against the Western political threat.[105] Reflecting colonial power relations and the Japanese media's own Euro-American-centric views, Japanese papers rarely talked about the Korean and Chinese commentaries on the conference, although they followed the coverage in English-language papers in Japan and the United States.

The first commentary on the Nagasaki conference appeared in the *New York Times*, which aptly suggested that in the context of Japan's policy of cooperation with Britain and the United States for peace in the East Asia and the Pacific, a pan-Asiatic congress did not seem advantageous for Japan's national interest. The same article described Asianism as a trend instigating revolutionary activities against the hegemony of whites in Asia among a number of disgruntled, weak nations, dismissing the movement as even less tenable than the pan-Europeanism of the 1920s.[106]

Further comments by the English-language press, including the *Chicago Tribune,* the *Times* and the *Advertiser,* repeated condescending commentaries belittling the Asianist movement and emphasizing the contradictions and weaknesses of its anti-Western ideology. Critics particularly focused on the fact that Asia was too diverse to be united and too Westernized to form a civilizational alternative.[107] They often contrasted Asia with Europe, noting that it never had the level of cohesion and cooperation that Europe possessed:

> Inter-Asiatic hostilities are fiercer than any Asian hostility towards Europe, and as for the cultural aspect of the matter, the Asiatics care a good deal for European culture but their regard for other Asiatic cultures is mainly a polite and political fiction. The Japanese enthusiasm for Chinese culture has long ago vanished, and nowadays manifests itself mainly in the love for lavish Chinese food occasionally. The Asiatic cultures have never learnt how to commingle and assimilate, like those of Europe, but live side by side, mighty interesting to observe, but hardly making for progress and social happiness.[108]

The Asianist claim to offer a civilizational alternative to the West attracted the second major line of critique from English- and Japanese-language papers, for which the vision of the "renaissance of Asia's cultures and civilization," as expressed in the final declaration of the conference, was a goal in conflict with Asia's urgent need to modernize itself. The *Japan Weekly Chronicle* underlined the contradiction between the anti-Westernization discourse of the Asianists and the successful Japanese experience of modernization through adoption of Western methods. "The assumption of all Pan-Asians is that the East is something morally and socially superior, which happens for the moment to be submerged beneath an inferior but more energetic system. Japan shows that it is merely a case of adopting the Western methods to become just like the Western powers, and rather more so. . . . To follow Japan's example will be simply to catch up to the Western powers in all those qualities, which it is the fashion to decry as materialistic, rapacious, or predatory.[109]

In short, the Nagasaki pan-Asiatic conference represented an attempt by Japanese pan-Asianists to reassert their vision for Asian solidarity and new world order. However, the hostile attitude of the Japanese government toward Asianist projects, the lack of any real representation from nationalist movements in Asia, and the denunciation of the conference by Chinese and Korean nationalists effectively demonstrated the weakness of pan-Asianism.

Japan's liberal internationalists during the 1920s never viewed the pan-Asiatic movement as a serious rival. For example, Zumoto Motosada, an ardent liberal internationalist, lecturing at a League of Nations–affiliated university in Geneva in 1926, sought to reaffirm Japan's liberal orientation in response to Western media attention to the Nagasaki pan-Asiatic conference.[110] He looked down on the pan-Asiatic movement in Japan, emphasizing its marginality and insignificance for both Japan's foreign policy and international politics:

> How faithfully Japan fulfills this self-imposed mission was shown in connection with the so-called Pan-Asiatic Congress held at Nagasaki at the beginning of August in the present year, about which more or less sensational press dispatches appear to have been printed in Europe and America. During the last twenty years Japan has been visited by a succession of radical leaders and political adventurers from different parts of Asia for the purpose of enlisting Japanese sympathy and assistance in various propaganda against one or another of the European powers. Always finding deaf ears turned to their pleadings, some of these indefatigable plotters recently struck upon the bright idea of realizing their aim under the inoffensive guise of promoting the Asiatic renaissance, and finally succeeded in interesting in their plan a few notoriety mongers of no standing in our public life. The result was the Nagasaki conference in question. It was an event of no consequence whatever, no person of any importance in any country taking part in it. And what is most significant, it was scarcely noticed by the press in Japan.
>
> (24–25)

Despite Zumoto Motosada's rejection of the pan-Asian political movement, however, his liberal internationalism was based on a discourse of civilization that was similar to the Asianist language on East-West relations. While it denied the idea of a race war and clash of civilizations, his internationalism did recognize the political relevance of civilizational identities. He noted that Japan "imposes upon herself the role of harmonizer between the civilizations of East and West" (9) to aid the cause of international peace within the framework of the League of Nations. Thus he proudly described a cultural awakening in Asia that was inspired first by the Japanese victory over Russia and then by the traumatic experience of the Great War in Europe. Zumoto saw rising liberalism and industrialization in Japan as compatible with elements of the renaissance of the Asian cultural legacy such as the revival of Buddhism, and he regarded this harmony as a positive contribution to world peace. Alfred Zimmern, deputy director of the League of Nations' Institute of Intellectual Cooperation, likened Zumoto Motosada to Nitobe Inazô in his commitment to an intellectual exchange between East and West and praised Japan's role in this civilizational dialogue (4).

CONCLUSION

Pan-Islamic and pan-Asian visions of the world did not fade away in the face of competition from the two "Western" alternatives to imperial world order, namely, Wilsonianism and socialism. When the rising tide of nationalism in post-WWI Asia continued to erode the legitimacy claims of the Western empires and imperial policies with their utilization of the principle of national self-determination, it also diminished the realpolitik value of pan-Islamic and pan-Asian visions of world order. The success of the Turkish Republic had inspired a pan-Islamic notion of triumph against Western colonialism, yet the new republic's decision to abolish the caliphate and disavow any leadership in the Islamic world undermined pan-Islamic visions. More important, neither pan-Islamism nor pan-Asianism had any practical political projects appropriated and supported by a state agency. The example of various pan-Islamic and pan-Asian congresses from 1924 to 1926 shows continued attempts based on a certain ideal but also vivid failures of organization, state support, and appeal. Pan-Islamism and pan-Asianism remained, during the 1920s, a network of ideas and critiques without any institutional and political backing.

Nevertheless, both pan-Islamic and pan-Asian thought continued as potential alternatives for expressing discontent with the interwar-era world order in the Muslim world and Asia. Their critiques of Wilsonian internationalism were based not on its ideals but on its implementation through the League of Nations, which was seen as being manipulated by imperial interests and white-race biases. In fact, the failure of the League of Nation system to fulfill its own proclaimed ideals of equality and fair membership in the international community, the continuing practice of racial discrimination in the international system, and the perpetuation of colonial rule in the Muslim world and Asia all contributed to the vitality of intellectual critiques informed by pan-Islamic and pan-Asian thought.

The intellectual vitality of pan-Asian visions based on the powerful notions of East-West civilizational discourses and the white race's continuing discrimination against the colored races helps explain one of the major paradoxes in the history of pan-Asianism. If pan-Asianism in Japan lacked any political support during the 1920s, why did it gradually gain official endorsement during the 1930s? Why and how did the Japanese government decide to revive the old notions of a Japan-centered pan-Asian internationalism by the late 1930s? The answer to these questions lies in the way the Japanese Empire utilized pan-Asianist thought, despite Asianism's anticolonial lineage, to solve the crisis of Japan's own imperialism in East Asia.

7

THE REVIVAL OF A PAN-ASIANIST VISION OF WORLD ORDER IN JAPAN (1931–1945)

ONE OF THE most striking aspects of the international history of the 1930s is the revival and official endorsement of a pan-Asian vision of regional world order in Japan. The pan-Asian discourse of East-West civilizational difference and comparison was influential in various intellectual circles in Asia. But, as a political project of Asian solidarity, it was irrelevant for Japan's foreign policy, and it did not have any international momentum or movement during the 1920s. Unexpectedly, the period after the Manchurian Incident in 1931 witnessed a process by which pan-Asianist ideas and projects became part of Japan's official foreign policy rhetoric.[1] After 1933, pan-Asian internationalism began to overshadow liberal internationalism, gradually becoming the mainstream vision of an alternative world order in Japan. This process culminated in the declaration of the Greater East Asia Coprosperity Sphere in 1940, a project that relied heavily on the rhetoric of pan-Asian internationalism. In 1943, seventeen years after the ineffectual 1926 Nagasaki pan-Asiatic conference that was ridiculed by official and liberal circles in Japan, the Japanese government itself hosted a Greater East Asia Conference to which it invited the leaders of the Philippines, Burma, the provincial government of India, the Nanking government of China, Manchukuo, and Thailand.

Given that pan-Asianist activists had regularly expressed strong opposition to Japan's foreign policy up to the 1930s and knowing the lack of political power of Asianist circles during the 1920s, Japan's apparent endorsement of pan-Asianism in its official "return to Asia" after 1933 raises a major question. How can we understand the predominance of pan-Asianist discourses in Japanese intellectuals circles during the 1930s? Why would Japan's political elite, with its proven record of cooperation with Western powers based on a realistic assessment of the trends of the time, choose to endorse an anti-Western discourse of Asianism as its official policy during the late 1930s?

EXPLAINING JAPAN'S OFFICIAL "RETURN TO ASIA"

A full examination of Japan's official "return to Asia" from the perspective of the government elite is beyond the scope of this study. In the previous literature, the process of transition from a policy of pro-Western capitalist internationalism in the 1920s to a very different policy aiming to create a regional order in East Asia has been attributed to a complex set of interrelated factors, both contingent and structural. For the sake of clarity, I categorize the explanations of the previous historiography into two groups, which are distinct but not necessarily opposed to one another: those that emphasize domestic political causes of the change and those that stress changes in the international environment.

According to domestic policy–driven explanations, Asianism was the foreign policy ideology espoused by the expansionist, militarist, and conservative segments of Japanese society. Frederick Dickinson has traced back to the period of WWI the origins of two distinct agendas for Japan's diplomacy and national mission, one liberal and pro-British and the other characterized by pro-German, anti-liberal, and Asianist tendencies. The Asianist and conservative group, mostly clustered around Yamagata Aritomo, could not implement its policy visions during the 1910s because the liberal group prevailed over it in domestic politics. By identifying two distinct visions of Japan's national identity and the two corresponding international policies in response to the opportunities presented by WWI, Dickinson's study successfully demonstrates that foreign policy decisions should not be regarded as automatic responses to international trends and immediate external challenges but rather be seen as results of the balance of power in domestic politics among groups that have competing visions of their national identity and mission. According to Dickinson, pan-Asianism was one such grand vision, which aimed to establish Japan's leadership in Asia by excluding Western powers from the region in the name of racial solidarity and civilizational harmony.[2]

Other studies on the 1920s have argued that members of the conservative antiliberal political camp, often identified with pan-Asianist inclinations, continued to agitate for an expansionist policy, even at a time when their voices were overshadowed by the liberalism of the Taishô democracy and the capitalist internationalism of Shidehara diplomacy. According to Richard Storry's early work, which offers a history of Japanese ultranationalism based on the materials of the Tokyo War Crimes Tribunal, the persistence and violence displayed by right-wing groups was able to weaken and eventually to overturn the prevailing atmosphere of the Taishô democracy and liberal diplomacy. For Storry, for example, pan-Asianist thinker Ôkawa Shûmei was one of the Asianist "double patriots" who influenced young military officers and played a great role in the transition to the expansionist 1930s.[3] Christopher Szpilman strengthened this argument in his study of Kokuhonsha, the main conservative organization of interwar Japan, noting that anti-Western and antiliberal trends in Japan had high-ranking supporters and strong organizational solidarity during the 1920s and thus were able to exert disproportionate influence as a result of their popularity among the bureaucratic and military elite.[4] In his research on the House of Peers, Genzo Yamamoto further demonstrated the appeal and predominance of what he described as an "illiberal" agenda among Japan's political elite from the 1920s to the late 1930s. Yamamoto's study shows that the illiberal ideas in both domestic and foreign policy had strong supporters at the top of the political elite during the 1920s, with their final triumph in domestic politics paralleling the adoption of an aggressive China policy.[5]

This focus on the domestic political components of the transition to the pan-Asianist policies of the 1930s has obvious merit. Asianism, however, could not always be uniquely identified as the expansionist ideology of conservative antiliberals, as Japan's liberals also envisioned a special role for Japan in Asia, whether as the disseminator of a higher civilization to backward areas or as the leading force in economic development and political cooperation in the region. Moreover, an aggressive policy in Manchuria was not the monopoly of Japanese Asianists. As demonstrated by Louise Young, there existed within Japanese society an overwhelming consensus concerning Japan's policy in Manchuria, which cut across the lines dividing the liberal and conservative camps.[6] The majority of Japan's political and intellectual elite, including the pro-Western internationalists, supported the new orientation in foreign policy symbolized by the withdrawal from the League of Nations. For example, Nitobe Inazô, reputed for his liberal internationalism, was willing to defend Japan's policy in China that led to the Manchurian Incident, even to the point of accepting Japan's withdrawal in 1932 from the League of Nations, in which he had served for so many years.[7] Another liberal internationalist, Zumoto Motosada, went on lecture tours in 1931 to Europe and the United States in an attempt to explain Japan's position in the Manchurian Incident. During his speeches, Motosada often referred to the idea of a Japan-led regional order in East Asia separate from the European-based league system. Just five years before the Manchurian Incident, Zumoto had affirmed Japan's pro-league internationalism in his critique of the Nagasaki pan-Asiatic conference of 1926. It seemed that Japan's liberal internationalists turned to pan-Asianism when they saw a tension between Japanese national interests and the decisions of the League of Nations.[8]

The Asianist discourse of Japan's transnational identity had many different versions, ranging from a doctrine of regional solidarity to anti-Western visions of civilizational revival, and it was not limited to conservative circles. For example, during the 1930s, many Japanese intellectuals who had no previous connection with conservative radical nationalist groups, such as the members of the Kyoto School of Philosophy or the semiofficial think tank Shôwa Ken-kyûkai, also utilized anti-Western rhetoric and advocated the revival of Japan's Asian identity.[9] This indicates an area of overlap in the worldviews of liberals and antiliberals with respect to Japan's Asian identity and its international mission in Asia, as well as their shared diagnosis of the international system during the 1920s. It also shows that the theories of the clash of civilizations and Japan's mission in Asia were part of a common vocabulary, which would then have different political connotations depending on the intellectual climate. For example, those advocating the U.S.-Japan friendship would frame their efforts as a dialogue of harmony among the different civilizations of the East and West, thus confirming a vision of the world as divided into different race and civilization groups beyond the nations. In that sense, many leading Japanese intellectuals who had no ties to the conservative radical nationalist groups ended up contributing to the legitimacy of the pan-Asianist program in some way, either through their theories on overcoming modernity and Eurocentrism or through their search for an alternative modernity in the Japanese and Asian cultural traditions.[10]

The second major approach to the question of Japan's adoption of Asianist rhetoric in foreign policy emphasizes that the structural transformations in the international system in East Asia complemented changes in the domestic power configurations to create a situation that led to the triumph of antiliberal and Asianist projects. Akira Iriye and James Crowley have argued that Japanese policies during the 1930s were largely a response to changes in the trends of the times as perceived by the Japanese elite. A perceived sense of an international legitimacy crisis and Japan's isolation after the Manchurian Incident was accelerated by the impact of changed world conditions. Regionalism became the trend of the time, making the creation of a regional order in East Asia a more feasible policy, in harmony with the flow of world opinion. As Akira Iriye noted, "by 1931 all indications seem to suggest that the neo-mercantilist world-view of Matsuoka was more realistic than Shidehara's rational, laissez-faire image, which had apparently failed to produce tangible results."[11] The capitalist internationalism of the 1920s was not only denied altogether by Fascist Germany and Socialist Russia but also half-abandoned in the concept of the pan-American trade bloc and economic nationalism of the United States and the idea of the sterling trade bloc in England.[12] In short, Japan's policy shift from liberal internationalism to Asian regionalism could be considered a function just as much of other powers' policies in the changing international system of the late 1930s as of Japan's own domestic politics.

The end of the party cabinet system in 1932 and the increasing power of the military in political decisions created a discontinuity in the history of Japan's domestic political order in terms of democratic participation and popular expression. Japan continued to be a constitutional state, however, with normally functioning domestic politics in accordance with the intricacies of the Meiji Constitution.[13] In his study on the 1930s, James Crowley refutes the idea of a conservative or right-wing takeover of the Japanese leadership by focusing on continuity in the "official mind" and the "decision-making process." Crowley shows that all the policy decisions of the Japanese government during the 1930s were made by responsible political and military leaders in the interest of national defense and national policy.[14]

The historiography that focuses on Japan's response to changes in the international environment attributes an important role to ideology and culture in shaping Japanese perceptions of world events, without limiting focus to right-wing or militarist groups. It is in this context that an Asianist worldview about world cultures and international order becomes relevant for determining the perceptions and decisions of Japanese leaders. Akira Iriye has discussed the role of key notions such as isolation and self-sufficiency in the psychology of Japanese decision makers, showing how the perception that Japan stood uneasily between East and West influenced the policy-making mood.

In this view, the notions that the Japanese elite held concerning the threats and opportunities presented to Japan by the new global developments should thus be regarded as more significant than the impact of antiliberal right-wing movements associated with pan-Asianism. A similar approach attributes Japan's turn to anti-Westernism not to the influence of pan-Asianist groups in particular but rather to the general characteristics of Japanese nationalism. Hayashi Fusao's controversial assertion that the "Pacific War was one phase of an Asian Hundred Years' War to drive out the Occidental invader" presents a generalized formulation that portrays Asianist ideas as a permanent part of mainstream Japanese nationalism.[15] This emphasis on the anti-Western historical memory of Japanese nationalism depicts Asianism as a widely held conception about Japan's transnational identity rather than an exclusively radical ideology monopolized by ultranationalists or conservatives. Mark Peattie and James Crowley concur with Hayashi Fusao's assessment of the importance of anti-Western historical memory embedded in Japanese nationalism as an ideological factor, although they do not share his revisionist agenda.[16]

Since we know, however, that mainstream nationalism in Japan had changing perceptions of the West, it would be inaccurate to characterize anti-Westernism as a single constant position in the history of Japanese nationalism from the

Opium War to the Greater East Asia War. Moreover, the Japanese intellectual elite remained closely linked to trends and ideas in Europe and the United States. During the 1930s, there was no new expansion of the West in Asia to which the surge in Japanese nationalism might be attributed; on the contrary, the West was perceived to be in a phase of global decline and retreat.[17] Thus the very assumption that there was a constant association between Japanese nationalism and resistance to Western expansion reflects the influence of the official pan-Asianist discourse of wartime Japan rather than accurately characterizing how images of the West and civilizational identity interacted with Japanese foreign policy.

WITHDRAWAL FROM THE LEAGUE OF NATIONS AS A TURNING POINT

There had been pan-Asianists in Japan since the turn of the twentieth century, and some continued to work for the cause they believed in from 1905 to the 1930s, especially under the umbrella of patriotic Asianist organizations such as Kokuryûkai and Genyosha. It is clear that these patriotic Asianists represented a minority, if not a marginal opinion, in the overall direction of Japanese foreign policy. They often complained about the neglect to which they had been subjected by the Japanese elite. In the aftermath of the Manchurian Incident of 1931 and Japan's withdrawal from the League of Nations the following year, however, traditional Asianists found a very receptive audience for their ideas among Japanese bureaucrats and army officers.

The story told by a Kokuryûkai Asianist who specialized in the Islamic world, Wakabayashi Han, is very telling in this regard. Wakabayashi became interested in the Muslim world after a visit to India with the Burmese Buddhist monk and anticolonial nationalist U. Ottama in 1912.[18] His discovery of Indian Muslims led him to undertake further research about Islam in Asia.[19] For twenty years, he worked closely with a small circle of Islam experts within Kokuryûkai led by Tanaka Ippei, arguing that if Japan could develop closer ties with the colonized Muslims of Asia, its efforts to become the leader of an awakening and independent Asia could benefit from Muslim support.[20] According to Wakabayashi, however, the activities of his small group neither achieved any result nor received any support from the government, and he became pessimistic about its future success.[21] Then in 1932 Tôyama Mitsuru and Uchida Ryôhei sent Wakabayashi to observe the meeting of the League of Nations in Geneva that addressed the question of recognizing the state of Manchukuo. There, Wakabayashi witnessed the vital decision of Japanese diplomats to withdraw from the league upon its refusal to recognize Japanese actions in Manchuria. It was only during his trip back to Japan, Wakabayashi notes, that he recognized a change of attitude to his group's Asianist ideas on the part of Japanese military officers. In the long trip from Europe to Japan, he had a chance to talk to Isogai Rensuke, a lieutenant-colonel in the Japanese army and explain to him the benefits that attention to the Muslim world could bring to Japan's East Asian policy. After his return to Japan, Isogai Rensuke later contacted Wakabayashi Han and introduced him to Army Minister Araki Sadao.[22] Wakabayashi's story of the developments that followed this meeting continues as a narrative of triumph, as the Japanese army began to implement a pan-Asianist Islam policy in China and supported the activities of the Kokuryûkai group. It is clear from his story that Japan's withdrawal from the League of Nations was a turning point in the Japanese government's attitude to the pan-Asianist ideas of Japan's cooperation with Muslim nationalities against the Western colonial presence. Autobiographical anecdotes of other pan-Asianist activists exhibit a similar pattern. Even the most influential pan-Asianist in Japan, Ôkawa Shûmei, had the similar experience of finding a surprising shift in Japanese official policy and intellectual life toward positions more to his liking in the mid-1930s, more than two decades after his initial commitment of the cause of Asianism.

Ôkawa's biography during the 1930s took an ironic turn, as he was put on trial and imprisoned for his involvement in a failed military coup to change Japan's domestic politics at the very time his Asianist projects were receiving the support of the Japanese government. Since Ôkawa was the head of the East Asia Economic Research Bureau of the Manchurian Railway Company after 1929, he naturally was familiar with Japanese interests in Manchuria. Frequently visiting Manchuria and China, Ôkawa came to know the leading military figures of the Kwantung Army personally. From 1929 onward, Ôkawa argued that a solution to the Manchurian problem was essential for both Asian revival and the reconstruction of Japan. In 1928 Ôkawa met with the Manchurian warlord Chang Hsüeh-liang in an effort to convince him to form a stronger political union with Japan based on "Confucian political values."[23] Both a respected scholar of colonial studies and a radical nationalist, Ôkawa once gave a lecture on the necessity of creating an independent Manchuria-Mongolia to an audience that included top military officers of the 1930s, most notably, Itagaki Seishirô, Nagata Tetsuzan, and Tôjô Hideki.[24] He went on a lecture tour in Japan before and after the Manchurian Incident, expressing his conviction that Manchuria was not only a legitimate economic and security sphere for Japan but actually represented the lifeline of Japan's national policy.

Like so many other Japanese intellectuals and leaders, Ôkawa was outspoken about the importance of protecting Japanese interests in Manchuria, and he favored radical action to secure these interests against the claims of Chinese nationalism. For Ôkawa, Japan's "sacrifice" in the Sino-Japanese and the Russo-

Japanese wars created the historical legitimacy for its treaty privileges in Man-churia. Criticizing the anti-Japanese movement in China, Ôkawa argued that if Japan did not act to protect its rights in Manchuria, it would endanger its position in Korea and Taiwan as well. He condemned the Japanese leaders of the late 1920s for not being able to show the courage and determination nec-essary to find a long-term solution to the Manchurian problem because of their submissive commitment to international cooperation with the Western powers. His arguments can clearly be construed as offering encouragement for the radical actions orchestrated by the Kwantung Army.[25] Citing these facts, the prosecution at the Tokyo War Crimes Tribunal argued a link between Ôkawa's pan-Asianist ideas and the Manchurian Incident, a key step in constructing the ideological background of the tribunal's thesis about the long-term Japanese conspiracy to invade Asia.[26]

Ôkawa Shûmei's support for the Japanese policy in Manchuria after 1931, however, was nothing but exceptionally Asianist. It is impossible to attribute the Manchurian Incident or post–Manchurian Incident Japanese policies spe-cifically to the ideology of the pan-Asianists. The fact that pan-Asianist Ôkawa had lectured on the issue of Manchuria and had known some of the military leaders did not necessarily make him an ideologue of the Manchurian Incident, since there were many others, including those identified as liberals at the time, who advocated a similarly radical policy in Manchuria.[27] It is helpful to com-pare Ôkawa Shûmei's arguments on Manchuria with the writings of Rôyama Masamichi (1895–1980), a liberal intellectual of the time who was well respected internationally and influential in Japanese policy circles. Rôyama's analysis of Japan's relations with Manchuria, which he presented to an international audi-ence affiliated with the Institute of Pacific Relations two years before the Man-churian Incident, argued that Japan's established interests in Manchuria de-served international approval.[28] In a later policy report on Manchuria, Rôyama placed blame for the Manchurian Incident on the existing international peace structures and the refusal to acknowledge the special relations between China and Japan, not on the actions of the Kwantung Army on the ground. Ôkawa's writings about the need to defend Japanese rights in Manchuria against Chi-nese nationalist demands did not differ substantially from Rôyama's insistence on the protection of Japan's vital interests.[29]

The nature of the pan-Asianist approach to the Manchurian Incident be-came apparent only after the incident, when intellectuals like Ôkawa formu-lated laudatory characterizations of the establishment of Manchukuo both as a victory against the corruption of business conglomerates (*zaibatsu*) and politi-cal parties at home and as a brave defense of Japan's continental policy against American, British, and Soviet opposition.[30] Ôkawa retroactively offered a moral justification for the Manchurian Incident within the framework of a pan-

Asianist critique of Japan's foreign policy between 1905 and 1931. His interpretation of the incident as a correction of the misguided course of pro-Western diplomacy, especially since the Russo-Japanese War, differed significantly from Rôyama Masamichi's justification of the Manchurian Incident as a practical response to the changing conditions of the region. Ôkawa wrote:

> Our victory over Russia inspired hope and courage in the countries exploited under the pressure of the Caucasian colonialists. But, before long, Japan gave in to the Franco-Japanese Agreement and the revised Anglo-Japanese Alliance, actions that shattered the hopes of noble Vietnamese and Indian patriots who sought independence for their countries. . . . However, the mistakes in Japanese policy were later rectified decisively by the foundation of Manchukuo. Japan abandoned cooperation with the Anglo-Americans, the chief instigators suppressing the Asian people. The foundation of Manchukuo was the first step in achieving a great "renascent Asia."[31]

Ôkawa similarly applauded Japan's withdrawal from the League of Nations.[32] As shown in the previous chapter, Ôkawa had always regarded the league as an instrument of Western colonial powers and often urged the Japanese government to create a League of Asian Nations as an alternative.[33] After Japan's withdrawal from the league in 1933, Ôkawa's ideas seemed in harmony with the policies of the Japanese government for the first time in the history of his Asianist activism, dating back to 1913.

As the foreign policy Ôkawa had envisioned began to be implemented, he was put on trial for his involvement in the May 15, 1932, assassination of Prime Minister Inukai Tsuyoshi.[34] After his arrest on June 15, 1932, the court found Ôkawa Shûmei guilty of providing guns and money to conspirators during the planning stage of the assassination. In February 1934, Ôkawa received a fifteen-year prison sentence. Because of a lenient system of appeals and paroles, however, he spent less than two years in prison, between June 1936 and October 1937.[35] In the four years between 1931 to 1935, the dominant visions of Japanese foreign policy and domestic politics changed so dramatically that, by the early 1935, Ôkawa Shûmei no longer needed to work through secretive radical organizations to achieve his ideological goals. In February 1935, he marked the end of his career as an activist promoting the Shôwa Restoration in domestic politics and pan-Asianism in foreign policy by disbanding the last organization he established, Jinmukai.[36] More important, however, Japan itself was approaching the state of military mobilization while endorsing an Asianist foreign policy agenda, making radical activism for the same purpose pointless.

After his release from prison in October 1937, Ôkawa Shûmei volunteered his services for Japan's new foreign policy projects that relied on the ideas and legitimacy of pan-Asianism. Although his image had been tarnished by his involvement in the May 15 assassination, shortly after his release from prison, Ôkawa was appointed to head the continental campus of Hôsei University. In May 1938, he was reinstated to his position as director of the East Asia Economic Research Bureau in Tokyo. Back in his position of managing one of the largest research institutes in Japan, he actively promoted a pan-Asianist agenda with the journal he edited, entitled *Shin Ajia* (New Asia). His position as editor allowed him to observe, comment on, and influence Japan's Asia policy in the period following the official declaration of the "New Order in East Asia" in November 1938.[37] In his first editorial, published just a month before the German invasion of Poland, Ôkawa predicted that the outbreak of war in Europe would usher in a new era in which nationalist movements in Asia would find their chance to achieve independence. He also urged the Japanese government to support these anticolonial movements with the goal of accelerating their process of national liberation and simultaneously creating future allies for Japan. Pointing out that Japan's mission in Asia was gaining greater urgency, Ôkawa expressed his hope that the Japanese public, which was not appropriately knowledgeable even about the recent developments in China, would become better informed about the conditions and peoples of Asia in general.[38]

As the Japanese government began to use the slogan "New Order in East Asia" to describe its foreign policy, Ôkawa Shûmei became concerned about the unpreparedness of the Japanese public, in terms of their knowledge about Asian societies and cultures, for a serious and official pan-Asian policy in Japan. In order to carry out a mission to educate young Japanese about the culture and politics of Asia and prepare them for positions in the service of Japan, Ôkawa received government funds to establish a special school offering instruction in Asian studies. The two-year professional school, the most concrete product of Ôkawa's Asianist vision, was established in May 1938 as a teaching institute affiliated with the East Asian Economic Research Bureau in Tokyo, with special funds from the Manchurian Railway Company, the army, and the Foreign Ministry. All the expenses of the admitted students were paid by the school, which was widely known as the Ôkawa Juku (Ôkawa School), although it was named the Shôwa Gogaku Kenkyûjo (Shôwa Language Institute). In return for receiving tuition and a stipend for two years, the students were obligated to work for the Japanese government in overseas regions such as Southeast Asia for approximately ten years. Each year, the school recruited twenty students around the age of seventeen. In their first year, students had to learn either English or French as their primary foreign language, along with an additional language to be selected from among Hindu, Urdu, Thai, and Malay. After the second year of the school, Arabic, Persian, and Turkish were added to the elective language course offerings.

The Ôkawa Juku represented a practical implementation of Ôkawa Shûmei's long-held pan-Asianist vision of merging a colonial cultural policy with anti-colonial ideology. He aimed to educate a body of Japanese bureaucrats who could understand the culture and language of Asian peoples and take a position of leadership among them. According to his students, Ôkawa often noted the apparent unreadiness of the Japanese Empire for a great pan-Asian cause, underlining the urgency and utility he perceived in his teaching mission for the Greater East Asia war. He encouraged his students to form personal friendship with Asian peoples and establish bonds of solidarity that would last even if Japan lost the war.[39] A retrospective assessment of Japan's wartime cultural policies in newly occupied Southeast Asia shows that, with a few exceptions, cultural policies were in fact developed ad hoc by administrators faced with the reality of ruling a large population they knew little about.[40] Ôkawa Juku complemented the other Asianist program that brought students from Southeast Asia to Japan for training. Most of the graduating students of Ôkawa Juku did find employment in the military administration of the Southeast Asian region during the era of the Greater East Asia Coprosperity Sphere.[41]

The content of pan-Asianist education at Ôkawa Juku reflected a synthesis between the scholarly-idealistic vision of Asian liberation and pragmatic goals of Japan's wartime military expansion. Ôkawa himself taught classes on colonial history, the "Japanese spirit," Islam, and Oriental history. His lecture notes for the classes entitled "History of Modern European Colonialism" and "Introduction to Islam" later became the basis for books with the same names. Students of the school praised Ôkawa as a dedicated educator, citing his informative and clear lectures, his hard work, and his close relationship with students.[42] From time to time, high-ranking army generals such as Doihara Kenji, Itagaki Seishirô, Matsui Iwane, Tôjô Hideki, and Okamura Seiji would visit the Ôkawa Juku and lecture students on Japan's Asia policy.[43] Indian nationalist Rash Behari Bose and Muslim immigrant from Russia Qurban Ali were among the part-time language and history instructors of the school, giving students a firsthand encounter with the anticolonial nationalist thinking of Asian exiles in Japan. It was during this time that Ôkawa pioneered Japan's rapidly growing field of Islamic studies not only through his own writings but also by supporting young scholars and purchasing library collections on Islamic studies from Europe under his authority as director of the East Asia Economic Research Institute.[44]

It would be mistaken to assume that, before Pearl Harbor, Japan's Asianists advocated a conflict with the United States based on their vision of East-West conflict. From the time of the China Incident in July 1937 to the Pearl Harbor attack in December 1941, for example, Ôkawa Shûmei cautioned against entering into conflict with the United States while advocating a southern advance by Japan that would target the colonies of Britain, France, and the Netherlands in Southeast Asia. With this goal in mind, he urged a quick resolution to the Sino-Japanese conflict. Particularly as pan-Asianists became aware of an approaching war in Europe, with all the implications that such a war carried for the colonized areas in Asia, they found renewed faith in Asia's ultimate rise to independence; destiny seemed to have presented Japan with an ideal opportunity to lead the liberation of Asia from Western colonialism. For pan-Asianists, a southern advance was as much a practical opportunity as it was a moral imperative, since neither the British nor the Dutch government were in a position to resist Japanese military pressure, particularly if Japan could act in cooperation with native nationalist movements in Southeast Asia. It is in this spirit that Ôkawa Shûmei proposed the creation of a Southeast [Asian] Common Cooperative Region (Tônan Kyôdôken) to secure the political and economic unity of liberated Southeast Asia with Japan. With this historical opportunity, there could emerge a new world order based on three regional blocs, Euro-Africa, America, and East-Southeast Asia.[45] Meanwhile, realizing the danger that cooperation between Europe and America could present to Japan, Ôkawa Shûmei advocated a policy of keeping the United States neutral.[46] He refrained from making anti-American arguments in his editorials and urged the improvement of economic ties, especially with joint projects in Manchuria and China, in a bid to secure U.S. neutrality in the event of a future British-Japanese conflict.

Thus, from 1938 up until the Pearl Harbor attack, Ôkawa Shûmei was involved in a project of developing trade ties between Japan and the United States. There had been an economic diplomacy toward the United States that aimed at cooperation in the industrialization of Manchuria between 1937 and 1940.[47] Endorsing Ishiwara Kanji's vision of the creation of a self-sufficient military industry in Manchukuo but recognizing the insufficiency of the machine tool industry in the region, military and industrial leaders in Manchuria aimed to attract a higher level of U.S. investment and technology. In fact, Manchuria became more heavily dependent on American capital and technology than it was on European investments. Beyond the goal of industrializing Manchuria, Ayukawa Yoshisuke, the president of the Manchurian Industrial Development Corporation and the founder of the Nissan conglomerate, also hoped to avoid war between the United States and Japan by fostering mutual economic ties.

Ôkawa Shûmei's personal commitment to the improvement of economic relations with the United States stemmed more from his interest in U.S. neutrality than from considerations of economic rationality. He believed it was possible for Japan to avoid U.S. involvement in its confrontation with the Chinese Nationalist government and the European colonial powers. It was Ôkawa's expectation that the strong trade relationships and joint investments they shared with Japan in Manchuria would lead the Americans to withdraw their support from the Nationalist government of China. In making these policy suggestions, Ôkawa relied on his assumptions about the American national character as being concerned primarily with business interests rather than principled foreign policies. He also considered that the United States would have less to lose by giving up its support for the government of Chiang Kai-shek than Britain did.[48] With these assessments and goals, Ôkawa became personally involved in an effort by the Pan-Pacific Trading and Navigation Company to barter mineral ores from China for gasoline from the United States. His project failed as a result of difficulties with the intricacies of U.S. trade regulations. Nevertheless, Ôkawa's desire to insulate the USA from Japan's war in China, in addition to his willingness to make use of U.S. trade in the development of Manchuria, should be noted as an indication that he was not, at least where practical policy matters were concerned, a consistent advocate of an inevitable war between the United States and Japan.[49]

Once the fighting between the United States and Japan began, however, Ôkawa Shûmei immediately took on the task of offering a historical justification for the war as Japan's response to a century of Anglo-American aggression in East Asia. He preferred the term "Anglo-American aggression" to "Western aggression," a contemporary expression that allowed pan-Asianist thinkers to exclude Germany from their anti-Western rhetoric. Even so, when Ôkawa discussed the historical and philosophical basis of the Greater East Asia War, he again spoke about the confrontation of East and West as if China did not belong to the East or Germany to the West. It was during his radio lectures on this topic delivered between December 14 and December 25 of 1941, that Ôkawa gave himself credit for the prophecy he had made back in 1925 of an inevitable war between Eastern and Western civilizations, represented by Japan and the United States:

> I published a book in 1924 under the title "Asia, Europe and Japan." It was a small book of less than one hundred pages in content. Not so in its significance, however. I wrote it to serve various purposes: first, to let the pacifists reconsider their wrong attitude by clarifying the historical significance of war; second, to show that world history, in its true sense of the word, is nothing but a chronicle of antagonism, struggle and unification between the Orient and the Occident; third, to reveal the cultural characteristics of the East and the West which had been blended into the history of the world; fourth, to give a logical foundation to Pan-Asianism; last, but not least, to point out that a war is inevitable between the East and the Anglo-American powers for the establishment of a new world. Moreover, I tried to clarify the sublime mission of Japan in the coming world war. I concluded the book as follows: "Now, East and West have respectively

attained their ultimate goals. . . . As history fully proves, in creating a new world, a life-and-death struggle between the champion of the East and that of the West is inevitable. This logic proved true when America challenged Japan." My prediction proved correct after the passage of 16 years.[50]

It was self-promoting references like this to his prediction of Japan's war with the United States that led to Ôkawa's indictment at the Tokyo War Crimes Tribunal.[51] During the trial, he pointed out that his writings in 1924 did not necessarily constitute a plan for a Japanese attack, as he was merely making a comment on the inevitability of war between civilizations based on the ideas of the Russian philosopher Soloviev.[52] In fact, he offered a more historical reinterpretation of his 1924 clash of civilization thesis while he was under U.S. interrogation. Albeit for opportunistic reasons, pan-Asianists opposed war with the United States before 1941. Moreover, in the aftermath of Immigration Act of 1924, theories of a clash between the USA and Japan was a popular topic beyond Asianist circles. Yet the easy transition by the pan-Asianists to clash of civilization theories to justify the war with the United States in the immediate aftermath of the Pearl Harbor attack also signifies the flexible utilization of the ideas of Eastern and Western civilization, and the historical memory of Western colonialism, for the ends of Japan's own imperial expansion.

ASIANIST JOURNALS AND ORGANIZATIONS

From the Manchurian Incident in 1931 to the end of WWII, Ôkawa Shûmei was only one of the many intellectual voices trying to clarify the content and goals of the ambivalent notion of Asian solidarity and Japan's Asian mission. Especially after Japan's withdrawal from the League of Nations, activities related to the ideals and discourse of pan-Asianism continuously gained momentum as support from the government, the military, and business circles increased. There was a significant gap, however, between the discourse of civilization reducing all global conflicts to a question of clashes between distinct races or major civilizations and the actual reality of the state of international affairs. Around the time of the Russo-Japanese War, a vision of racial solidarity and civilizational alliance seemed to be an appealing international strategy for the political projects of the rising nationalist movements, which perceived a united policy in the West of imperialism toward their Asian colonies. During the late 1930s, however, the Western world no longer seemed such a unified front as a result of sharp political and ideological divisions in Europe. And Japan's challenge to the international order was not based on racial divisions, either. Within East Asia, the major conflict was not between East and West but between Japanese imperialism, on the one hand, and Chinese and Korean nationalism, on the other.

From 1933 onward, there was a dramatic increase in the number of Asianist organizations, publications, and events in Japan. They aimed not only at demonstrating the sincerity of Japan's "return to Asia" but also at guarding against a perceived state of international isolation for Japan after its withdrawal from the League of Nations. Asianist publications and events also aimed at convincing both the Japanese public and Asian nationalists that civilizational and racial distinctions were in fact to be regarded as the primary consideration in international relations. But the empty repetition of slogans about the conflict between civilizations and races did not succeed in creating any substantial ideology able to account for the complex global politics of the 1930s, with Asianism instead becoming less and less credible in the face of Japan's full-scale war against Chinese nationalism. Realizing this, Asianists pursued ideological credibility by attempting to revive and reinvent the legacy of the early Asian internationalism dating back to the period from 1905 to 1914. At the same time, liberal and socialist converts to Asianism during the late 1930s infused new content and vigor into the nearly exhausted concept of Asian community and solidarity.

The reinvention of pan-Asianist ideology following the Manchurian Incident can best be seen in the sudden increase in the number of Asianist journals and organizations supported by military, political, and business authorities. In 1933, the same year Japan left the League of Nations, Rash Behari Bose and Qurban Ali, two Asianist exiles who had been living in Japan during the 1920s, began to receive funding for the purpose of publishing journals addressed to India and the Muslim World. Rash Behari Bose published *The New Asia–Shin Ajia*, a monthly periodical in a dual English- and Japanese-language format.[53] The government of India banned the entry and sale of *The New Asia* within the territories it controlled.[54] The journal seemed to have supporters in Southeast Asia, as evidenced by the contact between Indonesian nationalist leader Muhammed Hatta and Rash Behari Bose.[55]

Almost half of the journal *The New Asia* was devoted to coverage of news about the Indian independence movement, taking a tone sympathetic to the radical wing led by Subhas Chandra Bose.[56] Neither Japanese pan-Asianism nor *The New Asia*, however, received any attention or support from such prominent leaders of the Indian national movement as Gandhi, Nehru, Tagore, and Subhas Chandra Bose, all of whom were very critical of Japanese aggression in China. In the absence of interest in a Japan-centered pan-Asianist vision among Indian nationalists, the journal referred to the pro-Japanese statement by Tagore back in 1916, even though Tagore had radically changed his views of Japan by the 1930s.[57] Even Taraknath Das, the one Indian nationalist who bestowed great hopes on Japan's leadership of Asian nationalism during WWI, wrote to *The New Asia* that Japan had done nothing to improve Indo-Japanese relations for about two decades, expressing his skepticism over the motivations behind Japan's attempt to "return to Asia" after such a long period of indifference to nationalist movements.[58]

The New Asia included international news from the perspective of the East-West conflict and domestic news on the activities of various Asianist associations in Japan, such as the visits to Tokyo of African American or Asian figures of repute, or the awarding of scholarships to students from Asia.[59] The journal refrained from publishing any news or articles critical of the creation of Manchukuo and maintained silence on the subject of Chinese nationalism. After discussing the Sino-Japanese conflict in a tone of regret, Rash Behari Bose suggested that India should mediate between the two nations to reach a peaceful settlement.[60] With regard to the clash of civilizations and races, articles in *The New Asia* emphasized that what Asians wanted was their national liberation, with the possibility of a racial conflict thus depending entirely on the attitude that the Western powers chose to assume toward the independence movements:[61]

The non-white peoples are now conscious of the distressing fact that they have hitherto been mercilessly exploited and inhumanly humiliated. The intensity of this consciousness is the measure of their challenge to the white man. One thing is certain, and that is that the East and the West cannot coalesce, unless the West fully realizes its immeasurable folly of race-superiority consciousness, completely abandons its mischievous policy of exploitation, and immediately makes ample amends for the untold wrongs it has inflicted on the non-white peoples of the earth.[62]

In *The New Asia*'s editorials on Japanese foreign policy, Rash Behari Bose urged the Japanese government to cooperate with the United States, China, and the Soviet Union in a move to eliminate British colonial control in Asia. For him, Britain was the root of all problems in the region, including Japan's isolation in the international community. As early as 1934, Behari Bose warned that Japan needed to maintain good relations with the United States, as only Britain would benefit from a conflict between that country and Japan: "Britain is not able to fight Japan singly and therefore waiting for her opportunity, when Japan may be involved in a war with America. . . . An American-Japanese War will weaken these two great powers who are serious rivals of Great Britain. Those Americans and Japanese who are real patriots should do their best to promote American-Japanese friendship."[63]

While Rash Behari Bose edited a journal addressing primarily India, Qurban Ali was publishing *Yani Yapon Muhbiri* (New Japan Journal), which aimed its message at the Muslim world.[64] Although the journal was in Turkish, the cover page of the magazine included a Japanese subtitle, describing it as "the only journal that introduces Japan to the Muslim world." Several Japanese companies provided support to the small Muslim community in Tokyo for their efforts in the publication of *Yani Yapon Muhbiri*, which was seen as an effective means for the creation of an information network linking Japan and the Muslim world. In spite of the journal's limited circulation, the very fact that Tokyo was hosting a magazine published by Muslims was expected to have propaganda value in cultivating pro-Japanese sentiments within a Muslim audience.

Around the same time that *Yani Yapon Muhbiri* began publication in 1933, several other attempts at networking with the Muslim world were promoted with the support of the Japanese army in Manchuria. These new attempts benefited from the contacts Kokuryûkai had established in the Muslim world and the Turkish Tatar diaspora network in East Asia. In a daring experiment in 1933, a prince from the abolished Ottoman dynasty, Abdül Kerim Efendi (1904–1935) was invited to Japan, presumably to consider his potential contribution to Japan's policy toward the Muslims of Central Asia in case of a conflict with the Soviet Union. Although the plan was soon abandoned, it exemplified the reckless and unrealistic projects that Asianists were willing to consider at the expense of jeopardizing Japan's diplomatic relations with the Turkish Republic.[65] In the same year, Abdurreşid İbrahim, the famous pan-Islamist whose travel memoirs more than two decades earlier had popularized a pro-Japanese image in the Muslim world, currently leading an isolated and uneventful life in Turkey, received an invitation to visit Tokyo. İbrahim collaborated with the Asianist projects reaching out to the Muslim world until his death in 1944 in Tokyo.[66]

It was also in 1933 that several high-level military and civilian leaders established the Greater Asia Association (Dai Ajia Kyôkai).[67] The Greater Asia Association not only promoted regional unity in East Asia but also advocated solidarity among West and Southeast Asian societies. Konoe Fumimaro, General Matsui Iwane, and General Ishiwara Kanji were among its prominent members.[68] The Greater Asia Association published a monthly journal titled *Dai Ajia Shugi* (Greater Asianism), which became the most important pan-Asianist journal during that period, offering a wide range of news and opinion articles covering all of Asia, including Muslim West Asia, Southeast Asia, and Central Asia. Ôkawa Shûmei, Nakatani Takeyo,[69] Rash Behari Bose and many Asianist figures in the military frequently wrote for this journal. The content and discourse of *Dai Ajia Shugi* became an influential source in shaping the official language of pan-Asianism during the late 1930s, influencing the "New Order in East Asia" proclamation of the Konoe Fumimaro cabinet in 1938.[70]

The discourse of Asian identity represented in *Dai Ajia Shugi* was perfectly in harmony with the broader Asia view of Ôkawa Shûmei's ideology, as it seemed to regard India and the Muslim world as just as important as East and Southeast Asia. Taking this continental Asia perspective, *Dai Ajia Kyôkai* made an important contribution to Asianist thought with its introduction of news and information about the political, economic, and social trends of the entire Asian world, from China and India to Iran and Turkey.[71] In foreign policy, *Dai Ajia Shugi* was highly anti-British and, strikingly, not anti-American. Discussions of the conflict and clash of interests between England and Japan started as early as 1933,[72] and gradually the journal's call for a new world order turned to a more radical rejection of European hegemony in Asia. The journal, however, did not carry any vision of conflict with the United States that could have indicated the path to war. Beginning in 1938, it actively promoted the concept of "New Asia," offering enthusiastic intellectual support for the government's declaration of the "New Order in East Asia."[73]

Despite the journal's endorsement of cooperation among Asian nations, there was no genuine dialogue with Asian intellectuals and nationalist movements in the pages of *Dai Ajia Shugi*. When it claimed to present an Asian perspective, the journal always consulted the same small group of exiled nationalists in Japan.[74] This artificial perspective tended to give the journal a self-congratulatory tone, which became typical of Japanese pan-Asianism during the late 1930s; Japanese readers received the impression that Asian nationalists eagerly looked to Japan for leadership. In reality, expectation of Japanese leadership against Western colonialism was much weaker among the nationalist movements of the 1930s compared to the period in the aftermath of 1905. Still, the journal tried to convince the Japanese public that pan-Asianism could be a plausible and positive alternative to the declining Eurocentric world order in Asia.[75]

In addition to the boom of journals and organizations, an increasing degree of networking with different Asian countries took place, primarily involving students and intellectuals. When one of Indonesia's most prominent nationalist leaders, Muhammad Hatta, visited Japan in 1933, he was showered with media attention and received an enthusiastic welcome from the Greater Asia Association as the "Gandhi of the Netherlands East Indies." Hatta had previously expressed criticism of Japanese imperialism in China following the Manchurian Incident; however, after his trip, he moderated his position on the Japanese "return to Asia" and advocated Indonesian cooperation with the liberal, progressive, and idealistic segments of Japanese society, suggesting that Indonesian nationalists should challenge the Japanese to be sincere in their pan-Asianist rhetoric. During his visit to Japan in the fall of 1935, Ahmad Subardjo, another Indonesian nationalist leader, expressed his belief that Japan's withdrawal from the League of Nations and the revival of the pan-Asianist discourse represented a very positive turning point in Asian history. It is important to note that, despite their cautious approach to Japan's official Asianism, neither Hatta nor Subardjo had anything positive to say about the League of Nations.[76] Meanwhile, various Asianist organizations tried to increase the number of Indonesian students attending Japanese universities, with most of these students becoming members of pan-Asianist organizations during their stays in Japan.

In 1934 the Japanese government established a semiofficial agency, Kokusai Bunka Shinkōkai (Society for International Cultural Relations), with the purpose of introducing Japanese culture to other parts of the world and improving cultural ties with European, American, and Asian societies.[77] Although the initial focus of the organization emphasized Europe and the United States, Kokusai Bunka Shinkōkai gradually expanded the funding it devoted to cultural interactions with Asian societies.[78]

As the number of cultural and political associations, journals, and books focusing on Asia grew dramatically after 1933, the Japanese public's interpretation of international events began to be shaped more by their consciousness of racial difference and Asian identity. The best example of the power that an internationalist race identity held over the Japanese imagination was the popular reaction to the Italian invasion of Ethiopia, when strong pro-Ethiopian sentiments caused problems for Japan's diplomatic relations with Italy. The mainstream Japanese media was full of anti-Italian and pro-Ethiopian commentaries, with references to the conflict as another instance of the struggle between the white race and colored races.[79] Such overwhelming sympathy for the Ethiopian resistance caused diplomatic tension between Japan and Italy, despite the Japanese Foreign Ministry's policy of keeping good relations with Italy.[80] Meanwhile, the highly pro-Ethiopian public response to the Ethiopian crisis attracted the attention of African American intellectuals, prompting a visit to Japan by W. E. B. Du Bois. The warm reception Du Bois met during his visit to Manchuria and Japan, combined with his perception of a genuine Japanese public interest in the struggle of Africans and African Americans, convinced him of the sincerity behind Japan's claim for leadership of the colored races. Du Bois continued to write about the legitimacy of Japan's actions in Asia in the framework of the importance of race in international affairs, even in the face of Japanese atrocities in China. Predictably, pro-Japanese comments by Du Bois were given great coverage in Japanese papers in a self-righteous affirmation of Japanese policies.[81]

Overall, the small group of Japan's Asian collaborators, together with the Asian and African American intellectuals who expressed support for Japan's Asianist projects, were very important in allowing Japanese intellectuals to convince themselves that their ideas of the New Order in East Asia and the Greater East Asia Coprosperity Sphere were somehow different from Western imperialism. As Naoki Sakai has pointed out, the ideologues of Japan's official pan-Asianism manifested a kind of "narcissism" that impelled them repeatedly to quote those individuals who praised the Japanese or who hoped to receive support from Japan against Western colonial rule.[82] Through magnification of these manifestations of pro-Japanese expressions, many of which dated back to the decade after the Russo-Japanese War, Japanese leaders depicted the Japanese Empire as a Coprosperity Sphere that purported to represent the will of all its colonial subjects.

The very fact that such an elaborate attempt was made to find a moral explanation for Japanese expansionism in Asia stands as an indication that imperialism and the vision of a civilizing mission had already lost their currency in international diplomacy. When Japan first began the process of colonizing Taiwan and Korea and received rights in Manchuria, its policies could be justified in international law through references to the ideals of progress and development. In the starkly different international climate of the 1930s, the vocabulary of benevolent colonialism had to be replaced by the discourse of pan-Asian solidarity to justify Japanese imperialism. By 1940 there were many Japanese, especially in the young generation, who believed in their Asian identity and the discourses of Asian liberation propagated by multiple sources within Japan.[83]

ASIANIST IDEOLOGY OF THE 1930S

Pan-Asianism did not have a defined ideology or a systematic doctrine to which its followers and challengers could refer. Formulating an ideology that was both realistic and intellectually appealing proved to be the greatest challenge faced by official Asianism in the 1930s. Early pan-Asianism derived its appeal from its opposition to the intellectual foundations of the Eurocentric international order while claiming to be in harmony with Japan's national interest through the idea of regional leadership in the project of an Asian Monroe Doctrine. In the context of the 1930s, when pan-Asianist ideology took on a more assertive challenge to the Eurocentric world order, a new generation of intellectuals struggled to inject a degree of international legitimacy and realism into the idea of Asianism by modifying the content of the racial conflict thesis with reference to regionalism and geopolitics. Moreover, a strong tide of intellectual critiques of Western modernity during the 1930s ended up strengthening the anti-Western discourse of pan-Asianism.

The charter of Dai Ajia Kyôkai, promulgated in 1933 after Japan's withdrawal from the League of Nations, was a far cry from the cautious language of the early Asian Monroe Doctrine developed during the 1910s:

> In culture, politics, economics, geography, and race, Asia is a body of common destiny. The true peace, prosperity, and development of Asian peoples are fea-

sible only on the basis of their consciousness of Asia as one entity and an organic union thereof. . . . The heavy responsibility for reconstruction and ordering of Asia rests upon the shoulders of Imperial Japan. . . . Now the Manchurian Incident has provided another opportunity in human history for a great turning point. Imperial Japan has, happily, expanded the world-historical meaning of the Russo-Japanese War, and now is the time for Japan to concentrate all its cultural, political, economic, and organizational power to take one step toward the reconstruction and union in Asia. . . . The formulation of the Greater Asia Federation is the historical mission facing the Japanese people today.[84]

In the early stages after Japan's withdrawal from the League of Nations, scholars of international relations such as Kamikawa Hikomatsu and Rôyama Masamichi criticized the idea of Great Asianism advocated by Dai Ajia Kyôkai, calling it both unrealistic and anachronistic. They suggested that instead of pursuing an anti-Western vision of Asian solidarity, Japan should create a Far Eastern League using the League of Nations as its model. They devoted some attention to the idea of a regional version of the League of Nations in the Far East. This plan was based on a liberal internationalist agenda without any emphasis on the primacy of race and civilization.[85] At that stage, scholars like Rôyama Masamichi were maintaining their resistance to an increasingly pervasive Asianist tendency to analyze and reorder Japan's relations with the rest of the world in terms of racial and civilizational blocs and conflicts among them. Rôyama noted that he deliberately decided "not to give a leading position to the question of race and culture" in his writings and policy suggestions.[86] In the end, however, Rôyama Masamichi himself capitulated to this convention, offering realpolitik substance to the slogans of official pan-Asianism. He incorporated the idea of a distinct East Asian culture in his elaborate support of the New Order in East Asia, although it is true that the core of his arguments relied more on the concepts of regionalism.[87] Japan's liberal intellectuals could redefine the idea of East Asian community (kyôdôtai) as a form of regionalism that would bring about a rationalization of economic and social interaction in the region.[88]

Because of harsh critiques from leading Asian nationalists, such as Gandhi and Nehru, of Japanese policies in China during the 1930s, official Asianism was based on highly repetitive references to the events and ideas of the Asian internationalism of the 1905–1914 period, when there was an interest in Japanese leadership in different parts of Asia. One of the best examples of this attempt to overcome the emptiness of an imposed notion of Asian unity through references to early Asianism can be seen in the response Ôkawa Shûmei offered to the condemnation of Japanese Asianism by leaders of the Indian National Congress. Even at the time when Japan was sponsoring the Indian National Army's fight against British rule, both Gandhi and Nehru denounced Japanese colonialism in the name of Asian solidarity. In an open letter to them, Ôkawa recounted his experiences during WWI in joining Indian nationalists to campaign for the liberation of India, regardless of Japan's pro-Western policy at the time of the Anglo-Japanese Alliance. For Ôkawa, this historical background of Indian-Japanese collaboration showed that the ideals of official pan-Asianism during the Greater East Asia War had altruistic historical roots, reflecting a genuine interest in aiding the decolonization of Asia.[89] It was during such a search for the historical roots of Asianism that Okakura Tenshin was made an icon of pan-Asian thought. All of Okakura's works, including a previously unpublished manuscript from his 1901 trip to India called *Awakening of the East*, were published in both English and Japanese editions between 1938 and 1945.[90] In the same quest to reinvent early Asian internationalism, books by Ôkawa Shûmei, Paul Richard, and Taraknath Das from the period of WWI were reprinted after more than twenty years.[91]

    It was the presence of new converts from the socialist and liberal intellectual traditions, however, that succeeded in bringing new energy and vitality to Asianism. In the writings of Miki Kiyoshi, a leading member of the Shôwa Kenkyûkai, we can see the Asianist discourse of civilization in its most sophisticated formulation, polished with the German tradition of the philosophy of history.[92] According to Miki's representation, the over-Westernization of world cultures and the Eurocentric character of the social sciences posed a global political problem. Borrowing the self-critique of European thought during the interwar period, Miki expressed the conviction that Western civilization was in the process of self-destruction and could no longer dominate the fate of Asia. From this observation, he proceeded to the conclusion that Japan should uphold its civilizational mission to facilitate Asian unity and cooperation and eliminate Western colonialism. For Miki, Asian cooperation under Japanese leadership would serve the interests of peace and harmony, as well as liberation and racial equality.[93] Miki Kiyoshi's arguments drew on reflections on modernity and Eurocentrism in the writings of the interwar era in both Europe and Japan. Ultimately, however, they resembled the ideas of Okakura Tenshin and Ôkawa Shûmei in their basic tenet, namely, belief in the collapse of the Eurocentric world order and the corresponding necessity to offer an alternative order based on Asian values and political solidarity. Other converts to Asianism, such as the famous socialists Sano Manabu, Nabeyama Sadachika, and Akamatsu Katsumaro, offered their own interpretations of the content of pan-Asianist thought.[94] These former socialists described their perception of the world in terms of a division into a proletarian East and a bourgeois West. It was their belief that the fusion between the West, "reorganized by the proletariat," and the East, "awakened through the influence of Pan-Asianism," would create a new world order that would finally establish world peace and unity.[95] Their retreat from Comintern socialism was accompanied by a shift in allegiance to Asian internationalism.

What united the ideology of such diverse groups and figures as the Greater Asia Association, Ôkawa Shûmei, and the new converts to Asianism such as Miki Kiyoshi was the discourse of civilization central to all their arguments. Miwa Kimitada and Victor Koschmann have accounted for the differences among these pan-Asianist visions by making a distinction between esoteric and exoteric versions of Asianism. Popular organizations such as the Greater Asia Association presented the exoteric Asianism that had the power to appeal to Japanese public opinion, while Shôwa Research Institute intellectuals such as Miki Kiyoshi produced an esoteric version of Asianism that was more relevant to rational policy making and legitimization in the eyes of the presumed world public opinion. East-West civilization discourse, however, united both the more sophisticated scholarly elaborations of Asianism and those that appealed to the broader domestic public opinion. This explains the striking similarities between the pan-Asianist ideas of Ôkawa Shûmei and Miki Kiyoshi, despite their dramatically different intellectual and political backgrounds. Very much like Ôkawa Shûmei, Miki Kiyoshi based his argument on the conviction that Eurocentrism or Western civilization had to be overcome, while the civilizational legacy of Asia could become the basis for an alternative. Gradually, these ideas turned into well-known slogans, frequently repeated if not always clearly defined. The following ambiguous formulation by the Greater Asia Association summed up the slogans that were common to all versions of Asianism: "It goes without saying that the cultures of Europe are incapable of rescuing themselves any more, much less the world at large. The new potential power lies with the third civilization. It makes both Eastern and Western civilizations come alive through 'musubi' or harmonious combination. This is what can produce a new order in China, and Japan may rightfully serve as a catalyst for this combination."[96]

The central tension in world politics, according to this Asianist discourse of civilization, was between East and West, and thus Asianism helped serve to reduce all world conflicts to this reductionist framework. Once the war between Japan and the United States started, such rhetoric served a very useful political purpose by placing the focus on the conflict with the Western powers and covering up the sense of guilt some Japanese may otherwise have felt about their country's aggression in China. Thus a great number of Japanese intellectuals were relieved after the outbreak of war with the USA. They could mobilize their ideas for the glorification and justification of the Pacific War in the name of overcoming modernity and East-West confrontation. For example, the participants in the famous wartime conference "Overcoming Modernity" utilized a wide array of philosophies and theories to link Japan's military conflict with the intellectual attempts to overcome the problems of Eurocentric modernity.[97] It was thus the intellectual legacy of early Asianism in the form of a discourse of Asian civilization that created similarities between the ideology of old-time Asianists such as Ôkawa Shûmei and that of the new converts to Asianism during the 1930s, whose disparate beliefs converged in their obsessive and constant blaming of the imagined united West for the problems of the international order.

WARTIME ASIAN INTERNATIONALISM AND ITS POSTWAR LEGACY

Throughout the Pacific War, pan-Asianists like Ôkawa Shûmei devoted all their energies to the service of the Japanese state and the project of the Greater East Asia Coprosperity Sphere. In addition to publishing books and journals advocating the ideals of Asianism, Ôkawa continued to head the administration of the East Asian Economic Research Institute and to run his professional school.[98] Among these efforts, he saw it as particularly important to clarify Japan's war aims and explain the origins and goals of the Greater East Asia War. The main Asianist project Ôkawa Shûmei closely followed during the war was the establishment of the Indian National Army, an event that gave a sense of final achievement to Ôkawa as he had spent three decades advocating Japanese support for Indian independence.

The creation of the Indian National Army (INA) in 1942, with its ranks composed of Indian soldiers from the surrendered British troops in Singapore, became the most memorable project to embody pan-Asianist slogans. The INA was intended to fight alongside the Japanese army against the British forces at the Burmese-Indian border. It is now clear that the initial success of the Japanese plans for the creation of an Indian army can be attributed more to the contributions of idealistic Japanese figures on the ground than to any planning in Tokyo.[99] Major Fujiwara Iwaichi (1908–1986) gained the trust of Indian officers mainly through his own sincere commitment to the project. In fact, upon Fujiwara's departure, INA commander Mohan Singh soon disagreed with the new liaison officer and attempted to disband the 40,000-man army he had created.[100] The objection of Mohan Singh and other Indian officers to the appointment of Rash Behari Bose to the top position in the newly created army marked another point of crisis, one that shows the agency of Indian collaborators in the whole project.[101]

Subhas Chandra Bose's willingness to cooperate with Japan, followed by his secret submarine trip from Germany to Japan in 1942, saved the Indian National Army project, when it faced a crisis provoked by disagreement between the Japanese and Indian sides. Chandra Bose was a well-respected leader of the Indian nationalist movement who could both gain the loyalty of the Indian officers and assert authority over the Japanese liaison officers. For a long time, he had advocated cooperation with anti-British powers in order to win independence for India, in contrast to the policy of passive resistance advocated by Gandhi. He saw a great opportunity in German and Japanese support for the final liberation of India and willingly collaborated with both powers. Soon after his arrival in Singapore, Subhas Chandra Bose took over the leadership of the INA and formed the Provisional Government of Free India. Although the actual engagement between the Indian National Army and their British enemies at Imphal resulted in defeat for the Indian side, the mere existence of a provisional government and an army had a positive psychological impact on the Indian nationalist movement as a whole.[102]

From his arrival at Singapore until his death in a plane crash at the end of the Pacific War, Subhas Chandra Bose visited Tokyo several times during the course of the war. The speech he made as the leader of the Provisional Government of Free India at the Greater East Asia Conference in 1943 to the heads of state of six recognized independent nations of the Coprosperity Sphere (Japan, China, Manchuria, the Philippines, Burma, and Thailand) demonstrated the links between the failure of the League of Nations system and the New Order in East Asia that Japan had declared its intention to establish in the context of its war aims. Bose began his speech by recalling his frustration with the League of Nations: "My thoughts also went back to the Assembly of the League of Nations, that League of Nations along whose corridors and lobbies I spent many a day, knocking at one door after another, in the vain attempt to obtain a hearing for the cause of Indian freedom." [103] According to Bose, the Greater East Asia Conference organized by the Japanese government as an alternative to the League of Nations was receptive to nationalist voices in Asia in a way none of the European-centered international organizations had ever been. Meanwhile, Chandra Bose gave several radio speeches and lectured to the Japanese public, helping to enhance the popular Japanese confidence in the liberation mission of the Pacific War.

What pan-Asianists like Ôkawa Shûmei never realized was that, for nationalist leaders like Subhas Chandra Bose, pan-Asianism was merely one of the means to reach national independence, not a goal in itself.[104] In one of his conversations with Ôkawa Shûmei about the future of the Indian national movement, Subhas Chandra Bose talked about the possibility of receiving Soviet support against the British Empire if Germany was defeated on the European front. Ôkawa was surprised that Bose could think of cooperating with the Soviets and asked him why he would collaborate with the Soviet Union if he was against Communism. In response, Bose pointed out that he was prepared "to shake hands even with Satan himself to drive out the British from India."[105] It did not occur to Ôkawa that Japan might well be one Satan with whom Chandra Bose had to cooperate. In fact, Chandra Bose saw Japan as a different ally from Russia or Germany because of the Asian identity common to both India and Japan. In the end, however, Bose's nationalist agenda was the main motive for collaboration, rather than a vision of Asian regionalism under Japanese leadership. In a sense, the legitimacy of wartime pan-Asianism intimately depended on the idea of national self-determination.

For Ôkawa Shûmei, on the other hand, Asian decolonization was unthinkable in the absence of Japan's unique mission to lead the free Asia. He refrained, however, from stating specifically what kind Asian federation would replace the old order. Unsurprisingly, Ôkawa's vision of the future Asia was ambiguous, and his wartime writings focused more on the history and ideology of Asianism. The Japanese government, on the other hand, had to clarify its war aims and postwar visions much more clearly than Ôkawa did, especially in response to the appeal of the Atlantic Charter. Initially, the Japanese leaders defined the first stage of the new world order they envisioned for Asia—namely, the expulsion of Western hegemony and the elimination of Western interests—without actually specifying clearly what would happen after the Western powers were gone. They assumed that, once Western exploitation was over and trade between Asian nations was established, Asia would develop very fast. They also hoped that the new Asia would cooperate with a German-dominated Europe to create a world order based on regional economic blocs.[106] As Japanese leaders hoped to get the further cooperation of local nationalist movements during the later stages of the war, they eventually clarified their own war aims as an alternative to the Atlantic Charter.[107]

As the declarations of the 1926 Nagasaki pan-Asiatic conference had looked similar to the principles of the League of Nations, so the Greater East Asia Conference declaration also looked like a modification of the Atlantic Charter, with slight alterations affording sensitivity to the cultural traditions of non-Western societies. For example, the principles declared on November 7, 1943, in Tokyo affirmed the national self-determination of Asian societies, with the only major difference from the Atlantic Charter being a call for the "abolition of racial discrimination" and the cultivation of Asian cultural heritages.[108] During the Greater East Asia War, the fierce competition between the Allied Powers and Japan in propaganda battles and psychological warfare had accelerated the pace of decolonization. Not only did Japan feel the need to respond to the Atlantic Charter, but the Allied Powers also had to respond to the pan-Asianist challenge to the interwar period colonial order. For instance, the U.S. Office of Strategic Services (OSS) reports on the psychological warfare in the Southeast Asia held that Japan's Asianist propaganda was generally very successful. In response, the OSS suggested that the vision of a United Nations organization and a new world order should be emphasized, taking care not to make any reference to the continuation of the British, French, and Dutch empires.[109] More important, there was a growing awareness among the wartime leaders of the U.S. government, including President Roosevelt, that they had to counter the widespread pan-Asian notions of solidarity spread by Japan by offering a new vision of postwar order at least recognizing the national demands of India and China. There was also a second concern beyond the competition with Japan: how to get the support of China and later India in the postwar international order. These concerns led to recognition that the pre-WWII colonial discourses of racial inferiority and the reality of the colonial subjugation of India and China should not continue, even if Japan were punished by a national-racial isolation.[110] It is against the background of this concern with pan-Asianism that Roosevelt formulated his recommendations to Churchill to give India more self-government in order to improve the war efforts against Japan.[111]

As a matter of fact, after the end of the Greater East Asia War, the prewar imperial order would not be reestablished. When Ôkawa Shûmei listened to the emperor's radio announcement of Japan's surrender, on August 15, 1945, he thought that four decades of his work "toward the revival of Asia [had] disappeared like a soap bubble."[112] Yet, although it was true that Japanese pan-Asianism as a political movement would disappear, the decolonization of Asia would be completed by the 1950s. More important, the Asianist discourse of an East-West civilizational conflict would likewise survive the post-WWII period.

The period immediately after WWII witnessed nationalist revolutions in Indonesia and Vietnam fighting against the returning Dutch and French colonialism. Even in India, despite Chandra Bose's death in a plane crash and the dissolution of his army at the end of WWII, the Indian national movement rushed to the moral and legal defense of the officers of the Japanese-sponsored Indian National Army, who were indicted for treason against the British Empire. As Tilak Raj Sareen wrote, the trial of the INA officers revitalized the nationalist movement in India, actually creating a new turning point in the Indian national movement, demoralized after WWII.[113] Meanwhile, at the Tokyo War Crimes Tribunal, the whole legacy of the prewar Asian discourse of civilization came to be played out in full during the conflict of opinion between the Indian Radhabinod Pal and the other judges.

Ôkawa Shûmei was indicted as a Class A war criminal by the Tokyo War Crimes Tribunal based on his role as an ideologue of right-wing pan-Asianism. Both the prosecution and the final verdict used Ôkawa's writings extensively in the construction of their case charging the accused Japanese leaders with conspiracy to commit aggression, even though charges against Ôkawa himself were dropped when he was diagnosed with brain syphilis in the early stages of the tribunal. While the majority of judges found the accused Japanese leaders guilty of the charges, Judge Radhabinod Pal wrote a long dissenting opinion asserting that the Japanese decision-making leading up to the Pacific War did not constitute a crime in international law. It is a testimony to Radhabinod Pal's expertise in international law and his sharp political and legal acumen that his long dissenting opinion is now as well remembered as the Tokyo Tribunal itself. The substance of Pal's dissenting judgment derived from his ideas of international law and his commitment to a just trial untainted by the politics of "victor's justice." It is also evident, however, that Pal's background in colonial Bengal and his sympathies for the Indian National Army under the leadership of Subhas Chandra Bose had an impact on the content of his dissenting judgment. This background may have also influenced his failure to speak out against the use of his dissenting judgment by Japanese right-wing revisionists.

Richard Minear and John Dower have agreed with many of Pal's legal arguments in their discussion of the neocolonial context of the Tokyo Tribunal and their critique of the negative impact of the Tokyo trial on both international justice and Japan's acceptance of the responsibility for the Pacific War.[114] As Timothy Brook has demonstrated, however, Justice Pal's anticolonial sensibilities led him to refrain from making any meaningful judgment on Japan's responsibility for the Nanking Massacre.[115] Radhabinod Pal's anticolonial stance led him to withhold comment on Japan's war crimes against Chinese civilians in Nanking. The majority of the judges, on the other hand, condemned Japanese imperialism in the name of international justice at the same time that Western powers were trying to reestablish their colonial hegemony.[116] Thus, in a sense, the color lines that pan-Asianism emphasized were acted out in an ironic way on the benches of the Tokyo Tribunal, indicating one of the many ways the legacies of the pan-Asianist discourse of civilization and race survived in the postwar period, shaping the perception of both the cold war and decolonization in contemporary history.

CONCLUSION

Japanese pan-Asianism gained unprecedented official support among the elites of the Japanese Empire in the aftermath of the Manchurian Incident and Japan's decision to withdraw from the League of Nations. The Japanese government declared its "return to Asia" by appropriating an already existing pan-Asianist alternative to the Eurocentric world order only when its empire was challenged internally by nationalist movements and externally by the other great powers. The very fact that Japan's realist elites saw something practical and useful in the pan-Asian slogans and networks to help justify the multiethnic Asian empire of Japan indicates both the continuing intellectual vitality of Asianist critiques of the interwar-era world order and the potential appeal of the Asianist slogans of East-West relations and racial identity to broader Japanese public opinion. Pan-Asianism allowed the Japanese Empire to implement more rigorous and inclusive assimilation policies and exhibit a high level of international confidence and self-righteousness in an era when imperialism was globally delegitimized. Yet it was partly a nostalgic and narcissistic ideology, making frequent references to the post-1905 Asian nationalist admiration of Japan without recognizing the fact that both the nature of nationalism and the image of Japan had changed dramatically from 1905 to the late 1930s.

Japanese pan-Asianists saw a great opportunity in the unexpected patronage of their ideas by the Japanese government and military authorities after 1933. Throughout the 1930s, the radical anti-Western tradition within Asianism was focused on the end of European empires in Asia, especially on the weakness of British Empire, without advocating or recommending any Japanese challenge to the United States. Pearl Harbor was thus an undesirable development for pan-Asianists in Japan, even though they rushed to glorify and justify it via a discourse of East-West civilizational or yellow-white racial conflicts. Meanwhile, new converts to Asianism from different segments of Japanese intellectual life added practical and policy-oriented content to the ambivalent slogans of Asian solidarity via social science theories of regional cooperation and multiethnic communities. Despite its internal paradoxes and its tensions with the logic of Japanese imperialism, pan-Asianism nevertheless allowed Japan to conduct a relatively successful propaganda campaign against the Western imperialism in Southeast Asia while motivating numerous idealist Japanese activists and their collaborators. Pan-Asianist propaganda, accompanied by Japan's own imperial expansion during WWII, did contribute to the end of Western empires, partly by forcing the Allied powers to formulate and promise a more inclusive and nonimperialistic world order at the end of WWII.

8

CONCLUSION

THE IDEA OF the West was not first born in Europe and simply spread to other parts of the world. It was partly a product of reflection and rethinking by non-Western reformist intellectuals during the nineteenth century. While we are familiar with the grand theories on the civilization of the West formulated by Montesquieu and other European thinkers, we should recognize that non-Western intellectuals found these theories insufficient and noninclusive and insisted on a more universalist interpretation of the secrets of Europe's progress. The result, as best seen in the writings of Fukuzawa Yukichi and Namık Kemal during the 1870s, was an optimist reformist ideology of progress and civilization that refuted any permanent association of universal civilization with climate, Christianity, race, or even imperialism. This global vision of non-Western intellectuals tied their reform projects to a fine formulation of the relationship between a vision of universal civilization and the historical experience of Europe that exhibited the culmination of this universal process of progress. Their vision of a universal West was closely linked with a desire to become equal members of the perceived civilized international society and to benefit from the security and prosperity this globalizing international society promised.

From the 1870s onward, even when Ottoman and Japanese intellectuals formulated critiques of aspects of European and American policies and societies, they began to frame this critique with reference to abstract universal ideals that they thought the intellectuals of the Western world would support. After the modernist rupture in Ottoman and Japanese thought, there was no rejection or critique of the West as an other or threat unworthy of respect. The idea of a universal West could no longer be ignored or rejected, even when European states and the Westernization process were criticized.

Anti-Western visions of world order were born of this non-Western idea of a universal West around the 1870s. The contradictions of the civilizing mission ideology and the crisis in the legitimacy of the imperial world order spawned the alternative visions of pan-Islamic and pan-Asian thought. Modern anti-Western discourses emerged originally to criticize the imperialist West for violating its own proclaimed standards of civilization. With the era of high imperialism in European history, symbolized by the British occupation of Egypt in 1882 and the subsequent scramble for Africa, non-Western intellectuals observed a dramatic change in the character of international society and its legitimacy structures, perceiving a more aggressive imperial West that did not abide by the standards of civilization. More important, the strengthening of the Christian and white-race identity in Europe led to a new European discourse of civilization, which proclaimed that no matter what reforms Chinese, Muslims, and Japanese implemented, they could never be equal to the Western societies because of the inferiority of their religion or their standing as members of the colored races. Precisely when Ottoman and Japanese elites were asking to universalize the international society by making it inclusive of non-Christian and nonwhite members, the new discourse of European racial and civilizational superiority was utilized to justify a more aggressive imperial world order as well as a more Christian, white, Western-defined notion of progress and modernity.

The contradictions between the Orientalist and racial ideologies of the high age of imperialism and the demands and expectations of non-Western elites for equality, autonomy, and inclusion facilitated a global debate on the characters, merits, and values of multiple civilizations, such as Western, Islamic, Indian, and Chinese. The idea of the existence of multiple world civilizations, with varying capacities and values, was initially proposed by Orientalists and empire apologists in Europe intent on proving the superiority of the West. But non-Western reformists and anti-colonial nationalists soon redefined and reemployed these imperial ideologies of civilization, sometimes with the help of European scholarship, to assert the equality of non-Western civilizations to the ideal Western one. Thus Orientalist categories of knowledge that posited a sharp distinction between East and West, Islam and Christianity, and whites versus the colored races were preserved in the anti-Western critiques of Ottoman and Japanese intellectuals. In the global debates on multiple civilizations, the argument of a standard of civilization never disappeared. Yet it took a new form when Muslims sought to prove that certain seemingly uncivilized aspects of the Islamic civilization were either a result of Western misinterpretation and misrepresentation or a cultural difference that did not violate the essential compatibility between Islam and modern civilization. Similarly, Japanese intellectuals asserted Japan's equality with the West by emphasizing the legacy, greatness, and values of the Chinese or Asian civilization. In that sense, the literature on civilizations has always been intimately related to the debates on the normative values and power relations of a dynamic but unequal international order.

When the Eurocentric world order in the age of high imperialism experienced a loss of legitimacy, non-Western intellectuals developed two major lines of thinking and critique. On the one hand, both Ottoman and Japanese intellectuals separated the project of modernity from its Western application, thus further universalizing it. There were always different, and competing, projects of refashioning Eurocentric modernity among non-Western intellectuals. It was during this process that both a reactionary anti-Westernism and a naive West imitationism emerged as ideal-typical constructs that never matched the complexity of the process of translation and rethinking of the West in Ottoman Turkey and Japan. None of the Ottoman and Japanese intellectuals truly denied the necessity and inevitability of learning from Western modernity, even though many underlined the insufficiency of the West as a model for every aspect of reform. Similarly, no Ottoman and Japanese intellectuals believed they could completely transform into cloned Westerners in Eastern lands. Within the diversity of Ottoman and Japanese intellectuals, the ideal of locally reinterpreted and negotiated modernity became the mainstream position, first in practice and later on in theory as well.

On the other hand, as the process of refashioning modernity continued, through competing projects, pan-Islamic and pan-Asian intellectuals began to criticize the imperialist West for violating its own standards of civilization. Thus they used the legitimating values of Western hegemony, especially the notion of civilized norms, against the excesses of Western powers in international affairs. Many Ottoman and Japanese intellectuals were able to challenge the Western discourse of the civilizing mission with regard to their own societies, while they could easily mobilize the same discourse either in domestic reforms or in imperial expansion, a self-contradiction that accompanied anti-Western visions of world order. The critique of the imperialist West with reference to the ideals of the Enlightenment West, however, created synergies in the global public sphere that shaped the notion of a shared destiny of non-Western nations around the redefined metageographical categories of Eastern and Western civilization, facilitating identity bonds among Japanese, Chinese, and Muslim West Asian intellectuals.

It is against the background of a worldwide debate on the ideas of race, empire, civilization, progress, and humanity from the 1880s to the 1900s that the Russo-Japanese War in 1905 became a truly global moment, as interpretations of the meaning of the Japanese victory empowered non-Western nationalists and their critique of the Eurocentric world order. By shattering the discourse of the racial and civilizational superiority of the West over the East, and thus the legitimacy of European hegemony, the Russo-Japanese War confirmed that non-Western societies, if they followed the path Japan had taken, could indeed fulfill all the standards of civilization within a very short period of time. In some ways, the Japanese success in modernization proved that the promises of Western modernity were universal and applicable everywhere, irrespective of race, religion, and geography. In that sense, the moment of the Russo-Japanese War was Westernist, and it inspired pro-Western constitutionalist movements in Turkey, Iran, and China. The jubilant excitement of the Asian nationalists over the Japanese achievement was not about creating an alternative to the Western model of modernization. On the contrary, it was aimed at confirming the universality of modernity and the equality of all races in international affairs, a confirmation that contradicted the civilizing mission ideology of the European and American empires. The slogans of the "Asian Awakening," which was identified with the period from the Russo-Japanese War to the outbreak of WWI in the writings of both Asian nationalists and European observers of Asia, already signaled the impending end of the Eurocentric world order.

The idea of an Asian awakening symbolized by the Russo-Japanese War also strengthened the alternative discourses of civilization formulated by pan-Asianist and pan-Islamic thinkers and contributed to the decolonization process. The example of Japan's achievement of equality with the Western powers through military victory led to the view that Asian nationalists needed to gather military power through alliances against the Western powers in an international order devoid of moral principles. Intellectually, the Russo-Japanese War allowed nationalist and reformist intellectuals in Asia to resolve the tension between belief in the scientific values of social Darwinism and Spencerian determinism, on the one hand, and the desire to establish the equality of Asia with the West, on the other.

The impact of WWI on alternative visions of world order, especially pan-Islamic and pan-Asian thought, thus has to be considered from the standpoint of Asian understanding of the 1904–1914 period as an era of Asia's revival and awakening. By 1914 Ottoman and Japanese intellectuals had already developed their alternative discourse of civilization, which held that East and West both had value and their synthesis or harmony would result in a higher level of civilization in a Hegelian fashion. In that sense, Asian consciousness of the era as the "Awakening of the East" shaped the political implications of the perception of WWI as the "Decline of the West." Both pan-Islamic and pan-Asian thinkers believed in a potential East-West synthesis by non-Western nationalism. Gradually, together with the idea of Western decline, the value of the East in the ambiguous yet popular slogan of East-West synthesis increased. It is at this juncture that Ottoman and Japanese intellectuals refined their own notions of race, culture, civilization, nation, and universality, some more sophisticated than European theories in terms of addressing the question of both the indispensability and insufficiency of the European model.

The widespread perception of international relations as a conflict between Crescent and Cross or as an encirclement of the Muslim world by a modern European Crusade played a crucial role in convincing the Ottoman public and the Ottoman political elite finally to endorse pan-Islamic projects as a realist policy option. Disillusioned by the response of European international society to the Italian invasion of Libya in 1911 and the Balkan wars of 1912, segments of the Ottoman public-opinion elite depicted a realist pan-Islamism as a last resort of hope for the survival of the Ottoman state and the autonomy of the Muslim world. In fact, frequent critiques of the pro-Western Tanzimat diplomacy in the aftermath of the 1912 Balkan wars indicate the pessimistic mood of the Ottoman elite about the survival of the Ottoman state through appeals to international law and the policy of cooperation with the Western powers. This climate of opinion contributed to the Ottoman government's decision to enter WWI on the side of Germany against the British, French, and Russian empires, the three empires that had large populations of Muslims under their colonial rule.

The Ottoman government's utilization of pan-Islamism during WWI should not be seen as a triumph of the utopian and radical ideals of Islamic solidarity among the Western-educated Ottoman decision-making elite. It was rather an indication of the general legitimacy crisis of the world order, which pushed the Ottoman leaders, who came from a tradition of realist assessment of world trends and European diplomacy since the Tanzimat era, to decide that a pan-Islamic challenge to the Eurocentric world order, in alliance with Germany, was the only way to end the Western imperial assault on the Muslim world. The Ottoman government's turn to pan-Islamism was not a reflection of a Muslim conservative reaction against the West but rather a symbol of the failures of the Eurocentric international society, which had forced an important Muslim-ruled state member of this society to formulate a radical alternative.

A similar estrangement from the West occurred among Japanese intellectuals and elites during WWI, despite the fact that the Japanese government entered the Great War on the side of the British Empire and did not endorse any pan-Asianist project. Pan-Asianist arguments that advocated an end to cooperation with the great powers became influential in Japanese public opinion during WWI especially because of the perception that, as a yellow race, Japan would never be treated equally by its white superpower allies. Moreover, during WWI, pan-Asian thought shifted from defensive culturalism to the assertion of a distinct Asian civilizational identity as an equal alternative to the West. When wartime Japanese pan-Asianists like Ôkawa Shûmei or the Indian pan-Asianist

Rabindranath Tagore advocated the revival of Asian values and culture as an essential precondition for the decolonization of Asia and search for equality with the West, they were also relying on an influential current of romantic and pessimistic critiques of Western civilization in Europe and the United States, some representatives of which looked to Asia as a potential source of alternative civilization. In other words, the content of the discourse on the Asian civilization's alternative nature to the West was shaped partly by self-reflection and self-critiques within the West rather than by a general rejection of Western modernity.

The alternative discourse of civilization perpetuated by pan-Islamic and pan-Asianist thought via a reverse Orientalist notion of a morally superior East and a materialist West was confirmed by the collapse of imperial diplomacy and the civilized image of Europe on the modern battlefields of the war. Thus, on the one hand, WWI strengthened the confidence of Asian intellectuals that they could rely on their moral, spiritual, and religious traditions to create a new global modernity that could save not only Asia but also the decadent and declining European civilization. On the other hand, however, the emergence of two other internationalist alternatives to the imperial world order—the compromised version of Wilsonianism at the League of Nations and the socialist internationalism championed by the Soviet Union—weakened the appeal of pan-Islamic and pan-Asian internationalism for the rising nationalist movements of the 1920s.

Pan-Islamism lost its earlier practical focus when the Turkish parliament in Ankara abolished the institution of the caliphate in 1924. Similarly, pan-Asianist political projects seemed to face a dead end when no one in the government endorsed them and a new generation of nationalist leaders in Asia showed little interest in Japan-centered projects of Asian solidarity.

Two of the main arguments of the pan-Islamic and pan-Asian visions of world orders—namely, their emphasis on the illegitimacy of the imperial order and their vision of Eastern-Asian-Islamic civilization—became a property of the larger intellectual climate of Asia in the decade after the end of WWI. During the 1920s and 1930s, because of the high moral ground of rising nationalist movements, imperialism was already without any credible supporters. Moreover, the interwar-era discourse on Eastern and Western civilizations had become the property of various nationalist movements and was not necessarily anti-Western, as liberal internationalism and a whole array of new religious movements put forth the ideal of harmony among civilizations as their transcendent universal mission. For example, the so-called pro-Western liberal internationalists of Japan made no attempt to deny the importance and reality of racial differences and civilizational boundaries in the international relations of the post-WWI period. Liberals, however, diagnosed the tensions between civilizations and races as a problem to overcome through dialogue in the new international order. Pan-Asianists and pan-Islamists, on the other hand, believed that conflict between the West and Asia was inescapable, a thesis they based on their conviction that the white or Christian powers would never give up their superiority and imperial possessions in Asia through dialogue. In particular, interwar-era Japanese pan-Asianists believed in the inevitable victory of Asian nationalism against the "declining West" and saw an opportunity to defend national interests if Japan took a historical position on the winning side of this conflict, thus accelerating the "retreat of the West" to its own advantage.

The complex history of pan-Asian visions of world order and Japanese imperialism has to be considered within the changing notions of the legitimacy of the evolving world order. Pan-Asianism and the ideas of the Japanese national mission and interest did not seem contradictory before the emergence of Wilsonianism and socialist internationalism. After WWI, the contradiction between Japanese pan-Asianism and the practices of the Japanese Empire became more obvious parallel to the rise of anti-Japanese nationalist resistance in East Asia. During the 1920s, the Asianist political movement in Japan had to clarify its position with regard to Japanese colonial control over other Asian societies that were supposed to become comrades in the struggle against white/Western domination. Their inability to oppose Japan's own colonialism imperiled Japanese pan-Asianist attempts to establish links with rising nationalist movements, a fact best reflected in the failure of the Nagasaki pan-Asianist conference of 1926.

It would therefore be incorrect to characterize the official pan-Asianism of Japan after 1933 as a triumph of the Asian internationalism of the 1905–1914 period. Instead, its content should be viewed as a reinvention of Asianism in the context of Japan's post–Manchurian Incident legitimacy crisis. It is in this context that Japan's pan-Asianist links with non-Chinese Asia, including India, Indonesia, and the larger Muslim world, were supported, revived, and strengthened. The focus on Asianist links with West Asia, whether India or the Muslim world, became one of the ways to get around the obvious contradictions of Japan's policies in Korea and China. The official pan-Asianism of Japan after 1933 employed the internationalist legacy of Asianism but subverted it to legitimize Japanese imperialism. Imperialism itself had gone out of fashion, and in order to justify Japanese rule in China, other ideologies were needed. Pan-Asianism could claim that Japanese imperialism was fulfilling the longtime expectations of Asian nationalists and divert attention from Japan's own expansion in China to the memory of Asia's confrontation with Western expansion and to a general critique of Eurocentrism in history, social theory, and culture. Ironically, the best way for Japan to act as an imperialist power in the changed political and ideological climate of the 1930s was to adopt the language of anti-imperialism. Instead of seeing this as a peculiarity of Japanese imperial style, however, we should remember that all forms of internationalisms, including liberal and socialist ones, are susceptible to such utilization by imperial projects.

Overall, the histories of pan-Islamic and pan-Asianist visions of world order show that their anti-Westernism cannot be reduced to a conservative reaction against the liberal and democratic values of the West. Nor, however, can they be classified as automatic responses to Western imperialism. Both of these two opposing assessments have to be modified to accord with the changing imagery of the West in international history. The period from the mid-nineteenth century to the mid-twentieth century witnessed a radical transformation of both the global hegemony of the West and the meaning of Western civilization itself, a transformation that is crucial to understanding the anti-Western aspects of pan-Islamic and pan-Asianist thought.

The very fact that pan-Islamism and pan-Asianism developed as challenges to the European imperial expansion in Asia during the last quarter of the nineteenth century is not sufficient to understand its content and legacy. The rejection of the unequal power relations between Europe and Asia required a critique of the ethos of the West's "civilizing mission." Opposition to the Eurocentric imperial order through a critique of its legitimizing discourse of civilization created an enduring legacy of anti-Western thought. This defensive form of anti-Westernism, however, which was almost apologetic in its claims of equality between East and West, simultaneously endorsed the universality of Western modernity in its vision of future convergence between Europe and Muslim or non-Muslim Asia. Thus anti-Western visions of world order embodied in pan-Islamic and pan-Asian thought still made reference to universal values historically associated with the liberal and humanist traditions of the West, such as national autonomy, cultural diversity, and racial equality.

Anti-Westernism in Asia should also not be seen as a symptom of the Occidentalism virus originating in European romantic thought. Non-Western intellectuals developed several original ways of thinking about the West and its imperialism that later appropriated European romantic thought but could not be reduced to it. For example, it is only from the perspective of the global consciousness of non-Western intellectuals that we can understand why some of pan-Islamists and pan-Asianists were among the most enthusiastic admirers of Woodrow Wilson, despite their rejection of the League of Nations as an instrument for the reaffirmation of Western colonial hegemony. For them, the Wilsonian principles represented a moral critique of imperial power politics. Yet, at the same time, admiration of several representative figures of the Western world such as Wilson persisted alongside an essentializing rhetoric that saw the West as representing power politics devoid of universal ethics.

Several lessons from the history of pan-Islamic and pan-Asianist thought can help us understand the recent revival of civilizational identities and contemporary anti-Western discourses. The first warns us of the political repercussions of adopting the myth of homogeneity for any nation or civilization, an assumption that was central to both of these anti-Western visions of world order. The continental cultural geographies of East and West or the Islamic world and the Western world remained rigid, essential units in the internationalist imagination of pan-Asianists and pan-Islamists, though these civilizational categories were initially not their own inventions. Non-Western intellectuals' achievement in redefining and reemploying the discourse of civilization against Western hegemony in Asia made them very dependent on the epistemology of civilizational thinking.

Second, added to the myth of the homogeneity of Western civilization was the permanent association of the West with both modernity and the international order itself; this assumption, a legacy of the nineteenth-century ideology of Western supremacy, had become ingrained in pan-Islamic and pan-Asianist thought to the extent that all the critiques of the international system and the over-Westernization of global cultures were automatically phrased in terms of an anti-Western rhetoric. For pan-Islamists and pan-Asianists, the West did not just symbolize one culture out of a multitude of diverse global cultures. It also meant the global power of the white race and Christian Europe, an imperial international order, and an aggressive program of cultural change that could undermine the traditions of Asia or the Muslim world. For some non-Western intellectuals, this association engendered the practice of blaming the West for everything that went wrong in either the world system or the domestic social order.

Third, anti-Western critiques of pan-Asianists and pan-Islamists lost their progressive content when their audience became limited exclusively to the Japanese or Muslim public. Until 1914, some of the leading advocates of pan-Asianist and pan-Islamic thought, such as Rabindranath Tagore, Halil Halid, Said Halim Paşa, Sun Yat-sen, and Okakura Tenshin, were hoping to change Western policies toward the East by influencing Western public opinion through their progressive critiques. These non-Western critiques of the West did have some influence on European intellectuals. In fact, during the interwar period, many intellectuals in the West themselves became very critical of the imperial world order and the Westernization of the globe. Thus, when pan-Asianists like Ôkawa Shûmei wrote extensively about European colonialism and U.S. racism during the interwar period, they selectively overlooked the movements for self-reflection within the West. They followed the literature about the Western decline within Europe and the United States very closely but never treated this as an indication of the vibrancy and diversity of intellectuals and groups in the

West. Instead, they treated Western critiques of the West as confirmation of a holistic denial of Western civilization.

In general, given the lack of dialogue between Western and Asian intellectual communities, there was little opportunity for constructive and positive effects to arise from the pan-Islamic and pan-Asianists criticism of Western modernity and racism. In the absence of communication between critics and their targets, criticism merely affirms exclusionary loyalty to culture, nation, or immediate community. These problems were not specific to Ottoman or Japanese relations with the West, nor were pan-Islamists and pan-Asianists alone to blame for this state of mutual "dis-communication." Part of the problem can be located in the inequity that characterized the global public sphere and communication, which would not allow Asian or Muslim objections to Western violations of universal moral standards to reach Western audiences. In the absence of such international communication, all the progressive and humanist content in the non-Western critique of the West, rather than creating a dialogue that could represent a positive force of change, instead rebounded into a justification of nativist agendas.

Since the formative period of modern nationalist thought in the non-Western world occurred during the century extending from the 1860s to the 1960s, when Asian and African nationalists had to revolt against the West in order to fulfill the perceived and desired promises of universal modernity, various forms of the critiques of Western modernity, civilization, and imperialism became engraved into the foundational texts of non-Western nationalist thought. The memory of the imperial-era white race's injustice to the colored races or the historical memory of the Christian imperial injustice to the Muslim world became part of the narratives of state building and nationalist redemption in Asia. As these nationalist narratives about the imperial domination of the West over the East have been taught to new generations in postcolonial Asia, from Turkey, Egypt, and Iran to India, China, and even Japan, the memory of Western outsiders' humiliation of the yellow race or Muslims was kept alive throughout the postcolonial period. For example, when the leaders of the newly decolonized African and Asian nations met at the Afro-Asian Conference at Bandung in 1955, their speeches and statements reflected the continuing relevance of historical memories of colonial-era civilizational identities. Many delegates at the Bandung conference advocated the solidarity of non-Western peoples against the political collectivity called the West in a new pan-Arabic and pan-Asian rhetoric. Richard Wright, who attended the conference as the only African American journalist, expressed his astonishment at the speeches, characterizing the ideology of the conference in terms of a "Color Curtain," which, in his observation, had taken precedence in Asian politics even over the "Iron Curtain" of the cold war.[1] In the postcolonial period, the image of an untrustworthy and sinister West continued to exist as a trope in the intellectual histories of Asian societies, despite the fact that the international context that created this image had been radically transformed with the end of the Western empires.

The affirmation of a religious or racial identity, as seen in the emphasis on Islamic, Asian, or Eastern values, in the reverse Orientalist discourse of Eastern versus Western civilizations was both a strategic essentialism against the European discourses of race, Orient, and empire and a legacy of the universalism inherited from the non-Western humanistic traditions of Islam, Confucianism, or Buddhism. These intellectual imaginations contributed immensely to decolonization while becoming an essential part of the foundational texts of modern nationalism in Asia. It is therefore impossible to think of contemporary religious, national, and cultural movements in Asia without taking into account the legacy of the role played by pan-Islamic and pan-Asian discourses of civilization during nationalism's formative age, namely, the 1880s to the 1930s. In fact, the popularity of the theories of Toynbee and Huntington in the Middle East and East Asia derives from this historical thinking. Furthermore, this embedded legacy of reverse Orientalist narratives is at the heart of the controversies surrounding historical revisionism in Japan. Hayashi Fusao's claim that Japan's Greater East Asia War was a response to Western expansion after the Opium Wars and hence should be seen as a stage in a hundred-year Asian war benefits from the widespread acceptance of this East-West conflict narrative.[2] Both pan-Islamic and pan-Asian histories show that these narratives of a natural Eastern response to modern Western expansion are products of the 1890s and that the perception of events such as the Opium Wars, the invasion of Algeria, or the Indian Mutiny were different in their own times. In reality, the global image of the West changed several times, once around the 1880s and again at the end of WWI, though anti-Western formulations of the 1890s remained paradigmatic because of this era's stature as the formative age of nationalist thought.

Postwar moments of denying the legacy of pan-Islamic and pan-Asianist pasts by the Turkish and Japanese elites also reproduced the implicit Orientalist frameworks and became partly responsible for the revival of revisionism. Modern Turkey's attempt, in a "Leave the Muslim World" mood, to dissociate itself from the pan-Islamic experience of WWI still relied on an East-West civilizational framework, arguing that the Eastern-Islamic civilization was dead and could not be modern and thus there was no path for Turkey other than trying to become a member of the Western civilization. Similarly, post-WWII Japanese "Leave Asia" arguments, symbolized by the figure of Maruyama Masao, carried assumptions of Asia's inferiority in comparison to Japan's progress through Westernization. As Takeuchi Yoshimi has warned, this second "Leave Asia" movement, like the first one symbolized by Fukuzawa Yukichi, was as problematic as expansionist Asianism, because it carried the political implications of the paradigm of the progressive West versus the developing East.

When thinking about the international impact and intellectual contradictions of pan-Islamic and pan-Asian projects in history, there is a need to question the legacy of Orientalism that shaped both the content of these ideologies and our contemporary thinking about them. This book has tried to avoid reproducing the Orientalist dichotomy seen in the source material in two ways. First, I have tried to show the unrecognized parallels between the predominantly Muslim Middle East and non-Muslim East Asia and thus move the discussion away from the question of primordial religious and racial identities and demonstrate that modern Western colonialism and its intellectual justifications were neither a Christian conspiracy against Muslims nor a white-race conspiracy against the yellow race. The idea of a clash between the West and the Muslims or between the white and colored races was, rather, a product of global moments and processes in the age of high imperialism, and there can be a non-Orientalist reading of this history. Second, this book has tried to shed light on the genealogies of anti-Western discourses as well as the civilizational thinking around them by problematizing the strategies and contradictions of Asian intellectuals' reappropriation of Orientalism. From the 1880s onward, non-Western reformists became equally important in the global circulation of the ideas of East-West civilizational difference because they managed to employ the discourse of civilization for anticolonial and nationalist purposes.

The diagnosis of the problems in the international order that characterizes them as the product of conflicts and clashes among the values of different civilizational identities has survived through the end of the cold war. The overall completion of the decolonization process and opportunities for reconciliation and dialogue among intellectuals of colonized and colonizing nations could have dispelled the paradigms of the Christian West's injustice to the Muslim world and the humiliation of the colored races by the white race. In fact, there has been a concerted effort on the part of international institutions such as UNESCO to fight against the scientific pretensions and political legacies of racism. Yet, while we do not talk about the clash between the white and colored races anymore, the idea of a continuing conflict between Islam and the West never really disappeared during the cold war and notably reappeared during the 1990s in the context of discussions about a possible "clash of civilizations." The story of the survival and transformation of civilizational thinking about Islam and the West in the postcolonial period has complex reasons, ranging from the transmission of historical memory to the neocolonial realities of the post-WWII Muslim world, and as such it is a topic that deserves a separate monographic study.

The history of pan-Islamic and pan-Asian visions of world order until the 1940s, however, shows that anti-Westernism often reflected the global legitimacy crisis of the international system rather than a clash of civilizations. Similarly, the earlier period of anti-Westernism teaches us that, in understanding the contemporary roots of anti-Americanism, one should not focus attention only on marginal terrorist groups but listen to the critiques of mainstream Muslim intellectuals with regard to the failures of the international order and U.S. foreign policy. As the anti-Western thinkers of the earlier era emphasized the violation of so-called Western values by the Western powers, contemporary anti-American writings underline the contradiction between American values and American foreign policy. It is also true that there is an element of reverse Orientalism in both the anti-Westernism of the past and the anti-Americanism of today. The continuing reproduction of the polarity between East and West in contemporary critiques of the world system and its global inequalities relies on the legacy of the critique of Eurocentric hegemony by anticolonial nationalism and internationalism in Asia. Yet, beyond the discursive divisions, the response to both imperialism and anti-Western ideologies should rely on affirming shared universal values and strengthening international institutions that can implement global norms, not blaming one of the parties in the imagined civilizational geographies of the East or the West.

Culture and identity will continue to play a role in international relations and the perception of international problems. The idea of a dialogue of civilizations is therefore inspired by a noble goal and could play a role in defining and delimiting legitimate power. Yet the development of pan-Islamic and pan-Asianist thought teaches us that the very notion of civilizations in international affairs has a specific history that can be traced back to nineteenth-century globalization, imperialism, and decolonization. Awareness of this history and its legacy should alert us to common causes and shared values that bind our search for peace and equality in the international community despite and beyond the diversity of civilizational and religious identities.

NOTES

1. INTRODUCTION

1. For example, Bernard Lewis's best seller (*What Went Wrong? The Clash Between Islam and Modernity in the Middle East* [New York: Oxford University Press, 2002]) clearly emphasizes the argument of the essential incompatibility between Islam and modernity and claims that it was the legacy of a centuries-long Muslim-Christian conflict that led to contemporary Muslim anti-Westernism. For examples of books that relate anti-Westernism to responses to Western colonialism, see Stephen Kinzer, *All the Shah's Men: An American Coup and the Roots of Middle East Terror* (New York: Wiley, 2004), and Rashid Khalidi, *Resurrecting Empire: Western Footprints and America's Perilous Path in the Middle East* (New York: Beacon, 2005).

2. For an example of modern Chinese history, see Guy S. Alitto, *The Last Confucian: Liang Shu-ming and the Chinese Dilemma of Modernity* (Berkeley: University of California Press, 1986).

3. H. Bull, "The Revolt Against the West," in H. Bull and A. Watson, eds., *The Expansion of International Society* (Oxford: Oxford University Press, 1984), 217–228.

4. S. N. Hay, *Asian Ideas of East and West: Tagore and His Critics in Japan, China, and India* (Cambridge: Harvard University Press, 1970).

5. Ian Buruma and Avishai Margalit, *Occidentalism: The West in the Eyes of Its Enemies* (New York: Penguin, 2004).

6. For examples from Iranian history that show how colonialism and religious conservatism are not sufficient to explain the variant and complex roots of anti-Westernism, see Mehrzad Boroujerdi, *Iranian Intellectuals and the West: The Tormented Triumph of Nativism* (Syracuse, N.Y.: Syracuse University Press, 1996); Ali Gheissari, *Iranian Intellectuals in the 20th Century* (Austin: University of Texas Press, 1998); and Ali Mirsepassi, *Intellectual Discourse and the Politics of Modernization: Negotiating Modernity in Iran* (New York: Cambridge University Press, 2000).

7. As Richard W. Bulliet shows, the relationship between Islam and Christianity in history cannot justify any clash-of-civilization thesis. On the contrary, he makes a strong

case for understanding this relationship through the paradigm of a shared Islamo-Christian civilizational legacy. See Richard W. Bulliet, *The Case for Islamo-Christian Civilization* (New York: Columbia University Press, 2004).

8. Tetsuo Najita and Harry Harootunian, "Japanese Revolt Against the West: Political and Cultural Criticism in the Twentieth Century," in Bob Tadashi Wakabayashi, eds., *Modern Japanese Thought* (Cambridge: Cambridge University Press, 1998), 207–272.

9. Buruma and Margalit, *Occidentalism*.

10. Benedict Anderson, *Imagined Communities* (London: Verso, 1983). For a good discussion of the role of (mis)perceptions of the Other in international history, see Mark Bradley, *Imagining Vietnam and America: The Making of Postcolonial Vietnam: The Making of Postcolonial Vietnam, 1919–1950* (Chapel Hill: University of North Carolina Press, 2000).

11. Stefan Tanaka, *Japan's Orient: Rendering Pasts into History* (Berkeley: University of California Press, 1993); Furuya Tetsuo, ed. *Kindai Nihon no Ajia Ninshiki* (Kyoto: Jinbun Kagaku Kenkyûjô, 1994).

12. The writings of Norbert Elias, Oswald Spengler and Arnold Toynbee show the importance of the idea of civilization for relations both within Europe and with the rest of the world. See Norbert Elias, *The Civilizing Process: The Development of Manners* (New York: Urizen 1978); Oswald Spengler, *The Decline of the West,* ed. Arthur Helps (New York: Knopf, 1962); and Arnold Toynbee, *Civilization on Trial* (New York: Oxford University Press, 1948).

13. Jacob M. Landau, *The Politics of Pan-Islam: Ideology and Organization* (Oxford: Clarendon, 1990); Hans Kohn, *Pan-Slavism: Its History and Ideology* (New York: Vintage, 1960); P. Olisanwuche Esedebe, *Pan-Africanism: The Idea and Movement, 1776–1991* (Washington, D.C.: Howard University Press, 1994).

14. Takeuchi Yoshimi, "Hôhô to shite no Ajia," in *Nihon to Ajia* (Tokyo: Chikuma Gakujitsu Bunshô, 1993).

15. For the best discussion of the changing political nature of Japan's images of Asia, see Hashikawa Bunsô, "Japanese Perspectives on Asia: From Dissociation to Coprosperity," in Akira Iriye, ed., *The Chinese and the Japanese: Essays in Political and Cultural Interactions* (Princeton: Princeton University, 1980), 331–341.

16. Marius Jansen, *The Japanese and Sun Yat-sen* (Cambridge: Harvard University Press, 1954); Joyce Lebra, *Jungle Alliance: Japan and the Indian National Army* (Singapore: Donald Moore, for Asia Pacific Press, 1971); R. C. Bhardwaj, ed., *Netaji and the INA: A Commemorative Volume Brought Out to Mark the Golden Jubilee of the Indian National Army* (New Delhi: Lok Sabha Secretariat, 1994).

17. Prasanjit Duara, "The Discourse of Civilization and Pan-Asianism," *Journal of World History* 12, no. 1 (Spring 2001): 99–130.

18. This revisionism was popularized in *Puraido: Unmei no Shunkan* (Pride: The moment of destiny, Tôei Company, Tokyo, 1998), a recent and rather controversial movie on the Tokyo War Crimes Tribunal. The controversy the movie caused can best be followed through the editorial letters sent to the *Japan Times* by all the representative sides, including the Japanese right wing and Asian residents in Japan. For example, see "War Crimes Remain Unacknowledged," "Not Proud of a Nation in Denial," and

"First Seek Knowledge, then Speak Out" in "Letters to the Editor," *Japan Times,* June 2, 1999, 9.

2. THE UNIVERSAL WEST

1. Donald Keene, *Japanese Discovery of Europe, 1720–1830* (Stanford, Calif.: Stanford University Press, 1969); Bernard Lewis, *Muslim Discovery of Europe* (New York: Norton, 1982).

2. Locating the historical roots of the underdevelopment or late development of the Middle Eastern region in Ottoman arrogance and ignorance toward the Europe during the era of reformation, scientific revolution, and enlightenment was a predominant trope in the nationalist history writing of Turkey and postcolonial Arab states. For a harsh critique of Ottoman ignorance of Europe's scientific revolution by a late Ottoman and Republican era nationalist intellectual, see Adnan Adıvar, *Osmanlı Türklerinde İlim* (Istanbul: Remzi Kitabevi, 1982).

3. See Keene, *Japanese Discovery of Europe,* 123. Donald Keene quotes a conversation with Bernard Lewis as evidence of Muslim ignorance. Bernard Lewis's book on Muslim interest and representations of Europe carries the same basic argument of Muslim contempt and uninterest in Europe. See Lewis, *Muslim Discovery of Europe.*

4. Gabor Agoston, "Early Modern Ottoman and European Gunpowder Technology," in Ekmeleddin İhsanoğlu, Kostas Chatzis, and Efthymios Nicolaidis, eds., *Multicultural Science in the Ottoman Empire* (Turnhout, Belgium: Brepolis, 2003), 13–27.

5. For an example of the Ottomans' selective approach to European science and technology during the eighteenth century, see Ekmeleddin Ihsanoğlu, "The Introduction of Western Science to the Ottoman World: The Case Study of Modern Astronomy (1660–1860)," in Ekmeleddin Ihsanoğlu, ed., *Transfer of Modern Science and Technology to the Muslim World* (Istanbul: IRCICA, 1992), 1–44.

6. Niyazi Berkes, *The Development of Secularism in Turkey* (New York: Routledge, 1999).

7. Mustafa Sami Efendi, *Avrupa Risalesi* (Istanbul: Takvim-i Vekayi Matbaasi, 1840).

8. For an English language discussion of Yirmisekiz Mehmet Çelebi, see Fatma Müge Göçek, *East Encounters West: France and the Ottoman Empire in the Eighteenth Century* (New York: Oxford University Press, 1987).

9. Sadik Rıfat Paşa, *Müntehabat-i Asar* (Istanbul: Takvimhane-i Amire, 1858), 1–12.

10. Martin Bernal, *Black Athena: Afroasiatic Roots of Classical Civilization* (New Brunswick, N.J.: Rutgers University Press, 1987).

11. "The Concert of Europe" was a form of diplomacy established after the Congress of Vienna (1815) to maintain long-lasting peace in international politics. See Richard B. Elrod, "The Concert of Europe: A Fresh Look at an International System," *World Politics* 28, no. 2 (January 1976): 159–174.

12. For the universalist reflections of an eighteenth-century Ottoman intellectual and bureaucrat with regard to the Ottoman Empire and the emerging new world, see the discussion on the writings of Ahmed Resmi Efendi (1700–1783) in Virginia Aksan,

"Ottoman Political Writings, 1768–1808," *International Journal of Middle East Studies* 25, no. 1 (February 1993): 57–59.

13. Several contemporary historians interpreted the Westernism of Tanzimat leaders as deception of themselves and their subjects. See Coşkun Çakır, "Türk Aydınının Tanzimat'la İmtihanı: Tanzimat ve Tanzimat Dönemi Siyasi Tarihi Üzerine Yapılan Çalışmalar," *Türkiye Araştırmaları Literatür Dergisi* 2, no. 1 (2004): 13–15.

14. Aware of shared Hellenistic legacy with Europe, Ottoman intellectuals even translated Arabic versions of classical Greek texts during the 1718–1730 period to understand better the scientific developments in contemporary Europe. See Salim Aydüz, "Lâle Devri'nde Yapılan İlmi Faaliyetler," *Divan: İlmi Araştırmalar* 1, no. 3 (1997): 151–152.

15. H. L. Bulwer, *Life of Palmerston*, 3 vols. (London, 1870–1874), 2:298, quoted in M. E. Yapp, "Europe in the Turkish Mirror," *Past and Present*, No. 137, (November, 1992), 155.) For the connection and comparisons between Metternich and Ottoman reformists, see Ilber Ortaylı, "Tanzimat Bürokratları ve Metternich," in *Osmanlı İmparatorluğu'nda İktisadi ve Sosyal Değişim: Makaleler,* vol. 1 (Ankara: Turhan Kitabevi, 2000). Ortaylı rightly emphasizes that Tanzimat reformists were less reactionary and conservative than Metternich.

16. Berkes, *The Development of Secularism in Turkey,* 123–125.

17. Rifa'a Rafi' Tahtavi [Rifaah Rafi al-Tahtawi], *Paris Gözlemleri,* ed. Cemil Çiftçi (Istanbul: Ses Yayınları, 1992).

18. For a recent reassessment of Khayr al-Din Tunisi, see Syed Tanvir Wasti, "A Note on Tunuslu Hayreddin Paşa," *Middle Eastern Studies* 36, no. 1 (January 2000): 1–20.

19. Even in European definitions of interstate relations and international law, Hedley Bull notes a de-Christianization of language and identity during the first quarter of the nineteenth century. See Hedley Bull, *The Anarchical Society: A Study of Order in World Politics* (New York: Columbia University Press, 1995), 31–33.

20. Vasant Kaiwar and Sucheta Mazumdar, "Race, Orient, Nation in the Time-Space of Modernity," in Vasant Kaiwar & Sucheta Mazumdar, eds., *Antinomies of Modernity* (Durham, N.C.: Duke University Press, 2003), 270–271.

21. Ejder Okumuş, "İbn Haldun ve Osmanlı'da Çöküş Tartışmaları," *Divan: İlmi Araştırmalar* 4, no. 6 (1999): 183–209.

22. Montesquieu (1689–1755) wrote *The Spirit of Laws* (*De l'esprit des lois*) in 1752. See Charles de Secondat Montesquieu, *The Spirit of Laws* (Amherst, N.Y.: Prometheus, 2002).

François M. Guizot (1787–1874) first published *Histoire de la civilisation en Europe* in 1828. For a recent English language edition, see François M. Guizot, *The History of Civilization in Europe* (London: Penguin, 1997).

Henry Thomas Buckle's *History of Civilization in England* was first published in 1857 and became more influential for the intellectuals of the 1860s and 1870s. See below on the Japanese intellectual construction of a universal West.

23. Yapp, "Europe in the Turkish Mirror," 155; David Urquhart, *Turkey and Its Resources* (London: Saunders and Otley, 1833); Orhan Koloğlu, "Alexandre Blacque: Défenseur de l'état ottoman pour amour des libertés," in Hamit Batu and Jean-Louis Bacque-

Grammont, eds., *Empire Ottoman, la République de Turquie et la France*, (Istanbul: Isis, 1986), 179–95.

24. François, baron de Tott, *Memoirs, containing the state of the Turkish Empire and the Crimea, during the late war with Russia, with numerous anecdotes, facts, and observations, on the manners and customs of the Turks and Tartars* (London: G. G. J. and J. Robinson, 1786).

25. For the development of Ottoman interest in European civilization, see Ahmet Hamdi Tanpinar, *19uncu Asır Türk Edebiyatı Tarihi* (Istanbul: Çağlayan Yayınları, 1988), 37–128.

26. Tuncer Baykara, *Osmanlılarda Medeniyet Kavrami* (Izmir: Akademi Kitabevi, 1992).

27. Franz Rosenthal, *The Classical Heritage in Islam* (London: Routledge, 1992). For examples of the classical Muslim approach to a universal history of science and knowledge, one can look at the sections on pre-Islamic scientists, physicians, and philosophers in the classification of science and biography books in the Islamic tradition.

28. Cevdet Paşa's approach was partly shaped by Ibn Khaldun's legacy. Even his interest in Ibn Khaldun should be seen as deriving from an intellectual search to redefine universalism after the encounter with early nineteenth-century European liberal thought. See Ümid Meriç, *Cevdet Paşa'nin Cemiyet ve Devlet Görüşü* (Istanbul: Ötüken Yayınları, 1979).

29. Meriç, *Cevdet Paşa'nin Cemiyet ve Devlet Göörüşü*, 50–57, 84–85.

30. Perhaps recognizing this difficulty, Egyptian liberal reformist Rifaah Rafi al-Tahtawi used the term "*el-ümem'ül mutabarbire*" (barbarian nations) as the opposite of "civilization" and refrained from making any connections between savage peoples and Bedouin culture. See Nadia Abu-Zahra, "Al-Tahtawi as Translator of the Culture of Parisian Society: An Anthropological Assessment," in Ekmeleddin İhsanoğlu, ed., *Transfer of Western Science and Technology to the Muslim World* (Istanbul: IRCICA, 1992), 420.

31. Ussama Makdisi, "Ottoman Orientalism," *American Historical Review* 107, no. 3 (2002): 768–796.

32. Bull. *The Anarchical Society*, 32.

33. Bob Tadashi Wakabayashi, *Anti-Westernism and Western Learning in Early-Modern Japan: The New Theses of 1825* (Cambridge: Harvard University Press, 1986).

34. During the Tokugawa period, only Dutch merchants were allowed to trade between Europe and Japan, and some of them lived on a particular island off the port of Nagasaki. Dutch studies, *rangaku*, was the study of Dutch texts brought to Japan by those Dutch merchants, which triggered the interest in European knowledge.

35. Watanabe Hiroshi, "They Are Almost the Same as the Ancient Three Dynasties: The West as Seen Through Confucian Eyes in the Nineteenth-Century Japan," in Tu Wei-Ming, ed., *Confucian Traditions in East Asian Modernity* (Cambridge.: Harvard University Press 1996), 125–127.

36. In English translations of the Charter Oath, the Confucian term "Fair Way of Heaven and Earth" is usually translated as "just laws of Nature." See "Charter Oath," in Tsunoda Ryusaku, Wm. Theodore de Bary, and Donald Keene, eds., *Sources of Japanese*

Tradition (New York: Columbia University Press, 1958), 2:136–137. The original Japanese text, however, refers to the Confucian terms and concepts.

37. For an excellent discussion of the late Tokugawa background of the terms "bunmei and kaika," often translated as "civilization and enlightenment," see Watanabe Hiroshi, " 'Shimpo' to 'Chuka': Nihon no Baai," in Mizoguchi Yuzo, Hamashita Takeshi, Miyajima Hiroshi, and Hiraishi Naoaki, eds., *Kindaika Zô* (Tokyo: Tokyo University Press, 1994), 133–175.

38. It was published in the summer of 1866 and sold more than 250,000 copies that same year.

39. Fukuzawa Yukichi, *An Outline of a Theory of Civilization* [Bunmeiron no gairyaku], trans. David A. Dilworth and G. Cameron Hurst (Tokyo: Sophia University, 1973).

40. Takashi Fujitani, *Splendid Monarchy: Power and Pageantry in Modern Japan* (Berkeley: University of California Press, 1996).

41. Hirakawa Sukehiro, "Japan's Turn to the West," in Bob Tadashi Wakabayashi, ed., *Modern Japanese Thought* (Cambridge: Cambridge University Press: 1998), 47–71.

42. Robert S. Schwantes, "Christianity Versus Science: A Conflict of Ideas in Meiji Japan," *Far Eastern Quarterly* 12, no. 2. (February 1953): 123–124.

43. G. B. Sanson, *The Western World and Japan: A Study in the Interaction of European and Asiatic Cultures* (New York: Vintage, 1973), 475–476.

44. For the gradual redefinition of Buddhism as a universal religious alternative to Christianity, see James Edward Ketelaar, *Of Heretics and Martyrs in Meiji Japan* (Princeton: Princeton University Press, 1990), 136–220; and Judith Snodgrass, *Presenting Japanese Buddhism to the West: Orientalism, Occidentalism, and the Columbian Exposition* (Chapel Hill:University of North Carolina Press, 2003).

45. For the tensions between Christianity and science in Meiji thought, see Schwantes, "Christianity versus Science," 123–132.

46. Michael Burtscher, "Facing 'the West' on Philosophical Grounds: A View from the Pavilion of Subjectivity on Meiji Japan," *Comparative Studies of South Asia, Africa and the Middle East* 26, no. 3 (Fall 2006): 367–376.

47. Fukuzawa Yukichi, *An Encouragement of Learning* [Gakumon no Susume], trans. David A. Dilworth and Umeyo Hirano (Tokyo: Sophia University, 1969).

48. Matsumoto Sannosuke, "Profile of Asian Minded Man V: Fukuzawa Yukichi," *Developing Economies* 5, no. 1 (March 1967): 156–172.

49. Henry Thomas Buckle, *History of Civilization in England* (New York, Hearst's International Library, 1913). Originally written in 1857, it tried to explain the laws that governed the evolution of society and progress of humanity. For Buckle, the division between European and non-European civilizations was due to the fact that in Europe man is stronger than nature, while elsewhere nature is stronger than man, the consequence of which is that in Europe alone has man subdued nature to his service. The advance of European civilization is thus characterized by the continually diminishing influence of physical laws and the continually increasing influence of mental laws. The book made Buckle a social celebrity. Though his work was later criticized for its many fallacies, it provoked further discussion on the topic and became influential worldwide.

50. For a discussion of the implicit critiques of Western thinkers of civilization in Fuku-zawa's theorization, see Matsuzawa Hiroaki, "Varieties of Benmei Ron (Theories of Civilization)," in Hilary Conroy, Sandra T. W. Davis, and Wayne Patterson, eds., *Japan in Transition: Thought and Action in the Meiji Era* (London: Associated University Presses, 1984), 209–223.

51. See Earl H. Kinmonth, *The Self-Made Man in Meiji Japanese Thought: From Samurai to Salary Man* (Berkeley: University of California Press 1961). Samuel Smiles (1812–1904) wrote *Self-Help* in 1859. See Samuel Smiles, *Self-Help* (Chicago: Bedford and Clarke, 1884).

52. Marius B. Jansen, "Changing Japanese Attitudes Toward Modernization," in Marius B. Jansen, ed., *Changing Japanese Attitudes Toward Modernization* (Rutland: Tuttle, 1982), 67.

53. Tokutomi Sohô published *Dai Jyûkyûseiki Nihon no Seinen oyobi sono Kyôiku* (Japan's youth and its education in the nineteenth century) in 1885. Later editions of the book carried the shorter title *Shin Nihon no Seinen* (The youth of new Japan). For a discussion of the impact of this work, see Kenneth Pyle, *The New Generation in Meiji Japan: Problems of Cultural Identity, 1885–1895* (Stanford, Calif.: Stanford University Press, 1969), 32–36.

54. *Shôrai no Nihon* was first published in 1886. For its English translation, see Tokutomi Sohô, *The Future of Japan,* trans. and ed. Vinh Sinh (Edmonton, Canada: University of Alberta Press, 1989).

55. Pyle, *The New Generation in Meiji Japan.*

56. Ibid., 89–91.

57. Miwa Kimitada, "Fukuzawa Yukichi's 'Departure from Asia': A Prelude to the Sino-Japanese War," in Edmund Skrzypczak, ed., *Japan's Modern Century* (Tokyo: Sophia University, in cooperation with Tuttle, 1968), 1–26. This argument sought to separate the destiny of Japan, which was progressing rapidly toward civilization, from that of the rest of East Asia, which seemed to lag far behind. For the translation of Fukuzawa's article, see Fukuzawa Yukichi, "On De-Asianization," in *Meiji Japan Through Contemporary Sources* (Tokyo: Center for East Asian Cultural Studies, 1973), 3:129–133.

58. P. J. Vatikiotis, *The History of Modern Egypt: From Muhammad Ali to Mubarak* (Baltimore: Johns Hopkins University Press, 1980), 73.

59. For the Ottoman response to the Great Indian Revolt of 1857, see Azmi Özcan, "1857 Büyük Hind Ayaklanması ve Osmanlı Devleti," *İ. Ü. Islam Tetkikleri Dergisi* (Istanbul) 9 (1995): 269–280.

60. Moshe Gammer, *Muslim Resistance to the Tsar: Shamil and the Conquest of Chechnia and Daghestan* (London: Cass, 1994).

61. Anthony Reid, "Nineteenth Century Pan-Islam in Indonesia and Malaysia," *Journal of Asian Studies* 26, no. 2 (February 1967): 275–276. Reid's article demonstrates the role played by pilgrims, students, scholars, and merchants who connected Indonesia with Mecca, Cairo, and Istanbul and revived the notion of Islamic solidarity during the 1860s and 1870s.

62. Azmi Özcan, "İngiltere'de Hilafet Tartışmaları, 1873–1909," in İsmail Kara, ed., *Hilafet*

Risaleleri (Istanbul: Klasik Yayınları, 2002), 1:65–67. The reports noted that the number of pilgrims engaging in the hajj increased dramatically. Even though there was no immediate threat, the majority of the reports further noted that these developments had to be followed with special attention. Here, it is important to underline that pan-Islamic moves and gestures started during the reign of Ottoman sultan Abdulaziz (1830–1876), not Abdulhamid II (1842–1918), whose name was later identified with the Ottoman pan-Islamic projects. This shows that trends at the level of Ottoman government cannot be reduced to the personality of the sultan.

63. The Freedom and People's Rights Movement, Jyû Minken Undo, was a nationwide political movement during the early Meiji period that peaked in the 1870s and 1880s. It involved the participation of both former samurai and commoners and asked for the reform of the new Meiji government along the lines of Western participatory democratic models. The Freedom and People's Rights Movement contributed to the declaration of the Japanese constitution.

64. For an excellent discussion of Ottomans' perception of the external pressures and how they acted to protect their integrity and reforms in a delicate balance-of-power politics, see Engin Deniz Akarli's unpublished Ph.D. dissertation, now considered a classic in its field: "The Problems of External Pressures, Power Struggles, and Budgetary Deficits in Ottoman Politics under Abdulhamid II (1876–1909): Origins and Solutions" (Ph.D. diss., Princeton University, 1976), 10–76.

65. For a good discussion of the Ottoman liberal belief in Christian-Muslim equality, see Roderic H. Davison, "Turkish Attitudes Concerning Christian-Muslim Equality in the Nineteenth Century," *American Historical Review* 59, no. 4 (July 1954): 844–864.

66. For examples, see Namik Kemal, "Medeniyet," *Mecmua-i Ulum* 5 (1 Safer 1297/January 14, 1880): 381–383; and Münif Paşa, "Mukayese-i İlm ve Cehl," *Mecmua-i Fünün* 1 (Muharrem 1279/June 1862): 26–27.

67. Serif Mardin, *The Genesis of Young Ottoman Thought* (Princeton: Princeton University Press, 1962), 283–336.

68. Namık Kemal, "İttihad-ı Islam." *Ibret* (Istanbul), June 27, 1872.

69. Ali Suavi, "Democracy: Government by the People, Equality," *Ulum Gazetesi* (Paris), May 17, 1870, reprinted in Charles Kurzman, ed., *Modernist Islam, 1840–1940* (New York: Oxford University Press, 2002), 142.

3. THE TWO FACES OF THE WEST

1. Michael Adas, "High Imperialism and the New History," in Michael Adas, ed., *Islamic and European Expansion: The Forging of a Global Order* (Philadelphia: Temple University Press, 1993), 311.

2. Hannah Arendt, *The Origins of Totalitarianism* (New York: World, Meridian, 1962), 123.

3. Carl Schmitt, *The Nomos of the Earth in the International Law of the Jus Publicum Europaeum* (New York: Telos, 2003), 3.

4. Rudyard Kipling, "The White Man's Burden (1899)," in Jan Goldstein and John W.

Boyer, eds., *Nineteenth-Century Europe: Liberalism and Its Critics* (Chicago: University of Chicago Press, 1988), 544–545.

5. J. P. Lehmann, *The Image of Japan: From Feudal Isolation to World Power, 1850–1905* (London: Allen and Unwin, 1978).

6. For debates on imperialism, see Harrison M. Wright, ed., *The New Imperialism: Analysis of Late Nineteenth-Century Expansion* (Lexington, Mass.: Heath, 1976).

7. William Ewart Gladstone served as British prime minister on several occasions for a total of twelve years between the years 1868 and 1894. He was prime minister during the 1880–1885 period, when the crucial imperial policies were applied.

8. William Gladstone's anti-Islamic remarks have become legend in contemporary Islamic reformist thought. Though not verified by any historic evidence, many Muslims still believe that Gladstone, during his tenure as colonial secretary, declared his intention to discredit the Qur'an, since this was the only way the British could truly dominate the Muslim peoples. This anecdote is seemingly one of the transformative events in the biography of Muslim reformist Bediuzzaman Said Nursi. See Necmeddin Sahiner, *Bilinmeyen Taraflariyla Bediuzzaman Said Nursi* (Istanbul: Nesil Yayınları, 1997), 84.

9. For an economic history approach to explaining the changes in British policy toward the Middle East, see Resat Kasaba, "Up the Down Staircase: British Policy in the Near East, 1815–74," in Francisco O. Ramirez, ed., *Rethinking the Nineteenth Century: Contradictions and Movements* (New York: Greenwood, 1988), 149–160.

10. Ernest Renan's writings on Islam embodied this argument and will be discussed in the following section. For another example of the anti-Turkish writings that argued the impossibility of Turks becoming members of civilized Christian Europe, see Edward A. Freeman, *The Ottoman Power in Europe* (London: Macmillan, 1877).

11. For a comprehensive examination of Ahmed Midhat's writings on Western civilization and Islamic identity, see Orhan Okay, *Batı Medeniyeti Karşısında Ahmed Midhat Efendi* (Istanbul: Milli Eğitim Bakanliği Yayınları, 1991).

12. For a discussion of the critique of over-Westernization among the Ottoman intellectuals, see Şerif Mardin, "Tanzimat'tan Sonra Aşırı Batılılaşma," in *Makaleler*, vol. 4, *Türk Modernleşmesi* (Istanbul: İletişim Yayınları, 1992), 21–79.

13. Carter Vaughn Findley, "An Ottoman Occidentalist in Europe: Ahmed Midhat Meets Madame Gulnar, 1889," *American Historical Review* 103, no. 1 (1998): 15–49.

14. Findley, "An Ottoman Occidentalist in Europe," 49.

15. For the main outlines and diverse formulations of Muslim modernism, see Charles Kurzman, ed., *Modernist Islam, 1840–1940: A Sourcebook* (New York: Oxford University Press, 2002).

16. Kenneth Pyle, "Meiji Conservatism," in Marius B. Jensen, ed., *The Cambridge History of Japan* (Cambridge: Cambridge University Press, 1989), 5:674–720.

17. Shiba Shirô, *Kaisetsu Kajin no Kigu* (Tokyo: Jiji Tsushinsha, 1970).

18. Guohe Zeng, "From Patriotism to Imperialism: A Study of the Political Ideals of 'Kajin No Kigu,' a Meiji Political Novel" (Ph.D. diss., Ohio State University, 1997).

19. Suzuki Tadashi, "Profile of Asian Minded Man IX: Tôkichi Tarui," *Developing Economies* 6, no. 1 (March 1968): 79–100.

20. Liang Qichao (1873–1929) was a leading Chinese intellectual who advocated constitutionalism and reform. After becoming a disciple of Kang Youwei in 1890, he worked closely with Kang throughout the 1895–1898 reform movement. After the conservative coup of 1898 that ended the reforms, Liang spent fourteen years of exile in Japan. He returned to China in 1912, upon the collapse of the dynasty, and served in the cabinet of Yuan Shikai. He retired from politics in 1917 to pursue academic studies and writings.

21. Suzuki, "Profile of Asian Minded Man," 97–98.

22. Vladimir Tikhonov, "Korea's First Encounters with Pan-Asianism Ideology in the Early 1880s," *Review of Korean Studies* 5, no. 2 (December 2002): 195–232.

23. Richard Jaffe, "Seeking Sakyamuni: Travel and the Reconstruction of Japanese Buddhism," *Journal of Japanese Studies* 30, no. 1 (Winter 2004): 65–96.

24. Kenneth Pyle, *The New Generation in Meiji Japan: Problems of Cultural Identity, 1885–1895* (Stanford, Calif.: Stanford University Press, 1969), 150–153.

25. Michael Burtscher, "Facing 'the West' on Philosophical Grounds: A View from the Pavilion of Subjectivity on Meiji Japan," *Comparative Studies of South Asia, Africa and the Middle East* 26, no. 3 (Fall 2006).

26. For a broader world historical assessment of Ernest Renan's ideas on the Aryan race, see Vasant Kaiwar, "The Aryan Model of History and the Oriental Renaissance: The Politics of Identity in an Age of Revolutions, Colonialism, and Nationalism," in Vasant Kaiwar and Sucheta Mazumdar, eds., *The Antinomies of Modernity,* (Durham, N.C.: Duke University Press, 2003), 13–61.

27. Soon afterward, in the same year, the speech was published separately as a twenty-four-page booklet.

28. For the most comprehensive discussion of the direct and indirect refutations of Renan, see Dücane Cündioğlu, "Ernest Renan ve 'Reddiyeler' Bağlamında İslam-Bilim Tartişmalarina Bibliyografik bir Katki," *Divan* (Istanbul) 1, no. 2 (1996): 1–94.

29. Expectedly, there were immediate reactions from Muslim intellectuals, three of whom are well known: Jamal ad-Din al-Afghani, Namik Kemal, and Ataullah Bayezidof (mufti of Russia). For the discussion, see Ernest Renan, "Islamlik ve Bilim," in Ziya İhsan, ed. and trans., *Nutuklar ve Konferanslar* (Ankara: Sakarya Basimevi, 1946), 183–205. (For an English translation, see Ernest Renan, *The Poetry of the Celtic Races and Other Studies* [London: Walter Scott, 1896], 84–108.) For Namik Kemal's response, see Namik Kemal, *Renan Müdafaanamesi: Islamiyet ve Maarif* (Ankara: Milli Kültür Yayınları, 1962). For Afghani's response, see Jamal al-Afghani, "Answer of Jamal ad-Din to Renan," in Nikkie Keddie, ed., *An Islamic Response to Imperialism* (Berkeley: University of California Press, 1968), 181–187. For the response of Ataullah Bayezidof, see his *Islam ve Medeniyet* (Ankara: TDV Yayınları, Ankara, 1993). For an account of Afghani's relationship with Renan in Paris, see Elie Kedourie, *Afghani and Abduh* (London: Cass, 1966), 41–46.

30. Renan, "Islamlik ve Bilim," 201.

31. Michael Adas, *Machines as the Measure of Man: Science, Technology, and Ideologies of Western Dominance* (Ithaca: Cornell University Press, 1989), 11–12.

32. Münif Efendi, "Mahiyet ve Aksam-i Ulum," *Mecmua-ı Fünun*, no. 13 (June 1863): 7. For similar racist comments on blacks and natives of the West Indies, see Mehmed Şevki, "Avrupa Devletlerinin Ahval-i Hazirrasi," *Mecmua-ı Fünun*, no. 32 (October 1864): 305.

33. See Cündioğlu, "Ernest Renan ve 'Reddiyeler,'" 28.

34. Charles Mismer, *Soirées de Constantinople* (Paris: Hachette, 1870).

35. Interestingly, the first public response was an article by Charles Mismer: "L'Islamisme et la science," in *Revue de la Philosophie Positive* (May–June 1883). See Cündioğlu, "Ernest Renan ve 'Reddiyeler' Bağlamında İslam-Bilim Tartişmalarina Bibliyografik bir Katkı," 27–28.

36. Afghani, "Answer of Jamal ad-Din to Renan," 183.

37. Ibid., 184–185.

38. For the bibliography of all the Muslim refutations of Ernest Renan, see Cündioğlu, "Ernest Renan ve 'Reddiyeler' Bağlamında İslam-Bilim Tartişmalarina Bibliyografik bir Katkı," 87–92.

39. For an authoritative analysis of *salafi* modernism and its critique of historical Islam, see İsmail Kara, "Islamcıların Fikri Endişeleri," in İsmail Kara, ed., *Türkiye'de Islamcılık Düsüncesi*, 3d ed. (Istanbul: Kitabevi, 1997), 1:57–66. See also David Dean Commins, *Islamic Reform: Politics and Social Change in Late Ottoman Syria* (New York: Oxford University Press, 1990), 65–88.

40. See Cemil Aydin, "Beyond Culturalism? An Overview of the Historiography on Ottoman Science in Turkey," in Ekmeleddin İhsanoğlu, Kostas Chatzis, and Efthymios Nicolaidis, eds., *Multicultural Science in the Ottoman Empire* (Turnhout, Belgium: Brepols, 2003), 201–215.

41. See William Draper, *Niza-yı İlim ve Din*, trans. Ahmet Midhat (Istanbul: Tercümani Hakikat Matbaası, 1313/1896–1897).

42. Findley, "An Ottoman Occidentalist in Europe," 49.

43. Numan Kamil Bey, "Vérité sur l'Islamisme et l'Empire Ottoman," *Présentée au X. Congrès International des Orientalistes à Genève* (Paris: Charles Noblet et Fils, 1894).

44. Numan Kamil Bey, *Islamiyet ve Devlet-i Aliyye-i Osmaniye Hakkında Doğru bir Söz* (Istanbul: Tahir Bey Matbaasi, 1316/1898). For a current edition of the text, see Numan Kamil Bey, "Islamiyet ve Devlet-i Aliyye-i Osmaniye Hakkında Doğru bir Söz: Cenevre'de Müsteşrikin Kongresi'nde İrad Olunmuş bir Nutkun Tercümesidir," in İsmail Kara, ed., *Hilafet Risaleleri* (Istanbul: Klasik Yayınları, 2002–2004), 1:353–371.

45. Numan Kamil Bey, "Islamiyet ve Devlet-i Aliyye-i Osmaniye Hakkında Doğru bir Söz," 361.

46. Ibid., 368–369.

47. Ibid., 371.

48. Kara, *Hilafet Risaleleri*, 1:30.

49. For a history of the concept of the yellow peril, see Heinz Gollwitzer, *Die gelbe Gefahr: Geschichte eines Schlagwortes* (The yellow peril: Retracing a slogan), (Göttingen: Vandenhoeck and Ruprecht, 1962). A collection of German diplomatic documents

includes the text of a letter from Kaiser Wilhem to the czar of Russia, dated April 26, 1895; see *German Diplomatic Documents, 1871–1914*, ed. E. T. S. Dugdale, vol. 3, *The Growing Antagonism, 1898–1910* (New York: Harper and Brothers, 1930).

50. The name of the article was *Dôjinshu Dômei: Shina Mondai Kenkyû no Hitsuyô* (We must ally with those of the same race, and we must study the China problem). See Marius B. Jansen, "Konoe Atsumaro," in Akira Iriye, ed., *The Chinese and the Japanese: Essays in Political and Cultural Interactions,* ed. Akira Iriye (Princeton: Princeton University Press, 1980), 113.

51. Jansen, "Konoe Atsumaro," 113–115.

52. Yamamuro Shinichi, "Ajia Ninshiki no Kijiku," in Furuya Tetsuo and Yamamuro Shinichi, eds., *Kindai Nihon no Ajia Ninshiki* (Kyoto: Kyoto University Press, 1994), 33–34.

53. The Monroe Doctrine, introduced during President Monroe's seventh annual message to the U.S. Congress on December 2, 1823, was aimed at limiting European expansion into the Western hemisphere. Monroe proclaimed, "The American continents, by the free and independent condition which they have assumed and maintain, are henceforth not to be considered as subjects for future colonization by any European powers." The Monroe Doctrine became more important after the emergence of the United States as a world power in the late nineteenth century. See Dexter Perkins, *A History of the Monroe Doctrine* (Boston: Little, Brown, 1955).

54. A similar change of perspective occurred with regard to Japanese interests in Egypt. Immediately after the Meiji Restoration, the Japanese government became interested in Egypt, specifically in how Egypt dealt with the system of unequal treaties and mixed courts. Thirty years later, however, Japanese leaders looked at Egypt from the perspective of its British colonial rulers, hoping for lessons on how to design a new policy in colonizing Korea. See Nakaoka San-eki, "Japanese Research on the Mixed Courts of Egypt in the Earlier Part of the Meiji Period in Connection with the Revision of the 1858 Treaties," *Journal of Sophia Asian Studies* 6 (1988): 11–47; see also Ôkuma Shigenobu, preface to Cromer, *Saikin Ejiputo* [Modern Egypt] (Tokyo: Dainippon Bunmei Kyôkai, 1911), 1:12–13.

55. According to Takeuchi Yoshimi, since Asianism was nothing more than a trend of thought advocating Asian nations' solidarity under Japanese leadership for the purpose of resisting Western expansionism, it did not inherently possess any specific ideological characteristic as democracy or socialism did, and as such it could be allied with different forms of ideologies in different political contexts. See Takeuchi Yoshimi, "Nihon to Ajiashugi," in *Nihon to Ajia* (Tokyo: Chikuma Gakujitsu Bunshô, 1993), 337–340.

56. For the anticolonial and nonhegemonic Asianist idealism that Miyazaki Tôten advocated for China's political revival, see Miyazaki Tôten, *My Thirty-Three Years' Dream: The Autobiography of Miyazaki Tôten,* trans. Etô Shinkichi and Marius Jansen (Princeton: Princeton University Press, 1982).

57. G. B. Sansom, *The Western World and Japan: A Study in the Interaction of European and Asiatic Cultures* (New York: Vintage, 1973), 411–415.

58. Marius B. Jansen, "Japanese Imperialism: Late Meiji Perspectives," in Ramon H. Myers and Mark R. Peattie, eds., *Japanese Colonial Empire, 1895–1945* (Princeton: Princeton University Press, 1984), 61–79. See also Alexis Dudden, *Japan's Colonization of Korea: Discourse and Power* (Honolulu: University of Hawai'i Press 2004).

59. E. H. Norman, "The Genyôsha: A Study in the Origins of Japanese Imperialism," *Pacific Affairs* 17, no. 3 (September 1944): 261–284

60. The Chinese character denoting the Amur River gave the society its name.

61. Hiraishi Naoaki, "Kindai Nihon no Kokusai Chitsujyokan to Ajiashugi," in *20 Seiki Shisutemu* (Tokyo: Tokyo Daigaku Shuppankai, 1998), 1:195–197.

62. While their intelligence gathering, espionage, and covert operations did prove useful to imperial interests, both organizations were also a severe liability in domestic politics. Members even arranged an assassination attempt against Foreign Minister Ôkuma Shigenobu in 1889 in response to Ôkuma's perceived conciliatory posture toward Western powers on the issue of the revisions of unequal treaties.

63. Marius B. Jansen, *The Japanese and Sun Yat-sen* (Cambridge: Harvard University Press, 1954), 34–41. The main source of information on this society is its own history: Yoshihisa Kuzuu, ed., *Tôa Senkaku Shishi Kiden* (Tokyo: Kokuryûkai Shuppanbu, 1933–1936).

64. For the Asian Solidarity Society, see Rebecca Karl, "Creating Asia: China in the World at the Beginning of the Twentieth Century," *American Historical Review* 103, no. 4 (October 1998): 1096–1118.

65. Okakura Tenshin is usually referred to as the pioneer of Japanese pan-Asianism and Japan's intellectual revolt against the West. See Tetsuo Najita and Harry Harootunian, "Japanese Revolt Against the West: Political and Cultural Criticism in the Twentieth Century," in Bob Tadashi Wakabayashi, ed., *Modern Japanese Thought* (Cambridge: Cambridge University Press, 1998), 211–212. Initially, Okakura Tenshin's books were not widely known in Japan, as they were published in English and were addressed to educated Westerners interested in Asian art and to Indian nationalists, with whom Okakura became familiar during his trip to India in 1902. For example, and quite ironically, Europeans were the first to quote from Okakura Tenshin in Japan's Asianist publications. See James H. Cousins, "The Cultural Unity of Asia," *Asian Review* (Tokyo) 2, no. 3 (March–April 1921): 217–228.

66. Christopher Benfey, *The Great Wave: Gilded Age Misfits, Japanese Eccentrics, and the Opening of Japan* (New York: Random House, 2003), 75–108.

67. For Okakura's radically anticolonial rhetoric, see Okakura Tenshin, "The Awakening of the East," in Okakura Tenshin, ed., *Okakura Kakuzô: Collected English Writings* (Tokyo: Heibonsha, 1984), 134–168. This essay, written during Okakura's visit to India, was not published during his lifetime. Its Japanese translation was published in 1938, while the original English version was published in the context of the Japanese claim to leadership in Asia in 1940.

68. The term "Asiaphile" was coined by Stephen Hay to describe those Western critics of modern rationalism and materialism who searched for an alternative in Asian intellectual traditions. Sister Nivedita was in contact with Okakura Tenshin while he was

writing *The Ideals of the East*. Okakura's intellectual dialogues with Nivedita's master, Swami Vivekananda, intensified when the two were working together at the Boston Fine Arts Museum. The correspondence between Okakura and Tagore continued until Okakura's death in 1913.

69. Okakura Tenshin, "The Ideals of the East with Special Reference to the Art of Japan," in Okakura, *Okakura Kakuzô*, 122.

70. Okakura, *Okakura Kakuzô*, 136.

71. Okakura Tenshin, "Book of Tea," in Okakura, *Okakura Kakuzô*, 270.

72. For an extensive account of Okakura Tenshin's thought, including its paradoxes, see F. G. Notehelfer, "On Idealism and Realism in the Thought of Okakura Tenshin," *Journal of Japanese Studies* 16, no. 2 (Summer 1990): 309–355.

73. Miwa Kimitada, "Crossroads of Patriotism in Imperial Japan: Shiga Shigetaka 1863–1927, Uchimura Kanzô 1861–1930, and Nitobe Inazô 1862–1933" (Ph.D. diss., Princeton University, 1967).

74. See Okakura, "The Awakening of the East," 134–168.

75. For an assessment of Abdulhamid II's policies from a world historical perspective, see Engin Deniz Akarli, "The Tangled End of Istanbul's Imperial Supremacy," in Leila Fawaz and C. A. Bayly, eds., *Modernity and Culture from the Mediterranean to the Indian Ocean, 1890–1920* (New York: Columbia University Press, 2002), 261–284. Also see Selim Deringil, *The Well-Protected Domains: Ideology and the Legitimation of Power in the Ottoman Empire, 1876–1909* (London: I. B. Tauris, 1998).

76. See Azmi Özcan, "Peyk-i Islam: 1880'de Istanbul'da Çıkarılan Bir Gazete ve İngiltere'nin Kopardığı Fırtına," *Tarih ve Toplum,* no. 99 (March 1992): 169–173.

77. Jacob M. Landau, *The Politics of Pan-Islam: Ideology and Organization* (Oxford: Clarendon, 1990), 2.

78. For the most extensive documentation of the extraordinary diversity of ideas, personalities, and interpretations of pan-Islamism during the era of high imperialism, see ibid., 1–72.

79. For an English-language extract from the article on Muslim unity published in the journal *al-Urwa al-Wuthqa* in 1884, see ibid., 318–320.

80. Ibid., 59.

81. Thanks to İsmail Kara's editorial leadership, all the major texts of the caliphate debate are being published. See Kara, *Hilafet Risaleleri.*

82. Azmi Özcan, "İngiltere'de Hilafet Tartışmaları, 1873–1909," in Kara, *Hilafet Risaleleri,* 1:64–65.

83. J. W. Redhouse, *A Vindication of the Ottoman Sultan's Title on 'Caliph': Showing Its Antiquity, Validity and Universal Acceptance* (London: Effingham Wilson, 1877).

84. For a recent reprint of Blunt's 1882 book, see Wilfrid Scawen Blunt, *The Future of Islam* (Lahore, Pakistan: Sind Sagar Academy, 1975). The second chapter of this book, titled "The Modern Question of the Caliphate" (48–89), directly deals with the question of reforming and reviving Islam by moving the caliphate to Arabic Cairo away from Ottoman Istanbul.

85. For an extensive discussion of the predominantly Arab opposition to the Ottoman

caliphate during the early years of Abdulhamid II's reign, see Ş. Tufan Buzpınar, "II. Abdulhamit Döneminde Osmanlı Hilafetine Muhalefetin Ortaya Çıkışı: 1877–1882," in Kara, *Hilafet Risaleleri,* 1:37–61.

86. For an assessment of this question from the British perspective, see Özcan, "İngiltere'de Hilafet Tartışmaları," 63–91.

87. See Ş. Tufan Buzpınar, "The Repercussions of the British Occupation of Egypt on Syria, 1882–1883," *Middle East Studies* 36, no. 1 (January 2000): 82–91; and Selim Deringil, "The 'Residual Imperial Mentality' and the 'Urabi Paşa Uprising in Eygpt': Ottoman Reactions to Arab Nationalism," in *Studies on Turkish-Arab Relations Annual* (Istanbul: Foundations for Studies on Turkish-Arab Relations, 1986), 31–38.

88. For an article-length biography of Halil Halid, see Syed Tanvir Wasti, "Halil Halid: Anti-Imperialist Muslim Intellectual," *Middle Eastern Studies* 29, no. 3 (July 1993): 559–579.

89. Halil Halid wrote his own autobiography in the form of political and cultural essays on the Muslim society he grew up in and his experience in the West. See Halil Halid, *The Diary of a Turk* (London: A. C. Black, 1903).

90. Mustafa Uzun, "Halil Halid," in *TDV Islam Ansiklopedisi* (Istanbul: TDV, 1997), 15:313–316.

91. In 1912 Halil Halid entered the Ottoman parliament as a representative of Ankara for the Party of Union and Progress. He was appointed as the chief consul (*başşehbender*) to Bombay and developed very close ties with Indian Muslims during this assignment. In 1922 Halil Halid was appointed to Istanbul University to teach ethnography of Muslim peoples, Islamic philosophy, and introduction to anthropology.

Ahmed Rıza was another Ottoman intellectual who was involved in challenging the justifying ideology of the Eurocentric world order in defense of Muslim political entities. For examples of this work, see Ahmed Rıza, *La faillite morale de la politique occidentale en Orient* (1922; reprint, Tunis: Bouslama, 1979); and Ahmed Rıza and Ismayl Urbain, *Tolérance de l'Islam,* (Saint-Ouen, France: Centre Abaad, 1992).

92. It should be mentioned from the very beginning that Halid's arguments and explanations regarding the civilizational identities in world order relied primarily on sources in European languages and were initially addressed to the Western public as a critique of their governments' imperial foreign policy. European writers Halil Halid made reference to included F. Guizot, T. W. Arnold, J. W. Draper, Sir William Muir, Albert Reville, Ernest Renan, R. N. Cust, De Thiersan, John R. Nott, Carl Peters, Theodor Nöldeke, Stanley Lane-Poole, Meredith Townsend, Max Nordau, Thomas Carlyle, Gibbons, D. A. Forget, Ch. Latourneau, H. Wallon, Thomas R. R. Cobb, Cesare Lombroso, Henry Wheaton, Clarkson, G. P. Gooch, P. S. Reisch, J. B. Crozier, W. Howitt, J. L. de Lanessan, and H. C. Morris.

93. Halil Halid, *Hilal ve Salib Münazaasi* (Cairo: Matbaa-i Hindiye, 1907), 4–5. Although the original of this book was written in English, here I will usually refer to the Ottoman-language version, published in the same year. For the English version, see Halil Halid, *The Crescent Versus the Cross* (London: Luzac, 1907).

94. Three sections in Halil Halid's *Hilal ve Salib Münazaasi* are devoted to the issue of

women in Islam: "The Role of Women in Islam," "Polygamy," and "Divorce" (83–133). Two sections are devoted to the question of slavery: "Slavery in Christianity and Islam" and "Humanist Purpose in the Emancipation of Slaves" (134–149).

95. See Halil Halid, *A Study in English Turcophobia* (London: Pan-Islamic Society, 1904). An earlier version of this book was published in 1898 without reference to Halil Halid's name. See *A Study in English Turcophobia* (London: Pan-Islamic Society, 1898). The book was translated into Urdu by Muhammed Şuayb Arvi and published under the title *Heybeti Türki* in Calcutta in 1905. Its Arabic translation was published in the journal *al-Liva*.

96. Halil Halid refers to John William Draper's *A History of Intellectual Development of Europe* (New York: Harper and Brothers, 1862). J. W. Draper became well known among Ottoman intellectuals for his book *History of Conflict Between Religion and Science* (New York: D. Appleton, 1875).

97. Halid, *Hilal ve Salib Münazaasi*, 179–180.

98. Halid, *The Crescent Versus the Cross*, 194–197.

99. Halid, *Hilal ve Salib Münazaasi*, 181–182.

100. Ibid., 185–187.

101. Halid, *The Crescent Versus the Cross*, 210. Halil Halid quotes from the 1909 Nobel Peace Prize laureate Baron d'Estournelles de Constant's (1852–1924) work "Les congrégations religieuses chez les Arabes et la conquête de l'Afrique" (Paris, 1887), 70.

102. Halid, *The Crescent Versus the Cross*, 223.

103. For other Young Turk intellectuals who thought similarly to Halil Halid, see M. Şükrü Hanioğlu, *Preparation for a Revolution: The Young Turks, 1902–1908* (New York: Oxford University Press, 2001), 303–306.

4. THE GLOBAL MOMENT OF THE RUSSO-JAPANESE WAR

1. Prasenjit Duara, ed., *Decolonization: Perspectives from Now and Then* (London: Routledge, 2004), 2–3; Narangoa Li and Robert Cribbs, eds., *Imperial Japan and National Identities in Asia, 1895–1945* (London: Routledge, 2003), 2–3; Klaus Kreiser, "Der japanische Sieg über Rußland (1905) und sein Echo unter den Muslimen" [The Japanese victory over Russia (1905) and its echo in the Islamic world], in *Die Welt des Islam* [The world of Islam] 21 (1981): 209–239; Barbara Watson Andaya, "From Rum to Tokyo: The Search for Anticolonial Allies by the Rulers of Riau, 1899–1914," *Indonesia* 24 (1977): 123–156; Nagazumi Akira, "An Indonesian's View of Japan: Wahidin and the Russo-Japanese War,", in F. H. H. King, ed., *The Development of Japanese Studies in Southeast Asia: Proceedings of the Fourth Leverhulme Conference* (Hong Kong: Centre of Asian Studies, University of Hong Kong, 1969), 72–84.

2. Gesa Westermann, "Japan's Victory in the Russo-Japanese War (1904–05) from the Philippine, Vietnamese, and Burmese Perspectives," in Rotem Kowner, ed., *Rethinking the Russo-Japanese War: Centennial Perspectives* (Honolulu: University of Hawai'i Press, 2006); Michael Laffan, "Tokyo as a Shared Mecca of Modernity: Reading the Impact of the Russo-Japanese War in the Colonial Malay World," in Rotem Kowner,

ed., *The Impact of the Russo-Japanese War*, 219–238 (London: Routledge Curzon, 2006). The image of Japan in England and America differed according to the ideological perspective of the individual. While progressive anti-imperialist figures welcomed the rise of Japan as an obstacle to imperialism, right-wing figures lamented it as a dangerous yellow peril. For example, British socialist Henry Hyndman's journal *Justice* had many pro-Japanese articles. For a very sympathetic account of Japan's victory written by a Universalist minister, see Sidney L. Gulick, *The White Peril in the Far East: An Interpretation of the Significance of the Russo-Japanese War* (New York: Revell, 1905). For a very negative right-wing British account of Japan, see T. W. H. Crosland, *The Truth About Japan* (London: Richards, 1904).

3. For the most comprehensive work on Middle Eastern perceptions of Japan, see Renee Worringer, "Comparing Perceptions: Japan as Archetype for Ottoman Modernity, 1876–1918" (Ph.D. diss., University of Chicago, 2001). See also Anja Pistor-Hatam, "Progress and Civilization in Nineteenth-Century Japan: The Far Eastern State as a Model for Modernization," *Iranian Studies* 29, nos. 1–2 (1996): 111–126; and Sugita Hideaki, "Japan and the Japanese as Depicted in Modern Arabic Literature," *Studies of Comparative Culture*, no. 27 (March 1989): 21–40. For examples of primary sources of this literature, see Mustafa Kamil, *Al-Shams al-Mushriqah* (Cairo: Matbaat al-Liwa, 1904). For the reception of Mustafa Kamil's book on Japan in Southeast Asia, see Michael Laffan. "Watan and Negeri: Mustafa Kamil's 'Rising Sun' in the Malay World," *Indonesia Circle*, no. 69 (1996): 157–175.

4. Oka Yoshitake, "The First Anglo-Japanese Alliance in Japanese Public Opinion," in J. P. Lehmann, ed., *Themes and Theories in Japanese History* (London: Athlone, 1988), 185–193.

5. For example, Egyptian nationalist leader Mustafa Kamil argued that, despite the vested interest of Britain in the Japanese victory, "a victory for Japan is a victory for the yellow race" against the British Empire. See Mustafa Kamil, "Al-Harb al-Hadirah wa'l-Islam," *Al-Liwa*, February 18, 1904, 1. For a discussion of Mustafa Kamil's ideas, see Worringer, "Comparing Perceptions," 350–356.

6. For the African-American reaction to the Russo-Japanese War, see Marc Gallicchio, *Black Internationalism in Asia, 1895–1945: The African American Encounter with Japan and China* (Chapel Hill: University of North Carolina Press, 2000), 6–15.

7. Renee Worringer, "'Sick Man of Europe' or 'Japan of the Near East'? Constructing Ottoman Modernity in the Hamidian and Young Turk Eras," *International Journal of Middle Eastern Studies* 36, no. 2 (May 2004): 207–223; see also Roxane Haag-Higuchi, "A Topos and Its Dissolution: Japan in Some Twentieth-Century Iranian Texts," *Iranian Studies* 29, nos. 1–2 (1996): 71–83.

8. Henry Dyer, *Dai Nippon, the Britain of the East: A Study in National Evolution* (London: Blackie, 1904).

9. For direct military reports from the fronts, see Ali Fuad Erden, *Musavver 1904–1905 Rus-Japon Seferi* (Istanbul: Kitaphane-yi Islam ve Askeri, 1321/1905 or 1906). Japanese military power and history were well studied and written about by Ottoman military officer Pertev Bey, especially in his book *Rus-Japon Harbinden Alinan Maddi ve Manevi Dersler ve Japonlarin Esbabi Muzafferiyeti: Bir Milletin Tâli'i Kendi*

Kuvvetindedir! [Material and moral lessons taken from the Russo-Japanese War and the reasons for Japan's victory: A nation's good fortune from its own power!] (Istanbul: Kanâ'at Kütüphanesi ve Matbaasi, 1329/1911).

10. Jawaharlal Nehru, *An Autobiography* (Delhi: Oxford University Press, 1989), 16. See also Jawaharlal Nehru, *Toward Freedom* (Boston: Beacon, 1967), 29–30.

11. Prasenjit Duara, "Transnationalism and the Predicament of Sovereignty: China, 1900–1945," *American Historical Review* 102, no. 4 (1997): 1038.

12. Quoted in Hugh Tinker, *Race, Conflict, and the International Order* (New York: St. Martin's, 1977), 39.

13. Mehmed Sevki, "Japonya Memleketi," *Mecmua-i Fünun*, no. 41 (December 1866): 314.

14. Both the Japanese conception of *tôyô* and the Ottoman concept of *Şark* were connected to complex political dynamics that involved relations not only with the West but also with the Ottoman and Japanese Orients, but this topic lies outside the scope of this chapter. See Stefan Tanaka, *Japan's Orient: Rendering Pasts into History* (Berkeley: University of California Press, 1993); and Ussama Makdisi, "Ottoman Orientalism," *American Historical Review* 107, no. 3 (2002): 768–796.

15. Misawa Nobuo, "Relations Between Japan and the Ottoman Empire in the Nineteenth Century: Japanese Public Opinion About the Disaster of the Ottoman Battleship Ertuğrul (1890)," *Annals of Japan Association of Middle East Studies* 18, no. 2 (2003): 1–8.

16. Michael Penn, "East Meets East: An Ottoman Mission in Meiji Japan," *Princeton Papers: Interdisciplinary Journal of Middle Eastern Studies* 13, 33–62.

17. For the Ottoman imagination of Japan as an Eastern nation, see Cemil Aydin, "Nihon Wa Itsu Tôyô No Kuni Ni Natta No Ka? Chutô Kara Mita Kindai Nihon" [When did Japan become an "Eastern" nation? Modern Japan in the imagination of Middle Eastern nationalists], in *Atarashi Nihongaku no Kôchiku—Constructing Japanese Studies in Global Perspective* (Tokyo: Ochanomizu University, 1999), 81–86.

18. James Hevia, "Looting Beijing: 1860, 1900," in Lydia H. Liu, ed., *Tokens of Exchange: The Problem of Translation in Global Circulations* (Durham, N.C.: Duke University Press, 1999), 192–213. During the suppression of the Boxer Rebellion, Japan joined the Western coalition, composed of soldiers from the United States, Austria-Hungary, Britain, France, Germany, Italy, and Russia.

19. M. Şükrü Hanioğlu, *The Young Turks in Opposition* (New York: Oxford University Press, 1995), 210.

20. William Cleveland, *The Making of an Arab Nationalist: Ottomanism and Arabism in the Life and Thought of Sati' Al-Husri* (Princeton: Princeton University Press, 1971), 37–38.

21. Ahmed Rıza, "La Leçon d'une guerre," *Mechveret Supplément Français* 169 (November 1, 1905): 1–2. The translation is from Worringer, "Comparing Perceptions," 208.

22. Gerrit Gong quotes L. Oppenheim's *International Law: A Treatise* (London: Longmans, Green, 1905) as an example. See Gerrit Gong, *The Standard of "Civilization" in International Society* (New York: Oxford University Press, 1984), 57.

23. M. Şükrü Hanioğlu, *Preparation for a Revolution: The Young Turks, 1902–1908* (New York: Oxford University Press, 2001), 304.

24. Ibid., 304–305.

25. Nader Sohrabi, "Historicizing Revolutions: Constitutional Revolutions in the Ottoman Empire, Iran, and Russia, 1905–1908," *American Journal of Sociology* 100, no. 6 (July 1995): 1383–1447.

26. As an example, see R. P. Dua, *The Impact of the Russo-Japanese (1905) War on Indian Politics* (Delhi: S. Chand, 1966).

27. Mission Scientifique du Maroc first published the *Revue du Monde Musulman* was in November 1906; the last issue appeared in 1926. The founding editor, Alfred Le Chatelier, was appointed chair of Muslim sociology at the College de France in 1903. See Susan Bayly, "Racial Readings of Empire: Britain, France, and Colonial Modernity in the Mediterranean and Asia," in Leila Fawaz and C. A. Bayly, eds., *Modernity and Culture from the Mediterranean to the Indian Ocean, 1890–1920* (New York: Columbia University Press 2002), 296. See also Edmund Burke III, "The First Crisis of Orientalism," in Jean-Clause Vatin et al., eds., *Connaissances du Maghreb: Sciences sociales et colonisation* (Paris: CNRS, 1984), 213–226.

28. For some of the articles on pan-Islamism in the *Revue du Monde Musulman (RMM)*, see L. Bouvat, "La presse anglaise et le panislamisme," *RMM* 1, no. 3 (January 1907): 404–405; L. Bouvat, "Un projet de parlement musulman international," *RMM* 7, no. 2 (March 1909): 321–322; A. Fevret, "Le croissant contre la croix," *RMM* 2, no. 7 (May 1907): 421–425; Ismael Hamet, "Le Congrès Musulman Universal," *RMM* 4, no. 1 (January 1908): 100–107; and A. Le Chatelier, "Le pan-Islamisme et le progrès," *RMM* 1, no. 4 (February 1907): 145–68.

29. Bayly, "Racial Readings of Empire," 304.

30. For the English translation of *La psychologie du musulman,* see André Servier, *Islam and the Psychology of the Musulman,* trans. A. S. Moss-Blundell, pref. Louis Bertrand (New York: Scribner's, 1924). For a similar book by the same author, see André Servier, *Le nationalisme musulman en Egypte, en Tunisie, en Algerie: Le péril de l'avenir* (Constantine, Algeria: M. Boet, 1913).

31. For the importance of WWI in the history of decolonization, see Prasenjit Duara, "The Discourse of Civilization and Pan-Asianism," *Journal of World History* 12, no. 1 (Spring 2001): 99–130; and Michael Adas, *Machines as the Measure of Men: Science, Technology, and Ideologies of Western Dominance* (Ithaca: Cornell University Press, 1989).

32. "Luhmah buyna al-Sharqiyyin," *Al-Liwa,* October 11, 1904, 1.

33. Nitobe Inazô, *Bushido: The Soul of Japan. An Exposition of Japanese Thought* (Tokyo: Kodansha International, 1998), 188.

34. Leon Ostrorog, *Conférence sur la renaissance du Japon* (Istanbul: Ahmed Ihsan, 1327/ 1911). This work includes Ostrorog's published remarks during the proceedings as well as organizer M. Salih Gourdji's speech, which serves as a postscript on pages 86–91. An Arabic translation of the book was produced by the former Ottoman Army officer and later Iraqi officer Taha al-Hashimi in 1925. See *Nahdat al-Yaban wa Ta'thir Ruh al-Ummah fi'l-Nahdah* [The awakening of Japan and the influence of the

nation's spirit on the awakening] (Baghdad, 1925). For comments on this lecture, see also Worringer, "Comparing Perceptions", 267.

35. Hanioğlu, *Preparation for a Revolution*, 304.

36. For Gourdji, the three years since the constitutional revolution had not offered enough time for the constitution Ottoman regime to demonstrate comparable achievements; see Gourdji's postscript in Ostrorog, *Conference*, 86–88.

37. For example, Ahmet Münir İbrahim, who studied commerce at Waseda University, sent articles to *Sebilürreşad*. Münir reportedly became a member of the Progressive Asian Student Society at Waseda, joining other students from China, Korea, India, Siam, and Japan. See Ahmed Münir, "Hâricî Ticâret Vesile-i Sa'âdet-i Umûmidir," *Sebilürreşât* 12, no. 307 (1330/1914): 290–291; and idem, "Japonya Ticaret-i Bahriyesi," *Sebilürreşât* 1-8, no. 204 (1328/1912): 426–427. Münir also wrote a tribute to the Meiji emperor after his death: "Japonya Mikado'su Mutsuhito," *Sebilürreşât* 2-9, no. 213 (1328/1912): 96–98. Another student, Hasan Fehmi, wrote articles on the Japanese constitution and parliament emphasizing the key role played by the participatory political system in the empowerment of the Japanese nation. See Hasan Fehmi, "Şuyûn: Japonya," *Sebilürreşad* 12, no. 295 (1914): 167.

38. For the derivative modernity concept, see Partha Chatterjee, *Nationalist Thought and the Colonial World: A Derivative Discourse* (Minneapolis: University of Minnesota Press, 1986).

39. For a discussion of this topic, refer to the section in chapter 2 on the appropriation of history of civilization literature from Europe.

40. Stephen Vlastos, ed., *Mirror of Modernity: Invented Traditions of Modern Japan* (Berkeley: University of California Press, 1988).

41. Albert Hourani, *Arabic Thought in the Liberal Age, 1798–1939* (Cambridge: Oxford University Press, 1962), 205.

42. Even as late as the Balkan wars of 1911–1912, the example of Japanese women was invoked to ask for dedication and sacrifice from Ottoman Muslim women for the sake of the Ottoman state. See Zafer Toprak, *Milli Iktisat—Milli Burjuvazi* (Istanbul: Tarih Vakfı Yurt Yayınları, 1995), 175. For the "good wife, wise mother" ideology, see Sharon Nolte and Sally Hastings, "Meiji State's Policy Toward Women," in Gail Lee Bernstein, ed., *Recreating Japanese Women, 1600–1945* (Berkeley: University of California Press, 1991), 151–74.

43. Egyptian modernist Qasim Amin's famous work *Tahrir al-Mar'ah*, written in 1899, spoke of Japanese women as an ideal example for Muslim women. See Qasim Amin, *Tahrir al-Mar'ah* (Cairo: Dar al-Maarif, 1970). For the English translation, see idem, *The Liberation of Women: A Document in the History of Egyptian Feminism*, trans. Samiha Sidhom Peterson (Cairo: American University in Cairo Press, 1992).

44. See Niyazi Berkes, ed., Turkish Nationalism and Western Civilization: Selected Essays of Ziya Gökalp (New York: Allen and Unwin, 1959), 277. See also Uriel Heyd, Foundations of Turkish Nationalism: The Life and Teachings of Ziya Gökalp (London: Lucaz, 1950).

45. I discussed the shift in mood toward pessimism and radical ideologies of change in the last quarter of the twentieth century in my master's thesis; see Cemil Aydin, "Mec-

muai Fünün ve Mecmuai Ulum Dergilerinde Bilim ve Medeniyet Anlayişi" (master's thesis, Istanbul University 1995).

46. Worringer, "Comparing Perception," 222.

47. Indonesian nationalists metaphorically used the similarity between the words "Japanese" and "Javanese" to advance their claim that the Javanese could one day become independent and advanced as well. *Islamic Fraternity* (Tokyo) 2, no. 2 (May 15, 1911): 1–2.

48. F[ernand] Farjenel, "La Japon et l'Islam," *Revue du Monde Musulman* 1, no. 1 (November 1906): 101–114.

49. Abdurreşid İbrahim went to Japan in 1933 during the turbulant years after the post–Manchurian Incident reorientation in Japanese foreign policy. He participated in the Japanese public policy discussions about the Muslim world and died in Tokyo in 1944. See Selçuk Esenbel, "Japan's Global Claim to Asia and the World of Islam: Transnational Nationalism and World Power, 1900–1945," *American Historical Review* 109, no. 4 (October 2004): 1140–1170.

50. For information about its Japanese and Muslim members, see *Daitô* 4, no. 3 (March 1911): 64–65.

51. For examples, see "Japonya'da Daito Mecellesi ve Asya Gi Kai Cemiyetinin Beyannamesi," *Sirat-ı Müstakim* 6, no. 133 (1327/1911): 42–44. See also Barakatullah, "Japonya'da Islam Naşirleri," *Sirati Müstakim* 7, no. 158 (1327/1911).

52. The political and pan-Islamic focus of Abdurreşid İbrahim was in sharp contrast with the two previous great Muslim travelers, Ibn Batuta and Evliya Çelebi. Traveling in the fourteenth century from Morocco to China, Ibn Batuta experienced the scope of cosmopolitan Muslim networks of scholars and traders, as well as the power of the Arabic language. But he neither talked about Muslim unity nor interacted deeply with non-Muslims. Seventeenth-century traveler Evliya Çelebi preferred to remain mostly within Ottoman boundaries, or close to them, and engaged in conversations with and cultural observations of both Muslims and non-Muslims. Abdurreşid İbrahim's travels not only covered large areas of non-Muslim Asia but demonstrated a great sympathy for Koreans, Japanese, Chinese, and Hindus as the Asian-Eastern brothers of Muslims. He constantly urged unity against the common threat of Western hegemony. See Abdurreşid İbrahim, *Alem-i Islam ve Japonya'da İntişari Islamiyet* (Istanbul: Ahmed Saki Bey Matbaasi, 1327/1910–1911).

53. Mustafa Kamil, *Al-Shams al-Mushriqah* (Cairo: Matbaat al-Liwa, 1904).

54. Jacob M. Landau, *The Politics of Pan-Islam: Ideology and Organization* (Oxford: Clarendon, 1990), 128–129.

55. In his student years in Moscow (1865–1867), İsmail Gaspıralı was socially adopted by a famous pan-Slavist publisher and journalist, Mikhail Katkov, and witnessed the activities of the Moscow Slavic Benevolent Committee (which organized a pan-Slavic congress in 1867).

56. "İsmail Bey Gaspıralı'nın 'Müslüman Kongresi' ile ilgili olarak Osmanlı Padişahı II. Abdülhamid'e hitaben yazdığı mektubu," in Hakan Kırımlı and İsmail Türkoğlu, eds., *İsmail Bey Gaspıralı ve Dünya Müslümanları Kongresi,* Islamic Area Studies Project: Central Asian Research Series, no. 4 (Tokyo: Tokyo University, 2002), 7.

57. *Daitô* 3, no. 4 (December 1910): 2.

58. *The Islamic Fraternity* was edited and managed by Mohammad Barakatullah of Bhopal, India, in Tokyo from 1911 to 1912.

59. For an example of Kokuryûkai's increasing networking with Asian nationalists after the Russo-Japanese War, see Selçuk Esenbel, "Japanese Interest in the Ottoman Empire," in Bert Edstrom, ed., *The Japanese and Europe: Images and Perceptions* (Richmond, Surrey, U.K.: Curzon, 2000), 112–120; and El-Mostafa Rezrazi, "Pan-Asianism and the Japanese Islam: Hatano Uhô. From Espionage to Pan-Islamist Activity," *Annals of the Japan Association for Middle East Studies*, no. 12 (1997): 89–112.

60. Hatano Uho was an expert on Chinese Muslims and a graduate of Konoe Atsumaro's Tôa Dôbun Shoin in Shanghai.

61. Hatano [Uho], *Asya Tehlikede*, trans. Nakawa and [Abdurreşid] İbrahim (Istanbul: Sebilürreşad, 1328/1910).

62. İbrahim, *Alem-i Islam ve Japonya'da İntişari Islamiyet*. For an assessment of the Japanese contacts of Abdurreşid İbrahim and his pan-Asianism, see Selçuk Esenbel, Nadir Ozbek, İsmail Türköğlu, François Georgeon, and Ahmet Ucar, "Ozel Dosya: Abdurreşid İbrahim 2," *Toplumsal Tarih* 4, no. 20 (August 1995): 6–23.

63. Sakamoto Tsutomu, "The First Japanese Hadji Yamaoka Kôtaro and Abdurreşid İbrahim," in Selçuk Esenbel and Inaba Chiharu, eds., *The Rising Sun and the Turkish Crescent: New Perspectives on the History of Japanese-Turkish Relations*(Istanbul: Boğaziçi University Press, 2003), 105–121; and Nakamura Kojiro, "Early Japanese Pilgrims to Mecca," *Report of the Society for Near Eastern Studies in Japan* (Nippon Orient Gakkai) 12 (1986): 47–57. See also "Japonya'da İhtida," *Sirati Müstakim* 7, no. 174 (1327/1912), which discusses the conversions of Hatano and Baron Hiki.

64. See Selçuk Esenbel, "A 'fin de siècle' Japanese Romantic in Istanbul: The Life of Yamada Torajiro and His 'Toruko Gakan.'" *Bulletin of the School of Oriental and African Studies* 59, no. 2 (1996): 237–252.

65. Ibid., 247.

66. For the early stages of pan-Islamism, see Azmi Özcan, *Pan-Islamism: Indian Muslims, the Ottomans and Britain (1877–1924)* (Leiden: Brill, 1997). For the Buddhist links of pan-Asianism, see Stephan N. Hay, *Asian Ideas of East and West: Tagore and His Critics in Japan, China, and India* (Cambridge: Harvard University Press, 1970).

67. See Rebecca Karl, *Staging the World: Chinese Nationalism at the Turn of the Twentieth Century* (Durham, N.C.: Duke University Press, 2002).

68. Rebecca Karl, "Creating Asia: China in the World at the Beginning of the Twentieth Century," *American Historical Review* 103, no. 4 (October 1998): 1096–1118. Rebecca Karl analyzes an attempt by Chinese intellectuals at the beginning of the twentieth century to construct a radical meaning of "Asia, emphasizing how they tried to make Asia a site for anti-imperialist and antistate praxis and for cultural recovery. Karl traces the development of this "Asia" concept from the Chinese appropriation of the Philippine struggles against the United States for their own nationalist discourses to the founding of a small pan-Asianist society in 1907 by Japanese and Chinese socialists and anarchists, Indian nationalists, and Filipino and Vietnamese activists. Contrary to those who focus on state-centered pan-Asianism, particularly the figure

of Sun Zhongshan (Sun Yat-sen), she argues that this ultimately failed effort at radical Asianism was seminal in the articulation of new relationships among emerging concepts of culture, race, geography, and global solidarity. Karl also challenges the reification of "Asia" as a unit of historical analysis by historicizing this original radical impulse in regional construction. Her argument about Asia as a constructed rather than natural category not only illuminates developments in that part of the world at the beginning of the twentieth century but suggests how historians can analyze regional constructs in other times and places.

69. "Al-Yaban wa'l-Islam," Al-Muqtabas, February 18, 1910.

70. Daitô 3, no. 4 (December 1910): 2.

71. İbrahim, Alem-i Islam ve Japonya'da İntişari Islamiyet, 88

72. Islamic Fraternity 2, no. 2 (May 15, 1911).

73. In this context, Tokutomi Sohô (1863–1957) advocated a "yellow man's burden," giving voice to an alternative to the idea of the white man's burden inspired by Rudyard Kipling's famous poem of 1899. See Tokutomi Sohô, "Kôjin no omoni," Kokumin Shimbun (January 1906), quoted in Hirakawa Sukehiro, "Modernizing Japan in Comparative Perspective," Comparative Studies of Culture, no. 26 (1987): 29.

74. Yamamuro Shinichi, "Nihon Gaikô to Ajia Shugi no Kôsaku," in Seiji Gaku Nenpô (Tokyo: Iwanami Shoten, 1998), 26–27, taken from Tsurumi Yûsuke, Gotô Shinpei (Tokyo: Keisô Shôbo, 1965–1967), 960–961.

75. George Akita and Itô Takashi, "Yamagata Aritomo no 'jinshû kyôsô' ron" [Yamagata Aritomo's theory of racial conflict], in Nihon Gaikô no kiki ninshiki (Tokyo: Yamakawa Shuppansha, 1985), 95–118.

76. For example, Abdurreşid İbrahim was able to meet with Ôkuma Shigenobu, Itô Hirobumi and other leading statesmen of Japan, particularly because of the Japanese leaders' interest in meeting with a Muslim intellectual and pan-Islamist activist. For the records of his conversation with Ôkuma Shigenobu in 1909, see İbrahim, Alem-i Islam ve Japonya'da İntişari Islamiyet, 386–387. For Gotô Shinpei and Inukai Tsuyoshi's role in helping an Indian revolutionary in Tokyo in 1917, see Tapan Mukherjee, Taraknath Das: Life and Letters of a Revolutionary in Exile (Calcutta: National Council of Education in Bengal, 1997), 109–110. For the attention that Vietnamese nationalist Phan Boi Chau received from Inukai Tsuyoshi and Ôkuma Shigenobu, see David Marr, Vietnamese Anti-Colonialism, 1885–1925 (Berkeley: University of California Press, 1971), 113.

77. Yamamuro, "Nihon Gaikô to Ajia Shugi no Kôsaku," 26–27, taken from Tsurumi, Gotô Shinpei, 960–961.

78. Marr, Vietnamese Anti-Colonialism, 146, 154–155.

79. Miura Tôru, "Nihon no Chutô-Isuramu Kenkyû," Gekkan Hyakka, no. 365 (1993): 18–23. For Ôkuma Shigenobu's comments, see the preface to Cromer, Saikin Ejiputo [Modern Egypt] (Tokyo: Dainippon Bunmei Kyôkai, 1911), 1:12–13. For a recent English-language assessment of this topic, see Miura Tôru, "The Past and Present of Islamic and Middle Eastern Studies in Japan: Using the Bibliography of Islamic and Middle Eastern Studies in Japan 1868–1988," Annals of Japan Association for Middle East Studies 17, no. 2 (2002), 45–60.

80. Nitobe's famous work on Bushido ethics represented this interpretation; see Nitobe Inazô, *Bushido: The Soul of Japan. An Exposition of Japanese Thought* (Tokyo: Kodansha International, 1998). For the implications of Nitobe's argument, see Akira Iriye, *Cultural Internationalism and World Order* (Baltimore: Johns Hopkins University Press, 1997), 44. For insightful articles on Nitobe Inazô as both an internationalist and Japanese nationalist, see John F. Howes, ed., *Nitobe Inazô: Japan's Bridge Across the Pacific* (Boulder, Colo.: Westview, 1995).

81. See Okakura Kakuzo, *The Ideals of the East with Special Reference to the Art of Japan* (London: John Murray, 1903).

82. For an example of the popularity of this slogan among the Japanese political elite, see Joyce Lebra, "Ôkuma Shigenobu: Modernization and the West," in Edmund Skrzypczak, ed., *Japan's Modern Century* (Tokyo: Sophia University, in cooperation with Tuttle, 1968), 40. See also Ôkuma Shigenobu, *Tôzai Bunmei no Chôwa* (Tokyo: Waseda Daigaku Shuppansha, 1990).

5. THE IMPACT OF WWI ON PAN-ISLAMIC AND PAN-ASIANIST VISIONS OF WORLD ORDER

1. Celal Nuri, *İttihad-i İslam: İslamin Mazisi, Hali, İstikbali* (Istanbul: Yeni Osmanli Matbaasi, 1913),10–11. For an example of how Ottoman intellectuals perceived pan-Islamism as unrealistic around 1904 and 1905, see Yusuf Akçura, *Üç Tarzı Siyaset* (Ankara: Türk Tarih Kurumu Basımevi, 1987), 39–40. In his work *İttihad-ı İslam* (Muslim unity), Celal Nuri describes the objections of realist politicians of the Ottoman state to the rising tide of pan-Islamic ideas after the Balkan wars. Those against Ottoman leadership in the Muslim world saw the Ottoman state as an "old and sick grandfather [perhaps referring to the European notion of the "sick man of Europe"], in need of help himself" (ibid.) and believed that the Ottoman state was in no position to help liberate other Muslims.

2. The best example of this historiography can be found in Turkish school textbooks and military history books, prepared by the Turkish General Staff. For an example, see Turkish General Staff, *Osmanlı Imparatorluğu'nun Siyasi ve Askeri Hazırlıkları ve Harbe Giriş*, vol. 1, *Birinci Dünya Harbi'nde Türk Harbi* (Ankara: Genelkurmay Basımevi, 1991). Mustafa Aksakal attributes the origin of this official version of Turkish history to the writings of Yusuf Hikmet Bayur, especially his *Türk Inkılabı Tarihi* (Ankara: Türk Tarih Kurumu Basimevi, 1940–1967). For an assessment of this historiography, see Mustafa Aksakal, "Defending the Nation: The German-Ottoman Alliance of 1914 and the Ottoman Decision for War" (Ph.D. diss., Princeton University, 2003), 1–13.

3. This view is also part of official Turkish history textbooks. For examples of similar views in English-language literature, see Jacob M. Landau, *Pan-Turkism: From Irredentism to Cooperation* (Bloomington: Indiana University Press, 1995), 51–55.

4. Feroz Ahmad was the most articulate critic of this theory. For a summary of his views,

see Feroz Ahmad, "Ottoman Armed Neutrality and Intervention, August–November 1914," *Studies on Ottoman Diplomatic History* (Istanbul) 4 (1990): 41–69. Ahmad concluded this article with the following statement: "Turkey's intervention in 1914 was not the result of collusion between the Germans and the war party. It was mainly determined by the nationalist aspirations of the Unionists which Enver Paşa came to personify" (69).

5. Aksakal, "Defending the Nation."

6. Mustafa Aksakal puts emphasis on the triumph of nationalist feelings in the post–Balkan War period and connects it to the post-1923 Kemalist policies of nationalism. Aksakal's references to the writings of Özdemir and Habil Adem, the pseudonyms for Şehbenderzade Filibeli Ahmed Hilmi and İsmail Naci Pelister, suggest the connections between nationalism and pan-Islamism.

7. For the ideas and activities of Mehmet Akif Ersoy during the Balkan wars and WWI, see Ertuğrul M. Düzdağ, *Mehmet Akif Ersoy* (Ankara: Kültür ve Turizm Bakanlığı Yayınları, 1988).

8. Selim Deringil, *The Well-Protected Domains: Ideology and the Legitimization of Power in the Ottoman Empire, 1876–1909* (London: Tauris, 1998); Engin Deniz Akarli, "The Tangled End of Istanbul's Imperial Supremacy," in Leila Fawaz and C. A. Bayly, eds., *Modernity and Culture from the Mediterranean to the Indian Ocean, 1890–1920* (New York: Columbia University Press, 2002), 261–284.

9. Famous pan-Islamist activist Abdurreşid İbrahim's observation of the Muslim responses to the opening of the parliament in a small town in Russian Siberia is an illustrative example of the global impact of the Turkish constitutional revolution. Muslims in this remote Russian town gathered on the same evening to celebrate the new "liberty and freedom" in the Ottoman Empire and wanted to send a congratulatory telegraph to Istanbul. See Abdurreşid İbrahim, *İslam Dünyasi* (Istanbul: Yeni Asya Yayınları, 1987), 1:151–152. The anti-imperialist and modernist rhetoric of the Young Turks made them very popular among Muslims throughout the world. The coincidence that two prominent Egyptian and Albanian leaders of the twentieth century, Anwar Sadat and Anwar Hoja, received their names from parents celebrating the achievements of Young Turk leader Anwar Pasha is an indication of the popularity of the Young Turks' image among civilized modern Muslims.

10. Two Young Turk leaders, Ahmed Rıza and Dr. Nazim, mentioned the formula of making Turkey "The Japan of the Near East" in their interview with British foreign secretary Sir Edward Grey in 1908. See M. Şükrü Hanioğlu, *Preparation for a Revolution: The Young Turks, 1902–1908* (New York: Oxford University Press, 2001), 304 and 492; and Feroz Ahmed and Marian Kent, eds., *The Great Powers and the End of the Ottoman Empire* (London: Allen and Unwin, 1984), 13. The conversation clearly refers to the fact that Japan was an ally of Great Britain and a recognized great power in international affairs.

11. For an assessment of the activities and lack of support for a pan-Islamist intellectual during the early years of the Young Turk period, see Nadir Özbek, "From Asianism to Pan-Turkism: The Activities of Abdürreşid İbrahim in the Young Turk Era," in Selçuk

Esenbel and Inaba Chiharu, eds., *The Rising Sun and the Turkish Crescent: New Perspectives on the History of Japanese-Turkish Relations* (Istanbul: Boğaziçi University Press, 2003), 86–104.

12. *Sırat-ı Müstakim* (The straight way) was a weekly magazine that started on August 1908. Publication under that name ceased, but the journal continued under the name *Sebilürreşad* (The right way). It was edited by Mehmet Akif Ersoy and Eşref Edip.

13. Interestingly, Muhammad Barakatullah, a pan-Islamist activist who published *Islamic Fraternity* in Tokyo, reflected on the Muslim perception of the Italian invasion of Libya as a modern European crusade in his editorial titled "Christian Combination Against Islam," *Islamic Fraternity* (Tokyo) 3, no. 2 (June 1912): 1–2.

14. For the ethnic cleansing of the Muslims in the Balkans, see the sections on the Balkans wars in Justin McCarthy, *Death and Exile: The Ethnic Cleansing of Ottoman Muslims, 1821–1922* (Princeton, N.J.: Darwin, 1995), 135–164.

15. After about six months of negotiation, during which a second Balkan war occurred, the Treaty of London signed on May 30, 1913, ended the Balkan wars. With that treaty, Turkey ceded most of its territory in Europe.

16. For the most comprehensive biography of Ahmed Hilmi, see M. Zeki Yazıcı, "Şehbenderzade Ahmet Hilmi: Hayatı ve Eserleri" (Ph.D. diss., Istanbul University, 1997).

17. For the English translation of Şehbenderzade Ahmed Hilmi's novel on universal mystical thought, see Şehbenderzade Ahmed Hilmi, *Awakened Dreams: Raji's Journeys with the Mirror Dede* [Amak-i Hayal), trans. Refik Algan and Camille Helminski (Putney, Vt.: Threshold, 1993).

18. Şeyh Mihridin Arusi [Şehbenderzade Ahmed Hilmi], *Yirminci Asırda Alem-i İslam ve Avrupa—Müslümanlara Rehber-i Siyaset* (Istanbul, 1911). İsmail Kara has published a good selection from this work (2–11, 66–73, and 87–96) in his edited collection *Türkiye'de İslamcılık Düşüncesi* [Islamist thought in Turkey], 3d ed. (Istanbul: Kitabevi, 1997) 1:86–101.

19. See Kara, *Türkiye'de Islamcılık Düşüncesi,* 1:100–101.

20. Ibid., 1:86–87.

21. Özdemir [Şehbenderzade Ahmed Hilmi], *Türk Ruhu Nasıl Yapılıyor? Her Vatanperverden, Bu Eserciği Türklere Okumasını ve Anlatmasını Niyaz Ederiz* (How is the Turkish spirit formed? We ask that each patriot read and relate this pamphlet to the Turks) (Istanbul: Hikmet Matbaa-i İslamiyesi, 1913).

22. For Şehbenderzade Ahmed Hilmi's critique of Celal Nuri (İleri) for proposing a materialist interpretation of Islamic history, see Şehbenderzade Filibeli Ahmed Hilmi, *Huzur-ı Akl u Fende Maddiyyun Meslek-i Dalaleti: Tarih-i İstikbal'in Birinci Cildini Teşkil Eden Mesail-i Fikriyenin Tenkidi* (Istanbul, 1332/1913–1914).

23. The Arabic translation of this work was published in Cairo in 1920, the year of the Paris Peace Conference. See Celal Nuri Bey [Jalal Nuri Bek], *İttihad al-Muslimin: Al-Islam, madihi wa-hadiruhu wa mustaqbaluhu,* trans. Hamzah Tahir and Abd al-Wahhab 'Azzam (Cairo, 1920). Celal Nuri published a similar work on pan-Islamism on the eve of WWI but focused more on its potential relations with German grand

policy. See Celal Nuri Bey, *İttihad-i İslâm ve Almanya* (Istanbul: Yeni Osmanli Mat-baasi, 1914).

24. Especially during and after the Balkan wars, Celal Nuri wrote often and turned his articles into various books. He traveled to Russia, Scandinavian countries, and America in 1914. Nuri became a founding member of the Wilsonian Principles Society in 1918. In 1919 he was elected to the Ottoman parliament and helped in the preparation of the draft of the National Pact (Misak-i Milli). Exiled to Malta by the British occupation authorities, he later joined the parliament of the Ankara government.

25. Celal Nuri, *Kendi Noktai Nazarimizdan Hukuk-i Düvel* (Istanbul: Osmanlı Şirketi Matbaasi, 1911). Even in this early work, Celal Nuri argues that Muslims should cooperate with socialists in their struggle against Western imperialism.

James Lorimer (1818–1890) was the author of *The Institutes of the Law of Nations: A Treatise of the Jural Relations of Separate Political Communities* (1884). He occupied the chair of Law of Nature and of Nations in Edinburgh. An anti-Semite, he viewed Islam as a degenerate religion. Friedrich von Martens' book *Völkerrecht: Das internationale Recht der zivilisierten Nationen* (Law of nations: International law of civilized nations) was first published in 1882. Henri Bonfils (1835–1897) authored a book on international law, edited by Paul Fauchille (1858–1926), that existed in Ottoman translations. See Henri Bonfils and Paul Fauchille, *Hukuk-i umumiye-yi düvel*, trans. Ahmet Salahettin and Mehmet Cemil (Istanbul: Matbaa-i Jirayir-Keteon, 1908).

26. For Nuri's main writings on Islam and modernity, see Celal Nuri. *Mukadderat-ı Tarihiye: Tedenniyat-i Osmaniyenin Esbab ve Sevaik-i Tarihiyesi* (Istanbul: Matbaa-i İçtihad, 1912); and idem, *İştirak Etmediğimiz Harekat: Tarih-i Osmani ve Keşfiyat, Rönasans ve Reform Harakati* (Istanbul: Cemiyet Kütüphanesi, 1917).

27. Nuri, *İttihad-i İslam*, 3.

28. "Japanese and Chinese should not be separated in a time when Europe is conquering the whole world. On the contrary, the expansion and the penetration of the West will unite them in a serious and sincere way" (ibid., 139).

29. "Asia is now the home property of Europe. If it was not for the rise of the government of the 'Sun of the East [Japan],' and if Europeans were a little more capable of unity and cooperation among themselves, today China would be divided and fully colonized to be in the status of another India" (ibid., 139–140).

30. Celal Nuri perceived a common culture in Asia different from European culture and depicted the Asian civilization as older and more moderate, humanist, and spiritual (ibid., 141–142).

31. Celal Nuri seem to have been aware of Abdurreşid İbrahim's ideas about solidarity between the Muslim world and Japan. He thought that this rapprochement would create new era in Asia and further strengthen a shared cultural legacy. Nuri rejected the idea that the weak and backward Asia was already dead. For him, Asia was asleep until the beginning of the twentieth century, and the turn of the century symbolized the end of this long sleep and a new awakening. See ibid., 144.

32. Celal Nuri, *Kadinlarimiz; Umumiyet İtibarile Kadin Meselesi ve Tarihi, Müslüman ve Türk Kadinlari* (Istanbul: Matbaai Içtihat, 1912).

33. Aloys Sprenger (1813–1893), an Austrian Orientalist, was famous for his argument that Muhammad suffered from hysteria. After acting as the principal of a Muslim college in Delhi in 1857, he was naturalized as a British subject and left India to become a professor of Oriental languages at Bern University from 1858 to 1881. See Aloys Sprenger (1813–1893), *Das Leben und die Lehre des Mohammad* (Berlin: Nicolai, 1869).

Reinhart Dozy became a well-known Orientalist for his thesis that the Islamic faith spread with the help of the sword. See Reinhart Peter Dozy, *Essai sur l'histoire de l'Islamisme* (Paris: Maisonneuve, 1897). Because this work was perceived to be prejudiced in its representation of Islamic history, its Turkish translation in 1908 by Abdullah Cevdet attracted negative reactions, and its distribution was banned in 1910. See Reinhart Peter Dozy, *Tarih-i İslamiyet* (Mısır: Matbaa-i İçtihad, 1908). Dozy became a frequent reference in Muslim apologetic writings critical of European Orientalism.

34. Celal Nuri's biography of the Prophet, *Hatemül Enbiya,* was republished during the Republican period; see Cemal Kutay, *Tarih önünde İslam Peygamberi* (Istanbul: Aksoy Yayıncılık, 1998). Şehbenderzade Ahmed Hilmi severely criticized some of the ideas in the book; see Hilmi, *Huzur-ı Akl u Fende Maddiyyun Meslek-i Dalaleti.*

35. For Celal Nuri's critique of Abdullah Cevdet's pro-Westernism during the Balkan Wars, see Celal Nuri, *Müslümanlara, Türklere Hakaret, Düşmanlara Riayet ve Muhabbet* (Istanbul: Kader Matbaasi, 1914).

36. Belak [pseud.], *Mağlub Milletler Nasıl İntikam Alırlar,* trans. Habil Adem [pseud.] (Istanbul: Ikbal Kütübhanesi, 1332/1913–1914).

37. Jons Mul [pseud.], *Londra Konferansindaki Mes'elelerden: Anadoluda Türkiya Yaşayacak mi? Yaşamayacak mi?* trans. Habil Adem [pseud.] (Istanbul: Ikbal Kütüphanesi, n.d.).

38. Professor Vayt [pseud.], *Muharebeden Sonra: Hilafet Siyaseti ve Türklük Siyaseti,* trans. Habil Adem (Istanbul: Ikbal Kütüphanesi, 1915). İsmail Kara used selections (only pages 32 to 143) from an earlier version of the work, published in 1913 in Istanbul by Şems Matbaası, for a recent edition. See Professor Vayt, "Muharebeden Sonra: Hilafet Siyaseti ve Türklük Siyaseti," in İsmail Kara, *Hilafet Risaleleri* (Istanbul: Klasik, 2003), 3:329–383. İsmail Naci also wrote on pan-Germanism and pan-Slavism, indicating his interest in the politics of "pan-" ideologies in world affairs. See Habil Adem [pseud.], *Pan Cermanizm, Pan Islavizm* (Istanbul: Seda-yi Millet Matbaasi, 1916).

39. *Siyasetü'l-Etrak ve'l-Hilafe* (Istanbul: Matbaatu'l-Adl, 1331/1913).

40. Naci attributes the origins of the Tanzimat policies to European diplomats, not to Turkish bureaucrats; see Professor Vayt, "Muharebeden Sonra," 3:335–336.

41. Professor Vayt, "Muharebeden Sonra," 331–381.

42. Muhiddin Baha [Pars], "Halife Ordusu Mısır ve Kafkas'da," in İsmail Kara, ed., *Hilafet Risaleleri* (Istanbul: Klasik, 2003), 3:387.

43. İsmail Kara has underlined the exceptionality and originality of Said Halim Paşa's ideas in the history of Islamist thought. See Kara, *Türkiyede İslamcılık Düşüncesi,* 1:38–39.

44. Said Halim's seven essays, written between 1910 and 1919, were titled "Meşrutiyet" (Constitutionalism), "Mukallitliklerimiz" (Our emulation [of the West]); "Buhran-i Fikri-

miz" (Our intellectual crisis); "Taassub" (Dogmatism); "Buhran-i İçtimaimiz" (Our
social crisis); "İnhitat-i İslam Hakkında Bir Tecrübe-i Kalemiye" (An essay on the decline of Islam); and "İslamlaşmak" (On Islamization). All these essays were published
as one book under the title *Buhranlarımız* (Our crisis) in 1919. For a recent edition of
this work, see Said Halim Paşa, *Bütün Eserleri* (Istanbul: Anka, 1985). For other published books by Said Halim Paşa, see Said Halim Passa, *Intihat-i Islam Hakkinda Bir
Tecrübe-yi Kalemiye* (Istanbul: Matbaa-i Âmire, 1918); and Mehmet Said Halim Paşa,
L'Empire Ottoman et la guerre mondiale, 1863–1921 (Istanbul: Isis, 2000). See also Said
Halim Paşa, *Political Reform of Muslim Society* (Lahore: Islamic Publications, 1947).

45. See Kara, *Türkiyede İslamcılık Düsüncesi,* 1:193.

46. Jacob M. Landau, *The Politics of Pan-Islam: Ideology and Organization* (Oxford:
Clarendon, 1990), 92–94.

47. After he came to Istanbul, Abdurreşid İbrahim participated in the pan-Islamic campaigns against the colonization of the Muslim lands and joined the Libyan resistance
to the Italian invasion, where he developed his close ties with the Young Turk leadership. During WWI, İbrahim worked actively for the Ottoman/German government's
pan-Islamic campaigns.

48. Landau, *The Politics of Pan-Islam,* 105–142.

49. [Pars], "Halife Ordusu Mısır ve Kafkas'da." The play was originally written in 1915 and
published in Bursa.

50. For the English translation of this proclamation, see Geoffrey L. Lewis, "The Ottoman
Proclamation of Jihad in 1914," *Islamic Quarterly: A Review of Islamic Culture* (London) 19, no. 1–2 (January–June 1975): 157–163.

51. Feroz Ahmad, "1914–1915 Yıllarında İstanbul'da Hint Milliyetçi Devrimcileri," *Yapıt*
(Ankara), no. 6 (August–September 1984): 5–15.

52. This is the title of a British intelligence memorandum, dated July 15, 1917, about the
pan-Islamic activities in East Africa. See Landau, *The Politics of Pan-Islam,* 141.

53. İsmail Kara's edition of all the major writings on the issue of the caliphate demonstrates the intellectual lineage of the idea of the illegitimacy of the Ottoman caliphate
and the proposal of an alternative Arab caliphate from the early 1880s to the 1910s.
See İsmail Kara, *Hilafet Risaseleri,* 4 vols. (Istanbul: Klasik, 2002–2004).

54. The reports of the wartime Foreign Office from Tokyo indicate the increasing suspi-
cion and confusion of the British embassy with regard to the relationship between
Asianists and a number of influential politicians. See British Foreign Office, *Japan
Correspondence, 1914–1923,* Public Records Office Collection, FO 371.

55. Ôtsuka Takehiro, *Ôkawa Shûmei to Kindai Nihon* (Tokyo: Mokutakusha, 1990); idem,
Ôkawa Shûmei: Aru Fukkô Kakushin Shugisha no Shisô (Tokyo: Chûô Kôronsha,
1995); and Hashikawa Bunsô, "Kaisetsu," in Ôkawa Shûmei, *Ôkawa Shûmei Shû,* ed.
Hashikawa Bunsô (Tokyo: Chikuma Shobô, Tokyo 1975), 407.

56. Ôkawa's views on the inevitable conflict between Eastern and Western civilizations
were best formulated in his work "Ajia, Yoroppa, Nihon" [Asia, Europe, and Japan], in
Ôkawa Shûmei, *Ôkawa Shûmei Zenshû,* 7 vols., ed. Ôkawa Shûmei Zenshû Kankôkai
(Tokyo: Ôkawa Shûmei Zenshû Kankôkai, 1961–1974), 2:872–873. This article was
originally published in book form in 1925. See also Ôkawa Shûmei, "Yoroppa no

Rakuchô," *Tôyô* 32, no. 2 (1929). For references to Ôkawa Shûmei's ideas as evidence for a Japanese conspiracy to wage aggressive war, see *International Military Tribunal for the Far East, The Tokyo Major War Crimes Trial: The Transcripts of the Court Proceedings of the International Military Tribunal for the Far East*, ed. R. John Pritchard (Lewiston, N.Y.: Edwin Mellen, 1998).

57. See Ôtsuka, *Ôkawa Shûmei*, 66–72; and Hiraishi Naoaki, "Kindai Nihon no Kokusai Chitsujyokan to Ajiashugi," in *20 Seiki Shisutemu* (Tokyo: Tokyo Daigaku Shuppan-sha, 1998), 1:201–204.

58. Takeuchi Yoshimi, "Ôkawa Shûmei no Ajia Kenkyû," in Hashikawa Bunsô, ed., *Ôkawa Shûmei Shû* (Tokyo: Chikuma Shobô, 1982), 391–406. Because of the high quality of Ôkawa's scholarship on Asia and the recent interest in Islamic revivalism, two of his works were reprinted in the last decade. See Ôkawa Shûmei, *Fukkô Ajia no Shomondai* (1922; reprint, Tokyo: Chûô Kôronsha, 1993); and idem, *Kaikyô Gairon* (Tokyo: Keiô Shobô, 1942).

59. He seemed to be most fascinated by the ideas of Schleiermacher; see Ôtsuka, *Ôkawa Shûmei to Kindai Nihon*, 63–64. Most of the biographical information on Ôkawa's youth provided here relies on this book, unless noted otherwise.

60. He was especially interested in Kôtoku Shûsui and subscribed to the anarchist journal *Heimin Shinbun* (Commoner's news), which was an influential socialist weekly founded by Kôtoku Shûsui and Sakai Toshihiko, famous for its publication of Karl Marx's manifesto in 1904 and for taking a critical, pacifist stance toward the Russo-Japanese War. Its publication was suspended in January 1905. In 1904, before he started high school, Ôkawa visited Tokyo and attended lectures by leading socialists such as Kôtoku Shûsui, Sakai Toshihiko, and Abe Isoo. See Ôtsuka, *Ôkawa Shûmei to Kindai Nihon*, 23–24. Sakai Toshihiko (1871–1933) was a journalist and socialist thinker, and Abe Isoo (1965–1949) was a Christian-socialist educator. Together with Kôtoku Shûsui, they led the socialist movement, and all of them opposed the Russo-Japanese War.

61. For Ôkawa's involvement in Dôkai, see Ôtsuka, *Ôkawa Shûmei to Kindai Nihon*, 63–100. For the importance of Dôkai in the history of Christianity in Japan, see Mark R. Mullins, *Christianity Made in Japan: A Study of Indigenous Movements* (Honolulu: University of Hawai'i Press, 1998), 69–81. Like many other Japanese at that time, Matsumura Kaiseki encountered Christianity during his study of a foreign language, and he was later baptized as a member of the Dutch Reformed Church. Matsumura Kaiseki left the organized missionary church in 1881 because of disagreement with its "un-Japanese" and "irrational" interpretation of Christianity and, in particular, the white missionaries' disrespectful attitudes toward Japanese culture. While continuing his intellectual and spiritual search, he began to think of forging a Confucian Christianity that could be integrated with the new scientific theology that emerged in Europe. In connection with his new religion, Matsumura launched the magazine *Michi*. He published *A History of the Rise and Fall of Nations* in 1902 and *Modern European History* and *Saint Socrates* in 1903. When he decided to establish an independent church fostering a new, reformed Christianity for Japan, he initially called his

church the One Heart Association. In 1907 he renamed it Nihon Kyôkai (the Church of Japan) and finally dubbed it Dôkai (South Church) in 1912. The name changes reflected his realization that the movement had transformed from a reform movement within Christianity into a new religion independent of Christianity. According to his teachings, Matsumura Kaiseki was combining the basic truths contained in the sacred writings of Christianity, Buddhism, and Confucianism. He was convinced that it was possible to reduce the central truths of all major religions to the following four basic teachings: belief in God, cultivation of moral character, love of neighbor (interpreted broadly to mean responsibility for emperor, nation, and humankind), and belief in eternal life. Dôkai rejected the Christian beliefs of the Holy Trinity and original sin.

62. Sir Henry Cotton, *New India or India in Transition* (London: K. Paul, 1907).

63. Ôkawa, *Anraku no Mon*, in *Ôkawa Shûmei Zenshû*, 1:803–804.

64. See Ôkawa, *Fukkô Ajia no Shomondai*, 1–3.

65. Tetsuo Najita and Harry Harootunian, "Japanese Revolt Against the West: Political and Cultural Criticism in the Twentieth Century", in Bob Tadashi Wakabayashi, ed., *Modern Japanese Thought* (Cambridge: Cambridge University Press, 1998), 211–212.

66. See James H. Cousins, "The Cultural Unity of Asia," *Asian Review* (Tokyo) 2, no. 3 (March–April 1921): 217–228.

67. Ôkawa even wanted to translate some of Okakura's writings from English into Japanese. See Ôtsuka, *Ôkawa Shûmei*, 61–62.

68. See Anagarika Dharmapala, "Naite Nipponjin ni keikoku su" [A cry of warning to the Japanese], *Michi*, no. 65 (September 1913): 29–33; and Muhammad Barakatullah, "Yo ga Sokoku" (My motherland), *Michi*, no. 67 (November 1913): 42–47.

69. Kahawatte Siri Sumedha Thero, *Anagarika Dharmapala: A Glorious Life Dedicated to the Cause of Buddhism* (Sarnath, Varanasi: Maha Bodhi Society of India, 1999).

70. Tôa Dôbun Shoin was the Japanese school established in Shanghai in 1901 by the Asianist organization established by Konoe Atsumaro, Tôa Dôbunkai. It recruited students from Japan to study Chinese language and culture.

71. Anti-British agitation of *Islamic Fraternity* led to pressure from the British embassy to close down the journal, but because of its status as a religious journal, the Japanese government did not want to ban it. Finally, in 1912, the Home Ministry prohibited the publication of the journal, and in 1914 the Barakatullah's teaching contract was not renewed. See Gaimushô Gaikô Shiryôkan, Tokyo, Muhammad Barakatullah file. See also Ôkawa, *Fukkô Ajia no Shomondai*, 307.

72. The Ghadar Party was established in 1913 in San Francisco as a revolutionary party dedicated to achieving the full independence of India. It was led by Har Dayal. During WWI, Ghadar Party members cooperated with both Germany and the Ottoman government in attempts to form an army from imprisoned Indian soldiers, but they could not actualize these plans. For more details, see Harish K. Puri. *Ghadar Movement: Ideology, Organization, and Strategy* (Amritsar: Guru Nanak Dev University, 1993).

73. Lala Lajpat Rai was one of the leaders of a new generation of Indian nationalists who

advocated violence if repression became too strong. He was a prolific writer, and his book *Young India* made him famous. When he went to Japan in 1915, he often gave speeches with names such as "Asia for Asiatics," and he emphasized Japan's responsibility for helping its Asian neighbors. Rai predicted that the Great War would destroy European ethics and a worldwide revolution could occur. During his visit to Japan in 1915, Rai also published a book in Tokyo about the current nationalist movement in India; see Lala Lajpat Rai, *Reflections on the Political Situation in India with A Personal Note and Extracts from Indian and English Newspapers etc.* (Tokyo, 1915).

74. Ôtsuka, *Ôkawa Shûmei, Aru Fukkô,* 70.

75. For the text of Rai's speech, see Lala Lajpat Rai, "Ajia no Bunmei," *Michi,* no. 92 (December 1915): 31–34.

76. Nakajima Takeshi, *Nakamuraya no Bosu* (Tokyo: Hakusuisha, 2005), 81–98.

77. For the full text of Tagore's speech at Tokyo University, see Rabindranath Tagore, *The Message of India to Japan: A Lecture by Sir Rabindranath Tagore, Delivered at the Imperial University of Tokyo* (Tokyo, 1916). For a discussion of the response to Tagore's message in Japan, see Stephen N. Hay, *Asian Ideas of East and West: Tagore and His Critics in Japan, China, and India* (Cambridge: Harvard University Press, 1970).

78. Ôkawa Shûmei, *Indo ni Okeru Kokuminteki Undô no Genjyô oyobi sono Yurai,* in Hashikawa Bunsô, ed., *Ôkawa Shûmei Shû* (1916; reprint, Tokyo, Chikuma Shobô, 1975), 11–76. For a detailed assessment of this work as a contribution to the study of Indian nationalism, see Nagasaki Nobuko, "Ôkawa Shûmei no Shoki Indo Kenkyû, Indo Kankei no Ichi Sokumen," *Tôkyô Daikgaku Kyôyôbu Jinbun Kagaku Kiyô: Rekishi to Bunka,* no. 12 (March 1978): 116–120.

79. Rai, *Reflections on the Political Situation in India.* Ôkawa seemed to rely on two other works in the preparation of his book: Lala Lajpat Rai, *Young India: An Interpretation and a History of the Nationalist Movement from Within* (New York: B. W. Huebsch, 1916); and Paul Samuel Reinsch, *Intellectual and Political Currents in the Far East* (Boston: Houghton Mifflin, 1911).

80. Ôkawa, *Indo ni Okeru,* 75–76. Rai's book starts with a quotation from a Dr. Seton Watson about the aims of the allied powers in the war: "Our task is nothing less than the regeneration of Europe, the vindication of the twin principles of nationality and democracy and the emancipation of subject races from alien rule" (quoted in Rai, *Reflections on the Political Situation in India,* 1).

81. Ôkawa, *Indo ni Okeru,* 73–74. The quotation here is drawn from the English original published in the *Manchester Guardian.* This comment of Tagore's was frequently referenced in Japanese Asianist writings. For an example, see Taraknath Das, *Is Japan a Menace to Asia?* (Shanghai, 1917), i.

82. Taraknath Das left Bengal in 1905 and earned a master's degree from the University of Washington while remaining highly involved in organization and publication to popularize the cause of Indian nationalism. During the war, he went to Germany and Turkey but did his most fruitful work in Japan. He became a naturalized U.S. citizen. For the best study on his life, see Tapan Mukherjee, *Taraknath Das: Life and Letters of a Revolutionary in Exile* (Calcutta: National Council of Education in Bengal, 1997).

83. Mukherjee, *Taraknath Das,* 92–93.

84. Tarakunato Dasu [Taraknath Das], "Ajia no Kyôisha wa Hatashite Nihon Ka?" *Nippon Oyobi Nipponjin,* no. 706 (June 1, 1917): 68–75.

85. Mukherjee, *Taraknath Das,* 102–103.

86. An Asian Statesman [Taraknath Das], *The Isolation of Japan in World Politics* (Tokyo: Asiatic Association of Japan, 1918). The book included an introduction by Oshikawa Masayoshi, an M.P. in the Imperial Japanese Diet, and appendixes by Dr. Setsui Miyake, the editor of *Nippon Oyobi Nipponjin,* and Prof. Dr. Senga Tsurutaro of Kyoto Imperial University. The Japanese translation of the work, by Ôkawa Shûmei, was published earlier than its English original. See Dasu Tarakunato [Taraknath Das], *Kokusaikan ni Okeru Nihon no Koritsu* (Tokyo: Asiatic Association of Japan, 1917).

87. For other articles written by Das for the same purpose, see Taraknath Das, "The Orient and the Question of Race Superiority," *Asian Review* 1, no. 7 (October 1920): 712–717; and idem, "The European Peril," *Asian Review* 1, no. 8 (November–December 1920): 835–841.

88. Kuwajima Sho, *Indian Mutiny in Singapore (1915)* (Calcutta: Ratna Prakashan, 1991).

89. W. W. Pearson, *For India* (Tokyo: Asiatic Association of Japan, 1917). Pearson also wrote one of the first articles on Gandhi for the Japanese Asianist press; see idem, "A Character Study of M. K. Gandhi, Leader of the Non-Cooperation Movement in India," *Asian Review* 2, no. 5 (July–August 1921): 485–492.

90. Pearson, *For India,* 47–48.

91. Ôkawa Shûmei, "Sekai ni Okeru Nippon no Chii," *Dôwa,* no. 52 (August 1915): 40–44.

92. Ôkawa Shûmei, "Kunkoku no Shimei," *Michi,* no. 93 (January 1916): 47–55.

93. See chapter 3.

94. For a summary of Tokutomi Sohô's Asian Monroe Doctrine, see Iichirô Tokutomi, "Japan's Mighty Mission," appendix to Das, *Is Japan a Menace to Asia?* 122. The appendix by Tokutomi Sohô was originally published in the *Japan Chronicle* of January 19, 1917. Das reproduced the articles from the version published in the *Peking Post* on February 10, 1917.

95. Kodera Kenkichi, *Dai Ajiashugi Ron* (Tokyo: Hôbunkan, 1916), i–ix.

96. For a biography of Paul Richard by his son, see Michel Paul Richard, *Without Passport: The Life and Work of Paul Richard* (New York: Peter Lang, 1987).

97. Ôkawa Shûmei, "Kaisetsu," in Paul Richard, *Nipponkoku ni Tsugu* (1917; reprint, Tokyo: Seinen Shobô, 1941). Other works translated by Ôkawa Shûmei are Paul Richard, *Dai JûIchiJi* (1921), in Ôkawa Shûmei, *Ôkawa Shûmei Zenshû,* 1:881–993; and Paul Richard, *Eien no Chie* (Tokyo: Keiseisha, 1924).

98. Paul Richard, *Nipponkoku ni Tsugu* (Tokyo: Seinen Shobô, 1941). Paul Richard wrote this book at Ôkawa Shûmei's suggestion. Also see Kita Reikichi, "Waga Kuni no Daishimei—Pôru Risha shi no Nipponkoku ni Tsugu wo yomu," *Tôhô Jiron* 2, no. 12 (November 1917): 12.

99. Paul Richard, "Some Answers," *Asian Review* 1, no. 1 (February 1920): 42.

100. Paul Richard, introduction to Pearson, *For India,* iii–v.

101. Paul Richard, "Democracy," *Asian Review* 1, no. 3 (April 1920): 272–275.

102. Kuzuu Yoshihisa, "Farewell to Dr. Richard and Prof. Cousins, Advisors of the Asian Review," *Asian Review* 1, no. 3 (April 1920): 282.

103. Ishikawa Yoshihiro, "Tôzai Bunmeiron to Nihon no Rondan," in Furuya Tetsuo, ed., Kindai Nihon no Ajia Ninshiki (Kyoto: Kyoto University Press, 1994), 395–432.

6. THE TRIUMPH OF NATIONALISM?

1. Signed between the British and French empires in May 1916, The Sykes-Picot Agreement laid out how these two empires would share the Middle East after the dismemberment of the Ottoman state, dividing the Ottoman provinces of Syria, Iraq, Lebanon, and Palestine into various French- and British-administered areas. The agreement took its name from its negotiators, Sir Mark Sykes of Britain and Georges Picot of France.

2. Woodrow Wilson's "Fourteen Points" speech to the United States Congress on January 8, 1918, articulated what he considered the basic framework of a just and lasting peace after WWI. This included freedom of the seas and open covenants, the settlement of the boundaries of Eastern Europe according to the principle of self-determination, and a League of Nations that would enforce the peace. It constituted the only open statement by any of the belligerents of their war aims. The fourteen points thus became the basis for German and Ottoman surrender. Wilson asked for the settlement of competing claims for imperial territories based on the interest of the populations concerned and defined by the principle of "national self-determination." I discuss conflicting interpretations of the idea of "national self-determination" below.

3. See Michael Adas, "Contested Hegemony: The Great War and the Afro-Asian Assault on the Civilizing Mission Ideology," in Prasenjit Duara, ed., *Decolonization: Perspectives from Now and Then* (New York: Routledge, 2004), 78–100.

4. Arno Mayer, *Wilson vs. Lenin: Political Origins of the New Diplomacy, 1917–1918* (Cleveland: World Publishing, 1964).

5. Number 12 of Wilson's fourteen points read as follows: "The Turkish portion of the present Ottoman Empire should be assured a secure sovereignty, but the other nationalities which are now under Turkish rule should be assured an undoubted security of life and an absolutely unmolested opportunity of autonomous development, and the Dardanelles should be permanently opened as a free passage to the ships and commerce of all nations under international guarantees." For the full text of the fourteen points, see www.ourdocuments.gov/doc.php?doc=62.

6. Even Mustafa Kemal Paşa, later to become the leader of the national struggle against the British-led coalition, thought of establishing good relations with the British Empire after WWI. See Şerafettin Turan, "Mondros Mütarekesi Ertesinde Mustafa Kemal'in Orduya, Siyasete ve İngilizlerin Tutumuna İlişkin Düsünceleri," *Belleten* (Ankara) 46, no. 182 (1982): 346.

7. Egyptian leader Sa'ad Zaghlul, Vietnamese leader Ho Chi Minh, and Indian national-

ist leader Bal Tilak were some of the anticolonial leaders who aimed at gaining support for their cause at the Paris Peace Conference; see Erez Manela, "The Wilsonian
Moment: Self Determination and the International Origins of Anticolonial Nationalism, 1917–1920" (Ph.D. diss., Yale University, 2003).

8. Mine [Sümer] Erol, "Wilson Prensipleri Cemiyeti'nin Amerika Cumhurbaşkanı
Wilson'a Gönderdiği Muhtıra," in *Ankara Üniversitesi Dil ve Tarih Coğrafya Fakültesi
Tarih Araştırmaları Dergisi* 3, nos. 4–5 (1966): 237–245. See also Mehmet Şahingöz
and Vahdet Keleşyılmaz, "Milli Mücadele Dönemi Türk Basınında Wilson Prensipleri," *Atatürk Araştırma Merkezi Dergisi* (Temmuz) 12, no. 35 (July 1996): 357–378.

9. Mustafa Budak, *Idealden Gerçeğe: Misakı Milliden Lozan'a Dış Politika* (Istanbul: Küre
Yayınları, 2002), 64. In the first royal consultative assembly organized by the Ottoman government to discuss the crisis caused by the Greek invasion of Izmir (Birinci
Saltanat Şurası of May 26, 1919), delegates emphasized the importance of demanding
the implementation of the Wilsonian principles, reminding the great powers of the
promises of the civilized world. Several participants urged the Ottoman government
to chart a pro-British and pro-American policy, with appeals to Wilsonianism, to
receive their support for liberating Western Anatolian Muslims from Greek invasion.
It was agreed that the government should try to get an invitation to go to the Paris
Peace Conference to present its legitimate and just cause, under the twelfth point
of the Wilsonian principles, against the foreign occupation of the Muslim-majority
areas in Anatolia.

10. Mustafa Budak, "I. Dünya Savaşı Sonrası Uluslarası Düzen Kurma Sürecinde Osmanlı
Devleti'nin Tavrı: Paris Barış Konferansı'na Sunulan 23 Haziran 1919 Tarihli Muhtıra,"
Divan İlmi Araştırmalar Dergisi 4, no. 7 (1992): 191–215.

11. Budak, *Idealden Gerçeğe*, 86.

12. Mushir Hosain Kidwai was an Indian Muslim nationalist and a leading name in the
international pan-Islamic network of intellectuals, with connections to the Ottoman
government. He received a law education in England from 1897 to 1904. One of the
founders of a pan-Islamic society established in London in 1903, he received a deco-
ration from the Ottoman sultan, Abdulhamid II. Kidwai joined the Indian National
Congress and became a founding member of the Khuddam-ul-Ka'ba Society (the
organizational predecessor of the Khilafat movement). Living in England between
1913 and 1920, he served as the honorary secretary of the Central Islamic Society of
London

13. S. Mushir Hosain Kidwai, *The Future of the Muslim Empire: Turkey* (London: Central Islamic Society, 1919); idem, *The Sword Against Islam; or, A Defence of Islam's
Standard-Bearers* (London: Central Islamic Society, 1919).

14. S. Mushir Hosain Kidwai, *İslama çekilen kılıç, yahut, Alemdaran-ı İslamı müdafaa:
Osmanlı heyet-i murahhasasının sulh konferansına takdim ettiği muhtıra ve Paris sulh
konferansı onlar meclisi tarafından aldığı cevaba nazaran Osmanlı devlet İslamiyesi
meselesinin tenkidi* (London: Londra Cemiyet-i Merkeziye-i İslamiyesi, 1919).

15. Kidwai later wrote in support of socialist internationalism. See S. Mushir Hosain
Kidwai, *Pan-Islamism and Bolshevism* (London: Luzac, 1937).

16. See Mim Kemal Öke, *Hilafet Hareketleri* (Ankara: Türkiye Diyanet Vakfı Yayınları, 1991), 43–45. For a more comprehensive assessment of the Khilafat movement, see Gail Minault, *The Khilafat Movement: Religious Symbolism and Political Mobilization in India* (New York: Columbia University Press, 1982).

17. Muhammad Ali made this argument in a speech in London in 1920; see Jacob M. Landau, *The Politics of Pan-Islam: Ideology and Organization* (Oxford: Clarendon, 1990), 208.

18. Mustafa Necati, "Sevgili Payitahtımızın İşgali Karşısında," *İzmir'e Doğru*, no. 46 (March 24, 1920), quoted in Şahingöz and Keleşyılmaz, "Milli Mücadele Dönemi."

19. For a recent assessment of the Sèvres Treaty and its renegotiation from the perspective of the new world order established by the Paris Peace Conference, see Margaret Macmillan, *Paris 1919* (New York: Random House Trade Paperbacks, 2003), 427–455.

20. See Martin Kramer, *Islam Assembled: The Advent of the Muslim Congresses* (New York: Columbia University Press, 1986), 72–79.

21. British intelligence took note of this conference and reported in on September 14, 1921. For the activities of Ahmed al-Sharif al-Sanusi in connection with the Ankara government, see Anita L. P. Burdett, *Islamic Movements in the Arab World* (Slough: Archive, 1988), 1:146. For an assessment of the British intelligence reports during this period and the basis of their analysis of the pan-Islamic activities of Ankara government, see A. L. Macfie, "British Intelligence and the Turkish National Movement, 1919–1922," *Middle Eastern Studies* 37, no. 1 (January 2001), 1–16.

22. For the international pan-Islamic activism of the post-WWI period, see Landau, *The Politics of Pan-Islam*, 231–234.

23. Born in 1858, Ahmed Rıza joined the Young Turk opposition to Sultan Abdulhamid II in 1889 and for about nineteen years played a leadership role in the opposition movement. He became an important member of an international group of positivists in Paris. After the 1908 constitutional revolution, Ahmed Rıza entered parliament as a representative from Istanbul and later became the president of both the parliament and the senate.

24. Ahmed Rıza, *Meclisi Mebusan ve Ayan Reisi Ahmed Rıza Bey'in Anıları* (Istanbul: Arba Yayınları, 1988), pp. 76–80.

25. Using his personal contacts, he helped to arrange the mission to Ankara by Franclin Bouillon, who signed the first agreement between France and the nationalist government in Anatolia.

26. Ahmed Rıza, *La faillite morale de la politique occidentale en Orient* (Paris, 1922; reprint, Tunis: Bouslama, 1979).

27. Mustafa Kemal Atatürk, "Fransız Muharriri Maurice Pernot'ya Demeç (29/10/1923)," in Uygur Kocabaşoğlu, ed., *Modern Türkiye'de Siyasi Düşünce*, vol. 3, *Modernleşme ve Batıcılık* (Istanbul: İletişim Yayınları, 2002), 599–600.

28. Mustafa Kemal, "A Speech Delivered by Ghazi Mustapha Kemal, October 1927" (Leipzig: K. F. Koehler, 1929), microform, 586–587, quoted in Roderick Davison, "Turkish Diplomacy from Mudros to Lausanne," in *Essays in Ottoman and Turkish History, 1774–1923: The Impact of the West* (Austin: University of Texas Press, 1990), 586–587.

29. Erkan Türkmen, "M. İkbal'ın Gözüyle Türkiye ve Atatürk," in *Ata (Dergisi)*, no. 2 (1992): 18–29.

30. For the patterns of response of the Indian Muslims to the abolishment of the caliphate, see Mohammad Sadiq, *The Turkish Revolution and the Indian Freedom Movement* (Delhi: Macmillan India, 1983), 104–130.

31. Arnold Toynbee, *Survey of International Affairs, 1925,* vol. 1, *Islamic World Since the Peace Settlement* (Oxford: Oxford University Press, 1927), p. 53. For the caliphate's international importance, see also Arnold J. Toynbee and Kenneth P. Kirkwood, *Turkey* (London: E. Benn, 1926), 112.

32. Ali Satan, "Halifeliğin Kaldırılışı, 1919–1924" (M.A. thesis, Marmara Üniversitesi, Sosyal Bilimler Enstitutüsü, 2000).

33. The Ottoman newspaper *Vakit* noted that the League of Nations did not even have a modicum of power or initiative. If great powers experienced difficulties over second- and third-rate matters, they passed them on to the league. See Yücel Güçlü, "Turkey's Entrance into the League of Nations," *Middle Eastern Studies* 39, no. 1 (2003): 189. Though not a member of the league, Turkish delegates participated in various conferences and committees, such as the Preparatory Commission for the Disarmament Conference in 1928, the Advisory Convention on Traffic in Opium, the International Opium Convention, the International Labor Organization, and the Briand Commission of Enquiry for European Union.

34. The Mosul question was not resolved with the Lausanne Treaty but referred to the league by the British government, which argued that the league had given it the mandate over Iraq. Turkey saw the league as helping Britain to obtain in peacetime what it had been unable to get through war.

35. Ahmed Rıza, *The Moral Bankruptcy of Western Policy Towards the East* (Ankara: Ministry of Culture and Tourism Publications, 1988), 210.

36. See Halil Halid, *Türk Hakimiyeti ve Ingiliz Cihangirligi* (Istanbul: Yeni Matbaasi 1925).

37. Miwa Kimitada, "Japanese Opinions on Woodrow Wilson in War and Peace," *Monumenta Nipponica* 22, nos. 3–4 (1967): 368–389.

38. The Japanese name of the proposal means the abolition of racial discrimination, which does not exactly mean "race equality." Therefore, some scholars choose to name it the "racial nondiscrimination clause." In this work, I will follow the "racial equality proposal" translation of Naoko Shimazu, because the proposal was later interpreted as an attempt to make racial equality a tenet of the League of Nations, despite the initial Japanese wording and intention.

39. Naoko Shimazu, *Japan, Race and Equality: The Racial Equality Proposal of 1919* (London: Routledge, 1998), 66–67.

40. For an example of the dominance of this civilizational paradigm, see Hara Takashi, "Harmony Between East and West," in K. K. Kawakami, ed., *What Japan Thinks* (New York: Macmillan, 1921).

41. Frederick Dickinson, *War and National Reinvention: Japan in the Great War, 1914–1919* (Cambridge: Harvard University Press, 2001).

42. African-American intellectuals shared this critique of the league; see Marc Gallicchio,

Black Internationalism in Asia, 1895–1945: The African American Encounter with Japan and China (Chapel Hill: University of North Carolina Press, 2000), 21–29.

43. Ôkawa Shûmei, "Kôwa Kaigi ni Okeru Wiruson no Shippai," *Michi*, no. 138 (October 1919): 45–54.

44. "The League of Nations and Colored People," *Asian Review* 1, no. 4 (May–June 1920): 347–348.

45. Miwa, "Japanese Opinions on Woodrow Wilson," 382–385.

46. The Washington Conference system relied on the international agreement at the Washington Conference in February 1922 among Japan, France, Great Britain, and the United States to replace the Anglo-Japanese Alliance with a naval disarmament program and to establish international cooperation among them to respect the status quo in the Pacific Region. It allowed for a compromise between Japan's special interest in Manchuria and the open door policy of the USA. The conference agreement set the framework of power relations in the Pacific Region for almost a decade.

47. Ôtsuka Takehiro, *Ôkawa Shûmei: Aru Fukkô Kakushin Shugisha no Shisô* (Tokyo: Chûô Kôronsha, 1995), 92–93.

48. The final resolution of the conference was telegraphed, as the opinion of the Japanese people, to Georges Clemenceau, head of the Paris Peace Conference, and to the prime minister of Japan, Hara Takashi. See "Jinshuteki Sabetsu Teppai Kiseikai Undôki," *Ajia Jiron* 3, no. 3 (March 1919): 60–61.

49. For the texts of Paul Richard's speeches, see Paul Richard, "Jinshuteki Sabetsu Teppai Mondai to Nippon Kokumin no Tenshoku," *Ajia Jiron* 3, no. 4 (April 1919): 25. See also idem, "Mazu Ajia Renmei wo Jitsugen Seyo," *Ajia Jiron* 3, no. 5 (May 1919): 31–32.

50. Ôkawa Shûmei, "Indo Kokuminteki Undo no Yûrai," in *Ôkawa Shûmei Zenshû*, 7 vols., ed. Ôkawa Shûmei Zenshû Kankôkai (Tokyo: Ôkawa Shûmei Zenshû Kankôkai, 1961–1974), 2:508–510.

51. Among the Japanese Asianists, Miyazaki Tôten seems to have been one of the very few who agreed with Paul Richard. See Hiraishi Naoaki, "Kindai Nihon no Kokusai Chitsujyokan to Ajiashugi," in *20 Seiki Shisutemu* (Tokyo: Tokyo Daigaku Shuppankai, 1998), 1:196–197.

52. Ôkawa Shûmei, "Kroma Shi no Ejipto Tôji," in *Fukkô Ajia no Shomondai* (Tokyo: Daitôkaku, 1922; reprint, Tokyo: Chûô Kôronsha, 1993), 234–238.

53. The Baku Congress aimed to create cooperation between the anticolonial nationalist movements and the new Soviet Russia, advancing several unorthodox theses on national and colonial questions and ending with a revolutionary manifesto to the peoples of the East that urged them to unite against colonialism in order to bring about nationalist awakening. For the proceedings of the Baku Congress, see John Riddell, ed., *To See the Dawn: Baku, 1920—First Congress of the Peoples of the East* (New York: Pathfinder, 1993).

54. For Enver Paşa's cooperation with the Bolshevik government and his activities during the years of 1921 and 1922, see Suhnaz Yılmaz, "An Ottoman Warrior Abroad: Enver Paşa as an Expatriate," *Middle East Studies* 35, no. 4 (October 1999): 40–70.

55. Enver Paşa died in battle, on August 4, 1922, in one of the military confrontations in the Central Asian Basmachi resistance against the Bolshevik army.

56. B. Nicolaevsky, "Russia, Japan, and the Pan-Asiatic Movement to 1925," *Far Eastern Quarterly* 8, no. 3 (May 1949): 269.

57. Tan Malaka, "Communism and Pan-Islamism," *What Next: Marxist Discussion Journal,* no. 21 (2001), www.whatnextjournal.co.uk/Pages/Back/Wnext21/Panislam.html.

58. Ôkawa, *Fukkô Ajia,* 162–176.

59. For pan-Asianist Ôkawa's early positive ideas on the role of the Soviet Revolution in Asian revival, see ibid., chap. 7, 170–185. This sympathetic evaluation of Soviet policy in Asia was shared by Indian nationalists in Tokyo, who advocated an alliance between Asian nationalism and Bolshevism to purge white colonialism from Asia. Ôkawa's sympathy with the Bolshevik efforts to create a noncapitalist economy and his later advocacy of normalizing Japan's diplomatic ties with the Soviet Union became one of the reasons behind his disagreement with Kita Ikki, who remained a firm opponent of the new government in Russia. When Soviet envoy Joffe visited Tokyo in February 1923, Ôkawa Shûmei advocated Japanese rapprochement with the new socialist regime in opposition to Kita Ikki, who viewed Soviet Russia as a menace to Japan and the rest of Asia. See George M. Wilson, "Kita Ikki, Ôkawa Shûmei, and the Yûzonsha," *Papers on Japan,* no. 2 (1963): 161–162.

60. Takeuchi Yoshimi, "Nihon to Ajiashugi," in *Nihon to Ajia* (Tokyo: Chikuma Gakujitsu Bunshô, 1993), 337–340.

61. Ibid., 337–340; Ôgata Kôhei, ed., *Nippon to Indo* (Tokyo: Sanseidô, 1978), 61–66.

62. The polarization of right- and left-wing radical ideologies in domestic politics occurred from 1917 to 1921. Faced with the turmoil in the international order symbolized by the Russian Revolution and the significant domestic discontent in Japan near the end of WWI, Ôkawa Shûmei and Mitsukawa Kametarô organized a cosmopolitan study group, Rôsôkai (Old and Young Society), to discuss both world developments and social problems at home. Their group included a highly diverse array of individuals, including socialists and liberals, who would meet regularly to discuss the global trends created by the Great War. Well-known socialists such as Takabatake Motoyuki and Sakai Toshihiko, the agrarianist Gondô Seikyô, the populist nationalist Nakano Seigô and even the famous liberal Ôi Kentarô were members of Rôsôkai. When this study group ended its meetings after only one year, Ôkawa Shûmei, Mitsukawa Kametarô, and Kita Ikki organized a radical nationalist organization called Yûzonsha. The cofounders of Yûzonsha hoped to execute Kita Ikki's plan of national reorganization with the goal of fostering conditions in Japan that would aid Asian revival.

Mitsukawa Kametarô (1888–1936) was a pan-Asianist intellectual and activist who cooperated with Ôkawa throughout the 1920s and 1930s. For his most famous book on Asia, see Mitsukawa Kametarô, *Ubawaretaru Ajia* (Tokyo: Kôbundô Shoten, 1921); for his view of civilizational conflict, see idem, *Tôzai jinshu tôsô shikan* (Tokyo: Tôyô Kyôkai Shuppanbu, 1924).

63. The term "*yûzon*" comes from an ancient Chinese poem and means "to survive." In terms of its program for domestic politics, Yûzonsha advocated a state-controlled economy and limitations on the wealth of individuals. For a discussion of the economic ideas of Ôkawa Shûmei and Yûzonsha, see Ôtsuka, *Ôkawa Shûmei,* 199–200; and Wilson, "Kita Ikki, Ôkawa Shûmei and the Yûzonsha," 153–155.

64. Takeuchi Yoshimi was the first to emphasize this aspect; see Takeuchi Yoshimi, "Profile of Asian Minded Man X: Ôkawa Shûmei," *The Developing Economies* 7, no. 3 (September 1969): 368–369.

65. According to Ôkawa's argument, in spite of the heroic achievements of the Meiji Restoration, Japan had fallen behind its goals.

> To have the heart to die for the purpose of raising our country, and to spread justice to the four seas, was actually the real wish of our seniors who embodied the spirit of the Meiji Restoration. The nation of new Japan has to make this real wish a tradition and shoulder the responsibility of its job vigorously. For to undertake the leadership of Asia and create Asian unity is in fact the only way to bring justice to the four seas. This should be done for the sake of Japan, and for the sake of Asia, and for the sake of humanity.
>
> (ÔKAWA, FUKKÔ AJIA, 21)

66. Both Ôkawa and Kita Ikki used the metaphor of "the sword of Islam" to describe their mission: "It was about the same time when my heart became attracted to the faith of Muhammad, whose doctrines require a unity of religion and politics and whose religion puts an emphasis on the principle of 'either the sword or the Quran'" (Ôkawa, *Fukkô Ajia,* 21–22). In his later scholarly works on Islam, Ôkawa commented that this was an Orientalist depiction of Islam and had nothing to do with Islamic history. See Ôkawa Shûmei, *Kaikyô Gairon* (Tokyo: Keiô Shobô, 1942; reprint, Tokyo: Chûô Kôronsha, 1992), 10–11.

67. For the historical development of Bolshevik policies toward pan-Asiatic movements as well as nationalist movements in East Asia, see Nicolaevsky, "Russia, Japan and the Pan-Asiatic Movement," 259–295.

68. Bertrand Russell, *Roads to Freedom: Socialism, Anarchism and Syndicalism* (London: Allen and Unwin, 1918).

69. *Stolen Asia* was the title of a well-known book by Ôkawa's close friend and comrade Mitsukawa Kametarô (1888–1936). See Mitsukawa, *Ubawaretaru Ajia.*

70. For example, interest in Japan among leading Vietnamese nationalists from 1905 to 1914 was replaced by Wilsonian and socialist inclinations after World War I. For the pro-Japanese trend in mainstream Vietnamese nationalism, see David Marr, *Vietnamese Anti-Colonialism,1885–1925* (Berkeley: University of California Press, 1971), 113. Ho Chi Minh's biography illustrates the appeal of both Woodrow Wilson's principle of self-determination and socialist internationalism. See Mark Bradley, *Imagining Vietnam and America: The Making of Postcolonial Vietnam, 1919–1950* (Chapel Hill: University of North Carolina Press, 2000).

71. Mohammad Sadiq, *The Turkish Revolution and the Indian Freedom Movement* (Delhi: Macmillan India, 1983). For Chinese nationalist interest in the success of Turkish national movement, see Chin Tokujin and Yasui Sankichi, eds., *Sonbun Kôen Dai Ajia Shugi Shiryôshû: 1924 nen, 11 Gatsu Nihon to Chûgoku no Kiro* (Kyoto: Hôritsu Bunkasha 1989), 44–47.

72. Lothrop Stoddard, *The New World of Islam* (New York: Scribner's, 1921). The fact that Stoddard's book was translated into Arabic and Ottoman within a few years is indicative of the global circulation of ideas. In the Arabic translation, the extensive and far-ranging commentaries by pan-Islamic thinker Shakip Arslan made the translation almost a different work. See Lothrop Stoddard, *Yeni Alem-i Islam,* trans. Ali Riza Seyfi (Istanbul: Ali Şükrü Matbaasi, 1922). For the Arabic translation, see Lûthrub Stûdârd, *Hadir al-Alam al-Islami,* trans. 'Ajjâj Nuwayhid, ed. al-Amîr Shakîb Arslân (Cairo: Matbaa-i Salafiyah, 1924).

73. Ôkawa, *Fukkô Ajia,* 37–41.

74. *The Rising Tide of Color Against the White World Supremacy* was the title of an influential book by Lothrop Stoddard (1883–1950), first published in New York by Scribner's in 1920. Ôkawa often referred to Stoddard's works in his writings.

75. Ôkawa, *Fukkô Ajia,* 27–45.

76. For the diplomatic background of the Immigration Act of 1924 and its long-term consequences for the U.S.-Japanese relations, see Minohara Toshihiro, *Hainichi Iminho to Nichibei Kankei: "Hanihara Shokan" no Shinso to Sono "Judainaru Kekka"* (Tokyo: Iwanami Shoten, 2003), 259–266.

77. For a recent assessment of the impact of the 1924 Immigration Act on U.S.-Japanese relations, see Hirobe Izumi, *Japanese Pride, American Prejudice: Modifying the Exclusion Clause of the 1924 Immigration Act* (Stanford: Stanford University Press, 2001).

78. Minohara, *Hainichi Iminho to Nichibei Kankei,* 258–264.

79. Peter Duus, "Nagai Ryutaro and the 'White Peril,' 1905–1944," *Journal of Asian Studies,* 31, no. 1 (November 1971): 41–48.

80. In fact, the primary international publication of Kokuryûkai, the *Asian Review,* devoted its massive attention to both the racial equality proposal at the Paris Peace Conference and the issue of discrimination against Japanese immigrants in the USA. The *Asian Review* mailed its initial copies to Japan-related diplomats, politicians, and business leaders in the United States. It published editorials on issues of race equality and the status of Japanese immigrants in the USA in almost every issue. As examples, see Kaiichi Toda, "The Japanese in California," *Asian Review* 1, no. 4 (May–June 1920): 362–363; and Tokutomi Sohô, "America and Japan," *Asian Review* 2, no. 2 (February 1921): 134–138.

81. Ogata Sadako, "The Role of Liberal Nongovernmental Organizations in Japan," in Dorothy Borg and Okamoto Shumpei, eds., *Pearl Harbor as History* (New York: Columbia University Press, 1973): 459–486; and Yoichi Nakano, "East-West Harmony: The Immigration Controversy and the U.S.-Japan Relations Committee (1916–1932)" (unpublished paper submitted to History 1851 seminar at Harvard University, January 2000).

82. Ôkawa Shûmei, "Nichi-Bei Mondai," *Tôyô* 27 (June 1924), reprinted in idem, *Ôkawa Shûmei Kankei Monjo,* ed. Ôkawa Shûmei Kankei Monjo Kankôkai (Tokyo: Fuyô Shohô Shuppan, 1998), 194–196.

83. Prasenjit Duara, "Transnationalism and the Predicament of Sovereignty: China, 1900–1945," *American Historical Review* 102, no. 4 (October 1997): 1030–51; Kobayashi

Toshihiko, "Sun Yatsen and Asianism: A Positive Approach," in J. Y. Wong, ed., *Sun Yatsen: His International Ideas and International Connections* (Sydney, N.S.W.: Wild Peony, 1987), 15–38.

84. For the text (in multiple languages) and media coverage of Sun Yat-sen's Great Asianism speech, see Chin Tokujin and Yasui Sankichi, eds., *Sonbun Kôen Dai Ajia Shugi Shiryôshû: 1924 nen, 11 Gatsu Nihon to Chûgoku no Kiro* (Kyoto: Hôritsu Bunkasha, 1989).

85. Ibid., 11.

86. The American challenge to Japan referred to here is the anti-Japanese Immigration Act of 1924.

87. Ôkawa Shûmei, "Ajia, Yoroppa, Nihon" (1925), in *Ôkawa Shûmei Zenshû*, 2:872–873. The English translation is taken from the excerpt Ôkawa quoted in the English version of his post–Pearl Harbor lectures on the radio. See Ôkawa Shûmei, *A History of Anglo-American Aggression in East Asia*, trans. Yoshio Agawa and P. B. Clarke (Tokyo: Daitôa Shuppan Kabushiki Kaisha 1944), 2.

88. Ôkawa Shûmei, "Shin Tôyô Seishin," in *Ôkawa Shûmei Zenshû*, 2:946. Ôkawa did not specify when he first read Soloviev.

89. Ôkawa Shûmei, "Soloviev no Sensô Ron," *Gekkan Nihon*, June 1928, reprinted in *Ôkawa Shûmei Zenshû*, 4:543–560. See also Vladimir Sergeyevich Soloviev, *The Justification of the Good: An Essay on Moral Philosophy*, trans. Nathalie Duddington (New York: Macmillan, 1918); Paul Marshall Allen, *Vladimir Soloviev: Russian Mystic* (New York: Steiner, 1978).

90. Mark R. Peattie, "Forecasting a Pacific War, 1912–1933: The Idea of a Conditional Japanese Victory," in J. White, M. Umegaki, and T. Havens, eds., *The Ambivalence of Nationalism: Modern Japan Between East and West* (New York: University Press of America, 1990), 116.

91. Incidentally, two decades later, when Ôkawa's prosecutor questioned him about his advocacy of a war between Japan and the United States, Ôkawa responded that what he wrote was not a plan for Japanese aggression against the United States but rather a prediction of an American attack if Japan stood up for principles of Asian liberation. See *Exhibits of International Military Tribunal for the Far East*, 60 vols. (Tokyo, 1946–1948), vol. 31, exhibit 2177.

92. For ideas of a Muslim League of Nations or its variants, see Landau, *The Politics of Pan-Islam*, pp. 219 and 222.

93. Seiyûkai was one of the two major political parties in Japan during the interwar period. Zen Ajia Kyôkai had been founded in the aftermath of the anti-Japanese Immigration Act of 1926 under the leadership of Seiyûkai director Iwasaki Isao. See Mizuno Naoki, "Senkyûhyaku Nijû Nendai Nihon, Chôsen, Chûgoku ni okeru Ajia Ninshiki no Ichidaimen: Ajia Minzoku Kaigi o Meguru Sankoku no Ronchô," in Furuya Tetsuo, ed., *Kindai Nihon no Ajia Ninshiki* (Kyoto: Kyôto Daigaku Jinbun Kagaku Kenkyûjo, 1994), 509–544.

94. The organizing committee was composed of Won Kong-su, China; Lin Koi, China; R. B. Bose, India; Raja Pratap, Afghanistan; General Ricarte, Philippines; Ôkawa Shûmei, Tokyo; Gen Saroi, Annam; and J. Imazato.

95. Nakatani Takeyô, a young student and follower of Ôkawa Shûmei's Asianism, was among the seven members of the Japanese delegation in Shanghai. Two close friends of Ôkawa, Indian representative Rash Behari Bose and Afghanistan representative Pratap Mehandra, were other important figures at both conferences.

96. Upon a proposal by its most active delegate, the Indian nationalist Rash Behari Bose, the conference issued a note of appreciation to those who had done much to forward the cause of the Asian peoples. The list included not only nationalist leaders such as the king of Afghanistan, Amanullah Khan; Mustafa Kemal Pasha of Turkey; Sa'ad Zaghlul of Egypt; Gandhi of India; Aguinaldo of the Philippines; and Sun Yat-sen from China but also Tôyama Mitsuru and Inukai Tsuyoshi, two of the most prominent Asianist figures in Japan.

97. "Asiatic Conference: The Gathering at Nagasaki," *Japan Weekly Chronicle,* August 15, 1926, 158.

98. "Asiatic Congress," *Japan Weekly Chronicle,* July 29, 1926, 135–136.

99. "An Asiatic Congress," *Japan Weekly Chronicle,* July 22, 1926, 93–94. In Nagasaki, it was only on the third day of the conference that local Japanese attendance increased dramatically, mainly because of the international media coverage of the event on the days before. The meeting was held at the Young Men's Christian Association hall because of financial limitations.

100. Pratap was the second-closest Indian nationalist to Ôkawa after Behari Bose. For Ôkawa's critique of the Japanese government's unfriendly treatment of Mehandra Pratap, see Ôkawa Shûmei, "Pratap-kun wo Mukaeru," *Gekkan Nihon,* no. 3 (June 1925): 19–20.

101. Both Rash Behari Bose and Mehandra Pratap had little contact with the national leadership in India, even though Pratap traveled around the world for Asianist causes and received financial support from Afghanistan's King Amanullah Khan. See Raja Mehandra Pratap, *My Life Story of Fifty-five Years* (Dehradun: World Federation, 1947). One Filipino delegate to the Nagasaki conference, General Ricardo, was so out of touch with Filipino nationalism that, by the time he returned to the Philippines during the Japanese occupation, he could play no role in his home country in spite of his Japanese connections (private communication with Professor Nick Cullather of Indiana University, April 2001). Prince Cuong De of Vietnam, although he was unable to join the Nagasaki conference, had a similar experience because of his exile in Japan during the 1920s and 1930s. When Japanese occupation forces in Vietnam decided to end French colonial rule in 1945, Prince Cuong De found that he had become almost irrelevant to Vietnamese nationalism and could not take any part in the independence movement. See David Marr, *Vietnamese Anti-Colonialism, 1885–1925* (Berkeley: University of California Press, 1971), 238.

102. For an example, see "Letter to the Editor," *Japan Weekly Chronicle,* August 5, 1926, 157.

103. *Japan Weekly Chronicle,* July 15, 1926, 68.

104. *Japan Weekly Chronicle,* August 15, 1926, 158.

105. Mizuno, "Senkyûhyaku Nijû Nendai Nihon, Chôsen, Chûgoku ni okeru Ajia Ninshiki no Ichidaimen," 543–544.

106. *New York Times,* July 17, 1926.

107. *Japan Weekly Chronicle,* July 29, 1926, 121.
108. Ibid., 127.
109. *Japan Weekly Chronicle,* July 22, 1926, 94.
110. Zumoto Motosada, *Japan and the Pan-Asiatic Movement* (Tokyo: Japan Times, 1926). The book is based on Motosada's lecture at the Congress of the International University in Geneva in 1926.

7. THE REVIVAL OF A PAN-ASIANIST VISION OF WORLD ORDER IN JAPAN (1931–1945)

1. The Manchurian Incident of 1931 initiated a process that led to the establishment of a Japanese-controlled puppet government in Manchuria and Japan's withdrawal from the League of Nations. The Japanese Kwantung army guarding the South Manchurian Railways bombed parts of the railway in Mukden to create a pretext to occupy Manchuria with the ostensible purpose of providing security against Chinese nationalists in September 1931. Instead of withdrawing from the occupied territories, the Japanese government created the puppet state Manchukuo in February 1932. Nonrecognition of this state by the League of Nations, then, became the reason for Japanese withdrawal from the league in 1933.
2. Frederick Dickinson, *War and National Reinvention: Japan in the Great War, 1914–1919* (Cambridge: Harvard University Press, 2001).
3. Richard Storry, *The Double Patriots: A Study of Japanese Nationalism* (Boston: Houghton Mifflin, 1957).
4. Christopher Szpilman, "Conservatism and Its Enemies in Prewar Japan: The Case of Hiranuma Kiichirô and the Kokuhonsha," *Hitotsubashi Journal of Social Studies* 30, no. 2 (December 1998): 101–133.
5. Genzo Yamamoto, "Defending Japan's Civilization and Civilizing Mission in Asia: The Resilience and Triumph of Illiberalism in the House of Peers, 1919–1934" (Ph.D. diss., Yale University, 1999). See also Arima Tatsuo, *The Failure of Freedom: A Portrait of Modern Japanese Intellectuals* (Cambridge: Harvard University Press, 1969). For a previous work on this topic that focuses more on the failure of the liberals to fight the antiliberals, see Toru Takemoto, *The Failure of Liberalism in Japan: Shidehara Kijuro's Encounter with Anti-Liberals* (Washington, D.C.: University Press of America, 1978).
6. Louise Young, *Japan's Total Empire: Manchuria and the Culture of Wartime Empire* (Berkeley: University of California Press, 1998).
7. For Nitobe Inazô's arguments justifying Japan's Manchuria policy, see Thomas W. Burkman, "The Geneva Spirit," in John F. Howes, ed., *Nitobe Inazô: Japan's Bridge Across the Pacific* (Boulder, Colo.: Westview, 1995), 204–209. See also George Oshiro, "The End: 1929–1933," in Howes, *Nitobe Inazô,* 255–258.
8. For Zumoto's defense of the Manchurian Incident before international audiences in the United States and Europe, see Zumoto Motosada, *The Origin and History of the Anti-Japanese Movement in China* (Tokyo: Herald, 1932); and idem, *Japan in Manchuria and Mongolia* (Tokyo: Herald, 1931). For Nitobe Inazô's opinion on the Man-

churian Incident, see Nitobe Inazô, "Japan and the League of Nations," in *The Works of Nitobe Inazô* (Tokyo: University of Tokyo Press, 1972), 4:234–239; and idem, "The Manchurian Question and Sino-American Relations," in *The Works of Nitobe Inazô*, 4:221–233.

9. For a discussion of Shôwa Kenkyûkai, see J. Victor Koschmann, "Asianism's Ambivalent Legacy," in Peter J. Katzenstein and Takashi Shiraishi, eds., *Network Power: Japan and Asia* (Ithaca: Cornell University Press, 1997), 90–94. Shôwa Kenkyûkai (1933–1940) was labeled in the popular press as Konoe Fumimaro's brain trust. Especially during Konoe's tenure as prime minister (1937–1939, 1940–1941), Shôwa Kenkyûkai was preoccupied with formulating the East Asian Cooperative Body and the New Order Movement. The membership of the association was diverse and included scholars and journalists from different ideological backgrounds.

   For the anti-Western ideas of the Kyoto School philosophers, see John Dower, *War Without Mercy: Race and Power in the Pacific War* (New York: Pantheon, 1986), 227.

10. Harry Harootunian, *Overcome by Modernity: History, Culture, and Community in Interwar Japan* (Princeton: Princeton University Press, 2000); Stefan Tanaka, *Japan's Orient: Rendering Pasts into History* (Berkeley: University of California Press, 1993); Kevin Doak, *Dreams of Difference: The Japan Romantic School and the Crisis of Modernity* (Berkeley, University of California Press, 1994). There is an ongoing debate about the relationship of the pro-war nature of the Kyoto School philosophy and its vision of overcoming modernity. See Ueda Shizuteru, "Nishida, Nationalism, and the War in Question," in James Heisig and John Moraldo, eds., *Rude Awakenings: Zen, the Kyoto School, and the Question of Nationalism* (Honolulu: University of Hawai'i Press, 1995), 77–106; Yusa Michiko, "Nishida and Totalitarianism: A Philosopher's Resistance," in Heisig and Moraldo, *Rude Awakenings*, 107–131; and Andrew Feenberg, "The Problem of Modernity in the Philosophy of Nishida," in Heisig and Moraldo, *Rude Awakenings*, 151–173.

11. Akira Iriye, "The Failure of Economic Expansionism: 1918–1931," in Bernard S. Silberman and H. D. Harootunian, eds., *Japan in Crises: Essays on Taishô Democracy* (Princeton: Princeton University Press, 1974), 265.

12. James B. Crowley, "A New Asian Order: Some Notes on Prewar Japanese Nationalism," in Silberman and Harootunian, *Japan in Crises*, 273.

13. This continuity in change was theorized by Andrew Gordon as the transition from imperial democracy to imperial fascism. See Andrew Gordon, *Labor and Imperial Democracy in Prewar Japan* (Berkeley: University of California Press, 1991).

14. "Confronted by a formidable cluster of diplomatic, economic, and military problems, the Imperial government [of Japan] resorted to a series of potential solutions: Manchukuo, a Japanese Monroe Doctrine, Hirota's three principles, an advance to the South Seas, a national defense state, and the rejuvenation of China"; see James B. Crowley, "Intellectuals as Visionaries of the New Asian Order," in James W. Morley, ed., *Dilemmas of Growth in Prewar Japan* (Princeton: Princeton University Press, 1971), 395. Similarly, Ben-Ami Shillony has demonstrated that, even at the peak of the Pacific War, Japan did not deviate from the normal functioning of the Meiji

Constitution. See Ben-Ami Shillony, *Politics and Culture in Wartime Japan* (New York: Oxford University Press, 1981).

15. Hayashi Fusao, *Daitôa Sensô Kôteiron*, 2 vols. (Tokyo: Banchô Shobô, 1964–1965), cited in Crowley, "A New Asian Order," 297–298.

16. For example, Mark Peattie has argued that Ishiwara Kanji's views "were part of this surging anti-Western nationalism during the interwar period, and his concept of a Final War must be seen as a reinvigoration of a persistent, if long-muted, theme of challenge to the West throughout Japan's modern history to 1945" (Mark R. Peattie, *Ishiwara Kanji and Japan's Confrontation with the West* [Princeton: Princeton University Press, 1975], 368).

17. For a good example of the perception of Western retreat from Asia, see No-Yong Park, *Retreat of the West: The White Man's Adventure in Eastern Asia* (Boston: Hale, Cushman, and Flint, 1937).

18. U. Ottama (1879–1939) was an influential figure in Burmese nationalism. Influenced by both the Indian National Congress and the Japanese model, Ottama denounced British colonial rule. He was imprisoned by the British authorities for a very long time, ultimately dying in prison. For Ôkawa's praise of Ottama, see Ôkawa Shûmei, "Ottama Hôshi o Omou," in *Ôkawa Shûmei Zenshû*, 7 vols., ed. Ôkawa Shûmei Zenshû Kankôkai (Tokyo: Ôkawa Shûmei Zenshû Kankôkai, 1961–1974), 2:913–915.

19. Selçuk Esenbel, "Japanese Interest in the Ottoman Empire," in Bert Edstrom, ed., *The Japanese and Europe: Images and Perceptions* (Richmond, Surrey, U.K.: Curzon, 2000), 112–120; El-Mostafa Rezrazi, "Pan-Asianism and the Japanese Islam: Hatano Uhô. From Espionage to Pan-Islamist Activity," *Annals of the Japan Association for Middle East Studies,* no. 12 (1997): 89–112.

20. Tanaki Ippei was a scholar of China and Buddhism. He converted to Islam and performed pilgrimages to Mecca in 1925 and 1933. Wakabayashi describes Tanaka Ippei as a fighter for "Sonnô Yûkoku," meaning "Revere the Emperor, and be a Patriot," despite the fact that Tanaka became a Muslim and adopted the name Haji Nur Muhammad in 1918.

21. His brother, Wakabayashi Kyûman, worked for the same cause, operating undercover as a merchant among Chinese Muslims until he died in Changsha in 1924. For Wakabayashi's reflections on the history of the Kokuryûkai circle of Islam policy advocates, see Wakabayashi Han, *Kaikyô Sekai to Nihon* (Tokyo: Wakabayashi Han, 1937), 1–3.

22. Wakabayashi, *Kaikyô Sekai to Nihon*, 3–7. Araki Sadao (1877–1966) was a leader in the Imperial Way faction of the army.

23. Ôkawa Shûmei, "Cho Gakuryo Shi o Tazuneru no Ki" (November 1928), in *Ôkawa Shûmei Zenshû,* 4:591.

24. Christopher Szpilman, "The Dream of One Asia: Ôkawa Shûmei and Japanese Pan-Asianism," in H. Fuess, ed., *The Japanese Empire in East Asia and Its Postwar Legacy* (Munich: German Institute of Japanese Studies, 1998), 51.

25. Ôkawa Shûmei, "Manmô Mondai no Kôsatsu," *Gekkan Nihon,* no. 75 (June 1931), reprinted in *Ôkawa Shûmei Zenshû,* 2:649–683.

26. See Awaya Kentaro and Yoshida Yutada, eds., *International Prosecution Section (IPS)* (Tokyo: Tokyo Daigaku Shuppankai, 1980), 23:396–398. During the interrogation,

Ôkawa conceded that he knew something would happen but noted that many others at that time had the same knowledge and it was not a secret.

27. For instance, as the biography of Ishiwara Kanji, the military brain of the Manchurian Incident, confirms, ideas about a final war and East-West confrontation, which were very important in Ôkawa Shûmei's pan-Asianism, were commonly shared by other European, American, and Japanese thinkers, and Ôkawa was not the main inspiration for Ishiwara's plans. See Peattie, *Ishiwara Kanji*, 27–86.

28. William Miles Fletcher, *The Search for a New Order: Intellectuals and Fascism in Prewar Japan* (Chapel Hill: University of North Carolina Press, 1982), 29–30. For the detailed arguments of Rôyama on the issue of Manchuria policy, see also Rôyama Masamichi, *Japan's Position in Manchuria* (Tokyo: Institute of Pacific Relations–Japan Council, 1929).

29. Even in June 1931, shortly before the Manchurian Incident, when Ôkawa warned that a war could break out between China and Japan at a slight provocation and suggested the necessity of a radical change in policy in Manchuria, his ideas still were not exceptional enough to single him out as an instigator of Kwantung Army officers. See Ôkawa, "Manmô Mondai no Kôsatsu," 679–682.

30. Ôkawa Shûmei, "Nijyû no Nankyoku ni tai suru Kakugo," *Gekkan Nihon*, May 1932, reprinted in *Ôkawa Shûmei Zenshû*, 4:629–631; and idem, "Manshu Shin Kokka no Kensetsu," *Gekkan Nihon*, July 1932, in *Ôkawa Shûmei Kankei Monjo*, ed. Ôkawa Shûmei Kankei Monjo Kankôkai (Tokyo: Fuyô Shohô Shuppan, 1998), 244–248.

31. Ôkawa Shûmei, "Daitô Kyôeiken no Rekishiteki Konkyo," in Dai Nippon Genron Hôkokukai, ed., *Kokka to Bunka* (Tokyo: Dômei Tsûshinsha, 1943), 29–43.

32. For Ôkawa Shûmei's main article on the withdrawal from the League of Nations, see "Kokusai Renmei to Nihon," *Tôyô*, May 1932, reprinted in *Ôkawa Shûmei Kankei Monjo*, 232.

33. For Ôkawa's advocacy of the withdrawal from the league before the Manchurian Incident, see Ôkawa Shûmei, "Nihon no Kokusai Chii O Kokoromiru," *Daitô Bunka*, May 1929, reprinted in *Ôkawa Shûmei Kankei Monjo*, 234–243.

34. Inukai was assassinated by a group of radical nationalist army cadets and naval officers. Ôkawa Shûmei was indicted, and found guilty, of providing material assistance to this group. It is ironic that he ended up contributing to Inukai Tsuyoshi's assasination, as pan-Asianists usually viewed Inukai positively, and the 1926 Nagasaki pan-Asiatic conference honored him as one of the Asian politicians who aided the cause of Asian people's awakening.

35. The fifteen-year prison sentence Ôkawa received on February 3, 1934, was reduced to five years on October 24, 1935. Because of his health problems, he was allowed to postpone his prison term until June 16, 1936. He was finally paroled on October 13, 1937. See Ôtsuka Takehiro, *Ôkawa Shûmei to Kindai Nihon* (Tokyo: Mokutakusha, 1990), 220.

36. In the aftermath of the Manchurian Incident, Ôkawa established Jinmukai (Society of Jinmu) as a new nationalist organization, with the hopes of reaching a larger audience and creating a broader popular base for his radical nationalist and Asianist movement. Ôkawa Shûmei's trial and imprisonment must have played a role

in his decision to disband the group. Moreover, after the coup of February 26, 1936, an event that led to the execution of Kita Ikki as the civilian ideologue of the military conspirators, the authorities began to show less tolerance for radical nationalist organizations.

37. The journal was published by Mantetsu Tôa Keizai Chôsakyoku in Tokyo from August 1939 to February 1944.

38. Ôkawa Shûmei, editorial, *Shin Ajia* 1, no. 1 (August 1939): 2–3.

39. Tazawa Takuya, *Musurimu Nippon* (Tokyo: Sho Gakkan, 1998), 145–146.

40. See Grant K. Goodman, ed., *Japanese Cultural Policies in Southeast Asia During World War 2* (New York: St. Martin's, 1991), 2–5.

41. Gotô Ken'ichi, " 'Bright Legacy' or 'Abortive Flower': Indonesian Students in Japan During World War 2," in Goodman, *Japanese Cultural Policies in Southeast Asia During World War 2, 7–35.* See also Grant K. Goodman, *An Experiment in Wartime Inter-Cultural Relations: Philippine Students in Japan, 1943–1945* (Ithaca: Cornell University Southeast Asia Program, 1962).

42. Students of Ôkawa were the leading figures in Ôkawa Shûmei Kenshôkai and organized the publication of his collected works and other related materials. See Harada Kôkichi, *Ôkawa Shûmei Hakushi no shôgai* (Yamagata-ken Sakata-shi: Ôkawa Shûmei Kenshôkai, 1982).

43. For a personal account of the Ôkawa Juku from the memoirs of students, see Tazawa, *Musurimu Nippon,* 129–142.

44. For the evaluation of Ôkawa's Islamic studies, see Takeuchi Yoshimi, "Ôkawa Shûmei no Ajia Kenkyû," in Hashikawa Bunsô, ed., *Ôkawa Shûmei Shû;* (Tokyo: Chikuma Shobô, 1975), 391–394.

45. See Ôkawa Shûmei, "Taisen no Zento to Ajia no Shorai o Kataru Zadankai," *Shin Ajia* 2, no. 3 (August 1940): 126. See also Ôkawa Shûmei, "Nanhô Mondai," in Yoshioka Nagayoshi, ed., *Sekai no Dôkô to Tôa Mondai* (Tokyo: Zenrin Kyôkai, 1941), 384–385.

46. Ôkawa, editorial, *Shin Ajia* 1, no. 1 (August 1939): 3.

47. Haruo Iguchi, *Unfinished Business: Ayukawa Yoshisuke and U.S.-Japan Relations, 1937–1953* (Cambridge: Harvard East Asia Monographs, 2001).

48. See Ôtsuka Takehiro, *Ôkawa Shûmei: Aru Fukkô Kakushin Shugisha no Shisô* (Tokyo:, Chûô Kôronsha, 1995), 160–170; Kusunoki Seiichirô, "Ôkawa Shûmei no tai-Bei Seisaku," *Nihon Rekishi,* no. 474 (November 1987): 54–70.

49. See Ôtsuka Takehiro, "Shôwa Jyunendai no Ôkawa Shûmei," in *Ôkawa Shûmei to Kindai Nihon,* 227–252.

50. Ôkawa Shûmei, *A History of Anglo-American Aggression in East Asia,* trans. Yoshio Ogawa and P. B. Clarke (Tokyo: Daitôa Shuppan Kabushiki Kaisha, 1944), 1–3.

51. For the way the prosecution used this reference, see Awaya and Yoshida, *International Prosecution Section (IPS),* 23:319.

52. Ibid., 23:303–306.

53. *The New Asia,* edited by Rash Behari Bose in Tokyo from 1933 to 1937).

54. The content of *The New Asia* included many of the arguments expounded by Ôkawa Shûmei, unsurprisingly, given the close ties that had existed between Ôkawa and Bose since 1915. For example, the content in *The New Asia,* nos. 5–6 (September–October

1933): 1, is very similar to the writings of Ōkawa in *Fukkō Ajia no Shomondai* and *Ajia, Yoroppa, Nihon.*

55. For news about Muhammad Hatta, see *The New Asia,* nos. 13–14 (May–June 1934): 4.

56. *The New Asia,* nos. 17–18 (September–October 1934), contains extensive coverage of Chandra Bose's ideas.

57. *The New Asia,* nos. 5–6 (September–October 1933): 3.

58. *The New Asia,* nos. 7–8 (November–December 1933): 3.

59. News about the visit to Japan of the African American poet Langston Hughes was accompanied by information about the issue of white discrimination against blacks in the United States; see *Shin Ajia,* no. 4 (August 1933): 2. In another instance, the Pan-Asiatic Cultural Association declared its goal to invite students from Turkey, Afghanistan, Persia, India, and East Asian and Southeast Asian regions to Japan. See *Shin Ajia,* nos. 7–8 (November–December 1933): 4.

60. *Shin Ajia,* nos. 5–6 (September–October 1933): 2.

61. For a lengthy commentary on the rise of the colored and decline of the white races, see *Shin Ajia,* no. 17–18 (September-October 1934): 1.

62. *The New Asia,* nos. 7–8 (November–December 1933): 2. Indicating his color-blind loyalty to universal principles, Bose wrote about his admiration for Abraham Lincoln, describing him as the leader who taught the world the meaning of liberation. See *The New Asia,* nos. 23–24 (March–April 1935): 2.

63. *The New Asia,* nos. 13–14 (May–June 1934): 3. See also nos. 17–18 (September–October 1934): 4.

64. *Yani Yapon Muhbiri* was edited by Qurban Ali in Tokyo from 1933 to 1938. The journal often contained didactic articles about the history, economy, and culture of Japan, as well as carrying news about the Tatar Turkish diaspora living within the boundaries of the Japanese Empire. Since there was a large Tatar Muslim community in Manchuria, the journal included news about Manchukuo, the Manchu dynasty, and developments in China as well.

65. For the background of Abdül Kerim Efendi incident and other Muslim activists who visited Japan after 1933, see Selçuk Esenbel, "Japan's Global Claim to Asia and the World of Islam: Transnational Nationalism and World Power, 1900–1945," *American Historical Review* 109, no. 4 (October 2004): 1159–1162.

66. Abdurreşid İbrahim looked to a Japanese expansion in the north against the Soviet Union with the hope that this would allow the Muslim regions of Central Asia to achieve independence. Initially, this idea had many supporters within the Japanese army as well. However, clashes between Japanese and Soviet forces in Nomonhan, Mongolia, during the summer of 1939 convinced the military authorities of Japan that Soviet military power could not be easily challenged, strengthening the southern advance theory.

    For the relationship between Kokuryûkai and Abdurreşid İbrahim, see Selçuk Esenbel, "Japanese Interest in the Ottoman Empire," in Edstrom, *The Japanese and Europe,* 95–124; see also Selçuk Esenbel, Nadir Ozbek, İsmail Türkoğlu, François Georgeon, and Ahmet Ucar, "Ozel Dosya: Abdurresid Ibrahim (2)," *Toplumsal Tarih* 4, no. 20 (August 1995): 6–23.

67. See Storry, *The Double Patriots*, 149.

68. In fact, General Ishiwara Kanji's Tôa Renmei Kyôkai (East Asia League Association), founded in 1939, was based on ideas also advocated by Dai Ajia Kyôkai. See Peattie, *Ishiwara Kanji and Japan's Confrontation with the West*, 281–282.

69. Nakatani Takeyô became a prolific writer in Asianist publications of the 1930s. Nakatani was influenced by Ôkawa Shûmei during his student years at Tokyo University and later became a member of several organizations led by Ôkawa. He took a leading position in both Dai Ajia Kyôkai and its journals. For his memoirs, see Nakatani Takeyô, *Shôwa Dôranki no Kaisô—Nakatani Takeyô Kaikoroku*, 2 vols. (Tokyo: Tairyûsha, 1989).

70. Koschmann, "Asianism's Ambivalent Legacy," 89–90.

71. For example see, Okubô Kôji, "Shinkô Toruko No Kokumin Shugi Hyôshiki," *Dai Ajia Shugi* 5, no. 5 (May 1937): 5–10. By late 1934, the news section was divided into five parts, devoted to Manchuria, China, India, Southeast Asia, and West Asia.

72. See "Nichi Ei Shôtotsu no Hitsuyôsei," *Dai Ajia Shugi* 1, no. 12 (December 1933): 33–38.

73. See "Shin Ajia Kensetsu No Shin ShinNen," *Dai Ajia Shugi* 6, no. 1 (January 1938): 2–19. Both Ôkawa and Rash Behari Bose used the same "New Asia" as titles of their journals.

74. In a roundtable discussion on nationalist movements in Asia, four Indians (including Behari Bose), two Annamese, two Indonesians, and one Manchurian nationalist offered contributions. Naitô Chishû, Mitsukawa Kametarô, and Nakatani Takeyô, all three close to Ôkawa Shûmei, were among the ten participants representing the Japanese side of the organization. See "Ajia Minzoku Undo: Zadankai," *Dai Ajia Shugi* 3, no. 3 (March 1935): 51–62.

75. It was only during the Pacific War that the same circle of Japanese Asianists began to publish an English-language magazine in Shanghai, *Asiatic Asia,* in order to reach a larger non-Japanese readership with more participation from non-Japanese Asian intellectuals. Publication began in January 1941 and continued for at least five monthly issues.

76. Gotô Ken'ichi, "The Indonesian Perspective," in Akira Iriye, ed., *Pearl Harbor and the Coming of the Pacific War* (Boston: Bedford and St. Martin's, 1999), 207–219. Gotô's article is reprinted from Gotô Ken'ichi, *"Return to Asia": Japanese-Indonesian Relations, 1930s–1942* (Tokyo: Kyûkei Shosha, 1997), 300–312.

77. Akira Iriye, *Cultural Internationalism and World Order* (Baltimore: Johns Hopkins University Press, 1997), 119–122; Robert S. Schwantes, "Japan's Cultural Foreign Policies," in James Morley, ed., *Japan's Foreign Policy, 1868–1941: A Research Guide* (New York: Columbia University Press, 1974), 179–180.

78. Shibasaki Atsushi, *Kindai Nihon no Kokusai Bunka Kôryû: Kokusai Bunka Shinkôkai no Sôsetsu to Tenkai, 1934–1945* (Tokyo: Yûshindô Kôbunsha, 1999). For example, it was through the support of Kokusai Bunka Shinkôkai that two Muslim intellectuals, Amir Lahiri and Mian Abdul Aziz, were able to visit Japan to prepare books advocating Asian solidarity: Mian Abdul Aziz (former president of the All-India Moslem

League), *The Crescent in the Land of the Rising Sun* (London: Blades, 1941); and Amar Lahiri, *Japanese Modernism* (Tokyo: Hokuseido, 1939); idem, *Mikado's Mission* (Tokyo: Japan Times, 1940).

79. For example, the journal *Dai Ajia Shugi* printed articles on the Italian-Ethiopian conflict with a pro-Ethiopian character, including those sent by Japanese correspondents from Addis Ababa, in each of the twelve months of 1935. There was also regular news on Ethiopia in the section devoted to West Asia. As an example, see the five articles on Ethiopia in *Dai Ajia Shugi* 3, no. 8 (August 1935): 32–53.

80. J. Calvitt Clarke III, "Japan and Italy Squabble Over Ethiopia: The Sugimura Affair of July 1935," in *Selected Annual Proceedings of the Florida Conference of Historians* 6 (December 1999): 9–20.

81. Takemoto Yuko, "W. E. B. Dubois to Nihon," *Shien* 54, no. 2 (March 1994): 79–96. Also see Marc Gallicchio, *Black Internationalism in Asia, 1895–1945: The African American Encounter with Japan and China* (Chapel Hill: University of North Carolina Press, 2000), 74–75.

82. Naoki Sakai, "Tôyô no Jiritsu to daitô-A kyôeiken," *Jokyo*, no. 48 (December 1994): 13.

83. For a good example of a Japanese individual who embraced the liberation vision of pan-Asian identity, sometimes with highly critical views on the policies of the Japanese state, see Mariko Asano Tamanoi, "Pan-Asianism in the Diary of Morisaku Minato (1924–1945) and the Suicide of Mishima Yukio (1925–1970)," in Mariko Asano Tamanoi, ed., *Crossed Histories: Manchuria in the Age of Empire* (Honolulu: University of Hawai'i Press, 2005), 184–206.

84. Quoted in Thomas W. Burkman, "Nitobe Inazô: From World Order to Regional Order," in J. Thomas Rimer, ed., *Culture and Identity: Japanese Intellectuals During the Interwar Years* (Princeton: Princeton University Press, 1990), 211.

85. Ibid., 212–213. Burkman discusses an article by Kamikawa Hikomatsu, "Asia Rengô ka Kyokutô Renmei ka?" *Kokka Gakkai Zasshi* 47, no. 7 (July 1933): 90–100.

86. Rôyama Masamichi, *Tô-A to Sekai* (Tokyo: Kaizôsha, 1941), 141–142, quoted in Miwa Kimitada, "Japanese Policies and Concepts for a Regional Order in Asia, 1938–1940," in J. White, M. Umegaki, and T. Havens, eds., *The Ambivalence of Nationalism: Modern Japan Between East and West* (New York: University Press of America, 1990), 149.

87. Rôyama Masamichi, *Foreign Policy of Japan, 1914–1939* (Tokyo: Institute of Pacific Relations–Japanese Council, 1941).

88. For an argument that shows the proto-Asianist views of Japanese liberals during the 1920s, see Han Jung-Sun, "Rationalizing the Orient: The 'East Asia Cooperative Community' in Prewar Japan," *Monumenta Nipponica* 60, no. 4 (Winter 2005), 481–514.

89. Ôkawa Shûmei, "Gandhi wo Tô Shite Indojin ni Atau" and "Nehru o Tô Shite Indojin ni Atau" (1942), in *Shin Ajia Shôron* (Tokyo: Nihon Hyôronsha, 1944), reprinted in *Ôkawa Shûmei Zenshû*, 2:925–938.

90. For some examples of the flood of publications on Okakura, see Kiyomi Rokurô, *Okakura Tenshin den*, (Tokyo: Keizôsha, 1938); Okakura Kakuzô, *Okakura Tenshin*

Zenshû (Tokyo: Rikugeisha, 1939); and Kiyomi Rokurô, *Senkakusha Okakura Tenshin* (Tokyo: Atoriesha, 1942). See also Okakura Kakuzô, *Japan's Innate Virility: Selections from Okakura and Nitobe* (Tokyo: Hokuseido, 1943).

91. For examples of the publication and republication of the books of Das, Paul Richard, and Ôkawa after the post-1937 Japan-China war, see Taraknath Das, *Indo Dokuritsu Ron* (Tokyo: Hakubunkan, 1944); and [Paul] Risharu, *Tsugu Nihon Koku,* trans. Ôkawa Shûmei (Tokyo: Seinen Shobô, 1941).

92. For a recent assessment of Miki Kiyoshi's Asianist ideas, see Harootunian, *Overcome by Modernity,* 394–399. See also Koschmann, "Asianism's Ambivalent Legacy," 90–94.

93. Crowley, ""A New Asian Order," 278–279.

94. Germaine Hoston's study of the writings of post-tenko Sano Manabu shows the importance of her interest in Eastern spirituality and intellectual tradition, as well as her belief in Japanese exceptionalism, in leading her to search for a Japanese context for adopting certain core ideals of Marxism. See Germaine A. Hoston, "Ikkoku Shakai-Shugi: Sano Manabu and the Limits of Marxism as Cultural Criticism," in Rimer, *Culture and Identity,* 168–190.

95. George Beckmann, "The Radical Left and the Failure of Communism," in Morley, *Dilemmas of Growth in Prewar Japan,* 170.

96. From Miwa, "Japanese Policies and Concepts for a Regional Order in Asia," 142.

97. Minamoto Ryôen, "Symposium on 'Overcoming Modernity,'" in Heisig and Moraldo, *Rude Awakenings,* 197–229.

98. All the books Ôkawa published during the wartime years attempted to define the ideology of the Greater East Asia Coprosperity Sphere and Japan's war aims. See Ôkawa Shûmei, *Dai Tôa Chitsujyo Kensetsu* (Tokyo: Dai Ichi Shobô, 1943); idem, *Shin Ajia Shôron;* and idem, *Shin Tôyô Seishin* (Tokyo: Shinkyô Shuppan Kabushiki Kaisha, 1945).

99. For a description of the ideas of Asian solidarity as they functioned in Japanese collaboration with Indian and Burmese nationalists, see Louis M. Allen, "Fujiwara and Suzuki: Patterns of Asian Liberation," in William H. Newell, ed., *Japan in Asia* (Singapore: Singapore University Press, 1981), 83–103.

100. A similar idealist Asianism can be seen in the Japanese cooperation with the nationalist leadership of Burma. As Louis Allen has shown, a conflict emerged among Japanese officers involved in the Burmese government when Officer Suzuki Keiji from Minami Kikan took the side of Burmese nationalism and asked for immediate independence, while General Ishii objected to this on the grounds of military interest. See Allen, "Fujiwara and Suzuki."

101. Objection to the leadership of Rash Behari Bose is another indication of the ineffectiveness of Japanese pan-Asianists' political networks. Although Japan's Asianist circles had always presented Rash Behari Bose as the representative voice of Indian nationalism, it became apparent that he did not have a reputation sufficient to play a role in the project of the Indian National Army. See Tilak Raj Sareen, *Japan and the Indian National Army* (New Delhi: Mounto, 1996), 35–82. See also Fujiwara Iwaichi, *Japanese Army Intelligence Operations in South East Asia During World War II* (Singapore: Select, 1983).

102. Sareen, *Japan and the Indian National Army*, 228–236.

103. Quoted in Joyce Lebra, "Bose's Influence on the Formulation of Japanese Policy toward India and the INA," in *International Netaji Seminar* (Calcutta: Netaji Research Bureau, 1975), 361.

104. Ôkawa Shûmei, "Bosu-shi no Raichô," *Shin Ajia* 5, no. 7 (1943): 1.

105. Quoted in Lebra, "Bose's Influence on the Formulation of Japanese Policy," 368.

106. Akira Iriye, "Wartime Japanese Planning for Postwar Asia," in Ian Nish, ed., *Anglo-Japanese Alienation, 1919–1952* (Cambridge: Cambridge University Press, 1982): 77–91.

107. For the best description of the Japanese war aims, see Akira Iriye, *Power and Culture: The Japanese American War, 1941–1945* (Cambridge: Harvard University Press, 1981).

108. The Greater East Asia conference did not allow for any representation from not-yet-independent regions under Japanese occupation, such as Indonesia and Vietnam. Similar contradictions existed in the Atlantic Charter Alliance, however, which likewise had not been prepared to envision a fully decolonized Asia. In fact, immediately after the end of the war, the French, British, and Dutch governments rushed to regain their colonial possessions in Asia.

109. One report made the following suggestion as a means to win support for the Allied cause: "Play up American and United Nations war aims; play down our association with Great Britain in the East.... Do not refer to British Malaya since many inhabitants of Malaya will not wish to see Malaya revert to its old status under British control" (Office of Strategic Services, Research and Analysis Branch, "Japanese Attempts at Indoctrination of Youth in Occupied Areas," March 23, 1943, microfilm, 10).

110. Christopher Thorne, *Allies of a Kind: The United States, Britain and the War Against Japan, 1941–1945* (New York: Oxford University Press, 1978), 157–159.

111. Ibid., 242–243.

112. Ôkawa Shûmei, entry for August 15, 1945, *Ôkawa Shûmei Nikki* (Tokyo: Iwasaki Gakujitsu Shuppansha, 1986), 391.

113. Sareen, *Japan and the Indian National Army*, 234–236.

114. Richard Minear, *Victor's Justice: The Tokyo War Crimes Tribunal* (Princeton: Princeton University Press, 1971); John Dower, *Embracing Defeat* (New York: Norton, 1999), 443–484.

115. Timothy Brook, "The Tokyo Judgment and the Rape of Nanking," *Journal of Asian Studies* 60, no. 3 (August 2001): 693.

116. Radhabinod Pal became the hero of the revisionist Right in Japan in the postwar period. He himself revealed his long-lasting sympathies to Japan during his celebrated visit to Japan in 1966 upon the invitation of Japanese right-wing revisionist groups. Justice Pal declared how he had admired Japan since his youth because Japan had "consistently stood up against the West" with "the spirit of independence that can say 'no.'" Then, he urged the Japanese people once again to resist the "flood of Westernization" with inspiration from Eastern civilization. For Pal's speeches during his 1966 visit to Japan, see Radhabinod Pal, *Ai Rabu Japan: Paru Hakase Genkôroku*, ed. Paru Hakase Kangei Jimukyoju (Tokyo: Tôkyô Saiban Kankôkai, 1966).

8. CONCLUSION

1. Richard Wright, *The Color Curtain: A Report on the Bandung Conference* (Jackson: University Press of Mississippi, 1995).
2. James B. Crowley, "A New Asian Order: Some Notes on Prewar Japanese Nationalism," in Bernard Silberman and H. D. Harootunian, eds., *Japan in Crisis: Essays on Taisho Democracy* (Princeton: Princeton University Press, 1974), 297–298; and Hayashi Fusao, *Daitôa Sensô Kôteiron,* 2 vols. (Tokyo: Banchô Shobô, 1964–1965).

BIBLIOGRAPHY

Abdul Aziz, Mian. *The Crescent in the Land of the Rising Sun.* London: Blades, 1941.

Abu-Zahra, Nadia. "Al-Tahtawi as Translator of the Culture of Parisian Society: An Anthropological Assessment." In Ekmeleddin İhsanoğlu, ed., *Transfer of Western Science and Technology to the Muslim World,* 411–429. Istanbul: IRCICA, 1992.

Adas, Michael. "Contested Hegemony: The Great War and the Afro-Asian Assault on the Civilizing Mission Ideology." In Prasenjit Duara, ed., *Decolonization: Perspectives from Now and Then,* 78–100. New York: Routledge, 2004.

——. "High Imperialism and the New History." In Michael Adas, ed., *Islamic and European Expansion: The Forging of a Global Order,* 311–344. Philadelphia: Temple University Press, 1993.

——. *Machines as the Measure of Man: Science, Technology, and Ideologies of Western Dominance.* Ithaca: Cornell University Press, 1989.

Adem, Habil [pseud.]. *Pan Cermanizm, Pan Islavizm.* Istanbul: Seda-yi Millet Matbaasi, 1916.

Adıvar, Adnan. *Osmanlı Türklerinde İlim.* Istanbul: Remzi Kitabevi, 1982.

Afghani, Jamal al-. "Answer of Jamal ad-Din to Renan." In Nikkie Keddie, ed., *An Islamic Response to Imperialism,* 181–187. Berkeley: University of California Press, 1968.

Agoston, Gabor. "Early Modern Ottoman and European Gunpowder Technology." In Ekmeleddin İhsanoğlu, Kostas Chatzis, and Efthymios Nicolaidis, eds., *Multicultural Science in the Ottoman Empire,* 13–27. Turnhout, Belgium: Brepolis, 2003.

Ahmad, Feroz. "1914–1915 Yıllarında İstanbul'da Hint Milliyetçi Devrimcileri." *Yapıt* (Ankara), no. 6 (August–September 1984): 5–15.

——. "Ottoman Armed Neutrality and Intervention, August–November 1914." *Studies on Ottoman Diplomatic History* (Istanbul) 4 (1990): 41–69.

Ahmad, Feroz and Marian Kent, eds. *The Great Powers and the End of the Ottoman Empire.* London: Allen and Unwin, 1984.

Akarli, Engin Deniz. "The Problems of External Pressures, Power Struggles, and Budgetary

Deficits in Ottoman Politics under Abdulhamid II (1876–1909): Origins and Solutions." Ph.D. diss, Princeton University, 1976.

———. "The Tangled End of Istanbul's Imperial Supremacy." In Leila Fawaz and C. A. Bayly, eds., *Modernity and Culture from the Mediterranean to the Indian Ocean, 1890–1920*, 261–284. New York: Columbia University Press, 2002.

Akçura, Yusuf. *Üç Tarzı Siyaset*. Ankara: Türk Tarih Kurumu Basımevi, 1987.

Akita, George and Itô Takashi. "Yamagata Aritomo no 'jinshû kyôsô' ron." In *Nihon Gaikô no kiki ninshiki*, 95–118. Tokyo: Yamakawa Shuppansha, 1985.

Aksakal, Mustafa. "Defending the Nation: The German-Ottoman Alliance of 1914 and the Ottoman Decision for War." Ph.D. diss., Princeton University, 2003.

Aksan, Virginia. "Ottoman Political Writings, 1768–1808." *International Journal of Middle East Studies* 25, no. 1 (February 1993): 53–69.

Alitto, Guy S. *The Last Confucian: Liang Shu-ming and the Chinese Dilemma of Modernity*. Berkeley: University of California Press, 1986.

Allen, Louis M. "Fujiwara and Suzuki: Patterns of Asian Liberation." In William H. Newell, ed., *Japan in Asia*, 83–103. Singapore: Singapore University Press, 1981.

Allen, Paul Marshall. *Vladimir Soloviev: Russian Mystic*. New York: Steiner, 1978.

Amin, Qasim. *The Liberation of Women: A Document in the History of Egyptian Feminism*. Trans. Samiha Sidhom Peterson. Cairo: American University in Cairo Press, 1992.

———. *Tahrir al-Mar'ah*. Cairo: Dar al-Maarif, 1970.

An Asian Statesman [Taraknath Das]. *The Isolation of Japan in World Politics*. Tokyo: Asiatic Association of Japan, 1918.

Anderson, Benedict. *Imagined Communities*. London: Verso, 1983.

Arendt, Hannah. *The Origins of Totalitarianism*. New York: World, Meridian, 1962.

Arima Tatsuo. *The Failure of Freedom: A Portrait of Modern Japanese Intellectuals*. Cambridge: Harvard University Press, 1969.

Arusi, Şeyh Mihridin [Şehbenderzade Ahmed Hilmi]. *Yirminci Asırda Alem-i İslam ve Avrupa—Müslümanlara Rehber-i Siyaset*. Istanbul, 1911.

Atatürk, Mustafa Kemal. "Fransız Muharriri Maurice Pernot'ya Demeç (29/10/1923)." In Uygur Kocabaşoğlu, ed., *Modern Türkiye'de Siyasi Düşünce*, vol. 3, *Modernleşme ve Batıcılık*, 599–600. Istanbul: İletişim Yayınları, 2002.

Awaya Kentaro and Yoshida Yutada, eds. *International Prosecution Section (IPS)*. Tokyo: Tokyo Daigaku Shuppankai, 1980.

Aydin, Cemil. "Beyond Culturalism? An Overview of the Historiography on Ottoman Science in Turkey." In Ekmeleddin İhsanoğlu, Kostas Chatzis, and Efthymios Nicolaidis, eds., *Multicultural Science in the Ottoman Empire*, 201–215. Turnhout, Belgium: Brepols, 2003.

———. "Mecmuai Fünün ve Mecmuai Ulum Dergilerinde Bilim ve Medeniyet Anlayişi." Master's thesis, Istanbul University, 1995.

———. "Nihon Wa Itsu Tôyô No Kuni Ni Natta No Ka? Chutô Kara Mita Kindai Nihon" [When did Japan become an "Eastern" nation? Modern Japan in the imagination of Middle Eastern nationalists]. In *Atarashi Nihongaku no Kôchiku—Constructing Japanese Studies in Global Perspective*, 81–86. Tokyo: Ochanomizu University, 1999.

Aydüz, Salim. "Lâle Devri'nde Yapılan İlmi Faaliyetler." *Divan: İlmi Araştırmalar* 1, no. 3 (1997): 151–152.

Barakatullah, Muhammad. "Christian Combination Against Islam." *Islamic Fraternity* (Tokyo) 3, no. 2 (June 1912): 1–2.

———. "Yo ga Sokoku." *Michi*, no. 67 (November 1913): 42–47.

Bayezidof, Ataullah. *Islam ve Medeniyet*. Ankara: TDV Yayınları, 1993.

Baykara, Tuncer. *Osmanlılarda Medeniyet Kavrami*. Izmir: Akademi Kitabevi, 1992.

Bayly, Susan. "Racial Readings of Empire: Britain, France, and Colonial Modernity in the Mediterranean and Asia." In Leila Fawaz and C. A. Bayly, eds., *Modernity and Culture from the Mediterranean to the Indian Ocean, 1890–1920*, 285–313. New York: Columbia University Press, 2002.

Bayur, Yusuf Hikmet. *Türk Inkılabı Tarihi*. Ankara: Türk Tarih Kurumu Basimevi, 1940.

Belak [pseud.]. *Mağlub Milletler Nasıl İntikam Alırlar*. Trans. Habil Adem [pseud.]. Istanbul: Ikbal Kütübhanesi, 1332/1913–1914.

Benfey, Christopher. *The Great Wave: Gilded Age Misfits, Japanese Eccentrics, and the Opening of Japan*. New York: Random House, 2003.

Berkes, Niyazi, ed. *The Development of Secularism in Turkey*. New York: Routledge, 1999.

———. *Turkish Nationalism and Western Civilization: Selected Essays of Ziya Gökalp*. New York: Allen and Unwin, 1959.

Bernal, Martin. *Black Athena: Afroasiatic Roots of Classical Civilization*. New Brunswick, N.J.: Rutgers University Press, 1987.

Bhardwaj, R. C., ed. *Netaji and the INA: A Commemorative Volume Brought Out to Mark the Golden Jubilee of the Indian National Army*. New Delhi: Lok Sabha Secretariat, 1994.

Blunt, Wilfrid Scawen. *The Future of Islam*. Lahore, Pakistan: Sind Sagar Academy, 1975.

Bonfils, Henri and Paul Fauchille. *Hukuk-i umumiye-yi düvel*. Trans. Ahmet Salahettin and Mehmet Cemil. Istanbul: Matbaa-i Jirayir-Keteon, 1908.

Boroujerdi, Mehrzad. *Iranian Intellectuals and the West: The Tormented Triumph of Nativism*. Syracuse, N.Y.: Syracuse University Press, 1996.

Bouvat, L. "La presse anglaise et le panislamisme." *Revue du Monde Musulman* 1, no. 2 (January 1907): 404–405.

———. "Un projet de parlement musulman international." *Revue du Monde Musulman* 7, no. 3 (March 1909): 321–322;

Bradley, Mark. *Imagining Vietnam and America: The Making of Postcolonial Vietnam, 1919–1950*. Chapel Hill: University of North Carolina Press, 2000.

British Foreign Office. *Japan Correspondence, 1914–1923*. Public Records Office Collection, FO 371.

Brook, Timothy. "The Tokyo Judgment and the Rape of Nanking." *Journal of Asian Studies* 60, no. 3 (August 2001): 673–700.

Buckle, Henry Thomas. *History of Civilization in England*. New York: Hearst's International Library, 1913.

Budak, Mustafa. "I. Dünya Savaşı Sonrası Uluslarası Düzen Kurma Sürecinde Osmanlı Devleti'nin Tavrı: Paris Barış Konferansı'na Sunulan 23 Haziran 1919 Tarihli Muhtıra." *Divan İlmi Araştırmalar Dergisi* 4, no. 7 (1992): 191–215.

——. *Idealden Gerçeğe: Misakı Milliden Lozan'a Dış Politika.* Istanbul: Küre Yayınları, 2002.

Bull, Hedley. *The Anarchical Society: A Study of Order in World Politics.* New York: Columbia University Press, 1995.

——. "The Revolt Against the West." In Hedley Bull and A. Watson, eds., *The Expansion of International Society,* 217–228. Oxford: Oxford University Press, 1984.

Bulliet, Richard W. *The Case for Islamo-Christian Civilization.* New York: Columbia University Press, 2004.

Burdett, Anita L. P. *Islamic Movements in the Arab World.* Vol. 1. Slough: Archive, 1988.

Burke, Edmund III. "The First Crisis of Orientalism." In Jean-Claude Vatin et al., eds., *Connaissances du Maghreb: Sciences sociales et colonisation,* 213–226. Paris: CNRS, 1984.

Burkman, Thomas W. "The Geneva Spirit." In John F. Howes, ed., *Nitobe Inazô: Japan's Bridge Across the Pacific,* 203–214. Boulder, Colo.: Westview, 1995.

——. "Nitobe Inazô: From World Order to Regional Order." In J. Thomas Rimer, ed., *Culture and Identity: Japanese Intellectuals During the Interwar Years,* 209–222. Princeton: Princeton University Press, 1990.

Burtscher, Michael. "Facing 'the West' on Philosophical Grounds: A View from the Pavilion of Subjectivity on Meiji Japan." *Comparative Studies of South Asia, Africa and the Middle East* 26, no. 3 (Fall 2006): 367-376.

Buruma, Ian and Avishai Margalit. *Occidentalism: The West in the Eyes of Its Enemies.* New York: Penguin, 2004.

Buzpınar, Ş. Tufan. "II. Abdulhamit Döneminde Osmanlı Hilafetine Muhalefetin Ortaya Çıkışı: 1877–1882." In İsmail Kara, ed., *Hilafet Risaleleri,* 1:37–61. Istanbul: Klasik Yayınları, 2002.

——. "The Repercussions of the British Occupation of Egypt on Syria, 1882–1883." *Middle East Studies* 36, no. 1 (January 2000): 82–91.

Çakır, Coşkun. "Türk Aydınının Tanzimat'la İmtihanı: Tanzimat ve Tanzimat Dönemi Siyasi Tarihi Üzerine Yapılan Çalışmalar." *Türkiye Araştırmaları Literatür Dergisi* 2, no. 1 (2004): 13–15.

Celal Nuri Bey. *İştirak Etmediğimiz Harekat: Tarih-i Osmani ve Keşfiyat, Rönasans ve Reform Harakati.* Istanbul: Cemiyet Kütüphanesi, 1917.

—— [as Jalal Nuri Bek]. *İttihad al-Muslimin: Al-Islam, madihi wa-hadiruhu wa mustaqbaluhu.* Trans. Hamzah Tahir and Abd al-Wahhab'Azzam. Cairo, 1920.

——. *İttihad-i İslâm: İslamin Mazisi, Hali, İstikbali.* Istanbul: Yeni Osmanli Matbaasi, 1913.

——. *İttihad-i İslâm ve Almanya.* Istanbul: Yeni Osmanli Matbaasi, 1914.

——. *Kadinlarimiz: Umumiyet İtibarile Kadin Meselesi ve Tarihi, Müslüman ve Türk Kadinlari.* Istanbul: Matbaa-i İçtihad, 1912.

——. *Kendi Noktai Nazarimizdan Hukuk-i Düvel.* Istanbul: Osmanli Şirketi Matbaasi, 1911.

——. *Mukadderat-ı Tarihiye: Tedenniyat-i Osmaniyenin Esbab ve Sevaik-i Tarihiyesi.* Istanbul: Matbaa-i İçtihad, 1912.

——. *Müslümanlara, Türklere Hakaret, Düşmanlara Riayet ve Muhabbet.* Istanbul: Kader Matbaasi, 1914.

Chatterjee, Partha. *Nationalist Thought and the Colonial World: A Derivative Discourse.* Minneapolis: University of Minnesota Press, 1986.

Chin Tokujin and Yasui Sankichi, eds. *Sonbun Kôen Dai Ajia Shugi Shiryôshû: 1924 nen, 11 Gatsu Nihon to Chûgoku no Kiro.* Kyoto: Hôritsu Bunkasha, 1989.

Clarke, J. Calvitt III. "Japan and Italy Squabble Over Ethiopia: The Sugimura Affair of July 1935." *Selected Annual Proceedings of the Florida Conference of Historians* 6 (December 1999): 9–20.

Cleveland, William. *The Making of an Arab Nationalist: Ottomanism and Arabism in the Life and Thought of Sati' Al-Husri.* Princeton: Princeton University Press, 1971.

Commins, David Dean. *Islamic Reform: Politics and Social Change in Late Ottoman Syria.* New York: Oxford University Press, 1990.

Cotton, Sir Henry. *New India or India in Transition.* London: K. Paul, 1907.

Cousins, James H. "The Cultural Unity of Asia." *Asian Review* (Tokyo) 2, no. 3 (March–April 1921): 217–228.

Cromer. *Saikin Ejiputo* [Modern Egypt]. 2 vols. Tokyo: Dainippon Bunmei Kyôkai, 1911.

Crosland, T. W. H. *The Truth About Japan.* London: Richards, 1904.

Crowley, James B. "Intellectuals as Visionaries of the New Asian Order." In James W. Morley, ed., *Dilemmas of Growth in Prewar Japan,* 375–421. Princeton: Princeton University Press, 1971.

——. "A New Asian Order: Some Notes on Prewar Japanese Nationalism." In Bernard Silberman and H. D. Harootunian, eds., *Japan in Crisis: Essays on Taisho Democracy,* 270–298. Princeton: Princeton University Press, 1974.

Cündioğlu, Dücane. "Ernest Renan ve 'Reddiyeler' Bağlamında İslam-Bilim Tartişmalarina Bibliyografik bir Katkı." *Divan* (Istanbul) 1, no. 2 (1996): 1–94.

Das, Taraknath. "The European Peril." *Asian Review* 1, no. 8 (November–December 1920): 835–841.

——. *Indo Dokuritsu Ron.* Tokyo: Hakubunkan, 1944.

——. *Is Japan a Menace to Asia?* Shanghai, 1917.

——. "The Orient and the Question of Race Superiority." *Asian Review* 1, no. 7 (October 1920): 712–717.

Dasu Tarakunato [Taraknath Das]. "Ajia no Kyôisha wa Hatashite Nihon Ka?" *Nippon Oyobi Nipponjin,* no. 706 (June 1, 1917): 68–75.

——. *Kokusaikan ni Okeru Nihon no Koritsu.* Tokyo: Asiatic Association of Japan, 1917.

Davison, Roderic. *Essays in Ottoman and Turkish History, 1774–1923: The Impact of the West.* Austin: University of Texas Press, 1990.

Davison, Roderic H. "Turkish Attitudes Concerning Christian-Muslim Equality in the Nineteenth Century." *American Historical Review* 59, no. 4 (July 1954): 844–864.

Deringil, Selim. "The 'Residual Imperial Mentality' and the 'Urabi Paşa Uprising in Eygpt': Ottoman Reactions to Arab Nationalism." In *Studies on Turkish-Arab Relations Annual),* 31–38. Istanbul: Foundations for Studies on Turkish-Arab Relations, 1986.

——. *The Well-Protected Domains: Ideology and the Legitimation of Power in the Ottoman Empire, 1876–1909.* London: Tauris, 1998.

Dharmapala, Anagarika. "Naite Nipponjin ni keikoku su" [A cry of warning to the Japanese]. *Michi,* no. 65 (September 1913): 29–33.

Dickinson, Frederick. *War and National Reinvention: Japan in the Great War, 1914–1919.* Cambridge: Harvard University Press, 2001.

Doak, Kevin. *Dreams of Difference: The Japan Romantic School and the Crisis of Modernity.* Berkeley, University of California Press, 1994.

Dower, John. *Embracing Defeat.* New York: Norton, 1999.

——. *War Without Mercy: Race and Power in the Pacific War.* New York: Pantheon, 1986.

Dozy, Reinhart Peter. *Essai sur l'histoire de l'Islamisme.* Paris: Maisonneuve, 1897.

——. *Tarih-i İslamiyet.* Mısır: Matbaa-i İçtihad, 1908.

Draper, William. *History of Conflict Between Religion and Science.* New York: D. Appleton, 1875.

——. *Niza-yı Ilim ve Din.* Trans. Ahmet Midhat. Istanbul: Tercümani Hakikat Matbaasi, 1313/1896–1897.

Dua, R. P. *The Impact of the Russo-Japanese (1905) War on Indian Politics.* Delhi: S. Chand, 1966.

Duara, Prasenjit. "The Discourse of Civilization and Pan-Asianism." *Journal of World History* 12, no. 1 (Spring 2001): 99–130.

——. "Transnationalism and the Predicament of Sovereignty: China, 1900–1945." *American Historical Review* 102, no. 4 (October 1997): 1030–1051.

——, ed. *Decolonization: Perspectives from Now and Then.* London: Routledge, 2004.

Dudden, Alexis. *Japan's Colonization of Korea: Discourse and Power.* Honolulu: University of Hawai'i Press, 2004.

Duus, Peter. "Nagai Ryutaro and the 'White Peril,' 1905–1944." *Journal of Asian Studies,* 31, no. 1 (November 1971): 41–48.

Düzdağ, Ertuğrul M. *Mehmet Akif Ersoy.* Ankara: Kültür ve Turizm Bakanlığı Yayınları, 1988.

Dyer, Henry. *Dai Nippon, the Britain of the East: A Study in National Evolution.* London: Blackie, 1904.

Edip, Halide. *Türkün Atesle İmtihanı.* Istanbul: Can Yayınları, 1962.

Elias, Norbert. *The Civilizing Process: The Development of Manners.* New York: Urizen, 1978.

Elrod, Richard B. "The Concert of Europe: A Fresh Look at an International System." *World Politics* 28, no. 2 (January 1976): 159–174.

Erden, Ali Fuad. *Musavver 1904–1905 Rus-Japon Seferi.* Istanbul: Kitaphane-yi Islam ve Askeri, 1321/1905 or 1906.

Erol, Mine [Sümer]. "Wilson Prensipleri Cemiyeti'nin Amerika Cumhurbaşkanı Wilson'a Gönderdiği Muhtıra." In *Ankara Üniversitesi Dil ve Tarih Coğrafya Fakültesi Tarih Araştırmaları Dergisi* 3, no. 4–5 (1966), 237–245.

Esedebe, P. Olisanwuche. *Pan-Africanism: The Idea and Movement, 1776–1991.* Washington, D.C.: Howard University Press, 1994.

Esenbel, Selçuk. "A 'fin de siècle' Japanese Romantic in Istanbul: The Life of Yamada Torajiro and His 'Toruko Gakan.'" *Bulletin of the School of Oriental and African Studies* 59, no. 2 (1996): 237–252.

——. "Japan's Global Claim to Asia and the World of Islam: Transnational Nationalism and World Power, 1900–1945." *American Historical Review* 109, no. 4 (October 2004): 1140–1170.

——. "Japanese Interest in the Ottoman Empire." In Bert Edstrom, ed., *The Japanese and Europe: Images and Perceptions*, 95–124. Richmond, Surrey, U.K.: Curzon, 2000.

Esenbel, Selçuk, Nadir Ozbek, İsmail Türkoğlu, François Georgeon, and Ahmet Ucar, "Ozel Dosya: Abdurresid Ibrahim 2." *Toplumsal Tarih* 4, no. 20 (August 1995): 6–23.

Exhibits of International Military Tribunal for the Far East. 60 vols. Tokyo, 1946–1948.

Farjenel, F[ernand]. "La Japon et l'Islam." *Revue du Monde Musulman* 1, no. 1 (November 1906): 101–114.

Feenberg, Andrew. "The Problem of Modernity in the Philosophy of Nishida." In James Heisig and John Moraldo, eds., *Rude Awakenings: Zen, the Kyoto School and the Question of Nationalism*, 151–173. Honolulu: University of Hawai'i Press, 1995.

Fehmi, Hasan. "Şuyûn: Japonya." *Sebilürreşad* 12, no. 295 (1914): 167.

Fevret, A. "Le croissant contre la croix." *Revue du Monde Musulman* 2, no. 7 (May 1907): 421–425.

Findley, Carter Vaughn. "An Ottoman Occidentalist in Europe: Ahmed Midhat Meets Madame Gulnar, 1889." *American Historical Review* 103, no. 1 (1998): 15–49.

Fletcher, William Miles. *The Search for a New Order: Intellectuals and Fascism in Prewar Japan.* Chapel Hill: University of North Carolina Press, 1982.

Freeman, Edward A. *The Ottoman Power in Europe.* London: Macmillan, 1877.

Fujiwara Iwaichi. *Japanese Army Intelligence Operations in South East Asia During World War II.* Singapore: Select, 1983.

Fukuzawa Yukichi. *An Encouragement of Learning* [Gakumon no susume]. Trans. David A. Dilworth and Umeyo Hirano. Tokyo: Sophia University, 1969.

——. "On De-Asianization." In *Meiji Japan Through Contemporary Sources*, 3:129–133. Tokyo: Center for East Asian Cultural Studies, 1973.

——. *An Outline of a Theory of Civilization* [Bunmeiron no gairyaku]. Trans. David A. Dilworth and G. Cameron Hurst. Tokyo: Sophia University, 1973).

Furuya Tetsuo, ed. *Kindai Nihon no Ajia Ninshiki.* Kyoto: Jinbun Kagaku Kenkyûjô, 1994.

Gallicchio, Marc. *Black Internationalism in Asia, 1895–1945: The African American Encounter with Japan and China.* Chapel Hill: University of North Carolina Press, 2000.

Gammer, Moshe. *Muslim Resistance to the Tsar: Shamil and the Conquest of Chechnia and Daghestan.* London: Cass, 1994.

Genzo Yamamoto. "Defending Japan's Civilization and Civilizing Mission in Asia: The Resilience and Triumph of Illiberalism in the House of Peers, 1919–1934." Ph.D. diss., Yale University, 1999.

German Diplomatic Documents, 1871–1914. Ed. and trans. E. T. S. Dugdale. Vol. 3, *The Growing Antagonism, 1898–1910*, 1–13. New York: Harper and Brothers, 1930.

Gheissari, Ali. *Iranian Intellectuals in the 20th Century.* Austin: University of Texas Press, 1998.

Gollwitzer, Heinz. *Die gelbe Gefahr: Geschichte eines Schlagwortes* [The yellow peril: Retracing a slogan). Göttingen: Vandenhoeck and Ruprecht, 1962.

Gong, Gerrit. *The Standard of "Civilization" in International Society.* New York: Oxford University Press, 1984.

Goodman, Grant K. *An Experiment in Wartime Inter-Cultural Relations: Philippine Students in Japan, 1943–1945*. Ithaca: Cornell University Southeast Asia Program, 1962.

——, ed. *Japanese Cultural Policies in Southeast Asia During World War 2*. New York: St. Martin's, 1991.

Gordon, Andrew. *Labor and Imperial Democracy in Prewar Japan*. Berkeley: University of California Press, 1991.

Gotô Ken'ichi. "'Bright Legacy' or 'Abortive Flower': Indonesian Students in Japan During World War 2." In Grant G. Goodman, ed., *Japanese Cultural Policies in Southeast Asia During World War 2*, 7–35. New York: St. Martin's, 1991.

——. "The Indonesian Perspective." In Akira Iriye, ed., *Pearl Harbor and the Coming of the Pacific War*, 207–219. Boston: Bedford and St. Martin's, 1999.

——. *"Return to Asia": Japanese-Indonesian Relations, 1930s–1942*. Tokyo: Kyûkei Shosha, 1997.

Güçlü, Yücel. "Turkey's Entrance into the League of Nations." *Middle Eastern Studies* 39, no. 1 (2003): 186–206.

Guizot, François M. *The History of Civilization in Europe*. London: Penguin, 1997.

Gulick, Sidney L. *The White Peril in the Far East: An Interpretation of the Significance of the Russo-Japanese War*. New York: Revell, 1905.

Guohe Zeng. "From Patriotism to Imperialism: A Study of the Political Ideals of 'Kajin No Kigu,' a Meiji Political Novel." Ph.D. diss., Ohio State University, 1997.

Haag-Higuchi, Roxane. "A Topos and Its Dissolution: Japan in Some Twentieth-Century Iranian Texts." *Iranian Studies* 29, nos. 1–2 (1996): 71–83.

Halid, Halil. *The Crescent Versus the Cross*. London: Luzac, 1907.

——. *The Diary of a Turk*. London: A. C. Black, 1903.

——. *Hilal ve Salib Münazaasi*. Cairo: Matbaa-i Hindiye, 1907.

——. *A Study in English Turcophobia*. London: Pan-Islamic Society, 1898.

——. *Türk Hakimiyeti ve Ingiliz Cihangirligi*. Istanbul: Yeni Matbaasi, 1925.

Hamet, Ismael. "Le Congrès Musulman Universal." *Revue du Monde Musulman* 4, no. 1 (January 1908): 100–107.

Han Jung-Sun. "Rationalizing the Orient: The 'East Asia Cooperative Community' in Prewar Japan." *Monumenta Nipponica* 60, no. 4 (Winter 2005): 481–514.

Hanioğlu, M. Şükrü. *Preparation for a Revolution: The Young Turks, 1902–1908*. New York: Oxford University Press, 2001.

——. *The Young Turks in Opposition*. New York: Oxford University Press, 1995.

Kawakami, K. K., ed., *What Japan Thinks*. New York: Macmillan, 1921.

Harada Kôkichi. *Ôkawa Shûmei Hakushi no shôgai*. Yamagata-ken Sakata-shi: Ôkawa Shûmei Kenshôkai, 1982.

Harootunian, Harry. *Overcome by Modernity: History, Culture, and Community in Interwar Japan*. Princeton: Princeton University Press, 2000.

Haruo Iguchi. *Unfinished Business: Ayukawa Yoshisuke and U.S.-Japan Relations, 1937–1953*. Cambridge, Mass.: Harvard East Asia Monographs, 2001.

Hashikawa Bunsô. "Japanese Perspectives on Asia: From Dissociation to Coprosperity." In

Akira Iriye, ed., *The Chinese and the Japanese: Essays in Political and Cultural Interactions*, 331–341. Princeton: Princeton University, 1980.

——. "Kaisetsu," In Ôkawa Shûmei, *Ôkawa Shûmei Shû*, 405–448. Ed. Hashikawa Bunsô. Tokyo: Chikuma Shobô, 1975.

Hatano [Uho]. *Asya Tehlikede.* Trans. Nakawa and [Abdurreşid] İbrahim. Istanbul: Sebilürreşat, 1328/1910.

Hay, Stephan N. *Asian Ideas of East and West: Tagore and His Critics in Japan, China, and India.* Cambridge: Harvard University Press, 1970.

Hayashi Fusao. *Daitôa Sensô Kôteiron.* 2 vols. Tokyo: Banchô Shobô, 1964–1965.

Hevia, James. "Looting Beijing: 1860, 1900." In Lydia H. Liu, ed., *Tokens of Exchange: The Problem of Translation in Global Circulations*, 192–213. Durham, N.C.: Duke University Press, 1999.

Heyd, Uriel. *Foundations of Turkish Nationalism: The Life and Teachings of Ziya Gökalp.* London: Lucaz, 1950.

Hiraishi Naoaki. "Kindai Nihon no Kokusai Chitsujyokan to Ajiashugi." In *20 Seiki Shisutemu*, 1:176–211. Tokyo: Tokyo Daigaku Shuppankai, 1998.

Hirakawa Sukehiro. "Japan's Turn to the West." In Bob Tadashi Wakabayashi, ed., *Modern Japanese Thought*, 47–71. Cambridge: Cambridge University Press, 1998.

——. "Modernizing Japan in Comparative Perspective." *Comparative Studies of Culture*, no. 26 (1987): 1–22.

Hirobe Izumi. *Japanese Pride, American Prejudice: Modifying the Exclusion Clause of the 1924 Immigration Act.* Stanford, Calif.: Stanford University Press, 2001.

Hoston, Germaine A. "Ikkoku Shakai-Shugi: Sano Manabu and the Limits of Marxism as Cultural Criticism." In J. Thomas Rimer, ed., *Culture and Identity: Japanese Intellectuals During the Interwar Years*, 168–190. Princeton: Princeton University Press, 1990.

Hourani, Albert. *Arabic Thought in the Liberal Age, 1798–1939.* Cambridge: Oxford University Press, 1962.

Howes, John F., ed. *Nitobe Inazô: Japan's Bridge Across the Pacific.* Boulder, Colo.: Westview, 1995.

İbrahim, Abdurreşid. *Alem-i Islam ve Japonya'da İntişari Islamiyet.* Istanbul: Ahmed Saki Bey Matbaasi, 1327/1910–1911.

——. *İslam Dünyasi.* Vol. 1. Istanbul: Yeni Asya Yayınları, 1987.

Ihsanoğlu, Ekmeleddin. "The Introduction of Western Science to the Ottoman World: The Case Study of Modern Astronomy (1660–1860)." In Ekmeleddin Ihsanoğlu, ed., *Transfer of Modern Science and Technology to the Muslim World*, 1–44. Istanbul: IRCICA, 1992.

Iichirô Tokutomi. "Japan's Mighty Mission." Appendix to Taraknath Das, *Is Japan a Menace to Asia?* 121–127. Shanghai, 1917.

International Military Tribunal for the Far East, The Tokyo Major War Crimes Trial: The Transcripts of the Court Proceedings of the International Military Tribunal for the Far East. Ed. R. John Pritchard. Lewiston, N.Y.: Edwin Mellen, 1998.

Iriye, Akira. *After Imperialism: A Search for a New Order in the Far East, 1921–1931.* Cambridge: Harvard University Press, 1965.

——. *Cultural Internationalism and World Order.* Baltimore: Johns Hopkins University Press, 1997.

——. "The Failure of Economic Expansionism: 1918–1931." In Bernard S. Silberman and H. D. Harootunian, eds., *Japan in Crises: Essays on Taishô Democracy,* 239–269. Princeton: Princeton University Press, 1974.

——. *Power and Culture: The Japanese American War, 1941–1945.* Cambridge: Harvard University Press, 1981.

——. "Wartime Japanese Planning for Postwar Asia." In Ian Nish, ed., *Anglo-Japanese Alienation, 1919–1952,* 77–91. Cambridge: Cambridge University Press, 1982.

Ishikawa Yoshihiro. "Tôzai Bunmeiron to Nihon no Rondan." In Furuya Tetsuo, ed., *Kindai Nihon no Ajia Ninshiki,* 395–432. Kyoto: Kyoto University Press, 1994.

Jaffe, Richard. "Seeking Sakyamuni: Travel and the Reconstruction of Japanese Buddhism." *Journal of Japanese Studies* 30, no. 1 (Winter 2004): 65–96.

Jansen, Marius B. "Changing Japanese Attitudes Toward Modernization." In Marius B. Jansen, ed., *Changing Japanese Attitudes Toward Modernization,* 43–89. Rutland, Vt.: Tuttle, 1982.

——. *The Japanese and Sun Yat-sen.* Cambridge: Harvard University Press, 1954.

——. "Japanese Imperialism: Late Meiji Perspectives." In Ramon H. Myers and Mark R. Peattie, eds., *Japanese Colonial Empire, 1895–1945,* 61–79. Princeton: Princeton University Press, 1984.

——. "Konoe Atsumaro." In Akira Iriye, ed., *The Chinese and the Japanese: Essays in Political and Cultural Interactions,* 107–123. Princeton: Princeton University Press, 1980.

"Jinshuteki Sabetsu Teppai Kiseikai Undôki." *Ajia Jiron* 3, no. 3 (March 1919): 60–61.

Kaiichi Toda. "The Japanese in California." *Asian Review* l, no. 4 (May–June 1920): 362–363.

Kaiwar, Vasant. "The Aryan Model of History and the Oriental Renaissance: The Politics of Identity in an Age of Revolutions, Colonialism, and Nationalism." In Vasant Kaiwar and Sucheta Mazumdar, eds., *The Antinomies of Modernity,* 13–61. Durham, N.C.: Duke University Press, 2003.

Kaiwar, Vasant and Sucheta Mazumdar, eds. *Antionomies of Modernity.* Durham, N.C.: Duke University Press, 2003.

Kamikawa Hikomatsu. "Asia Rengô ka Kyokutô Renmei ka?" *Kokka Gakkai Zasshi* 47, no. 7 (July 1933): 90–100.

Kamil, Mustafa. "Al-Harb al-Hadirah wa'l-Islam." *Al-Liwa,* February 18, 1904, 1.

——. *Al-Shams al-Mushriqah.* Cairo: Matbaat al-Liwa, 1904.

Kara, İsmail. "İslamcıların Fikri Endişeleri." In İsmail Kara, ed., *Türkiye'de İslamcılık Düsüncesi,* 1:57–66. 3d ed. İstanbul: Kitabevi, 1997.

——, ed. *Hilafet Risaleleri.* 4 vols. Istanbul: Klasik Yayınları, 2002–2004.

——. *Türkiye'de İslamcılık Düşüncesi.* Vol. 1. 3d ed. Istanbul: Kitabevi, 1997.

Karl, Rebecca. "Creating Asia: China in the World at the Beginning of the Twentieth Century." *American Historical Review* 103, no. 4 (October 1998): 1096–1118.

——. *Staging the World: Chinese Nationalism at the Turn of the Twentieth Century.* Durham, N.C.: Duke University Press, 2002.

Kasaba, Resat. "Up the Down Staircase: British Policy in the Near East, 1815–74." In Francisco O. Ramirez, ed., *Rethinking the Nineteenth Century: Contradictions and Movements*, 149–160, New York: Greenwood, 1988.

Kedourie, Elie. *Afghani and Abduh*. London: Cass, 1966.

Keene, Donald. *Japanese Discovery of Europe, 1720–1830*. Stanford, Calif.: Stanford University Press, 1969.

Ketelaar, James Edward. *Of Heretics and Martyrs in Meiji Japan*. Princeton: Princeton University Press, 1990.

Khalidi, Rashid. *Resurrecting Empire: Western Footprints and America's Perilous Path in the Middle East*. New York: Beacon, 2005.

Kidwai, S. Mushir Hosain. *The Future of the Muslim Empire: Turkey*. London: Central Islamic Society, 1919.

——. *İslama çekilen kılıç, yahut, Alemdaran-ı İslamı müdafaa: Osmanlı heyet-i murahhasasının sulh konferansına takdim ettiği muhtıra ve Paris sulh konferansı onlar meclisi tarafından aldığı cevaba nazaran Osmanlı devlet İslamiyesi meselesinin tenkidi*. London: Londra Cemiyet-i Merkeziye-i İslamiyesi, 1919.

——. *Pan-Islamism and Bolshevism*. London: Luzac, 1937.

——. *The Sword Against Islam; or, A Defence of Islam's Standard-Bearers*. London: Central Islamic Society, 1919.

Kinmonth, Earl H. *The Self-Made Man in Meiji Japanese Thought: From Samurai to Salary Man*. Berkeley: University of California Press, 1961.

Kinzer, Stephen. *All the Shah's Men: An American Coup and the Roots of Middle East Terror*. New York: Wiley, 2004.

Kipling, Rudyard. "The White Man's Burden (1899)." In Jan Goldstein and John W. Boyer, eds., *Nineteenth-Century Europe: Liberalism and Its Critics*, 544–545. Chicago: University of Chicago Press, 1988.

Kırımlı, Hakan and İsmail Türkoğlu. *İsmail Bey Gaspıralı ve Dünya Müslümanları Kongresi*. Islamic Area Studies Project: Central Asian Research Series, no. 4. Tokyo: Tokyo University, 2002.

Kita Reikichi. "Waga Kuni no Daishimei—Pôru Risha shi no Nipponkoku ni Tsugu wo yomu." *Tôhô Jiron* 2, no. 12 (November 1917): 12.

Kiyomi Rokurô. *Okakura Tenshin den*. Tokyo: Keizôsha, 1938.

——. *Senkakusha Okakura Tenshin*. Tokyo: Atoriesha, 1942.

Kobayashi, Toshihiko. "Sun Yatsen and Asianism: A Positive Approach." In J. Y. Wong, ed., *Sun Yatsen: His International Ideas and International Connections*, 15–38. Sydney, N.S.W.: Wild Peony, 1987).

Kodera Kenkichi. *Dai Ajiashugi Ron*. Tokyo: Hôbunkan, 1916.

Kohn, Hans. *Pan-Slavism: Its History and Ideology*. New York: Vintage, 1960.

Koloğlu, Orhan. "Alexandre Blacque: Défenseur de l'état ottoman pour amour des libertés." In Hamit Batu and Jean-Louis Bacque-Grammont, eds., *Empire Ottoman, la République de Turquie et la France*, 179–95. Istanbul: Isis, 1986.

Koschmann, J. Victor. "Asianism's Ambivalent Legacy." In Peter J. Katzenstein and Takashi Shiraishi, eds., *Network Power: Japan and Asia*, 83–110. Ithaca: Cornell University Press, 1997.

Kramer, Martin. *Islam Assembled: The Advent of the Muslim Congresses.* New York: Columbia University Press, 1986.

Kreiser, Klaus. "Der japanische Sieg über Rußland (1905) und sein Echo unter den Muslimen." *Die Welt des Islam* 21 (1981): 209–239.

Kurzman, Charles, ed. *Modernist Islam, 1840–1940: A Sourcebook.* New York: Oxford University Press, 2002.

Kusunoki Seiichirô. "Ôkawa Shûmei no tai-Bei Seisaku." *Nihon Rekishi,* no. 474 (November 1987): 54–70.

Kutay, Cemal. *Tarih önünde İslam Peygamberi.* Istanbul: Aksoy Yayıncılık, 1998.

Kuwajima Sho. *Indian Mutiny in Singapore (1915).* Calcutta: Ratna Prakashan, 1991.

Laffan, Michael. "Tokyo as a Shared Mecca of Modernity: Reading the Impact of the Russo-Japanese War in the Colonial Malay World." In Rotem Kowner, ed., *The Impact of the Russo-Japanese War,* 219–238. London: Routledge Curzon, 2006.

——. "Watan and Negeri: Mustafa Kamil's 'Rising Sun' in the Malay World." *Indonesia Circle,* no. 69 (1996): 157–175.

Lahiri, Amar. *Japanese Modernism.* Tokyo: Hokuseido, 1939.

——. *Mikado's Mission.* Tokyo: Japan Times, 1940.

Landau, Jacob M. *Pan-Turkism: From Irredentism to Cooperation.* Bloomington: Indiana University Press, 1995.

——. *The Politics of Pan-Islam: Ideology and Organization.* Oxford: Clarendon, 1990.

Le Chatelier, A. "Le pan-Islamisme et le progrès." *Revue du Monde Musulman* 1, no. 4 (February 1907): 145–168.

Lebra, Joyce. "Bose's Influence on the Formulation of Japanese Policy toward India and the INA." In Sisir K. Bose, ed., *International Netaji Seminar,* 317–328. Calcutta: Netaji Research Bureau, 1975.

——. *Jungle Alliance: Japan and the Indian National Army.* Singapore: Donald Moore, for Asia Pacific, 1971.

——. "Ôkuma Shigenobu: Modernization and the West." In Edmund Skrzypczak, ed., *Japan's Modern Century.* Tokyo: Sophia University, in cooperation with Tuttle, 1968.

Lehmann, J. P. *The Image of Japan: From Feudal Isolation to World Power, 1850–1905.* London: Allen and Unwin, 1978.

Lewis, Bernard. *Muslim Discovery of Europe.* New York: Norton, 1982.

——. *What Went Wrong? The Clash Between Islam and Modernity in the Middle East.* New York: Oxford University Press, 2002.

Lewis, Geoffrey L. "The Ottoman Proclamation of Jihad in 1914." *Islamic Quarterly: A Review of Islamic Culture* (London) 19, no. 1–2 (January–June 1975): 157–163.

McCarthy, Justin. *Death and Exile: The Ethnic Cleansing of Ottoman Muslims, 1821–1922.* Princeton, N.J.: Darwin, 1995.

Macfie, A. L. "British Intelligence and the Turkish National Movement, 1919–1922." *Middle Eastern Studies* 37, no. 1 (January 2001): 1–16.

Macmillan, Margaret. *Paris 1919.* New York: Random House Trade Paperbacks, 2003.

Makdisi, Ussama. "Ottoman Orientalism." *American Historical Review* 107, no. 3 (2002): 768–796.

Malaka, Tan. "Communism and Pan-Islamism." *What Next: Marxist Discussion Journal,* no. 21 (2001). www.whatnextjournal.co.uk/Pages/Back/Wnext21/Panislam.html. Accessed June 10, 2006.

Manela, Erez. "The Wilsonian Moment: Self Determination and the International Origins of Anticolonial Nationalism, 1917–1920." Ph.D. diss., Yale University, 2003.

Mardin, Serif. *The Genesis of Young Ottoman Thought.* Princeton: Princeton University Press, 1962.

——. "Tanzimat'tan Sonra Aşırı Batılılaşma." In *Makaleler,* vol. 4, *Türk Modernleşmesi,* 21–79. Istanbul: İletişim Yayınları, 1992.

Marr, David. *Vietnamese Anti-Colonialism, 1885–1925.* Berkeley: University of California Press, 1971.

Matsumoto Sannosuke. "Profile of Asian Minded Man V: Fukuzawa Yukichi." *Developing Economies* 5, no. 1 (March 1967): 156–172.

Matsuzawa Hiroaki. "Varieties of Benmei Ron (Theories of Civilization)." In Hilary Conroy, Sandra T. W. Davis, and Wayne Patterson, eds., *Japan in Transition: Thought and Action in the Meiji Era,* 209–223. London: Associated University Presses, 1984.

Mayer, Arno. *Wilson vs. Lenin: Political Origins of the New Diplomacy, 1917–1918.* Cleveland: World Publishing, 1964.

Meriç, Ümid. *Cevdet Paşa'nin Cemiyet ve Devlet Görüşü.* Istanbul: Ötüken Yayınları, 1979.

Minamoto Ryôen. "Symposium on 'Overcoming Modernity.'" In James Heisig and John Moraldo, eds., *Rude Awakenings: Zen, the Kyoto School, and the Question of Nationalism,* 197–229. Honolulu: University of Hawai'i Press, 1995.

Minault, Gail. *The Khilafat Movement: Religious Symbolism and Political Mobilization in India.* New York: Columbia University Press, 1982.

Minear, Richard. *Victor's Justice: The Tokyo War Crimes Tribunal.* Princeton: Princeton University Press, 1971.

Minohara Toshihiro. *Hainichi Iminho to Nichibei Kankei: "Hanihara Shokan" no Shinso to Sono "Judainaru Kekka."* Tokyo: Iwanami Shoten, 2003.

Mirsepassi, Ali. *Intellectual Discourse and the Politics of Modernization: Negotiating Modernity in Iran.* New York: Cambridge University Press, 2000.

Misawa Nobuo. "Relations Between Japan and the Ottoman Empire in the Nineteenth Century: Japanese Public Opinion About the Disaster of the Ottoman Battleship Ertuğrul (1890)." *Annals of Japan Association of Middle East Studies* 18, no. 2 (2003): 1–8.

Mismer, Charles. *Soirées de Constantinople.* Paris: Hachette, 1870.

Mitsukawa Kametarô. *Tôzai jinshu tôsô shikan.* Tokyo: Tôyô Kyôkai Shuppanbu, 1924.

——. *Ubawaretaru Ajia.* Tokyo: Kôbundô Shoten, 1921.

Miura Tôru. "Nihon no Chutô-Isuramu Kenkyû." *Gekkan Hyakka,* no. 365 (1993): 18–23.

——. "The Past and Present of Islamic and Middle Eastern Studies in Japan: Using the *Bibliography of Islamic and Middle Eastern Studies in Japan 1868–1988.*" *Annals of Japan Association for Middle East Studies* 17, no. 2 (2002): 45–60.

Miwa Kimitada. "Crossroads of Patriotism in Imperial Japan: Shiga Shigetaka 1863–1927, Uchimura Kanzô 1861–1930, and Nitobe Inazô 1862–1933." Ph.D. diss., Princeton University, 1967.

——. "Fukuzawa Yukichi's 'Departure from Asia': A Prelude to the Sino-Japanese War." In

Edmund Skrzypczak, ed., *Japan's Modern Century*, 1–26. Tokyo: Sophia University, in cooperation with Tuttle, 1968.

——. "Japanese Opinions on Woodrow Wilson in War and Peace." *Monumenta Nipponica* 22, nos. 3–4 (1967): 368–389.

——. "Japanese Policies and Concepts for a Regional Order in Asia, 1938–1940." In J. White, M. Umegaki, and T. Havens, eds., *The Ambivalence of Nationalism: Modern Japan Between East and West*, 133–156. New York: University Press of America, 1990.

Miyazaki Tôten. *My Thirty-Three Years' Dream: The Autobiography of Miyazaki Tôten*. Trans. Etô Shinkichi and Marius Jansen. Princeton: Princeton University Press, 1982.

Mizuno Naoki. "Senkyûhyaku Nijû Nendai Nihon, Chôsen, Chûgoku ni okeru Ajia Ninshiki no Ichidaimen: Ajia Minzoku Kaigi o Meguru Sankoku no Ronchô." In Furuya Tetsuo, ed., *Kindai Nihon no Ajia Ninshiki*, 509–544. Kyoto: Kyôto Daigaku Jinbun Kagaku Kenkyûjo, 1994.

Montesquieu, Charles de Secondat. *The Spirit of Laws*. Amherst, N.Y.: Prometheus, 2002.

Müge Göçek, Fatma. *East Encounters West: France and the Ottoman Empire in the Eighteenth Century*. New York: Oxford University Press, 1987.

Mukherjee, Tapan. *Taraknath Das: Life and Letters of a Revolutionary in Exile*. Calcutta: National Council of Education in Bengal, 1997.

Mul, Jons [pseud.]. *Londra Konferansindaki Mes'elelerden Anadoluda Türkiya Yaşayacak mi? Yaşamayacak mi?* Trans. Habil Adem [pseud.]. Istanbul: Ikbal Kütüphanesi, n.d.

Mullins, Mark R. *Christianity Made in Japan: A Study of Indigenous Movements*. Honolulu: University of Hawai'i Press, 1998.

Münif Efendi. "Mahiyet ve Aksam-i Ulum." *Mecmua-ı Fünun*, no. 13 (June 1863): 7–9.

Münir, Ahmet. "Hâricî Ticâret Vesile-i Sa'âdet-i Umûmidir." *Sebilürreşât* 12, no. 307 (1330/1914): 290–291.

——. "Japonya Mikado'su Mutsuhito." *Sebilürreşât* 2–9, no. 213 (1328/1912): 96–98.

——. "Japonya Ticaret-i Bahriyesi." *Sebilürreşât* 1–8, no. 204 (1328/1912): 426–427.

Mustafa Sami Efendi. *Avrupa Risalesi*. Istanbul: Takvim-i Vekayi Matbaasi, 1840.

Nagasaki Nobuko. "Ôkawa Shûmei no Shoki Indo Kenkyû, Indo Kankei no Ichi Sokumen." *Tôkyô Daikgaku Kyôyôbu Jinbun Kagaku Kiyô: Rekishi to Bunka*, no. 12 (March 1978): 116–120

Nagazumi Akira. "An Indonesian's View of Japan: Wahidin and the Russo-Japanese War." In F. H. H. King, ed., *The Development of Japanese Studies in Southeast Asia: Proceedings of the Fourth Leverhulme Conference*, 72–84. Hong Kong: Centre of Asian Studies, University of Hong Kong, 1969.

Nakajima Takeshi. *Nakamuraya no Bosu*. Tokyo: Hakusuisha, 2005.

Nakamura Kojiro. "Early Japanese Pilgrims to Mecca." *Report of the Society for Near Eastern Studies in Japan* 12 (1986): 47–57.

——. *Renan Müdafaanamesi: Islamiyet ve Maarif*. Ankara: Milli Kültür Yayınları, 1962.

Nakaoka San-eki. "Japanese Research on the Mixed Courts of Egypt in the Earlier Part of the Meiji Period in Connection with the Revision of the 1858 Treaties." *Journal of Sophia Asian Studies* 6 (1988): 11–47.

Nakatani Takeyô. *Shôwa Dôranki no Kaisô—Nakatani Takeyô Kaikoroku*. 2 vols. Tokyo: Tairyûsha, 1989.

Namik Kemal. "Medeniyet." *Mecmua-i Ulum* 5 (1 Safer 1297/January 14, 1880): 381–383.

Naoko Shimazu. *Japan, Race and Equality: The Racial Equality Proposal of 1919.* London: Routledge, 1998.

Narangoa Li and Robert Cribbs, eds. *Imperial Japan and National Identities in Asia, 1895–1945.* London: Routledge, 2003.

Nehru, Jawaharlal. *An Autobiography.* Delhi: Oxford University Press, 1989.

——. *Toward Freedom.* Boston: Beacon, 1967.

Nicolaevsky, B. "Russia, Japan, and the Pan-Asiatic Movement to 1925." *Far Eastern Quarterly* 8, no. 3 (May 1949): 259–295.

Nitobe Inazô. *Bushido: The Soul of Japan. An Exposition of Japanese Thought.* Tokyo: Kodansha International, 1998.

——. "Japan and the League of Nations." In *The Works of Nitobe Inazô,* 4:234–239. Tokyo: University of Tokyo Press, 1972.

——. "The Manchurian Question and Sino-American Relations." In *The Works of Nitobe Inazô,* 4:221–233. Tokyo: University of Tokyo Press, 1972.

Nolte, Sharon and Sally Hastings. "Meiji State's Policy Toward Women." In Gail Lee Bernstein, ed., *Recreating Japanese Women, 1600–1945,* 151–174. Berkeley: University of California Press, 1991.

Norman, E. H. "The Genyôsha: A Study in the Origins of Japanese Imperialism." *Pacific Affairs* 17, no. 3 (September 1944): 261–284.

Notehelfer, F. G. "On Idealism and Realism in the Thought of Okakura Tenshin." *Journal of Japanese Studies* 16, no. 2 (Summer 1990): 309–355.

Numan Kamil Bey. *Islamiyet ve Devlet-i Aliyye-i Osmaniye Hakkında Doğru bir Söz.* Istanbul: Tahir Bey Matbaasi, 1316/1898.

——. "Islamiyet ve Devlet-i Aliyye-i Osmaniye Hakkında Doğru bir Söz: Cenevre'de Müsteşrikin Kongresi'nde İrad Olunmuş bir Nutkun Tercümesidir." In İsmail Kara, ed., *Hilafet Risaleleri,* 1:353–371. Istanbul: Klasik Yayınları, 2002.

——. "Vérité sur l'Islamisme et l'Empire Ottoman." *Présentée au X. Congrès International des Orientalistes à Genève.* Paris: Charles Noblet et Fils, 1894.

Office of Strategic Services (OSS), Research and Analysis Branch. "Japanese Attempts at Indoctrination of Youth in Occupied Areas." March 23, 1943.

Ôgata Kôhei, ed. *Nippon to Indo.* Tokyo: Sanseidô, 1978.

Ogata Sadako. "The Role of Liberal Nongovernmental Organizations in Japan." In Dorothy Borg and Okamoto Shumpei, eds., *Pearl Harbor as History,* 459–486. New York: Columbia University Press, 1973.

Oka Yoshitake. "The First Anglo-Japanese Alliance in Japanese Public Opinion." In J. P. Lehmann, ed., *Themes and Theories in Japanese History,* 185–193. London: Athlone, 1988.

Okakura Kakuzô. *The Ideals of the East with Special Reference to the Art of Japan.* London: Murray, 1903.

——. *Japan's Innate Virility: Selections from Okakura and Nitobe.* Tokyo: Hokuseido, 1943.

——. *Okakura Tenshin Zenshû.* Tokyo: Rikugeisha, 1939.

Okakura Tenshin. "The Awakening of the East." In *Okakura Kakuzô: Collected English Writings,* 134–168. Tokyo: Heibonsha, 1984).

——. *Okakura Kakuzô: Collected English Writings.* Tokyo: Heibonsha, 1984.

Ôkawa Shûmei. "Bosu-shi no Raichô." *Shin Ajia* 5, no. 7 (1943): 1.

——. *Dai Tôa Chitsujyo Kensetsu.* Tokyo: Dai Ichi Shobô, 1943.

——. "Daitô Kyôeiken no Rekishiteki Konkyo." In Dai Nippon Genron Hôkokukai, ed., *Kokka to Bunka,* 29–43. Tokyo: Dômei Tsûshinsha, 1943.

——. *Fukkô Ajia no Shomondai.* Tokyo: Daitôkaku, 1922. Reprint, Tokyo: Chûô Kôronsha, 1993.

——. *A History of Anglo-American Aggression in East Asia.* Trans. Yoshio Agawa and P. B. Clarke. Tokyo: Daitôa Shuppan Kabushiki Kaisha, 1944.

——. *Kaikyô Gairon.* Tokyo: Keiô Shobô, 1942. Reprint, Tokyo: Chûô Kôronsha, 1992.

——. "Kunkoku no Shimei." *Michi,* no. 93 (January 1916): 47–55.

——. "Nanhô Mondai." In Yoshioka Nagayoshi, ed., *Sekai no Dôkô to Tôa Mondai,* 384–385. Tokyo: Zenrin Kyôkai, 1941.

——. *Ôkawa Shûmei Kankei Monjo.* Ed. Ôkawa Shûmei Kankei Monjo Kankôkai. Tokyo: Fuyô Shobô Shuppan, 1998.

——. *Ôkawa Shûmei Nikki.* Tokyo: Iwasaki Gakujitsu Shuppansha, 1986.

——. *Ôkawa Shûmei Shû.* Ed. Hashikawa Bunsô. Tokyo: Chikuma Shobô, 1975.

——. *Ôkawa Shûmei Zenshû.* 7 vols. Ed. Ôkawa Shûmei Zenshû Kankôkai. Tokyo: Iwasaki Shoten 1961–1974.

——. *Shin Ajia Shôron.* Tokyo: Nihon Hyôronsha, 1944.

——. *Shin Tôyô Seishin.* Tokyo: Shinkyô Shuppan Kabushiki Kaisha, 1945.

Okay, Orhan. *Batı Medeniyeti Karşısında Ahmed Midhat Efendi.* Istanbul: Milli Eğitim Bakanliği Yayınları, 1991.

Öke, Mim Kemal. *Hilafet Hareketleri.* Ankara: Türkiye Diyanet Vakfı Yayınları, 1991.

Okubô Kôji. "Shinkô Toruko No Kokumin Shugi Hyôshiki." *Dai Ajia Shugi* 5, no. 5 (May 1937): 5–10.

Ôkuma Shigenobu. Preface to Lord Cromer, *Saikin Ejiputo* [Modern Egypt]. 1:12–13. Tokyo: Dainippon Bunmei Kyôkai, 1911).

——. *Tôzai Bunmei no Chôwa.* Tokyo: Waseda Daigaku Shuppanbu, 1990.

Okumuş, Ejder. "İbn Haldun ve Osmanlı'da Çöküş Tartışmaları." *Divan: İlmi Araştırmalar* 4, no. 6 (1999): 183–209.

Oppenheim, L. *International Law: A Treatise.* London: Longmans, Green, 1905.

Ortaylı, Ilber. *Osmanlı İmparatorluğu'nda İktisadi ve Sosyal Değişim: Makaleler.* Ankara: Turhan Kitabevi, 2000.

Ostrorog, Leon. *Conférence sur la renaissance du Japon.* Istanbul: Ahmed Ihsan, 1327/1911.

Ôtsuka Takehiro. *Ôkawa Shûmei to Kindai Nihon.* Tokyo: Mokutakusha, 1990.

——. *Ôkawa Shûmei: Aru Fukkô Kakushin Shugisha no Shisô.* Tokyo: Chûô Kôronsha, 1995.

Özbek, Nadir. "From Asianism to Pan-Turkism: The Activities of Abdürreşid İbrahim in the Young Turk Era." In Selçuk Esenbel and Inaba Chiharu, eds., *The Rising Sun and the Turkish Crescent: New Perspectives on the History of Japanese-Turkish Relations,* 86–104. Istanbul: Boğaziçi University Press, 2003.

Özcan, Azmi. "1857 Büyük Hind Ayaklanması ve Osmanlı Devleti." *İ. Ü. Islam Tetkikleri Dergisi* 9 (1995) 269–280.

——. "İngiltere'de Hilafet Tartışmaları, 1873–1909." In İsmail Kara, ed., *Hilafet Risaleleri*, 1:63–91. Istanbul: Klasik Yayınları, 2002.

——. *Pan-Islamism: Indian Muslims, the Ottomans and Britain (1877–1924)*. Leiden: Brill, 1997.

——. "Peyk-i Islam: 1880'de Istanbul'da Çıkarılan Bir Gazete ve İngiltere'nin Kopardiği Fırtına." *Tarih ve Toplum*, no. 99 (March 1992): 169–173.

Özdemir [Şehbenderzade Ahmed Hilmi]. *Türk Ruhu Nasıl Yapılıyor? Her Vatanperverden, Bu Eserciği Türklere Okumasını ve Anlatmasını Niyaz Ederiz*. Istanbul: Hikmet Matbaa-i İslamiyesi, 1913.

Pal, Radhabinod. *Ai Rabu Japan: Paru Hakase Genkôroku*. Ed. Paru Hakase Kangei Jimukyoju. Tokyo: Tôkyô Saiban Kankôkai, 1966.

Park, No-Yong. *Retreat of the West: The White Man's Adventure in Eastern Asia*. Boston: Hale, Cushman, and Flint, 1937.

[Pars], Muhiddin Baha. "Halife Ordusu Mısır ve Kafkas'da." In İsmail Kara, ed., *Hilafet Risaleleri*, 3:383–426. Istanbul: Klasik, 2003.

Paşa, Münif. "Mukayese-i İlm ve Cehl." *Mecmua-i Fünün* 1 (Muharrem 1279/June 1862): 26–27.

Pearson, W. W. "A Character Study of M. K. Gandhi, Leader of the Non-Cooperation Movement in India." *Asian Review* 2, no. 5 (July–August 1921): 485–492.

——. *For India*. Tokyo: Asiatic Association of Japan, 1917.

Peattie, Mark R. "Forecasting a Pacific War, 1912–1933: The Idea of a Conditional Japanese Victory." In J. White, M. Umegaki, and T. Havens, eds., *The Ambivalence of Nationalism: Modern Japan Between East and West*, 115–132. New York: University Press of America, 1990.

——. *Ishiwara Kanji and Japan's Confrontation with the West*. Princeton: Princeton University Press, 1975.

Penn, Michael. "East Meets East: An Ottoman Mission in Meiji Japan." Michael Penn, "East Meets East: An Ottoman Mission in Meiji Japan," *Princeton Papers: Interdisciplinary Journal of Middle Eastern Studies* 13 (forthcoming in fall 2006).

Perkins, Dexter. *A History of the Monroe Doctrine*. Boston: Little, Brown, 1955.

Pertev Bey. *Rus-Japon Harbinden Alinan Maddi ve Manevi Dersler ve Japonlarin Esbabi Muzafferiyeti: Bir Milletin Tâli'i Kendi Kuvvetindedir!* Istanbul: Kanâ'at Kütüphanesi ve Matbaasi, 1329/1911.

Pistor-Hatam, Anja. "Progress and Civilization in Nineteenth-Century Japan: The Far Eastern State as a Model for Modernization." *Iranian Studies* 29, nos. 1–2 (1996): 111–126.

Pratap, Raja Mehandra. *My Life Story of Fifty-five Years*. Dehradun: World Federation, 1947.

Professor Vayt [pseud.]. *Muharebeden Sonra: Hilafet Siyaseti ve Türklük Siyaseti*. Trans. Habil Adem. Istanbul: Ikbal Kütüphanesi, 1915.

Puri, Harish K. *Ghadar Movement: Ideology, Organization, and Strategy*. Amritsar: Guru Nanak Dev University, 1993.

Pyle, Kenneth. "Meiji Conservatism." In Marius B. Jansen, ed., *The Cambridge History of Japan*, 5:674–720. Cambridge: Cambridge University Press, 1989.

——. *The New Generation in Meiji Japan: Problems of Cultural Identity, 1885–1895.* Stanford, Calif.: Stanford University Press, 1969.

Rai, Lala Lajpat. "Ajia no Bunmei." *Michi,* no. 92 (December 1915): 31–34.

——. *Reflections on the Political Situation in India with a Personal Note and Extracts from Indian and English Newspapers etc.* Tokyo, 1915.

——. *Young India: An Interpretation and a History of the Nationalist Movement from Within.* New York: Huebsch, 1916.

Redhouse, J. W. *A Vindication of the Ottoman Sultan's Title on 'Caliph': Showing Its Antiquity, Validity and Universal Acceptance.* London: Effingham Wilson, 1877.

Reid, Anthony. "Nineteenth Century Pan-Islam in Indonesia and Malaysia." *Journal of Asian Studies* 26, no. 2 (February 1967): 275–276.

Reinsch, Paul Samuel. *Intellectual and Political Currents in the Far East.* Boston: Houghton Mifflin, 1911.

Renan, Ernest. "İslamlik ve Bilim." In Ziya İhsan, ed. and trans., *Nutuklar ve Konferanslar,* 183–205. Ankara: Sakarya Basimevi, 1946.

——. *The Poetry of the Celtic Races and Other Studies.* London: Walter Scott, 1896.

Rezrazi, El-Mostafa. "Pan-Asianism and the Japanese Islam: Hatano Uhô. From Espionage to Pan-Islamist Activity." *Annals of the Japan Association for Middle East Studies,* no. 12 (1997): 89–112.

Richard, Michel Paul. *Without Passport: The Life and Work of Paul Richard.* New York: Peter Lang, 1987.

Richard, Paul. *Dai JûIchiJi* (1921). Trans. Ôkawa Shûmei. In *Ôkawa Shûmei Zenshû,* 1:881–993. Tokyo: Ôkawa Shûmei Zenshû Kankôkai, 1961.

——. "Democracy." *Asian Review* 1, no. 3 (April 1920): 272–275.

——. *Eien no Chie.* Trans. Ôkawa Shûmei. Tokyo: Keiseisha, 1924.

——. Introduction to W. W. Pearson, *For India,* iii–v. Tokyo: Asiatic Association of Japan, 1917.

——. "Jinshuteki Sabetsu Teppai Mondai to Nippon Kokumin no Tenshoku." *Ajia Jiron* 3, no. 4 (April 1919): 25.

——. "Mazu Ajia Renmei wo Jitsugen Seyo. *Ajia Jiron* 3, no. 5 (May 1919): 31–32.

——. *Nipponkoku ni Tsugu.* Tokyo: Seinen Shobô, 1941.

——. "Some Answers." *Asian Review* 1, no. 1 (February 1920): 42.

—— [as Risharu]. *Tsugu Nihon Koku.* Trans. Ôkawa Shûmei. Tokyo: Seinen Shobô, 1941.

Riddell, John, ed. *To See the Dawn: Baku, 1920—First Congress of the Peoples of the East.* New York: Pathfinder, 1993.

Rıfat Paşa, Sadik. *Müntehabat-i Asar.* Istanbul: Takvimhane-i Amire, 1858.

Rıza, Ahmed. *La faillite morale de la politique occidentale en Orient.* Paris, 1922. Reprint, Tunis: Bouslama, 1979.

——. "La Leçon d'une guerre." *Mechveret Supplement Français* 169 (November 1, 1905): 1–2.

——. *Meclisi Mebusan ve Ayan Reisi Ahmed Rıza Bey'in Anıları.* Istanbul: Arba Yayınları, 1988.

——. *The Moral Bankruptcy of Western Policy Towards the East.* Ankara: Ministry of Culture and Tourism Publications, 1988.

Rıza, Ahmed and Ismayl Urbain. *Tolérance de l'Islam*. Saint-Ouen, France: Centre Abaad, 1992.

Rosenthal, Franz. *The Classical Heritage in Islam*. London: Routledge, 1992.

Rôyama Masamichi. *Foreign Policy of Japan, 1914–1939*. Tokyo: Institute of Pacific Relations–Japan Council, 1941.

——. *Japan's Position in Manchuria*. Tokyo: Institute of Pacific Relations–Japan Council, 1929.

——. *Tô-A to Sekai*. Tokyo: Kaizôsha, 1941.

Russell, Bertrand. *Roads to Freedom: Socialism, Anarchism and Syndicalism*. London: Allen and Unwin, 1918.

Sadiq, Mohammad. *The Turkish Revolution and the Indian Freedom Movement*. Delhi: Macmillan India, 1983.

Sahiner, Necmeddin. *Bilinmeyen Taraflariyla Bediuzzaman Said Nursi*. Istanbul: Nesil Yayınlari, 1997.

Şahingöz, Mehmet and Vahdet Keleşyılmaz. "Milli Mücadele Dönemi Türk Basınında Wilson Prensipleri." *Atatürk Araştırma Merkezi Dergisi* (Temmuz) 12, no. 35 (July 1996): 357–378.

Said Halim Paşa. *Bütün Eserleri*. Istanbul: Anka, 1985.

——. *İntihat-i Islam Hakkinda Bir Tecrübe-yi Kalemiye*. Istanbul: Matbaa-i Âmire, 1918.

——. *Political Reform of Muslim Society*. Lahore: Islamic Publications, 1947.

Said Halim Paşa, Mehmet. *L'Empire Ottoman et la guerre mondiale, 1863–1921*. Istanbul: Isis, 2000.

Sakamoto Tsutomu. "The First Japanese Hadji Yamaoka Kôtaro and Abdürreşid İbrahim." In Selçuk Esenbel and Inaba Chiharu, eds., *The Rising Sun and the Turkish Crescent: New Perspectives on the History of Japanese-Turkish Relations*, 105–121. Istanbul: Boğaziçi University Press, 2003.

Sansom, G. B. *The Western World and Japan: A Study in the Interaction of European and Asiatic Cultures*. New York: Vintage, 1973.

Sareen, Tilak Raj. *Japan and the Indian National Army*. New Delhi: Mounto, 1996.

Satan, Ali. "Halifeliğin Kaldırılışı, 1919–1924." M.A. thesis, Marmara Üniversitesi, Sosyal Bilimler Enstitutüsü, 2000.

Schmitt, Carl. *The Nomos of the Earth in the International Law of the Jus Publicum Europaeum*. New York: Telos, 2003.

Schwantes, Robert S. "Christianity Versus Science: A Conflict of Ideas in Meiji Japan." *Far Eastern Quarterly* 12, no. 2 (February 1953): 123–132.

——. "Japan's Cultural Foreign Policies." In James Morley, ed., *Japan's Foreign Policy, 1868–1941: A Research Guide*, 179–180. New York: Columbia University Press, 1974.

Şehbenderzade Ahmed Hilmi. *Awakened Dreams: Raji's Journeys with the Mirror Dede*. [Amak-i Hayal]. Trans. Refik Algan and Camille Helminski. Putney, Vt.: Threshold, 1993.

Şehbenderzade Filibeli Ahmed Hilmi. *Huzur-ı Akl u Fende Maddiyyun Meslek-i Dalaleti: Tarih-i İstikbal'in Birinci Cildini Teşkil Eden Mesail-i Fikriyenin Tenkidi*. Istanbul, 1332/1913–1914.

Servier, André. *Islam and the Psychology of the Musulman.* Trans. A. S. Moss-Blundell. Preface by Louis Bertrand. New York: Scribner, 1924.

——. *Le nationalisme musulman en Egypte, en Tunisie, en Algérie: Le Péril de l'avenir.* Constantine, Algeria: M. Boet, 1913.

Shiba Shirô. *Kaisetsu Kajin no Kigu.* Tokyo: Jiji Tsushinsha, 1970.

Shibasaki Atsushi. *Kindai Nihon no Kokusai Bunka Kôryû: Kokusai Bunka Shinkôkai no Sôsetsu to Tenkai, 1934–1945.* Tokyo: Yûshindô Kôbunsha, 1999.

Shillony, Ben-Ami. *Politics and Culture in Wartime Japan.* New York: Oxford University Press, 1981.

Smiles, Samuel. *Self-Help.* Chicago: Bedford and Clarke, 1884.

Snodgrass, Judith. *Presenting Japanese Buddhism to the West: Orientalism, Occidentalism, and the Columbian Exposition.* Chapel Hill: University of North Carolina Press, 2003.

Sohrabi, Nader. "Historicizing Revolutions: Constitutional Revolutions in the Ottoman Empire, Iran, and Russia, 1905–1908." *American Journal of Sociology* 100, no. 6 (July 1995): 1383–1447.

Soloviev, Vladimir Sergeyevich. *The Justification of the Good: An Essay on Moral Philosophy.* Trans. Nathalie Duddington. New York: Macmillan, 1918.

Sources of Japanese Tradition. Vol. 2. Ed. Tsunoda Ryusaku, Wm. Theodore de Bary, and Donald Keene. New York: Columbia University Press, 1958.

Spengler, Oswald. *The Decline of the West.* Ed. Arthur Helps. Abridged ed. New York: Knopf, 1962.

Sprenger, Aloys. *Das Leben und die Lehre des Mohammad.* Berlin: Nicolai, 1869.

Stoddard, Lothrop [as Stûdârd, Lûthrub]. *Hadir al-Alam al-Islami.* Trans. 'Ajjâj Nuwayhid. Ed. al-Amîr Shakîb Arslân. Cairo: Matbaa-i Salafiyah, 1924.

——. *The New World of Islam.* New York: Scribner's, 1921.

——. *The Rising Tide of Color Against the White World Supremacy.* New York: Scribner's, 1920.

——. *Yeni Alem-i Islam.* Trans. Ali Riza Seyfi. Istanbul: Ali Şükrü Matbaasi, 1922.

Storry, Richard. *The Double Patriots: A Study of Japanese Nationalism.* Boston: Houghton Mifflin, 1957.

Suavi, Ali. "Democracy: Government by the People, Equality." *Ulum Gazetesi* (Paris), May 17, 1870. Reprinted in Charles Kurzman, ed., *Modernist Islam, 1840–1940),* 142. New York: Oxford University Press, 2002.

Sugita Hideaki. "Japan and the Japanese as Depicted in Modern Arabic Literature." *Studies of Comparative Culture,* no. 27 (March 1989): 21–40.

Suzuki Tadashi. "Profile of Asian Minded Man IX: Tôkichi Tarui." *Developing Economies* 6, no. 1 (March 1968): 79–100.

Szpilman, Christopher. "Conservatism and Its Enemies in Prewar Japan: The Case of Hiranuma Kiichirô and the Kokuhonsha." *Hitotsubashi Journal of Social Studies,* 30, no. 2 (December 1998): 101–133.

——. "The Dream of One Asia: Ôkawa Shûmei and Japanese Pan-Asianism." In H. Fuess, ed., *The Japanese Empire in East Asia and Its Postwar Legacy,* 49–63. Munich: German Institute of Japanese Studies, 1998.

Tagore, Rabindranath. *The Message of India to Japan: A Lecture by Sir Rabindranath Tagore, Delivered at the Imperial University of Tokyo.* Tokyo, 1916.

Tahtavi, Rifa'a Rafi'. *Paris Gözlemleri.* Ed. Cemil Çiftçi. Istanbul: Ses Yayınları, 1992.

Takashi Fujitani. *Splendid Monarchy: Power and Pageantry in Modern Japan.* Berkeley: University of California Press, 1996.

Takemoto Yuko. "W. E. B. Dubois to Nihon." *Shien* 54, no. 2 (March 1994): 79–96.

Takeuchi Yoshimi. *Nihon to Ajia.* Tokyo: Chikuma Gakujitsu Bunshô, 1993.

——. "Ôkawa Shûmei no Ajia Kenkyû." In Ôkawa Shûmei, *Ôkawa Shûmei Shû,* 391–406. Ed. Hashikawa Bunsô. Tokyo: Chikuma Shobô, 1975.

——. "Profile of Asian Minded Man X: Ôkawa Shûmei." *Developing Economies* 7, no. 3 (September 1969): 368–369.

Tamanoi, Mariko Asano. "Pan-Asianism in the Diary of Morisaku Minato (1924–1945) and the Suicide of Mishima Yukio (1925–1970)." In Mariko Asano Tamanoi, ed., *Crossed Histories: Manchuria in the Age of Empire,* 184–206. Honolulu: University of Hawai'i Press, 2005.

Tanaka, Stefan. *Japan's Orient: Rendering Pasts into History.* Berkeley: University of California Press, 1993.

Tanpinar, Ahmet Hamdi. *19uncu Asır Türk Edebiyatı Tarihi.* Istanbul: Çağlayan Yayınları, 1988.

Tazawa Takuya. *Musurimu Nippon.* Tokyo: Sho Gakkan, 1998.

Tetsuo Najita and Harry Harootunian. "Japanese Revolt Against the West: Political and Cultural Criticism in the Twentieth Century." In Bob Tadashi Wakabayashi, ed., *Modern Japanese Thought,* 207–272. Cambridge: Cambridge University Press, 1998.

Thero, Kahawatte Siri Sumedha. *Anagarika Dharmapala: A Glorious Life Dedicated to the Cause of Buddhism.* Sarnath, Varanasi: Maha Bodhi Society of India, 1999.

Thorne, Christopher. *Allies of a Kind: The United States, Britain, and the War Against Japan, 1941–1945.* New York: Oxford University Press, 1978.

Tikhonov, Vladimir. "Korea's First Encounters with Pan-Asianism Ideology in the Early 1880s." *Review of Korean Studies* 5, no. 2 (December 2002): 195–232.

Tinker, Hugh. *Race, Conflict, and the International Order.* New York: St. Martin's, 1977.

Tokutomi Sohô. "America and Japan." *Asian Review* 2, no. 2 (February 1921): 134–138.

——. *The Future of Japan* [Shôrai no Nihon]. Trans. and ed. Vinh Sinh. Edmonton, Canada: University of Alberta Press, 1989.

Toprak, Zafer. *Milli Iktisat—Milli Burjuvazi.* Istanbul: Tarih Vakfi Yurt Yayınları, 1995.

Toru Takemoto. *The Failure of Liberalism in Japan: Shidehara Kijuro's Encounter with Anti-Liberals.* Washington, D.C.: University Press of America, 1978.

Tott, François, baron de. *Memoirs, containing the state of the Turkish Empire and the Crimea, during the late war with Russia, with numerous anecdotes, facts, and observations, on the manners and customs of the Turks and Tartars.* London: G. G. J. and J. Robinson, 1786.

Toynbee, Arnold. *Civilization on Trial.* New York: Oxford University Press, 1948.

——. *Survey of International Affairs, 1925.* Vol. 1, *Islamic World Since the Peace Settlement.* Oxford: Oxford University Press, 1927.

Toynbee, Arnold J. and Kenneth P. Kirkwood. *Turkey.* London: E. Benn, 1926.

Tsurumi Yûsuke. *Gotô Shinpei.* 4 vols. Tokyo: Keisô Shôbo, 1965–1967.

Ueda Shizuteru. "Nishida, Nationalism, and the War in Question." In James Heisig and John Moraldo, eds., *Rude Awakenings: Zen, the Kyoto School, and the Question of Nationalism,* 77–106. Honolulu: University of Hawai'i Press, 1995.

Urquhart, David. *Turkey and Its Resources.* London: Saunders and Otley, 1833.

Uzun, Mustafa. "Halil Halid." In *TDV Islam Ansiklopedisi,* 15:313–316. Istanbul: TDV, 1997.

Vatikiotis, P. J. *The History of Modern Egypt: From Muhammad Ali to Mubarak.* Baltimore: Johns Hopkins University Press, 1980.

Vlastos, Stephen, ed., *Mirror of Modernity: Invented Traditions of Modern Japan.* Berkeley: University of California Press, 1988.

Wakabayashi, Bob Tadashi. *Anti-Westernism and Western Learning in Early-Modern Japan: The New Theses of 1825.* Cambridge: Harvard University Press, 1986.

Wakabayashi Han. *Kaikyô Sekai to Nihon.* Tokyo: Wakabayashi Han, 1937.

Wasti, Syed Tanvir. "Halil Halid: Anti-Imperialist Muslim Intellectual." *Middle Eastern Studies* 29, no. 3 (July 1993): 559–579.

——. "A Note on Tunuslu Hayreddin Paşa." *Middle Eastern Studies* 36, no. 1 (January 2000): 1–20.

Watanabe Hiroshi. " 'Shimpo' to 'Chuka': Nihon no Baai." In Mizoguchi Yuzo, Hamashita Takeshi, Miyajima Hiroshi, and Hiraishi Naoaki, eds., *Kindaika Zô,* 133–175. Tokyo: Tokyo University Press, 1994.

——. "They Are Almost the Same as the Ancient Three Dynasties: The West as Seen Through Confucian Eyes in the Nineteenth-Century Japan." In Tu Wei-Ming, ed., *Confucian Traditions in East Asian Modernity,* 119–131. Cambridge: Harvard University Press, 1996.

Watson Andaya, Barbara. "From Rum to Tokyo: The Search for Anticolonial Allies by the Rulers of Riau, 1899–1914." *Indonesia* 24 (1977): 123–156.

Westermann, Gesa. "Japan's Victory in the Russo-Japanese War (1904–05) from the Philippine, Vietnamese, and Burmese Perspectives." In Rotem Kowner, ed., *Rethinking the Russo-Japanese War: Centennial Perspectives.* Honolulu: University of Hawai'i Press, 2006.

Wilson, George M. "Kita Ikki, Ôkawa Shûmei, and the Yûzonsha." *Papers on Japan,* no. 2 (1963): 139–181.

Worringer, Renee. "Comparing Perceptions: Japan as Archetype for Ottoman Modernity, 1876–1918." Ph.D. diss., University of Chicago, 2001.

——. " 'Sick Man of Europe' or 'Japan of the Near East'?: Constructing Ottoman Modernity in the Hamidian and Young Turk Eras." *International Journal of Middle Eastern Studies* 36, no. 2 (May 2004): 207–223.

Wright, Harrison M., ed. *The New Imperialism: Analysis of Late Nineteenth-Century Expansion.* Lexington, Mass.: Heath, 1976.

Wright, Richard. *The Color Curtain: A Report on the Bandung Conference.* Jackson: University Press of Mississippi, 1995.

Yamamuro Shinichi. "Ajia Ninshiki no Kijiku." In Furuya Tetsuo and Yamamuro Shinichi, eds., *Kindai Nihon no Ajia Ninshiki,* 3–46. Kyoto: Kyoto University Press, 1994.

——. "Nihon Gaikô to Ajia Shugi no Kôsaku." In *Seiji Gaku Nenpô,* 3–32. Tokyo: Iwanami Shoten, 1998.

Yapp, M. E. "Europe in the Turkish Mirror." *Past and Present,* no. 137 (November 1992): 155.

Yazıcı, M. Zeki. "Şehbenderzade Ahmet Hilmi: Hayatı ve Eserleri." Ph.D. diss., Istanbul University, 1997.

Yılmaz, Suhnaz. "An Ottoman Warrior Abroad: Enver Paşa as an Expatriate." *Middle East Studies* 35, no. 4 (October 1999): 40–70.

Yoichi Nakano. "East-West Harmony: The Immigration Controversy and the U.S.-Japan Relations Committee (1916–1932)." Unpublished paper submitted to the History 1851 seminar at Harvard University, January 2000.

Yoshihisa Kuzuu. "Farewell to Dr. Richard and Prof. Cousins, Advisors of the Asian Review." *Asian Review* 1, no. 3 (April 1920): 281–283.

——, ed. *Tôa Senkaku Shishi Kiden.* Tokyo: Kokuryûkai Shuppanbu, 1933–1936.

Young, Louise. *Japan's Total Empire: Manchuria and the Culture of Wartime Empire.* Berkeley: University of California Press, 1998.

Yusa Michiko. "Nishida and Totalitarianism: A Philosopher's Resistance." In James Heisig and John Moraldo, eds., *Rude Awakenings: Zen, the Kyoto School and the Question of Nationalism,* 107–131. Honolulu: University of Hawai'i Press, 1995.

Zumoto Motosada. *Japan and the Pan-Asiatic Movement.* Tokyo: Japan Times, 1926.

——. *Japan in Manchuria and Mongolia.* Tokyo: Herald, 1931.

——. *The Origin and History of the Anti-Japanese Movement in China.* Tokyo: Herald, 1932.

JOURNALS

Ajia Jiron
Asian Review
Asiatic Asia
Dai Ajia Shugi
Daitô
Islamic Fraternity
Isuramu Bunka
Kaikyô Jijyo
Kaikyô Sekai
Kaikyôken
Michi
The New Asia
Nihon Oyobi Nihonjin
Shin Ajia
Tôa
Tôyô
Yani Yapon Muhbiri

INDEX

251*n*36; on Korean self-determination, 144–45; on League of Nations, 142; on Manchurian policy, 167–68, 250*n*26, 251*n*27, 251*n*29; Okakura Tenshin's influence on, 113; pan-Asianism of, 118–19, 186; post-imprisonment career of, 169–70; relationship with Paul Richard, 121–23; on relations with U.S., 171–73; response to Indian condemnation of Japanese Asianism, 181–82; Rôsôkai and, 243*n*62; on shift in official policy to pan-Asianism, 167; socialist movement and, 234*n*60; on Soviet threat to Japanese interests, 148; sword of Islam metaphor, 244*n*66; sympathy toward Bolshevik Revolution, 146–47, 243*n*59; on Turkish nationalism and pan-Islamic revival, 150; on U.S. racial discrimination against Asians, 152; wartime Asianist activities of, 184; on Western colonialism and racism, 199; writings for *Dai Ajia Shugi,* 177; on Yûzonsha goals, 147–48

Ôkuma Shigenobu, 90, 117, 118, 217*n*62, 227*n*76

Old and Young Society (Rôsôkai), 243*n*62

Opium Wars, 25, 34, 74, 201

Orientalism: Ahmet Midhat on, 42; critiques of, 9, 47; on Islamic inferiority to Christianity, 47; legacy of, 202–203; on multiple civilizations, 192; Muslim participation in Orientalist congresses, 53–54; Muslim reformism challenging beliefs in European superiority, 49; politics of, 53; post-Russo-Japanese War challenges to, 77; racism and, 6, 10; reverse narratives of, 201; universalist, 22

"Oriental Society" (Tôho kyôkai), 46

Oshikawa Masayoshi, 117–18

OSS (Office of Strategic Services, U.S.), 186–87, 257*n*109

Ostrorog, Leon, 80, 223*n*34

Ottama, U., 166–67, 250*n*18

Ottoman caliphate: abolition by Turkish Republic, 137–39, 154, 196; Arab caliphate as alternative to, 233*n*53; legitimacy and influence of, 33, 60, 62–63, 211*n*62; successors to, 139

Ottoman Empire: acceptance of universal West, 15, 18–21; alliance with Germany, 10, 94–95, 228*n*4; avoiding challenges to Eurocentric world order, 93–94; civilizationism as protection against European interventions, 34–35; constitutional reform, 35, 62, 77, 194, 229*n*9; cooperation with 19th century European empires, 32; decoupling Christianity from universal civilization, 21–24, 208*n*19; engagement with Orientalists, 53–54; European public opinion about, 18–19; foreign policy, 96–97, 105–106, 195; Industrial Revolution impact and, 17; international relations of, 101–102; Japanese model for reforms, 78–80; as "Japan of the Near East," 96, 229*n*10; loss of Balkan territories, 96, 230*n*15; as Muslim state, 10, 16, 19; national self-determination as basis for peace, 130–32, 239*n*9; nineteenth-century views of the West, 7; optimism about Wilsonian principles and favorable peace agreement, 128–29; pan-Islamic propaganda in World War I, 109; pan-Islamism of, 5, 31–34, 93–99; pre-19th century ignorance about Europe, 16–17, 207*nn*2–3; privileges of Christians in, 31–32; reforms of Mahmud II, 20; Russo-Japanese War and Asian identity of, 73–74; Second Constitutional Period, 96; strategic use of universal civilization, 23–24; support for Aceh against Dutch, 33; Tanzimat Proclamation acknowledging Eurocentric world order, 19–20; wartime ideologies of, 3, 5, 93; Westernization criteria, 41. *See also* Turkish Republic

Ottoman National Pact (1920), 134